Ethics, Safety, and Regulation of AI-Enabled Infrastructure

by

ant

Table of Contents

Chapter 1: The Dawn of AI-Infused Infrastructure

AI-enabled infrastructure represents a profound shift in how we design, build, and operate the foundational systems that underpin modern society. It is not merely about augmenting existing infrastructure with a sprinkle of artificial intelligence, but about fundamentally transforming its intelligence, adaptability, and operational paradigms. At its core, AI-enabled infrastructure refers to systems where artificial intelligence, particularly machine learning and its subfields, is an integral component responsible for core functionalities, decision-making, or optimization, directly impacting the system's behavior and performance. This integration moves beyond simple automation or rule-based systems; it involves systems that can learn, adapt, and make predictions or decisions based on vast amounts of data, often in real-time and with a degree of autonomy. The "AI-enabled" aspect signifies that the system's capabilities, efficiency, and even its very nature are critically dependent on its AI components, rather than these components being merely peripheral add-ons.

To grasp this concept fully, it's essential to move from abstract definitions to concrete examples that illustrate the breadth and depth of AI's integration into infrastructure. Consider the evolution of **smart grids**. Traditional power grids were largely unidirectional, with centralized control and limited real-time visibility into demand or supply fluctuations at the granular level. The introduction of AI transforms this into a dynamic, responsive ecosystem. AI algorithms can analyze vast streams of data from sensors deployed across the grid – including weather patterns, historical consumption data, renewable energy generation (solar, wind), and even social media trends that might indicate unusual demand spikes. This data allows AI to predict energy demand with far greater accuracy, optimize the dispatch of power from various sources (balancing efficiency, cost, and carbon footprint), detect anomalies indicative of equipment failure or cyber threats before they escalate, and even manage distributed energy resources like home batteries to stabilize the grid. The AI isn't just controlling switches; it's orchestrating the complex, multi-variate dance of energy production, distribution, and consumption in near real-time, making decisions that a human operator or a simpler automated system could not possibly manage. This is a synergistic integration: the AI makes the grid smart, and the smart grid provides the data and operational context for the AI to function effectively.

Autonomous transportation networks offer another compelling illustration. Beyond self-driving cars, this encompasses the complex orchestration of traffic flow in entire cities. AI systems can process real-time data from traffic cameras, road sensors, vehicle GPS, and even passenger demand for ride-sharing services. They can dynamically adjust traffic light timings to optimize flow, reroute vehicles to avoid congestion or accidents, predict the need for maintenance on road infrastructure, and manage the integration of various modes of transport, including autonomous vehicles, public transit, and micro-mobility solutions. The safety and efficiency of moving people and goods rely on AI's ability to perceive, predict, decide, and act across a highly dynamic and complex environment. The AI doesn't just follow pre-programmed routes; it constantly learns from the urban environment, adapts to unexpected events, and makes decisions that aim to balance speed, safety, and energy efficiency. This goes beyond adding GPS to a car; it's about creating an intelligent, self-optimizing transportation fabric.

In the realm of
predictive maintenance systems, AI is revolutionizing how we keep industrial machinery, infrastructure, and equipment operational. Instead of relying on scheduled maintenance or waiting for equipment to fail, AI-powered systems continuously monitor the operational data (vibration, temperature, pressure, acoustic signatures, electrical load) from critical assets. Machine learning models are trained on this data, alongside historical failure records, to identify subtle patterns that precede a breakdown. For example, an AI might detect a minuscule increase in

vibration frequency in a particular bearing on a turbine, combined with a slight temperature anomaly, and predict a failure within the next 100 hours of operation. This allows maintenance to be scheduled proactively during planned downtime, preventing costly unexpected shutdowns, extending asset life, and ensuring operational continuity. This is synergistic because the AI's predictive power is amplified by the continuous stream of sensor data, and the ability to act on these predictions fundamentally changes the maintenance paradigm from reactive to proactive.

Intelligent public safety platforms represent a more intricate and sensitive application. AI can be employed to analyze diverse data sources such as emergency call data, social media feeds, sensor networks (e.g., gunshot detection systems), weather forecasts, and historical crime patterns. This analysis can help predict areas where crime is more likely to occur, optimize the deployment of emergency services, detect emerging threats like traffic accidents or fires more rapidly, and even assist in managing large-scale emergencies by providing real-time situational awareness and resource allocation recommendations. For instance, an AI could correlate unusual patterns in social media posts with sensor data to predict a potential public disturbance or identify bottlenecks in evacuation routes during a natural disaster. The integration here is complex, as it requires the AI to not only process vast amounts of data but also to do so in a manner that respects privacy, avoids bias, and supports human decision-makers under immense pressure.

What unites these diverse examples is the **inherent complexity arising from the integration of machine learning models with traditional engineering systems**. Traditional infrastructure was built on principles of deterministic behavior, well-defined physical laws, and predictable material properties. Engineering safety and reliability were achieved through rigorous design, robust materials, redundancy, and extensive testing of components and systems. The introduction of AI, however, brings new layers of complexity:

Probabilistic Nature: AI models, particularly machine learning models, are inherently probabilistic. They don't offer deterministic outputs in the way a traditional thermostat does. Their predictions come with a degree of uncertainty, and their behavior is governed by statistical relationships learned from data, not just immutable physical laws. This probabilistic nature requires a fundamental shift in how we define and verify safety and reliability.

Data Dependency: The performance and behavior of AI systems are critically dependent on the quality, quantity, and representativeness of the data they are trained on and operate with. Data drift, bias in data, or missing data can lead to degraded performance or erroneous decisions, which are harder to anticipate and manage than traditional component failures.

Opacity and Explainability: Many powerful AI models, especially deep neural networks, are often referred to as "black boxes." Understanding precisely why an AI made a particular decision can be challenging. This lack of transparency complicates debugging, auditing, and assigning accountability, especially when safety is at stake.

Emergent Behavior: Complex systems, especially those with learning components that interact with their environment and each other, can exhibit emergent behaviors. These are behaviors that were not explicitly programmed or anticipated by the designers. In AI-enabled infrastructure, these emergent behaviors can manifest as unforeseen system interactions or unintended consequences that impact safety or operational integrity.

Continuous Evolution: Unlike traditionally static engineered systems, AI components can continuously learn and adapt based on new data. While this adaptability can be a significant advantage, it also means the system's behavior can change over time, potentially in ways that compromise safety or performance if not managed meticulously.

This leads to the crucial point that AI integration is **synergistic rather than purely additive**. It's not like adding a new sensor or a better pump. The AI doesn't just perform a specific task; it influences the entire operational logic, decision-making process, and adaptive capabilities of the infrastructure. The smart grid isn't just a grid with an AI module; it's a fundamentally different kind of grid whose intelligence is woven into its fabric by the AI. This synergy means that the benefits (increased efficiency, greater adaptability, enhanced predictive capabilities) are amplified, but so too are the risks if the integration is not managed with a deep understanding of AI's unique characteristics and potential failure modes. The complexity and the synergistic nature of this integration set the stage for the critical discussions that follow, particularly concerning the imperative for responsible deployment and the adaptation of engineering principles to this new era of AI-infused infrastructure.

The advent of AI-enabled infrastructure represents a paradigm shift that necessitates a re-evaluation of traditional engineering and operational paradigms. The integration of artificial intelligence, particularly machine learning, into the backbone of our societal systems—from energy grids and transportation networks to manufacturing floors and public safety systems—introduces unprecedented capabilities. However, it also brings with it a unique set of complexities and challenges that demand a deliberate, thoughtful, and ethically grounded approach to deployment. Simply bolting on AI components to existing infrastructure is insufficient; the true potential, and indeed the necessary safety, lies in the synergistic fusion of AI's learning and adaptive capabilities with the robust, established principles of engineering.

Let us delve deeper into what constitutes AI-enabled infrastructure by examining its manifestations across key sectors. In the

smart grid, AI is the brain that orchestrates a complex, distributed network. Consider the challenges of integrating variable renewable energy sources like solar and wind power, which are inherently intermittent. Traditional grids struggle with this variability. AI, however, can ingest real-time data from weather forecasts, grid sensors, and market prices to predict energy generation and demand with remarkable granularity. Machine learning models can forecast the output of a wind farm hours in advance, anticipate localized demand spikes due to extreme weather events, and dynamically adjust power distribution. This involves sophisticated optimization algorithms that decide which power sources to activate, how to store excess energy (e.g., in battery farms or by adjusting demand response programs), and how to route power across the network to minimize transmission losses and prevent overloads. For example, an AI might detect a pattern of increased air conditioner usage in a specific neighborhood during a heatwave, correlating it with forecast temperatures and historical data. It then proactively dispatches power from the most efficient and cost-effective sources, potentially drawing from a local solar farm or a pumped-storage hydroelectric facility, while also initiating demand-response signals to encourage consumers to reduce non-essential usage during peak hours. This isn't simple automation; it's intelligent, predictive resource management that ensures grid stability and reliability in the face of dynamic and uncertain conditions. The synergy here is profound: the AI's predictive and optimization capabilities breathe intelligence into the grid, while the grid's extensive sensor network and control points provide the AI with the necessary data and levers to act upon.

Autonomous transportation networks are another vivid example. This extends far beyond the individual self-driving car to encompass the entire ecosystem of urban mobility. AI systems are essential for managing traffic flow across an entire city. Imagine a complex urban intersection where AI analyzes data from lidar, radar, cameras, and vehicle-to-infrastructure (V2I) communication systems. It can dynamically adjust traffic signal timings in real-time, not just based on predictable daily patterns, but on actual traffic density, pedestrian presence, and even the urgency of approaching emergency vehicles. Furthermore, AI can optimize the routing of autonomous delivery vehicles, public transport, and ride-sharing fleets to minimize travel times, reduce fuel consumption, and alleviate congestion. For instance, if an AI system detects a significant traffic jam caused by an accident, it can instantly recalculate optimal routes for thousands of vehicles, rerouting them through less congested arteries and communicating these changes dynamically. It can also predict where demand for ride-sharing services will surge next, preemptively repositioning vehicles to meet that demand efficiently. The safety aspect is paramount; AI must continuously monitor for potential hazards, predict the behavior of human-driven vehicles and pedestrians, and make split-second decisions to avoid collisions. This is a synergistic relationship where the AI's sophisticated perception, prediction, and decision-making capabilities are intrinsically linked to the real-time data streams and control mechanisms of the transportation infrastructure.

In
predictive maintenance systems, AI transforms industrial operations. Consider a large manufacturing plant with thousands of interconnected machines, each generating terabytes of operational data. AI algorithms can analyze vibrations, temperature, pressure, acoustic signatures, and electrical currents from these machines. By training on historical data of both normal operation and past failures, these algorithms can detect subtle anomalies that are precursors to equipment malfunction. For example, an AI monitoring a critical robotic arm on an assembly line might detect a fractional increase in motor current combined with a specific pattern of harmonic vibration. These are often imperceptible to human operators and difficult to detect with traditional threshold-based alerts. The AI, however, recognizes this pattern as indicative of an impending bearing failure. It can then predict that the component has a 90% probability of failing within the next 72 hours. This allows the maintenance team to schedule a replacement during a planned downtime

window, avoiding an unexpected shutdown that could halt production for days, costing millions in lost output and repairs. This synergy lies in the AI's ability to interpret complex, multi-modal sensor data for early anomaly detection, thereby enhancing the predictive power of maintenance efforts. The system is more than just a collection of machines; it's an intelligent entity capable of self-monitoring and anticipating its own needs.

Intelligent public safety platforms represent a domain where AI integration is both powerful and fraught with ethical considerations. AI can be used to analyze a wide array of data sources to enhance situational awareness and response. For instance, during a large-scale event like a music festival or a natural disaster, AI can process feeds from CCTV cameras, social media, emergency responder communications, and sensor networks to identify emerging safety concerns. It might detect unusual crowd density patterns that indicate a potential stampede, identify locations where emergency services are most needed based on call volume and incident reports, or predict the spread of a fire based on wind patterns and building layouts. In a more proactive context, AI can analyze historical crime data, demographic information, and even environmental factors to predict areas with a higher likelihood of certain types of crime, enabling law enforcement agencies to allocate resources more effectively. For example, an AI might identify that during specific weather conditions and at certain times of day, a particular park sees a statistically significant increase in reported petty theft. This insight, when combined with other data, can inform patrol strategies. The synergy here involves the AI's capacity to fuse and interpret vast, heterogeneous datasets to provide actionable intelligence that supports human decision-makers, augmenting their ability to protect public safety.

These diverse applications underscore a critical characteristic of AI-enabled infrastructure: the

inherent complexity arising from the integration of machine learning models with traditional engineering systems. Traditional infrastructure engineering has long relied on principles of determinism, predictability, and robustness derived from physics and material science. Components are designed, tested, and validated against known failure modes and performance envelopes. Safety is often achieved through over-engineering, redundancy, and adherence to strict design codes.

The introduction of machine learning, however, fundamentally alters this landscape by introducing elements that are less predictable and more dynamic:

Probabilistic and Statistical Reasoning: Unlike deterministic systems that follow fixed rules, ML models operate on probabilities. Their outputs are predictions or classifications based on patterns learned from data, and these predictions are often accompanied by confidence scores. This means that even when operating "correctly" according to its training, an AI system might still produce an incorrect outcome with a certain probability. Understanding and managing this inherent uncertainty is a core challenge for AI safety engineers. For instance, a self-driving car's perception system might correctly identify 99.9% of road signs, but that 0.1% of missed signs, especially in critical situations, can have severe consequences.
Data-Driven Behavior and Brittleness: ML models are only as good as the data they are trained on. If the training data is biased, incomplete, or unrepresentative of the real-world operational environment, the model's performance can suffer significantly. This phenomenon, known as "brittleness," means AI systems can fail unexpectedly when encountering situations or data distributions that deviate from their training experience. For example, a facial recognition system trained predominantly on lighter skin tones may perform poorly on darker skin tones, leading to discriminatory outcomes. Similarly, an AI system

designed to predict equipment failure based on sensor data might falter if a new, unanticipated type of failure mode emerges that was not present in its training set.

Opacity and the "Black Box" Problem: Many advanced AI models, such as deep neural networks, achieve high performance through complex internal architectures with millions or billions of parameters. This complexity can make it exceedingly difficult to understand precisely why a model made a specific decision. This lack of interpretability, often referred to as the "black box" problem, poses significant challenges for debugging, auditing, validating safety claims, and building trust. When an AI-driven system makes an incorrect or unsafe decision, identifying the root cause within the model's internal workings can be an arduous task. For example, if an AI-powered medical diagnostic tool misidentifies a benign anomaly as cancerous, tracing the exact algorithmic pathway that led to this misdiagnosis can be extremely challenging, hindering both correction and accountability.

Emergent Behaviors and Interactions: As AI systems become more complex and interconnected, they can exhibit emergent behaviors—unforeseen patterns of interaction or functionality that arise from the system's components and their environment. In AI-enabled infrastructure, these emergent behaviors can be a source of novel risks. For example, in a smart grid with multiple AI agents managing different segments, unexpected interactions between these agents could lead to oscillatory behavior, instability, or unintended power diversions. Similarly, in a complex autonomous transportation network, the collective decision-making of many AI-driven vehicles could lead to emergent traffic patterns that were not predicted by individual vehicle algorithms.

Continuous Learning and Adaptation: A key strength of AI is its ability to learn and adapt over time, improving performance as it encounters new data. However, this continuous evolution introduces a new dynamic: the system is not static. If not carefully managed, this adaptation can lead to gradual degradation of performance, drift away from desired safety parameters, or the emergence of unintended behaviors without clear breakpoints or version control. For instance, an AI system in a wastewater treatment plant that continuously adjusts chemical dosages based on incoming water quality might, over time, drift into a state where it is no longer effectively meeting environmental discharge regulations, even if its immediate operational efficiency appears to be improving.

These factors collectively highlight that the integration of AI into infrastructure is not merely an additive process; it is **synergistic**. The AI doesn't just perform a function; it fundamentally reshapes the intelligence, adaptability, and decision-making capabilities of the entire infrastructure. This synergy means that the benefits of AI—enhanced efficiency, greater resilience, improved prediction, and novel capabilities—are amplified. However, it also means that the risks are amplified and transformed. The failure modes of AI are different from those of traditional mechanical or software systems, and their impact can be more widespread and less predictable due to their interconnected and adaptive nature. This fundamental shift from deterministic to probabilistic and adaptive systems, mediated by complex data-driven models, necessitates a profound rethinking of how we engineer, deploy, and govern these critical infrastructures. This sets the stage for understanding the imperative for responsible deployment, as traditional approaches to safety and reliability are no longer sufficient. The challenge ahead is to harness the power of AI while mitigating its unique risks, ensuring that the infrastructure of the future is not only intelligent and efficient but also safe, secure, and trustworthy.

The integration of AI into critical infrastructure transcends simple technological upgrades; it represents a fundamental reimagining of how these systems operate, learn, and interact with their environments and with us. This synergistic fusion of machine intelligence with physical and digital systems creates what we term **AI-enabled infrastructure**. Unlike traditional infrastructure that relies on predetermined logic, mechanical principles, and human oversight for explicit commands, AI-enabled infrastructure incorporates components capable of perception, learning, prediction, and autonomous decision-making. These AI components are not peripheral add-ons; they are integral to the system's core functionality, directly influencing its behavior, efficiency, and safety.

To truly grasp this concept, it is crucial to move beyond abstract notions and examine tangible examples across diverse sectors. Consider the transformation of
smart grids. Traditionally, power grids operated on a centralized, one-way model of generation and distribution, with limited real-time visibility into granular demand or supply. AI revolutionizes this by enabling a dynamic, responsive ecosystem. AI algorithms continuously analyze vast streams of data from grid sensors, weather patterns, historical consumption trends, and even real-time market prices. This data empowers the AI to predict energy demand with unprecedented accuracy, optimize the dispatch of power from a heterogeneous mix of sources (balancing efficiency, cost, and environmental impact), detect subtle anomalies indicative of impending equipment failure or cyber threats before they escalate, and manage distributed energy resources like residential solar panels and battery storage systems to stabilize the grid. For instance, an AI might forecast a significant increase in energy demand in a specific region due to an upcoming sporting event and a heatwave, simultaneously predicting a dip in solar power generation due to cloud cover. It can then proactively adjust power flow, drawing from baseload power plants, activating energy storage facilities, and potentially initiating demand-response programs to mitigate peak load without compromising reliability. This isn't mere automation; it's intelligent orchestration, a synergistic partnership where the AI's learning and predictive capabilities are indispensable for the grid's modern operational demands.

Autonomous transportation networks provide another compelling illustration. This extends beyond individual autonomous vehicles to encompass the intelligent management of urban mobility systems. AI systems process real-time data from traffic cameras, road sensors, vehicle telemetry, and GPS to dynamically adjust traffic signal timings, optimize vehicle routing to alleviate congestion, predict maintenance needs for road infrastructure, and seamlessly integrate various transport modes, including autonomous shuttles, public transit, and personal mobility devices. Imagine an AI system managing city-wide traffic flow during rush hour. It analyzes traffic density, speed, and accident reports to dynamically adjust signal phases, reroute vehicles around incidents, and even communicate optimal routes to connected autonomous vehicles. This system learns from traffic patterns, adapting its strategies based on real-time feedback and historical data. The safety and efficiency of moving people and goods are thus intrinsically linked to the AI's ability to perceive, predict, decide, and act across a highly complex and dynamic environment. The synergy is evident: the AI's sophisticated decision-making capabilities are directly integrated into the operational fabric of the transportation network, enabling a level of optimization and responsiveness unattainable through traditional means.

In the domain of
predictive maintenance systems, AI is fundamentally altering how industrial assets are managed. Instead of relying on time-based schedules or reactive repairs after a failure, AI-powered systems continuously monitor operational data from machinery—vibration, temperature, pressure, acoustic signatures, power consumption, and more. Machine learning models analyze this data, learning to identify subtle patterns that signal impending failure. For example, an AI monitoring a critical pump in a chemical plant might detect a specific, unusual harmonic frequency in its vibration signature, combined with a slight increase in operational temperature. These anomalies, imperceptible to human operators, might indicate a developing bearing wear issue. The AI, trained on historical data of similar failures, can then predict that the component has a high probability of failing within the next 72 hours. This allows maintenance to be scheduled proactively during planned downtime, preventing catastrophic failures, extending the lifespan of the equipment, and

ensuring continuous operation. This is a synergistic integration: the AI's analytical prowess transforms raw sensor data into actionable predictive intelligence, fundamentally enhancing the maintenance process from reactive to proactive.

Intelligent public safety platforms showcase the intricate application of AI in safeguarding communities. AI can analyze diverse data streams—emergency dispatch logs, social media feeds, surveillance camera footage, weather forecasts, and anonymized location data—to enhance situational awareness and optimize resource allocation. For instance, during a natural disaster, an AI might process incoming emergency calls and social media reports to pinpoint areas with the most urgent need for rescue or supplies, predict the spread of wildfires based on wind patterns and topography, and recommend optimal routes for emergency vehicles considering road closures and traffic conditions. In urban environments, AI can assist in identifying potential threats by analyzing unusual patterns in crowd movement or traffic flow. For example, an AI system might detect an anomalous convergence of vehicles in an area where no event is scheduled, or flag suspicious activity captured on surveillance cameras, alerting human operators for further investigation. The synergy lies in the AI's ability to fuse and interpret vast, often disparate, data sources, providing human decision-makers with critical insights to enhance safety and operational efficiency in high-stakes scenarios.

These examples—smart grids, autonomous transportation, predictive maintenance, and public safety—underscore a profound characteristic of AI-enabled infrastructure: the **inherent complexity arising from the integration of machine learning models with traditional engineering systems**. Traditional infrastructure engineering has been built on principles of deterministic behavior, well-understood physical laws, and predictable material properties. Safety and reliability are achieved through rigorous design, robust materials, redundancy, and exhaustive testing within defined operational parameters.

The introduction of AI, particularly machine learning, fundamentally challenges these established paradigms by introducing elements that are inherently probabilistic, data-dependent, and potentially opaque:

Probabilistic Nature: Machine learning models do not operate on absolute certainties. Their outputs—predictions, classifications, or decisions—are typically probabilistic, reflecting a learned statistical relationship within the data. This means that even when functioning "as intended" based on its training, an AI system can still make an incorrect prediction or decision with a certain probability. For example, an AI system designed to predict traffic congestion might be highly accurate, but it cannot guarantee 100% accuracy, meaning unexpected jams can still occur. Managing this inherent uncertainty and its implications for safety-critical operations is a significant engineering challenge.

Data Dependency and Brittleness: The performance and behavior of AI systems are inextricably linked to the data they are trained on and the data they encounter during operation. If training data is biased, incomplete, or unrepresentative of real-world conditions, the AI model can exhibit "brittleness"—failing unexpectedly when presented with novel inputs or scenarios outside its training distribution. For instance, an AI system trained to identify infrastructure damage from aerial imagery might fail to recognize damage caused by an entirely new type of event not present in its training set. Similarly, biases in training data can lead to discriminatory outcomes, as seen in facial recognition systems that perform less accurately for certain demographic groups.

Opacity and the "Black Box" Problem: Many sophisticated AI models, particularly deep neural networks, operate as "black boxes." Their internal decision-making processes are complex and often lack straightforward interpretability. While techniques like LIME or SHAP can offer post-hoc explanations, fully understanding why an AI made a specific decision can be challenging. This opacity complicates debugging, auditing, validating safety claims, and assigning accountability when errors occur. In critical infrastructure, a lack of transparency can hinder root cause analysis and trust.

Emergent Behaviors: Complex systems, especially those involving multiple interacting AI agents or AI interacting with a dynamic environment, can exhibit emergent behaviors—unforeseen functionalities or interactions that arise from the system's components rather than being explicitly programmed. In AI-enabled infrastructure, these emergent behaviors can introduce novel failure modes or unintended consequences. For instance, multiple AI-driven traffic management systems in different city zones might interact in unexpected ways, leading to unforeseen congestion patterns or signal conflicts.

Continuous Learning and Adaptation: A hallmark of AI is its capacity for continuous learning and adaptation based on new data and operational feedback. While this adaptability enhances performance and responsiveness, it also means that the system's behavior can evolve over time. Without careful management, this evolution can lead to drift—a gradual deviation from initial performance benchmarks, safety parameters, or intended functionality. For example, an AI managing energy distribution might, over time, adapt its strategies in ways that inadvertently compromise grid stability during extreme weather events if not properly constrained.

These complexities underscore that the integration of AI into infrastructure is
synergistic rather than purely additive. AI is not merely a new component; it fundamentally reshapes the intelligence, adaptability, and decision-making core of the infrastructure. This synergy amplifies not only the potential benefits—enhanced efficiency, predictive capabilities, resilience—but also the risks. The unique failure modes of AI, coupled with the complexity of their integration, necessitate a proactive and robust approach to safety and governance, moving beyond traditional

engineering paradigms to address the novel challenges posed by intelligent, adaptive systems. This sets the crucial context for understanding why responsible deployment is paramount.
The integration of artificial intelligence into the foundational systems that support modern society—our infrastructure—is not merely an evolutionary step; it is a transformative leap. As we discussed, this infusion of AI promises unprecedented gains in efficiency, resilience, and adaptability across sectors as diverse as energy, transportation, and public safety. The potential societal benefits are indeed profound. Imagine smart grids that seamlessly balance renewable energy sources with demand, minimizing waste and carbon emissions while ensuring uninterrupted power supply. Consider transportation networks that predict and alleviate congestion, making commutes safer and more efficient, and enabling the seamless integration of autonomous vehicles. Envision public safety systems that can anticipate and respond to emergencies with greater speed and precision, enhancing the security and well-being of our communities. These are not abstract fantasies but tangible possibilities unlocked by the intelligent capabilities of AI. The ability of AI systems to process vast datasets, identify complex patterns, make predictions, and even act autonomously offers the prospect of optimizing resource allocation, reducing operational costs, and improving the overall quality of life.

However, this transformative potential is inextricably linked to a commensurate increase in the stakes. The very complexity and interconnectedness that make AI-enabled infrastructure so powerful also amplify the potential consequences of failure. Traditional infrastructure, while subject to failures, often operates with a degree of isolation and predictability. A localized power outage, a bridge collapse, or a traffic signal malfunction, while disruptive, typically has contained impact. In contrast, AI-enabled infrastructure systems are characterized by their interconnectedness and their dynamic, often adaptive, nature. A failure in one part of an AI-controlled system can cascade through interconnected components, leading to widespread and unpredictable disruptions.

The unique characteristics of AI systems, as we have begun to explore, introduce failure modes that are fundamentally different from those encountered in traditional engineering. The probabilistic nature of machine learning models means that even when functioning correctly according to their training, they can produce erroneous outputs. This is not a simple bug to be fixed; it is an inherent characteristic of statistical inference. When these probabilistic decisions are integrated into safety-critical systems like autonomous vehicles or power grid management, the implications are significant. A slight miscalculation in an autonomous vehicle's perception system, or a suboptimal decision by an AI managing grid load, can have immediate and severe consequences. The brittleness of AI, its susceptibility to performing poorly when encountering data outside its training distribution, means that unforeseen events or novel environmental conditions can trigger unexpected and potentially dangerous behaviors.

Furthermore, the opacity of many advanced AI models—the "black box" problem—poses a significant challenge to ensuring safety and reliability. When an AI system fails, understanding precisely why it failed can be an arduous, if not impossible, task. This lack of interpretability hinders root cause analysis, making it difficult to implement effective corrective measures and to build trust in the system. Without a clear understanding of how an AI arrives at its decisions, it becomes challenging to rigorously verify its safety, especially under novel or edge-case conditions that may not have been present in the training data. This is particularly concerning in domains where human lives or critical services are at stake.

Moreover, the emergent behaviors that can arise from complex, interacting AI systems introduce an entirely new category of risk. These are not failures that can be traced to a single faulty component or a predictable bug. Instead, they are often systemic and unpredictable, arising from the intricate interplay of multiple AI agents or between AI systems and their environments. For instance, imagine a city's AI-managed traffic control system that, when interacting with the AI systems of individual autonomous vehicles and public transport, begins to exhibit oscillations in traffic flow or unintended traffic jams in areas that were previously clear. These emergent behaviors are difficult to anticipate during the design phase and even harder to diagnose once they manifest. The continuous learning and adaptation capabilities of AI, while beneficial, also introduce the risk of system drift—a gradual, insidious degradation of performance or safety parameters over time as the AI continuously updates its models based on new data. This dynamic evolution means that a system deemed safe at deployment may become less safe over time if its learning processes are not carefully monitored and constrained.

These unique failure modes and the amplified consequences arising from their integration into complex, interconnected systems underscore a critical imperative: the need for a deliberate and ethical approach to the deployment of AI in infrastructure. Simply applying traditional engineering safety paradigms, which were developed for deterministic and predictable systems, is no longer sufficient. While principles of robustness, redundancy, and testing remain vital, they must be augmented with new methodologies and frameworks specifically designed to address the probabilistic, data-dependent, and adaptive nature of AI.

The discussion must therefore pivot towards the responsible deployment of AI-enabled infrastructure. This means moving beyond the excitement of technological advancement to a sober assessment of the risks and the development of robust strategies to mitigate them. It requires a multidisciplinary approach that brings together AI researchers, engineers, ethicists, policymakers, and domain experts to ensure that these powerful technologies are developed and deployed in ways that prioritize human safety, security, and well-being. This is not an optional consideration; it is an ethical and practical necessity. The foundations of our society are increasingly reliant on these intelligent systems, and their responsible deployment is paramount to building a future that is both technologically advanced and fundamentally safe and trustworthy.

The inherent complexity and the synergistic nature of AI integration into infrastructure necessitate a profound rethinking of how we approach safety, reliability, and risk management. Traditional engineering practices, honed over decades for systems governed by predictable physical laws and deterministic logic, are proving insufficient for the nuanced challenges posed by AI. These challenges stem from the probabilistic underpinnings of machine learning, the critical dependence on data quality and representation, the inherent opacity of complex models, the potential for emergent behaviors in interconnected systems, and the dynamic evolution of AI through continuous learning.

Consider the stark reality of failure in AI-enabled systems. A failure in a traditional bridge might result in localized structural collapse, leading to immediate and observable damage. The cause is often traceable to material fatigue, design flaws, or external forces, all within the realm of established physics and engineering principles. The response is typically focused on repair, reconstruction, and adherence to stricter building codes. However, a failure in an AI-managed power grid could lead to cascading blackouts affecting millions, potentially for days, with the root cause being an algorithmic misinterpretation of sensor data during an unprecedented weather event, or an unforeseen interaction between multiple AI controllers designed for different grid segments. The problem might not be a physical defect but a logical one, embedded within the statistical patterns learned by the AI, making diagnosis and correction far more intricate.

Similarly, a failure in an AI-powered transportation network could manifest not as a single accident, but as widespread traffic gridlock, unsafe driving behaviors emerging from collective AI decisions, or even a systemic vulnerability to cyberattack that paralyzes movement across an entire city. The challenge here is that the AI's "decision-making" process is not a straightforward sequence of commands but a complex inference based on vast datasets and learned correlations. If these correlations are flawed, incomplete, or exploited, the entire system can enter an unstable state. The opacity of deep learning models exacerbates this; when an autonomous vehicle makes an incorrect decision—say, to brake too late or to swerve into an unexpected lane—pinpointing the exact algorithmic pathway that led to that decision can be a monumental task. This makes it difficult to guarantee that such a failure will not recur, especially under different but similar circumstances.

The risks are further amplified by the interconnectedness of these systems. An AI managing traffic flow might interact with an AI controlling public transit schedules, which in turn relies on real-time data from sensors that are part of the smart city's broader data infrastructure. If one of these AI components behaves unexpectedly, or if a vulnerability is exploited, the ripple effects can propagate through the entire ecosystem. This interconnectedness means that a localized AI failure, or a subtle algorithmic bias, can escalate into a widespread systemic risk, impacting multiple critical services simultaneously. For example, a bias in an AI used for predictive policing, if deployed across various domains of public safety, could inadvertently lead to discriminatory resource allocation and disproportionate enforcement in certain communities, reinforcing existing societal inequalities.

The imperative for responsible deployment, therefore, is not merely a matter of adhering to ethical guidelines; it is a fundamental requirement for the very viability and trustworthiness of AI-infused infrastructure. It demands a proactive and precautionary approach, one that anticipates potential failure modes and builds in safeguards from the outset. This requires a paradigm shift in how we think about engineering safety. Instead of solely relying on proving that a system will perform correctly under known conditions, we must also focus on ensuring that it behaves safely and predictably even when faced with novel, unexpected, or adversarial inputs—the so-called "unknown unknowns."

This necessitates the development and adoption of new engineering frameworks. These frameworks must go beyond traditional verification and validation methods to incorporate techniques for assessing the robustness of AI models, for understanding and mitigating biases, for ensuring transparency and explainability where possible, and for establishing mechanisms to detect and respond to emergent behaviors and system drift. The goal is not to eliminate risk entirely—an impossible feat in any complex system—but to ensure that risks are understood, managed, and communicated effectively, and that the potential consequences of failure are minimized to acceptable levels.

The very definition of "safety" needs to evolve. In traditional engineering, safety is often defined in terms of preventing catastrophic physical failures or ensuring reliability within specified operational parameters. In the context of AI, safety must also encompass algorithmic safety—ensuring that the AI's decision-making processes are sound, unbiased, and robust to manipulation or unexpected inputs. It must also consider ethical safety—guaranteeing that the AI's deployment does not lead to discriminatory outcomes, privacy violations, or other societal harms.

The development of such specialized frameworks is an urgent necessity. We are building the nervous system of our future society with AI, and just as a biological nervous system requires careful development and protection to function healthily, so too does our AI-infused infrastructure. Failure to establish these responsible deployment practices risks not only the efficacy and efficiency of these systems but also their public acceptance and, most critically, their ability to serve humanity safely and equitably. The pursuit of innovation must be tempered with the wisdom of caution, ensuring that the foundations we build are not only intelligent and adaptable but also fundamentally sound and secure.

The challenges posed by AI-enabled infrastructure are not merely technical; they are deeply intertwined with societal values and ethical considerations. The transition from traditional, deterministic systems to probabilistic, adaptive AI necessitates a re-evaluation of our established safety engineering principles. Where traditional approaches relied on exhaustive testing of components and systems against known failure modes, AI introduces a realm of uncertainty and emergent properties that defy such straightforward analysis. The imperative for responsible deployment stems from this fundamental divergence, demanding new paradigms to ensure that the societal benefits of AI-infused infrastructure are realized without compromising safety, equity, or trustworthiness.

This imperative is further amplified by the potential for AI failures to have disproportionately large and cascading impacts. Consider the power grid, a quintessential example of critical infrastructure. A failure in a traditional component, such as a transformer, might lead to localized outages. However, an AI managing grid stability could misinterpret sensor data during an extreme weather event, leading to a decision that causes a much wider and longer-lasting blackout. The cause might not be a physical defect but a flaw in the AI's predictive model, its inability to account for an unprecedented scenario, or even an adversarial attack designed to exploit the AI's learning mechanisms. The consequences—disruption of essential services, economic losses, and even threats to public health and safety—are magnified by the interconnected and intelligent nature of the system.

In the realm of transportation, the deployment of autonomous vehicles and AI-managed traffic systems promises enhanced safety by removing human error. Yet, a single critical error in an AI's perception or decision-making module, especially one that propagates across a network of vehicles, could lead to catastrophic multi-vehicle accidents. Traditional safety measures like airbags and anti-lock brakes are physical and deterministic. Ensuring the safety of AI in vehicles requires addressing algorithmic robustness, cybersecurity vulnerabilities, and the predictable behavior of complex learning systems under a vast array of real-world conditions, many of which may not have been fully represented in training data. The opacity of many AI models makes it difficult to certify their safety with the same rigor as traditional mechanical systems. If an autonomous vehicle causes an accident, understanding precisely why it made the erroneous decision—whether it was a sensor failure, a software bug, a data bias, or an unexpected environmental factor—is crucial for preventing recurrence, but often exceedingly difficult to ascertain.

The integration of AI into public safety systems, while offering the promise of more efficient resource allocation and faster response times, introduces a unique set of ethical and safety concerns. AI systems used for predictive policing, for example, can inadvertently perpetuate and amplify existing societal biases if trained on historical data that reflects discriminatory practices. This can lead to over-policing in certain communities, undermining public trust and potentially leading to unjust outcomes. The safety imperative here extends beyond preventing physical harm; it includes ensuring that AI systems do not systematically discriminate against certain populations or erode civil liberties. Moreover, the reliance on AI for critical decisions in emergency situations demands a high degree of reliability and accountability. If an AI system fails to correctly identify a threat, misallocates emergency resources, or misinterprets critical data during a crisis, the consequences can be dire.

These scenarios highlight why conventional engineering safety paradigms are insufficient. They were designed for systems where components have well-defined failure modes and predictable behavior. AI systems, on the other hand, are characterized by their data-driven, probabilistic, and adaptive nature. Their "failures" might not be outright malfunctions but rather gradual degradations in performance, unintended emergent behaviors, or decisions that are statistically sound but contextually inappropriate or ethically unsound.

Therefore, the imperative for responsible deployment necessitates the development of new approaches to safety assurance. This includes:

Robustness Testing and Validation: Moving beyond standard testing to include adversarial testing, stress testing under extreme conditions, and formal verification methods tailored for AI. This involves actively trying to "break" the AI in controlled environments to understand its limits and vulnerabilities.
Explainability and Interpretability: Developing techniques to understand why an AI makes a particular decision. While complete transparency may be impossible for some complex models, methods that provide insights into the decision-making process are crucial for debugging, auditing, and building trust. This is essential for accountability and for ensuring that AI aligns with human values.

Bias Detection and Mitigation: Implementing rigorous processes to identify and correct biases in training data and AI models. This is critical for ensuring fairness and preventing AI from perpetuating or exacerbating societal inequalities. The development of fairness metrics and auditing tools is paramount.

Continuous Monitoring and Governance: Establishing systems for ongoing monitoring of AI performance and behavior in real-world deployment. This is necessary to detect system drift, emergent issues, and potential vulnerabilities that may arise over time as the AI interacts with its environment and adapts. Strong governance frameworks are needed to oversee these systems, define acceptable risk levels, and ensure accountability.

Human-AI Collaboration and Oversight: Designing systems where AI augments, rather than entirely replaces, human judgment, especially in safety-critical applications. This involves ensuring that human operators have the necessary information, tools, and authority to intervene when an AI system exhibits concerning behavior or makes potentially erroneous decisions. The synergy between human expertise and AI capabilities needs to be carefully managed.

Ethical Frameworks and Standards: Developing clear ethical guidelines and industry-wide standards for the design, development, and deployment of AI in infrastructure. These standards should address issues of safety, fairness, privacy, security, and accountability, providing a common ground for responsible innovation.

The transition to AI-enabled infrastructure is an exciting frontier, promising significant advancements. However, this promise can only be fully and safely realized if we proactively address the unique challenges it presents. The imperative for responsible deployment is not a brake on innovation, but rather a necessary compass, guiding us toward a future where intelligent infrastructure enhances human well-being and societal progress without introducing unacceptable risks. It demands a collective commitment from researchers, developers, policymakers, and the public to prioritize safety, ethics, and trustworthiness in every stage of AI integration. Without this deliberate and ethical approach, the very systems designed to safeguard and advance society could inadvertently become sources of unforeseen risks and systemic vulnerabilities.

The profound integration of artificial intelligence into the fabric of our critical infrastructure, as we have established, presents a paradigm shift with immense potential for societal advancement. However, this transformative power is inextricably linked to an amplified responsibility. The foundational principles of engineering have always included a commitment to safety and reliability, but the unique characteristics of AI necessitate a deliberate and robust ethical framework to guide its development and deployment within these vital systems. This is not an abstract philosophical exercise; it is a pragmatic requirement for ensuring that AI-infused infrastructure truly serves humanity, enhancing our lives without introducing unacceptable risks.

At the heart of this ethical imperative lie several core principles, adapted from broader bioethics and applied to the domain of AI engineering. The principle of
beneficence compels us to design and deploy AI systems that actively promote human well-being and societal good. For infrastructure, this translates into ensuring that AI-driven improvements in efficiency, sustainability, and accessibility actually translate into tangible benefits for all citizens. For instance, an AI-managed smart grid should not only optimize energy distribution for cost savings but also ensure equitable access to reliable power, particularly for vulnerable communities that might otherwise be underserved. Similarly, an AI system for traffic management should not just reduce congestion for commuters but also enhance safety for pedestrians and cyclists, demonstrating a clear and demonstrable benefit to public welfare.

Complementary to beneficence is the principle of
non-maleficence, often summarized as "do no harm." In the context of AI-engineered infrastructure, this demands a rigorous proactive

identification and mitigation of potential harms. This extends beyond traditional safety concerns like structural integrity or mechanical failure. It encompasses algorithmic harm, such as the introduction or amplification of biases that lead to unfair or discriminatory outcomes. It also includes systemic harm, where the complex interactions of AI systems could lead to cascading failures or unforeseen negative externalities. For example, an AI system designed to optimize public transport routes for efficiency might, if not carefully designed, inadvertently reduce service to less affluent neighborhoods, thereby causing harm through decreased accessibility. The engineering challenge then becomes not just about optimizing a given metric but about ensuring that the optimization process itself does not violate the principle of non-maleficence.

The principle of
justice is equally critical, demanding fairness and equity in the design, deployment, and impact of AI-infused infrastructure. This has several dimensions. Distributive justice concerns how the benefits and burdens of AI are shared. Will the efficiency gains from AI-powered systems lead to job displacement without adequate retraining or social support? Will the advanced capabilities be accessible to all, or will they exacerbate existing digital divides, creating a two-tiered society where some benefit immensely while others are left behind? Procedural justice requires that the processes by which AI systems are developed and governed are fair, transparent, and accountable. This means ensuring diverse voices are included in the design and decision-making processes and that there are clear mechanisms for redress when AI systems cause harm. Algorithmic justice, a more specific application, addresses the inherent biases that can be encoded into AI models. If an AI system for resource allocation, such as water distribution or emergency services deployment, is trained on biased historical data, it can perpetuate and even amplify existing inequities, leading to unjust outcomes for certain demographic groups. The engineering task here is to actively audit for and correct these biases, striving for algorithms that are fair by design and by operation.

Finally, the principle of **autonomy** warrants careful consideration. In the context of infrastructure, this relates to the autonomy of the system itself, the autonomy of the individuals interacting with it, and the autonomy of society in shaping its technological future. For engineered systems, it means ensuring that AI components operate within well-defined boundaries and that their adaptive capabilities do not lead to unpredictable or uncontrollable behavior that undermines human oversight. For individuals, it means respecting their right to understand how AI systems affect them and, where appropriate, to make choices about their interaction with these systems. For society, it means fostering informed public discourse and democratic control over the direction of AI deployment in critical infrastructure. The development of transparent interfaces, clear user agreements, and robust public consultation processes are all facets of upholding this principle.

These foundational principles—beneficence, non-maleficence, justice, and autonomy—provide a crucial compass for navigating the complex ethical landscape of AI-infused infrastructure. However, translating these abstract ideals into concrete engineering practices requires confronting specific, recurring ethical dilemmas.

One of the most pervasive challenges is **algorithmic bias**. As mentioned, AI systems learn from data, and if that data reflects historical societal biases, the AI will likely perpetuate and even amplify them. This is not a theoretical concern; it has tangible implications for infrastructure. Consider an AI system designed to manage the allocation of resources for road maintenance. If historical data shows that certain neighborhoods have received less maintenance than others, an AI trained on this data might continue to deprioritize those areas, even if the underlying need is greater. This leads to a widening gap in infrastructure quality and disproportionately affects the residents of those communities, violating principles of justice and beneficence. The engineering challenge lies in developing methods to detect and mitigate these biases. This involves rigorous data auditing, exploring fairness-aware machine learning algorithms, and implementing post-deployment monitoring to identify and correct emergent biases. It requires engineers to move beyond simply optimizing for accuracy to optimizing for fairness metrics alongside performance metrics.

Another significant ethical hurdle is the
lack of transparency and explainability, often referred to as the "black box" problem. Many advanced AI models, particularly deep neural networks, operate in ways that are opaque even to their creators. When an AI system makes a critical decision—perhaps rerouting power during a surge, or adjusting traffic light timing in an emergency—understanding precisely *why* it made that decision can be incredibly difficult. This opacity poses a direct threat to accountability and trust. If an AI-managed system fails, and we cannot understand the root cause, it is hard to assign responsibility, learn from the failure, and prevent its recurrence. In safety-critical infrastructure, this lack of understanding is unacceptable. Imagine an autonomous vehicle involved in an accident; if investigators cannot ascertain the precise algorithmic reasoning that led to the erroneous action, it hampers both legal accountability and future safety improvements. The engineering response involves developing and deploying explainable AI (XAI) techniques, even if they introduce a slight performance trade-off. This could involve using inherently more interpretable models where feasible, developing post-hoc explanation methods, or designing interfaces that provide meaningful insights into the AI's decision-making process for human operators.

The potential for
unintended consequences is a broad category of ethical risk inherent in complex, interconnected AI systems. Because AI can learn and adapt, and because AI-infused infrastructure is increasingly interconnected, emergent behaviors can arise that were not foreseen by the designers. For

example, an AI that optimizes traffic flow in a city might, by subtly adjusting signal timings, inadvertently create patterns of sound pollution in residential areas or redirect traffic through sensitive ecological zones. These are not direct bugs but indirect, emergent effects of the AI's optimization process interacting with the environment. The engineering challenge here is one of foresight and systemic thinking. It requires moving beyond component-level testing to embrace system-level analysis, simulation of complex interactions, and the development of robust risk assessment methodologies that explicitly account for emergent properties. It also underscores the importance of iterative development and continuous monitoring, allowing engineers to identify and address unintended consequences as they emerge in real-world deployment.

Related to unintended consequences is the challenge of **system drift**. AI models are trained on data from a specific period and context. As the real world changes—environmental conditions shift, user behavior evolves, or new threats emerge—the AI's performance may degrade if it cannot adapt appropriately. However, uncontrolled adaptation can lead to undesirable outcomes. An AI managing a water purification system, for instance, might continue to operate based on historical data about contaminant levels, failing to adapt to a new, previously unencountered pollutant. Conversely, an AI that adapts too aggressively might become unstable or develop new, unforeseen failure modes. The ethical imperative is to ensure that AI systems remain safe and effective over their entire lifecycle. This requires sophisticated monitoring systems that detect performance degradation or drifts away from desired parameters. It also necessitates careful design of the learning and adaptation mechanisms, possibly incorporating human oversight or predetermined "safety anchors" that prevent the AI from deviating too far from its original safe operating envelope.

Another critical ethical dilemma arises from the

dual-use nature of AI technologies. AI developed for beneficial infrastructure applications can often be repurposed for harmful ends. For instance, advanced AI for predictive maintenance in power grids could, in the wrong hands, be used to identify vulnerabilities for cyberattacks. Sophisticated AI for traffic management could be manipulated to create deliberate chaos or to facilitate surveillance. The engineering challenge here involves building security and resilience into AI systems from the ground up. This means robust cybersecurity measures, but also designing AI such that its core functionalities are inherently resistant to misuse or manipulation. It requires a proactive approach to threat modeling, considering not just accidental failures but malicious intent, and embedding security and ethical considerations into the very architecture of the AI.

The question of
accountability and responsibility is fundamental. When an AI-infused infrastructure system causes harm, who is responsible? Is it the developers who trained the model, the engineers who deployed it, the operators who managed it, or the company that owns it? The distributed nature of AI development and deployment, coupled with the opacity of some models, can make it difficult to establish clear lines of accountability. This is not just a legal issue; it is an ethical one. Without clear accountability, there is less incentive to prioritize safety and ethics, and victims may lack recourse. Engineering solutions can contribute to addressing this. By demanding greater transparency and explainability, we make it easier to trace the causes of failure. By implementing robust logging and auditing mechanisms, we create a record of system behavior and decision-making. Developing clear governance frameworks that delineate responsibilities for AI system oversight and maintenance is also crucial.

Furthermore, the sheer
complexity of AI-infused infrastructure presents a unique ethical challenge. As systems become more interconnected and intelligent, their

behavior becomes less predictable. A seemingly minor change in one part of the system could have cascading and unforeseen effects elsewhere. This complexity can overwhelm traditional risk assessment methods. The ethical responsibility of engineers is to acknowledge this complexity and to develop new methodologies for managing it. This might involve developing sophisticated simulation environments to test interactions between different AI components, employing formal methods to prove certain safety properties of AI algorithms, or adopting a more precautionary approach, where new functionalities are introduced incrementally and with extensive validation.

Finally, the **human element** in AI-infused infrastructure cannot be overlooked. While AI promises automation, human operators remain essential for oversight, intervention, and complex decision-making. However, the integration of AI can change the role and skills required of these human operators. There is a risk of "automation complacency," where operators become less vigilant because the AI is perceived as infallible, leading to missed alerts or delayed responses when the AI does falter. Conversely, the AI might provide information in ways that are difficult for humans to interpret, leading to misjudgments. The ethical engineering challenge is to design human-AI interfaces that promote effective collaboration. This involves ensuring that AI provides clear, actionable insights, that human operators are adequately trained and empowered to intervene, and that the overall system design fosters a healthy skepticism and vigilance towards AI's outputs, rather than blind trust.

Addressing these ethical dilemmas is not an optional add-on to AI engineering; it must be an integral part of the design and development process. This requires a shift in mindset, where ethical considerations are not an afterthought but a primary design constraint. It means embedding ethical reasoning into the engineering curriculum and fostering a culture within organizations that prioritizes responsible innovation. The development of AI-infused infrastructure is a journey into uncharted territory. By grounding our efforts in robust ethical principles and proactively addressing the inherent dilemmas, we can ensure that this journey leads to a future that is not only more intelligent and efficient but also more just, equitable, and safe for all. The engineering of our future infrastructure demands not just technical prowess, but profound ethical wisdom.

The successful and responsible integration of artificial intelligence into our critical infrastructure hinges on a comprehensive understanding of the diverse array of individuals and groups who have a vested interest in these systems. This understanding is not merely an academic exercise; it forms the bedrock of effective governance and ethical deployment. Identifying these stakeholders is the crucial first step in ensuring that AI-infused infrastructure is developed and operated in a manner that is not only technically sound but also socially equitable and trustworthy. Without this foundational step, even the most technically brilliant solutions risk being misaligned with societal needs, engendering distrust, or, worse, causing unintended harm.

Stakeholders, in this context, are any individuals, groups, or organizations that can affect, be affected by, or perceive themselves to be affected by the development, deployment, or operation of AI-infused infrastructure. This definition is intentionally broad, encompassing a wide spectrum of interests and perspectives. At the most immediate level are the **end-users** of the infrastructure. For a smart grid, these are the households and businesses relying on electricity. For AI-enhanced transportation networks, it includes commuters, freight operators, and public transit riders. Their primary concern is reliable service, affordability, and safety. However, as AI introduces new functionalities, their concerns may expand to include privacy related to their data usage, the fairness of service distribution, and their ability to understand and interact with AI-driven systems that impact their daily lives.

Moving beyond direct users, we must consider the

operators and maintainers of these AI-infused systems. These are the engineers, technicians, and operational staff responsible for the day-to-day functioning, monitoring, and upkeep of the infrastructure. Their engagement is vital because they possess intimate knowledge of the system's practicalities, its limitations, and its real-world performance. They are often the first to identify emergent issues or deviations from expected behavior. Their concerns typically revolve around the usability of AI interfaces, the clarity of AI outputs, the training required to manage AI systems effectively, and the clarity of roles and responsibilities when AI is involved in operational decisions. The "automation complacency" risk, for example, is a direct concern for operators, and their feedback is essential for designing systems that maintain human vigilance.

A critical group of stakeholders are the **regulators and policymakers**. These entities are responsible for establishing the legal and regulatory frameworks that govern infrastructure development and operation. They are concerned with public safety, national security, economic competitiveness, and ensuring that new technologies align with societal values and objectives. Their engagement is paramount for ensuring that AI-infused infrastructure adheres to existing laws and that new regulations are developed to address the unique challenges posed by AI, such as data privacy, algorithmic accountability, and fair competition. Policymakers need to understand the capabilities and limitations of AI, as well as its potential risks, to craft effective and forward-looking governance.

Furthermore, we must actively engage with **affected communities**. This category is particularly nuanced and essential for upholding principles of justice and equity. Affected communities are those that may not directly operate or use the infrastructure but are nevertheless impacted by its presence and operation. This can include:

Local residents living near infrastructure facilities: They may be concerned about environmental impacts, noise pollution, or changes to their neighborhoods.
Vulnerable populations and historically marginalized groups: These groups are often disproportionately affected by infrastructure decisions and may face amplified risks or be excluded from benefits if AI systems are not designed with equity in mind. For instance, an AI-powered resource allocation system for emergency services must be carefully scrutinized to ensure it does not deprioritize underserved areas.
Environmental advocacy groups: Concerned with the ecological footprint of infrastructure and the sustainability implications of AI-driven optimization.
Labor unions and worker representatives: Concerned with job security, workforce training, and the impact of AI on employment conditions.

These communities often possess invaluable local knowledge and a deep understanding of the social and environmental context in which infrastructure operates. Their inclusion ensures that the potential for unintended consequences and the distribution of benefits and burdens are considered from a human-centered perspective.

The **developers, researchers, and technology providers** who create the AI systems are also key stakeholders. They possess the technical expertise and are responsible for the design and implementation of the AI algorithms and hardware. Their engagement is crucial for understanding the state of the art, the inherent limitations of current AI technologies, and the ethical considerations that arise during the development process. Their concerns often relate to intellectual property, the feasibility of implementing ethical guidelines within technical constraints, and the potential for their innovations to be misused. Fostering a culture of responsible innovation within these groups is paramount.

Beyond these core groups, other stakeholders can include:

Academics and ethicists: Providing critical analysis, theoretical frameworks, and independent research on the societal implications of AI.
Non-governmental organizations (NGOs) and civil society groups: Advocating for public interest, human rights, and environmental protection.
Insurance providers: Assessing and underwriting the risks associated with AI-infused infrastructure.
Investors and financial institutions: Providing capital and influencing project viability based on risk and return, including considerations of social and environmental impact.
Emergency services and disaster response organizations: Relying on the resilience and reliability of infrastructure during critical events.

Identifying these diverse stakeholders is only the first step. The subsequent and perhaps more challenging phase is **meaningful engagement**. It is not enough to simply acknowledge their existence; their voices must be actively sought, heard, and genuinely considered. Meaningful engagement goes beyond superficial consultations; it aims to foster genuine dialogue and collaboration throughout the entire lifecycle of AI-infused infrastructure, from initial concept and design through deployment, operation, and decommissioning.

Several strategies can facilitate this engagement:

Firstly, **establishing clear communication channels** is fundamental. This involves creating platforms and forums where stakeholders can easily access information and provide feedback. For end-users, this might involve intuitive user interfaces with accessible explanations of AI functionality, feedback mechanisms within apps, or public information campaigns. For affected communities, it might mean town hall meetings in accessible locations and at convenient times, dedicated community liaisons, and translated materials. For regulators, ongoing dialogue through working groups and official consultations is essential.

Secondly,
transparency in intent and process builds trust. Stakeholders need to understand what AI is intended to achieve, how it will operate, and what data it will use. This does not necessarily mean revealing proprietary algorithms, but rather providing clear, understandable explanations of the system's purpose, its decision-making logic (to the extent possible), and the safeguards in place. For instance, when an AI is used to optimize the deployment of public resources like snow plows, affected residents should be informed about the criteria used for prioritization and how the AI responds to unexpected events. The principle of explainable AI (XAI) becomes crucial here, not just for technical operators but for communicating with the public.

Thirdly,
adopting a participatory design approach can be highly effective. This involves actively involving stakeholders in the design and development process itself. For example, when designing an AI system for managing urban water distribution, involving representatives from local residents, environmental groups, and water utility operators in co-design workshops can ensure that critical needs and potential issues are identified early. This approach moves beyond mere consultation to co-creation, where stakeholders have a tangible influence on the system's architecture and functionality. This is particularly important for ensuring that justice and non-maleficence principles are embedded from the outset, rather than being retrofitted later.

Fourthly,
iterative feedback loops are vital for continuous improvement. The deployment of AI-infused infrastructure is not a one-time event. It is an ongoing process that requires continuous monitoring, evaluation, and adaptation. Establishing mechanisms for ongoing feedback collection and ensuring that this feedback leads to demonstrable changes is crucial. For example, if users report that an AI-powered public transport app is providing inaccurate real-time arrival information, a responsive system would not only acknowledge the feedback but also visibly address the underlying technical issue and communicate the resolution. This iterative process helps build long-term trust and ensures that systems remain aligned with evolving needs and contexts.

Fifthly,
building capacity and providing education is essential for informed engagement. Not all stakeholders have the technical expertise to understand complex AI systems. Therefore, providing accessible educational resources and training can empower them to participate more effectively. This could involve workshops for community leaders on understanding AI's impact, plain-language guides on data privacy, or training modules for operators on AI oversight. This investment in understanding fosters a more equitable and informed dialogue.

Building trust and fostering collaboration are not merely desirable outcomes; they are fundamental prerequisites for the socially responsible deployment of AI-infused infrastructure. When stakeholders feel that their concerns are genuinely heard and acted upon, they are more likely to trust the systems that govern their lives. This trust is fragile and can be eroded by a single instance of perceived unfairness, lack of transparency, or unaccountable failure. Therefore, a proactive and sustained commitment to inclusive engagement is paramount.

The process of stakeholder identification and engagement can be visualized as a continuous cycle. It begins with broad identification, followed by systematic engagement activities. The insights gained from engagement then inform the design, development, and operational adjustments of the AI systems. This cycle repeats, with feedback from ongoing operations and evolving societal needs leading to further refinement. For example, an AI system managing a city's power grid might be initially designed with input from utility operators and regulators. However, during operation, feedback from a community group about its impact on local businesses during peak demand periods could lead to adjustments in its load-balancing algorithms, ensuring both efficiency and equity.

Moreover, it is important to recognize that stakeholder interests can sometimes be in conflict. For instance, a regulator might prioritize stringent safety standards that increase development costs, while a technology provider might push for faster deployment to gain market share. Affected communities might advocate for environmental protections that could limit operational flexibility. The process of meaningful engagement is not about finding a solution that satisfies everyone perfectly, but about facilitating constructive dialogue to navigate these competing interests, seeking compromises that uphold core ethical principles while enabling progress. This requires skilled facilitation, a commitment to open-mindedness, and a shared understanding that the ultimate goal is to build infrastructure that serves the broader public good.

In conclusion, the journey towards AI-infused infrastructure must be undertaken with a profound awareness of the human element. This means meticulously identifying all relevant stakeholders, from the end-users and operators to regulators, affected communities, and developers.

Crucially, it requires moving beyond mere identification to embrace a commitment to meaningful, transparent, and participatory engagement. By actively listening to diverse voices, incorporating their concerns into the design and operational lifecycle, and fostering genuine collaboration, we can build not only smarter and more efficient infrastructure but also a more just, equitable, and trustworthy future for all. This commitment to inclusive governance is not an optional extra; it is an indispensable pillar of responsible technological advancement.

The integration of artificial intelligence into the very fabric of our critical infrastructure, while promising unprecedented efficiencies and capabilities, is occurring within a complex and dynamically evolving regulatory and policy environment. This landscape is not a static, well-defined map, but rather a constantly shifting terrain, shaped by rapid technological advancements, diverse societal expectations, and the inherent challenges of governing emergent technologies. For engineers, project managers, and indeed anyone involved in the design, deployment, and operation of AI-infused infrastructure, understanding this evolving ecosystem is not merely a matter of compliance; it is a strategic imperative. It dictates the feasibility of projects, the timelines for implementation, and crucially, the long-term viability and trustworthiness of the systems we build.

At present, the direct, AI-specific legislative frameworks are largely in their nascent stages globally. Many jurisdictions are grappling with how to adapt existing laws – those designed for physical infrastructure, data protection, and broader consumer rights – to encompass the unique characteristics of artificial intelligence. This often means that initial deployments of AI in infrastructure must navigate a patchwork of regulations. For example, in sectors like transportation, existing safety standards for autonomous vehicles are being developed or adapted, but the integration of AI into traffic management systems might fall under a different set of rules governing public utilities or data privacy. Similarly, smart grid technologies powered by AI must comply with energy sector regulations, cybersecurity mandates, and potentially data governance laws that predate the widespread use of machine learning for grid optimization.

The challenge for policymakers is immense. The pace of AI innovation far outstrips the traditional legislative cycles. By the time a law is drafted, debated, and enacted, the underlying technology may have evolved significantly, rendering the legislation either too restrictive, too permissive, or simply obsolete. This necessitates a more agile and adaptive approach to governance. We are seeing a rise in "soft law" mechanisms, such as industry standards, best practice guidelines, and voluntary ethical frameworks, which can offer more flexibility and quicker adaptation than formal legislation. Organizations are increasingly looking to bodies like the International Organization for Standardization (ISO) or national standards institutes for guidance on AI safety, reliability, and ethical considerations.

Consider the domain of AI in water management systems. While the physical infrastructure of pipes, pumps, and treatment plants is heavily regulated, the AI algorithms used for leak detection, demand forecasting, or optimizing chemical treatment might operate in a regulatory grey area. Policymakers are now actively exploring frameworks for AI auditing, algorithmic transparency, and accountability for AI-driven decisions that impact public services. This includes developing methodologies to assess the fairness of resource allocation algorithms, the robustness of AI systems against adversarial attacks, and the potential for bias in predictive models used for infrastructure maintenance scheduling.

The adaptation of existing industry standards is another crucial aspect of this evolving landscape. Regulators and industry bodies are not starting from scratch. They are examining established practices in areas like functional safety (e.g., IEC 61508 for electrical/electronic/programmable electronic safety-related systems), cybersecurity (e.g., NIST Cybersecurity Framework), and reliability engineering. The challenge lies in translating these principles to the context of AI. For instance, a traditionally designed control system might have well-understood failure modes that can be rigorously tested. An AI system, particularly one that learns and adapts over time, presents a more complex challenge for assurance and verification. How does one guarantee the safety of an AI that may exhibit emergent behaviors not present in its training data?

This has led to the development of new standards specifically addressing AI. For example, efforts are underway to create standards for AI testing and validation, focusing on data quality, model performance metrics, and the evaluation of AI systems in real-world operational environments. Standards related to AI explainability (XAI) are also gaining traction, aiming to provide mechanisms for understanding how AI systems arrive at their decisions, which is critical for debugging, auditing, and building user trust. In the context of AI-infused infrastructure, this could mean developing standards for how an AI controlling a power grid explains its load-balancing decisions to grid operators or how an AI managing autonomous public transport systems justifies its route choices or emergency braking actions.

Furthermore, the international dimension of AI governance cannot be overstated. AI is a global technology, and its infrastructure impacts transcend national borders. This necessitates international cooperation to avoid regulatory fragmentation and to establish common principles. Initiatives from organizations like the OECD, UNESCO, and the IEEE are working towards establishing global norms and ethical guidelines for AI development and deployment. This collaborative effort is essential for fostering trust and ensuring that AI-infused infrastructure serves humanity universally, rather than creating new geopolitical divides or technological dependencies.

The practical implications for engineers and managers are significant. They must develop a keen awareness of the regulatory horizon. This involves not only understanding the current legal and standards landscape but also actively monitoring proposed legislation, participating in industry working groups, and staying abreast of research and development in AI governance. For instance, a project manager overseeing the deployment of an AI-powered traffic management system needs to be aware of potential future requirements for data anonymization, algorithmic impact assessments, or mandatory reporting of AI system performance.

Anticipating future requirements is key to avoiding costly retrofits or project delays. This proactive approach involves adopting "privacy by design" and "safety by design" principles from the outset, integrating ethical considerations and robustness into the very architecture of the AI systems. It means building flexibility into systems to accommodate evolving regulatory requirements. For example, designing data pipelines that can be easily reconfigured to meet new data privacy standards or developing AI models that are inherently more interpretable.

The financial sector and insurance industry are also playing an increasingly influential role in shaping this landscape. As AI-infused infrastructure becomes more prevalent, insurers are developing new risk assessment models and underwriting practices. This can incentivize companies to adopt more robust AI safety and security measures, as these will directly impact their insurance premiums and insurability. Investment firms and venture capitalists are also increasingly scrutinizing the ethical and regulatory compliance of AI projects, viewing these as critical indicators of long-term success and risk mitigation. This financial pressure can act as a powerful catalyst for responsible AI development and deployment.

The challenge of keeping pace is compounded by the rapid iteration cycles of AI development. Unlike traditional infrastructure projects that might have multi-decade lifespans with relatively stable technological foundations, AI systems are often updated, retrained, and improved continuously. This presents a dilemma for regulators: how can they provide effective oversight for systems that are constantly changing? This points towards the need for regulatory approaches that focus on process and outcomes rather than rigid technical specifications. For example, instead of dictating specific algorithms, regulators might focus on ensuring that robust processes are in place for AI model validation, bias detection, and continuous monitoring of performance and safety in real-world conditions.

The concept of "algorithmic accountability" is central to these discussions. When an AI system makes a decision that leads to a negative outcome – whether it's a power outage, a traffic accident, or an unfair distribution of resources – who is responsible? Is it the developers, the operators, the data providers, or the AI system itself? Existing legal frameworks often struggle to assign responsibility in such complex scenarios. Therefore, new approaches to accountability are being explored, which may involve mandatory incident reporting, independent auditing of AI systems, and clear lines of responsibility established through contracts and service level agreements.

For managers of AI-infused infrastructure, this means fostering a culture of meticulous record-keeping, comprehensive documentation of AI model development and deployment, and establishing clear internal processes for incident investigation and response. It also means investing in training for personnel to understand the implications of AI and to be equipped to handle situations where AI systems behave unexpectedly. The human oversight component remains critically important; AI is a tool, and humans must remain in the loop for critical decision-making and for ensuring that the AI's actions align with societal values and legal requirements.

In conclusion, the journey of integrating AI into critical infrastructure is intrinsically linked to navigating a complex, dynamic, and often uncertain regulatory and policy environment. It is a domain where established legal traditions meet cutting-edge technology, where innovation must be tempered with foresight and responsibility. For those at the forefront of building and managing these AI-infused systems, a deep engagement with this evolving landscape is not optional. It requires a proactive, adaptive, and ethically grounded approach to anticipate challenges, ensure compliance, foster trust, and ultimately, harness the transformative power of AI for the betterment of society. This understanding is foundational for ensuring that the infrastructure of tomorrow is not only intelligent and efficient but also safe, equitable, and resilient.

Chapter 2: Principles of AI Safety Engineering

The integration of artificial intelligence into critical systems, from autonomous vehicles to smart grids and medical diagnostics, presents a profound challenge and opportunity for the field of safety engineering. For decades, safety engineers have developed rigorous methodologies to ensure the reliable and secure operation of complex systems, drawing upon hard-won experience in domains characterized by high stakes and unforgiving environments. Fields such as aerospace, nuclear power, and chemical processing have pioneered systematic approaches to identifying, analyzing, and mitigating hazards, establishing robust frameworks for the design and operation of safety-critical systems. These established principles, built on a foundation of deterministic logic, well-understood physical laws, and predictable failure modes, offer a crucial starting point for developing AI safety engineering. However, the very nature of AI, particularly machine learning-based systems, introduces fundamental differences that necessitate a thoughtful adaptation, rather than a wholesale rejection, of these traditional paradigms.

At the heart of traditional safety engineering lies the concept of hazard analysis. This systematic process involves identifying potential sources of harm, understanding the scenarios under which these hazards could manifest, and evaluating the severity and likelihood of the resulting accidents. Techniques like Failure Mode and Effects Analysis (FMEA), Fault Tree Analysis (FTA), and Hazard and Operability Studies (HAZOP) have been instrumental in dissecting complex systems into their constituent components and identifying potential failure pathways. In traditional systems, failure modes are often discrete and predictable. For example, a mechanical component might fail due to wear and tear, a sensor might drift out of calibration, or a software bug might cause a specific, reproducible error. The goal of hazard analysis is to identify all such credible failure modes, estimate their probability, and implement controls or redundancies to reduce the overall risk to an acceptable level.

Risk assessment, a natural extension of hazard analysis, quantifies the potential for harm. It typically involves characterizing hazards, assessing their likelihood of occurrence, and estimating the severity of their consequences. This process allows engineers to prioritize safety efforts, focusing resources on the most significant risks. The output of risk assessment is often a risk matrix or a quantitative risk value, which then informs the establishment of safety requirements. These requirements are typically specific, measurable, achievable, relevant, and time-bound (SMART), detailing the necessary design features, operational procedures, and performance criteria to ensure safety. For instance, a safety requirement might stipulate that a critical valve must close within 100 milliseconds of a specific trigger event, or that a backup power system must activate within 50 milliseconds of a primary power failure. The assurance of these requirements is often achieved through exhaustive testing, verification, and validation, often involving formal proofs or extensive simulation under a wide range of expected operating conditions.

However, when we turn our attention to AI-enabled systems, the direct application of these traditional methodologies encounters significant hurdles. The probabilistic and data-driven nature of AI, particularly deep learning models, fundamentally alters the landscape of predictability and determinism. Instead of well-defined, discrete failure modes, AI systems can exhibit subtle, emergent behaviors that are difficult to anticipate or enumerate exhaustively. A common example is the "brittleness" of machine learning models, where a slight perturbation in input data, perhaps imperceptible to a human, can lead to a catastrophic misclassification or decision. This contrasts sharply with traditional systems where failure modes are often more robustly understood and less sensitive to minor input variations.

Consider the application of FMEA to a deep neural network used for image recognition in an autonomous vehicle. While we can analyze the potential failures of the underlying hardware (e.g., sensor malfunction, computational unit failure), analyzing the failure modes of the neural network's decision-making process is far more complex. What constitutes a "failure mode" for a system that learns from data? It might not be a single, identifiable bug, but rather a statistical anomaly in its predictive capabilities under specific, perhaps rare, circumstances. The vast number of parameters in a modern neural network (millions or even billions) makes it infeasible to individually analyze the impact of each parameter on the system's overall behavior. Furthermore, the internal workings of these models are often opaque, making it challenging to pinpoint the exact cause of a failure once it occurs. This "black box" problem, where the internal logic is not easily interpretable, is a major departure from traditional systems where the operational logic is typically transparent and auditable.

Fault Tree Analysis, which starts with an undesirable outcome (e.g., a collision) and works backward to identify the combinations of component failures that could lead to it, also faces challenges. For an AI system, the "component failure" might not be a physical breakdown, but a conceptual one – a failure to generalize from its training data, a susceptibility to adversarial attacks, or an unintended bias learned from biased training data. The combinatorial explosion of potential causal factors in complex AI systems can render traditional FTA intractable. For example, a collision might be caused not by a single sensor failure, but by a confluence of factors: a particular lighting condition, a novel object on the road that the AI has not encountered in its training set, and a subtle misinterpretation of sensor data due to these novel conditions. Tracing all such potential causal chains is an immense undertaking.

The probabilistic nature of AI also complicates risk assessment. Traditional methods often rely on estimating the probability of discrete events. While we can quantify the probability of a specific component failing, quantifying the probability of an AI system exhibiting a particular undesirable behavior in a novel, unseen scenario is far more challenging. Generative adversarial networks (GANs) and other techniques can produce highly realistic but entirely novel inputs, and it is often impossible to predict how a trained AI will react to these inputs. This means that the "likelihood" of a hazardous event might not be a fixed value, but rather a function of the distribution of encountered data and the AI's capacity to generalize. The concept of "unknown unknowns" becomes particularly salient in AI safety, where the learning and adaptive capabilities of the system can lead to behaviors that were not conceived of during the design and analysis phase.

Consequently, the traditional approach to safety requirements, which often focuses on deterministic performance guarantees, needs to be re-evaluated. Instead of specifying that an AI system must "never" make a certain type of error (an often impossible guarantee for probabilistic systems), safety requirements might need to focus on bounding the probability of errors, ensuring graceful degradation of performance, or guaranteeing that the system can be safely overridden or shut down. For example, a safety requirement for an AI-powered medical diagnostic system might shift from "must correctly identify all instances of disease X with 100% accuracy" to "must achieve an accuracy of at least 99% on known datasets, and provide a confidence score for all diagnoses, with a mechanism to flag low-confidence diagnoses for human review." This introduces the concept of "bounded uncertainty" and emphasizes human-AI collaboration as a crucial safety mechanism.

The challenge of verification and validation (V&V) for AI systems is also significantly different. Traditional V&V often relies on testing against specifications. For AI, the "specification" is implicitly learned from data. This means that testing must go beyond verifying adherence to pre-defined rules; it must involve evaluating the AI's performance across a vast and representative range of real-world scenarios, including edge cases and adversarial examples. Techniques like formal verification, which mathematically proves the correctness of a system, are extremely difficult to apply to complex neural networks due to their non-linear and emergent properties. Instead, V&V for AI is increasingly reliant on empirical testing, statistical analysis of performance, and rigorous monitoring in operational environments. This leads to a greater emphasis on continuous V&V throughout the lifecycle of the AI system, rather than a one-time validation event.

Furthermore, the dynamic and adaptive nature of AI systems necessitates a shift in the safety engineering lifecycle. Traditional safety engineering often assumes a relatively static system once deployed. However, many AI systems are designed to learn and adapt over time, through continuous retraining or online learning. This means that a system that was deemed safe at the time of deployment may become unsafe later due to drift in data distributions, changes in the environment, or the introduction of new vulnerabilities. This requires a paradigm shift towards continuous safety monitoring, adaptive risk management, and robust mechanisms for detecting and responding to emergent unsafe behaviors. The concept of "safety as a continuous process" rather than a static state becomes paramount.

The principles of functional safety, as embodied in standards like IEC 61508, provide a useful conceptual framework. These standards define different Automotive Safety Integrity Levels (ASILs) or Safety Integrity Levels (SILs) that categorize systems based on their risk and required level of safety assurance. While these levels are typically defined for deterministic systems, the underlying concept of risk-based safety assurance can be adapted. For AI systems, the ASIL or SIL might not be assigned based on well-defined failure probabilities, but rather on the potential impact of system failure, the confidence in the AI's performance, and the robustness of its safety mechanisms. This might involve developing new metrics for AI safety integrity, focusing on factors like robustness to adversarial inputs, performance under distributional shift, and the effectiveness of oversight mechanisms.

Another crucial adaptation is the increased importance of data governance and quality in AI safety. In traditional systems, the reliability of inputs is often taken for granted or ensured through robust sensor calibration and filtering. For AI, however, the quality, integrity, and representativeness of training data are directly linked to the safety of the resulting model. Biased, incomplete, or corrupted data can lead to AI systems that are unfair, inaccurate, or unsafe. Therefore, data management practices, including data provenance, bias detection, and data validation, must be elevated to the same level of importance as the design and verification of the AI algorithms themselves. Safety requirements must extend to the data pipelines that feed and update AI systems.

In summary, while the fundamental goals of safety engineering – identifying hazards, assessing risks, defining requirements, and ensuring reliable operation – remain constant, their application to AI systems demands significant adaptation. The probabilistic, data-driven, and emergent nature of AI challenges traditional deterministic approaches to hazard analysis, risk assessment, and verification. Novel methodologies are required to address the "black box" problem, quantify bounded uncertainty, develop robust V&V techniques for adaptive systems, and ensure continuous safety monitoring. The focus must shift from guaranteeing absolute correctness to bounding uncertainty, ensuring robustness, facilitating human oversight, and maintaining safety as an ongoing process. This evolution represents a critical frontier in AI safety engineering, one that requires interdisciplinary collaboration and a willingness to innovate upon established principles.

Understanding AI Failure Modes

The fundamental objective of safety engineering, regardless of the technological domain, is to anticipate, understand, and mitigate potential failures that could lead to harm. While traditional safety engineering has a long history of dealing with predictable, often mechanical or software-logic-based failures, the advent of artificial intelligence introduces a spectrum of failure modes that are often emergent, probabilistic, and deeply intertwined with the system's learning and operational environment. A thorough understanding of these AI-specific failure modes is not merely an academic exercise; it is the bedrock upon which robust AI safety engineering practices must be built. Without this granular insight, our efforts to design, test, and deploy AI systems safely will be akin to building a dam without understanding the nature of the water it is meant to contain.

One of the most prominent and concerning categories of AI failure modes arises from
adversarial attacks. Unlike traditional software vulnerabilities that might exploit coding errors or security flaws, adversarial attacks target the very fabric of machine learning models: their reliance on statistical patterns in data. These attacks involve subtly manipulating input data in ways that are often imperceptible to human observers but are designed to trigger incorrect and potentially catastrophic outputs from the AI. For instance, a self-driving car's perception system, trained to recognize traffic signs, might be fooled by a sticker or a slight alteration to a stop sign that causes it to be misclassified as a speed limit sign, or worse,

completely ignored. Similarly, in the realm of cybersecurity, adversarial attacks can be used to bypass sophisticated spam filters or trick facial recognition systems. The danger here lies in the fact that these attacks can be deliberate, sophisticated, and designed to exploit the specific vulnerabilities of a deployed model. The challenge for safety engineers is that these inputs lie *outside* the expected distribution of normal operating data, yet they can induce failures with severe consequences. Techniques used to generate these adversarial examples often involve sophisticated optimization algorithms that search for the smallest possible perturbation to an input that will cause a misclassification. This can include small, carefully crafted noise patterns added to images, or minor modifications to audio signals. The existence and effectiveness of such attacks highlight the need for AI systems to be not just accurate on typical data, but also robust against malicious or unexpected inputs that can mimic legitimate data but lead to drastically different interpretations.

Another critical failure mode stems from **data drift**, also known as concept drift or covariate shift. AI models, particularly those based on machine learning, are trained on a specific dataset, and their performance is intrinsically linked to the statistical properties of that data. However, the real world is dynamic. Over time, the underlying distribution of the data to which the AI is exposed can change, a phenomenon known as data drift. This can happen for a multitude of reasons: societal trends, seasonal variations, changes in user behavior, or even evolving environmental conditions. When the deployed AI encounters data that significantly deviates from its training distribution, its performance inevitably degrades. Imagine a medical diagnostic AI trained on X-rays taken with a particular type of scanner. If hospitals begin using a newer scanner with slightly different image characteristics, the AI's accuracy may drop because the new images no longer conform to the patterns it learned. Similarly, a financial fraud detection system trained on historical transaction data might become less effective as fraudsters develop new, previously unseen methods of operation. The subtle nature of data drift makes it particularly insidious. It doesn't typically manifest as a sudden, obvious system crash, but rather as a gradual erosion of accuracy and reliability. Detecting and mitigating data drift requires continuous monitoring of the AI's performance in production, along with mechanisms to identify shifts in incoming data and, if necessary, retrain or adapt the model. This necessitates a paradigm shift from static deployment to continuous adaptation and vigilance, treating safety as an ongoing process rather than a one-time achievement.

The very nature of learning in AI systems can also lead to unique failure modes.
Catastrophic forgetting, for instance, is a phenomenon observed in certain types of neural networks, particularly those that are continually learning or being updated. When a model is trained on a new task or a new dataset, it can sometimes overwrite or drastically impair its ability to perform previously learned tasks. This is akin to a student cramming for a new exam and completely forgetting material they had mastered for a previous one. For an AI system deployed in a critical application, this could mean that a system designed to perform multiple functions might lose proficiency in one crucial area after learning a new skill. Consider an AI assistant that manages a smart home. If it learns a new voice command for a novel device, it might inadvertently forget how to control the primary lighting system. In more critical applications, such as robotics or autonomous systems that require a broad range of skills acquired over time, catastrophic forgetting represents a significant safety concern. Ensuring that AI systems can learn new information without catastrophically losing old knowledge is an active area of research, often involving techniques like incremental learning, replay mechanisms, or specialized network architectures designed to preserve past learning.

A related but distinct failure mode is the
brittle performance of AI systems outside their training distributions. While data drift refers to changes in the distribution of *expected* data over time, brittleness refers to the AI's inherent inability to generalize or perform reliably when faced with inputs that are simply

different from what it encountered during training, even if those inputs are not deliberately adversarial. This often manifests as unexpected and illogical outputs for inputs that are only slightly novel or unusual. For example, an image recognition system trained on a diverse set of cat breeds might fail to recognize a common house cat if it's shown in an unusual pose or under peculiar lighting conditions that were not part of its training set. This fragility is often a consequence of the complex, high-dimensional feature spaces learned by deep learning models. They may latch onto superficial correlations in the training data that do not hold true in slightly different, real-world scenarios. This means that even if the data hasn't "drifted" in a statistical sense, the AI can still fail when encountering variations that were simply not represented in its training data. Testing AI systems for robustness requires deliberately exposing them to a wide array of edge cases and out-of-distribution examples, far beyond what might be considered typical. Techniques like data augmentation, transfer learning, and domain adaptation aim to improve generalization, but achieving true robustness across all possible novel scenarios remains a significant challenge.

Perhaps the most challenging AI failure mode to address is the occurrence of
emergent unintended behaviors. These are behaviors that were not explicitly programmed into the AI and were not predicted or anticipated by its designers. They often arise from complex interactions between the AI's learned objectives, its environment, and its internal decision-making processes. Because AI systems learn to optimize for specific reward functions or objectives, they can discover novel and sometimes counter-intuitive strategies to achieve those goals. In research settings, this has been observed in game-playing AIs that exploit loopholes in the game's physics or rules to win in ways never conceived by the game designers. In real-world applications, this could manifest as an AI optimizing for a metric that indirectly leads to undesirable outcomes. For instance, an AI tasked with maximizing user engagement on a social media platform might learn to amplify divisive or sensational content, inadvertently

contributing to societal polarization, because such content happens to generate more clicks and interactions. Or, an autonomous robot tasked with tidying a room might learn to simply push all clutter under the bed to "clear" the visible floor space, thereby fulfilling its objective without achieving the intended outcome of a truly tidy room. Identifying and preventing emergent unintended behaviors requires a deep understanding of the AI's reward function, its learning dynamics, and its interaction with the environment. It often involves meticulous code review, extensive simulation, and rigorous oversight to catch these emergent strategies before they lead to harm. The "alignment problem"—ensuring that AI goals are perfectly aligned with human values and intentions—is fundamentally about preventing such emergent unintended behaviors.

Furthermore, the complex interplay of these failure modes can lead to compounding risks. For example, an AI system might be susceptible to adversarial perturbations
and suffer from data drift. If its performance is already degraded due to drifting data, it might become even more vulnerable to adversarial attacks, as the subtle manipulations required to fool it might be more effective on a weakened model. This highlights the interconnectedness of different failure modes and the need for a holistic approach to AI safety. Simply addressing one type of failure might not be sufficient if others remain unaddressed.

The opacity of many modern AI models, often referred to as the "black box" problem, exacerbates the difficulty in understanding and addressing these failure modes. When an AI system fails, it can be challenging to pinpoint the exact cause. Was it a subtle adversarial input, a consequence of data drift, a learned bias, or an emergent property of its complex internal state? Without clear interpretability, diagnosing the root cause of failure and implementing effective corrective measures becomes significantly more difficult. This underscores the importance of ongoing research into AI interpretability and explainability techniques, which aim to shed light on the internal workings of AI models and provide insights into their decision-making processes.

In conclusion, the landscape of AI failure modes is far richer and more complex than that of traditional engineered systems. Adversarial attacks, data drift, catastrophic forgetting, brittleness outside training distributions, and emergent unintended behaviors represent distinct yet often interconnected challenges. Recognizing, categorizing, and thoroughly understanding each of these modes is the indispensable first step in the journey of AI safety engineering. It is only through this deep comprehension that we can begin to develop the sophisticated strategies, robust architectures, and vigilant monitoring systems required to ensure that AI systems operate safely and beneficially in our world.

The preceding discussion has laid bare the multifaceted nature of AI failure modes, from the insidious creep of data drift to the deliberate machinations of adversarial attacks and the unsettling emergence of unintended behaviors. Understanding these vulnerabilities is the crucial preamble to a more proactive stance: the deliberate engineering of AI systems that are not only functional but fundamentally *robust* and *resilient*. This section delves into the principles and techniques that empower us to construct AI that can withstand the inevitable turbulence of the real world, continuing to operate predictably and safely even when confronted with noise, unexpected inputs, or subtle shifts in its operational environment. It's about moving beyond merely reacting to failures and towards building systems that are intrinsically fortified against them.

At the core of robust AI design lies the imperative to minimize sensitivity to small, seemingly insignificant variations in input data. Traditional machine learning models, especially deep neural networks, can exhibit remarkable fragility. A single pixel altered in an image, a fractional change in a sound wave, or a minute adjustment to numerical data can, under certain circumstances, lead to a drastically incorrect output. To counteract this, we employ techniques that aim to make models less susceptible to such perturbations. One of the most potent strategies is **adversarial training**. This involves augmenting the standard training dataset with carefully generated adversarial examples. These are not simply random noisy inputs, but rather inputs that have been specifically crafted to fool the model. By exposing the AI to these deceptive inputs during the training phase, and importantly, by teaching it the correct output for these adversarial examples, the model learns to become more resilient. It develops a more discerning internal representation, learning to disregard superficial features that can be easily manipulated and focusing instead on more fundamental, invariant characteristics of the data. The process is iterative: an adversarial example is generated for the current version of the model, the model is then trained on this example, and the process repeats, progressively hardening the model against a wider range of adversarial attacks. While computationally intensive, adversarial training has proven remarkably effective in improving the robustness of image classifiers, speech recognition systems, and other AI components against a significant class of adversarial perturbations. It's akin to vaccinating the AI against specific forms of deception, making it more resistant to sophisticated manipulation.

Beyond directly training against adversarial examples, another layer of defense involves
input sanitization and validation. This approach acts as a gatekeeper, scrutinizing incoming data before it even reaches the AI model. For structured data, this might involve checking for expected ranges, formats, and consistency. For unstructured data like images or text, it can be more nuanced. Techniques might include noise reduction filters, de-noising algorithms, or data normalization processes that aim to clean up or standardize inputs. For example, before an image recognition system processes a photograph, a de-noising algorithm might be applied to remove random sensor noise that could otherwise lead to misclassification. Similarly, natural language processing systems might

employ techniques to correct common spelling errors or normalize variations in punctuation. The goal is to present the AI with data that is as close as possible to the clean, well-behaved data it was trained on, thereby reducing the likelihood of unexpected behavior triggered by noisy or malformed inputs. This is particularly important in environments where data quality might be variable or where sensors are prone to introducing artifacts. Input sanitization can be seen as a first line of defense, attempting to scrub away potential sources of error before they can propagate through the AI's decision-making process.

A crucial aspect of ensuring predictable and safe operation, especially in systems with high stakes, is the ability of the AI to **quantify its uncertainty**. Many standard AI models, when faced with inputs that are novel or significantly different from their training data, will still produce a confident prediction. This is problematic because it can mask a potential failure. A more desirable characteristic is for the AI to indicate when it is unsure. **Uncertainty quantification** aims to equip AI models with a mechanism to express their confidence in their predictions. This can manifest in several ways. Bayesian neural networks, for instance, inherently model probability distributions over their parameters, allowing them to estimate the uncertainty associated with their outputs. Other methods involve ensemble techniques, where multiple models are trained and their collective disagreement can serve as a measure of uncertainty. For example, if a self-driving car's perception system is tasked with identifying an object and several independent models within an ensemble strongly agree on its classification, the system can have high confidence. If there is significant disagreement among the models, it signals uncertainty, prompting a more cautious response, such as slowing down or requesting human intervention. This explicit signaling of uncertainty allows downstream systems or human operators to react appropriately. Instead of blindly trusting a potentially erroneous output, the system can leverage the uncertainty estimate to adopt a safer operational mode, thereby contributing to overall system resilience. This is critical for applications where a wrong decision can have severe consequences, such as in medical diagnostics, autonomous navigation, or financial trading.

The principle of **graceful degradation** is central to building resilient AI. Rather than failing abruptly and completely when encountering challenging conditions, a gracefully degrading system experiences a gradual decline in performance. This means that even if the AI cannot perform its task perfectly under extreme circumstances, it should still be able to provide a useful, albeit degraded, output or transition to a safe state. For instance, an autonomous drone operating in high winds might not be able to maintain its precise positioning, but it should still be able to navigate to a designated landing zone or return to its base. This contrasts with brittle systems that might immediately lose control or shut down unpredictably. Achieving graceful degradation often involves designing AI systems with fallback mechanisms or simpler, more robust models that can take over when complex, high-performance models encounter out-of-distribution data or other challenging conditions. It also implies a design philosophy where the system prioritizes safety over optimal performance when uncertainty is high. This might involve implementing thresholds for uncertainty, below which the AI is permitted to operate normally, and above which it triggers a more conservative, safety-focused mode of operation. For critical infrastructure, such as power grids or traffic control systems, graceful degradation ensures that even if an AI component experiences difficulties, the overall system does not collapse, but rather maintains a reduced level of functionality, preventing cascading failures.

Furthermore, building resilience requires a deep understanding of the AI's operational context and the potential *distributional shifts* it might encounter. While adversarial attacks are often deliberate, distributional shifts are natural, evolutionary changes in the data landscape. This can range from seasonal variations affecting sensor readings to evolving user behavior patterns. **Domain adaptation** and

transfer learning are powerful techniques that help AI models generalize to new, but related, domains or adapt to shifts in data distribution without requiring a complete retraining from scratch. Domain adaptation techniques aim to bridge the gap between a source domain (where the model was trained) and a target domain (where it will be deployed), even if the data distributions differ. Transfer learning leverages knowledge gained from a related task to improve performance on a new task. For example, an image recognition model trained on a vast dataset of everyday objects can have its learned features transferred to a new task, such as identifying specific types of industrial equipment, significantly reducing the amount of data and training time required for the new, specialized task. By incorporating these techniques, AI systems can be made more adaptable and resilient to the gradual, often unpredictable, changes that characterize real-world deployments. This reduces the likelihood of performance degradation simply because the environment has subtly changed.

The concept of
regularization plays a subtle but vital role in enhancing AI robustness. Regularization techniques, such as L1 and L2 regularization or dropout, are primarily used to prevent overfitting – where a model learns the training data too well, including its noise and specific idiosyncrasies, and thus fails to generalize to new data. By penalizing complex models or randomly dropping units during training, regularization encourages the model to learn simpler, more generalizable patterns. This inherent tendency towards simplicity can contribute to robustness, as simpler models are often less sensitive to small perturbations in the input and less likely to latch onto spurious correlations that might not hold true in slightly different scenarios. A more generalized model is inherently more resilient to variations in data that were not explicitly present in the training set.

Another consideration for resilience is the design of

interpretable and modular AI systems. While not directly a training technique, the ability to understand how an AI makes decisions and to break down complex AI functionalities into smaller, more manageable modules can significantly enhance robustness and facilitate debugging. If a complex AI system fails, a black box model offers few clues as to why. However, a modular system, where each module has a clear function and potentially interpretable outputs, allows engineers to isolate the faulty component more easily. This diagnostic capability is crucial for quickly identifying the root cause of a failure and implementing a fix, thereby restoring system resilience. Furthermore, interpretable models, even if less complex, can sometimes be inherently more robust because their decision-making logic is more transparent and less prone to unexpected emergent properties. This transparency allows for better validation and verification of the AI's behavior against safety requirements.

The integration of
formal verification techniques also contributes to a more resilient AI. While traditional formal methods have been extensively applied to software, their application to the probabilistic and learning-based nature of AI is an active and challenging area of research. However, for critical components or specific properties of an AI system, formal methods can offer strong guarantees. For instance, one might formally verify that an AI system will never output a critical safety violation under a defined set of conditions, or that its response time will always remain within acceptable bounds. These methods provide mathematical proofs of correctness for specific aspects of the AI's behavior. When applied to safety-critical logic or decision pathways within an AI system, formal verification can significantly bolster confidence in its reliability and resilience, particularly in deterministic aspects of its operation.

Finally, the development of AI systems that can
monitor their own performance and detect anomalies is a key aspect of resilience. This involves incorporating mechanisms within the AI system itself to continuously assess its own outputs and compare them

against expected patterns or historical performance metrics. If the AI detects a significant deviation, it can trigger an alert, initiate a diagnostic procedure, or switch to a fallback mode. This self-monitoring capability allows the AI to detect issues like data drift or the onset of performance degradation in real-time, often before they lead to critical failures. It transforms the AI from a static entity into a dynamic system capable of self-assessment and adaptation, a crucial step towards true resilience in complex and evolving environments. This proactive approach to identifying and responding to internal deviations is fundamental to maintaining operational integrity over extended periods.

In essence, building robust and resilient AI is not a single technique but a holistic engineering discipline. It requires a combination of sophisticated training methodologies like adversarial training, careful data pre-processing through input sanitization, probabilistic modeling for uncertainty quantification, thoughtful system design for graceful degradation, advanced learning techniques for adaptation, and rigorous verification and self-monitoring capabilities. These principles, when applied diligently, move us closer to creating AI systems that are not only intelligent but also dependable and safe, capable of navigating the unpredictable currents of the real world with confidence.

The preceding discussion has established the critical importance of building AI systems that are not only performant but also inherently robust and resilient to the complexities and uncertainties of real-world operation. We have explored strategies for mitigating failure modes, from adversarial training and input sanitization to uncertainty quantification and graceful degradation, all aimed at fortifying AI against unforeseen circumstances. However, the journey from a trained model to a deployed, trustworthy AI system necessitates a rigorous process of verification and validation (V&V). This V&V process is not merely a final checkpoint; it is an integral part of the engineering lifecycle, ensuring that the AI behaves as intended, meets its safety specifications, and can be trusted in its operational environment.

Traditional software verification and validation often rely on exhaustive testing, where every possible input-output path can, in principle, be traced and verified. This paradigm is built upon the deterministic nature of conventional code. If a bug exists, it is a specific flaw in logic that can, with sufficient effort, be pinpointed and fixed. The process of testing involves executing the software with a defined set of inputs and comparing the actual outputs against expected outputs. Formal methods can even provide mathematical proofs of correctness for certain properties. However, AI systems, particularly those based on machine learning, introduce a profound departure from this established framework. Their behavior is emergent, learned from data, and inherently probabilistic. This probabilistic nature, coupled with the immense complexity of modern AI models like deep neural networks, means that exhaustive testing is not just impractical; it is fundamentally impossible. A neural network with millions or billions of parameters can process an astronomical number of input combinations, rendering a complete enumeration of all possible scenarios an unattainable goal.

This inherent difficulty demands a rethinking of V&V strategies. We must move beyond simply asking "Does it work?" to a more nuanced inquiry: "How well does it work under a defined range of conditions, and what are the acceptable margins of error?" This shift requires embracing new methodologies that are tailored to the unique characteristics of AI. One of the most promising avenues is the adaptation of **formal methods** for machine learning. While classic formal verification techniques, which rely on mathematical logic and proofs, are difficult to apply directly to the entirety of a neural network, they can be incredibly valuable when applied to specific, critical aspects of an AI system. For instance, formal methods can be used to verify properties of the underlying algorithms, the decision logic of certain components, or the adherence to safety constraints within a defined operational envelope. For example, in an autonomous vehicle, formal verification might be used to prove that the braking system, controlled by an AI, will always engage within a specific time frame under certain speed and distance conditions, or that the AI will never issue a command that violates a fundamental traffic law. Research is actively exploring how to "lift" formal verification techniques to handle the probabilistic and often non-differentiable nature of neural network computations. This involves developing new logical frameworks and verification tools that can reason about the behavior of learned models, often by approximating their behavior or by focusing on crucial decision boundaries. Techniques like abstract interpretation, model checking, and satisfiability modulo theories (SMT) solvers are being adapted to provide guarantees, albeit often under specific assumptions or for simplified versions of the AI model. The goal is to provide a higher level of assurance for critical functionalities, complementing empirical testing with a layer of mathematical rigor.

Complementing formal methods,
simulation-based testing emerges as a cornerstone of AI V&V. Simulations offer a controlled, repeatable, and scalable environment to expose AI systems to a vast array of scenarios, including those that are rare, dangerous, or expensive to replicate in the real world. The power of simulation lies in its ability to generate and explore an almost limitless number of test cases. For autonomous driving systems, this means simulating diverse weather conditions, lighting variations, road types, traffic densities, and the behavior of myriad other road users (pedestrians, cyclists, other vehicles). It allows engineers to create "edge cases" – rare but critical situations that might occur only once in a million miles of real-world driving. For example, a simulation could be designed to test how an AI perceives a specific type of obstacle under heavy fog, or how it reacts to a sudden, unpredictable maneuver by another vehicle. The key to effective simulation-based testing is achieving
comprehensive scenario coverage. This involves not just generating random scenarios but strategically designing test cases that probe specific vulnerabilities, stress particular functionalities, and cover the operational domain comprehensively. Techniques like fuzzing, which involves

generating random or semi-random inputs to uncover unexpected behaviors, can be applied in simulation. Generative adversarial networks (GANs) can also be employed to create realistic, yet novel, simulation environments and scenarios that push the AI to its limits. Furthermore, simulations can be used to test the AI's performance under distributional shifts, by gradually altering environmental parameters to mimic real-world changes. The fidelity of the simulation is also crucial; a simulation that is too simplistic might not accurately reflect real-world complexities, leading to a false sense of security. Therefore, continuous refinement and validation of simulation environments against real-world data are essential.

However, even with advanced simulation, the sheer complexity and probabilistic nature of AI outputs mean that simply checking for exact matches becomes problematic. This is where **statistical validation techniques** become indispensable. Instead of verifying that an AI produces *the* correct output for every input, statistical validation focuses on verifying that the AI's outputs fall within acceptable statistical bounds and that its performance metrics meet predefined criteria over a large number of trials. This involves defining **clear performance metrics and acceptance criteria** upfront. For a classification task, this might include metrics like accuracy, precision, recall, F1-score, and Receiver Operating Characteristic (ROC) curves. For regression tasks, mean squared error (MSE) or R-squared values are common. Crucially, these metrics need to be contextualized. An accuracy of 90% might be excellent for recommending movies but catastrophically insufficient for diagnosing a life-threatening disease. Therefore, acceptance criteria must be directly tied to the safety and reliability requirements of the AI's application. Statistical validation involves running the AI system on large, representative datasets (often distinct from the training and validation sets) and analyzing the distribution of its outputs and performance metrics. Confidence intervals are used to quantify the uncertainty around these metrics. For example, instead of stating an accuracy of 95%, a validation report might state "with 95%

confidence, the accuracy is between 94.5% and 95.5%." This statistical rigor allows engineers to understand the reliability of the AI's performance and to make informed decisions about its deployment. Techniques like hypothesis testing can be used to formally compare the performance of a new AI model against a baseline or to assess whether performance has degraded over time. Bootstrapping methods can be employed to estimate the variability of performance metrics when the available test data is limited.

A critical aspect of statistical validation is the careful design of test datasets. These datasets must be representative of the real-world deployment environment and should include a diverse range of examples, including those that are out-of-distribution or represent edge cases. Simply testing on data that is very similar to the training data will not reveal potential failure modes. Therefore, the process of data curation for testing is as important as data curation for training. Furthermore, for AI systems that learn and adapt over time, validation is not a one-time event. Continuous monitoring and periodic re-validation are essential to ensure that performance does not degrade due to data drift or other environmental changes. This brings us to the concept of **model interpretability and explainability** as a V&V tool. While not a direct validation technique, the ability to understand *why* an AI makes a particular decision is invaluable for debugging and for building trust. Techniques like LIME (Local Interpretable Model-agnostic Explanations) and SHAP (SHapley Additive exPlanations) can help identify which input features were most influential in a given decision. If an AI makes an incorrect prediction, an explanation might reveal that it was relying on spurious correlations or irrelevant features, thus pinpointing a weakness that might not be apparent from performance metrics alone. This can guide further targeted testing and model improvement. For safety-critical systems, the ability to explain decisions is often a regulatory requirement and a prerequisite for human oversight.

The probabilistic nature of AI outputs also necessitates a re-evaluation of

what constitutes a "failure." In traditional software, a failure is often a binary event: the program either works correctly or it doesn't. For an AI, a "failure" might encompass a range of outcomes, from a minor inaccuracy to a critical safety violation. Therefore,
defining hierarchical or graded failure modes is crucial for effective V&V. This involves categorizing potential errors based on their severity and impact. For instance, in a medical imaging AI, a slight misclassification of a benign lesion might be a low-severity error, while failing to detect a malignant tumor altogether would be a critical failure. Acceptance criteria can then be set differently for each category. Statistical validation can be used to estimate the probability of occurrence for each failure category. This granular approach allows for more precise risk assessment and for tailoring V&V efforts to the most critical failure modes.

Another dimension of V&V for AI is the
testing of system integration. AI models rarely operate in isolation; they are typically part of larger, complex systems. The V&V process must therefore extend to how the AI model interacts with other software components, hardware interfaces, and human operators. This includes testing for communication errors, data format incompatibilities, and cascading failures that might arise from unexpected interactions. For example, an AI perception system in an autonomous robot needs to reliably feed data to the path planning module, and any latency or corruption in this data could lead to operational failure. Integration testing ensures that the AI component functions correctly within its broader operational context.

Furthermore, the development of
AI-specific testing frameworks and tools is an ongoing and vital area of research and development. These tools are designed to address the unique challenges of AI V&V, offering capabilities such as automated scenario generation, sophisticated performance monitoring, uncertainty visualization, and integration with formal verification engines. Examples

include libraries for adversarial robustness testing, tools for exploring the decision boundaries of neural networks, and platforms for managing and executing large-scale simulation-based tests. The goal is to provide engineers with the necessary infrastructure to conduct thorough and efficient V&V of AI systems.

In summary, verifying and validating AI systems is a complex, multifaceted undertaking that diverges significantly from traditional software engineering. It requires a strategic blend of adapted formal methods for critical guarantees, extensive simulation-based testing for scenario coverage, and robust statistical validation techniques to account for probabilistic outputs. The emphasis shifts from exhaustive enumeration to principled sampling and statistical inference, underpinned by clearly defined performance metrics and acceptance criteria that are commensurate with the AI's intended application and associated risks. Moreover, the V&V process must be continuous, embracing interpretability, hierarchical failure modes, and rigorous integration testing to ensure that AI systems are not only intelligent but also demonstrably safe, reliable, and trustworthy across their operational lifespan.

The integration of artificial intelligence into complex systems is seldom an isolated endeavor. More often than not, these AI-driven infrastructures are designed to operate in concert with human beings, whether as end-users, operators, or collaborators. This pervasive human-AI interaction necessitates a distinct set of safety engineering considerations, focusing on the interfaces and dynamics that govern how humans and AI systems engage with each other. Ensuring the safety of these interactions is not merely about the AI's internal performance; it is about building systems that humans can understand, trust, and effectively control, especially in high-stakes environments. This subsection delves into the critical principles and practices for engineering safety into human-AI interfaces.

At the heart of safe human-AI interaction lies the principle of

user-centered design. This approach prioritizes the needs, capabilities, and limitations of the human operator or user throughout the entire design and development lifecycle. It is an iterative process that involves deep empathy for the user, understanding their cognitive load, their domain expertise, and their potential for error. For an AI system that assists air traffic controllers, for example, user-centered design would involve extensive consultation with experienced controllers to understand their workflow, their decision-making processes under pressure, and the types of information they find most critical. This understanding informs how the AI presents information, how it signals its recommendations, and what level of autonomy it is granted. A poorly designed interface, even with a perfectly functioning AI, can lead to confusion, misinterpretation, and ultimately, unsafe actions. This might manifest as information overload, where the AI bombards the operator with too much data, or conversely, as under-specification, where critical information is obscured or absent. Therefore, the interface must be intuitive, providing a clear and concise representation of the AI's state, its intentions, and the environment it perceives. This often involves leveraging established human-computer interaction (HCI) best practices, such as consistent visual language, clear feedback mechanisms, and logical information hierarchy. The goal is to minimize cognitive burden on the human, allowing them to focus their attention on higher-level decision-making and oversight.

A crucial element in fostering safe human-AI collaboration is the **clear communication of AI intent and limitations**. AI systems, especially those employing machine learning, can exhibit emergent behaviors that are not always easily predictable or understandable, even to their developers. For a human operator to safely interact with such a system, it is paramount that the AI can articulate its reasoning, its confidence levels, and its boundaries of operation. This goes beyond simply displaying output; it involves providing context and justification. For instance, in a diagnostic AI used in healthcare, if the AI suggests a particular diagnosis, it should ideally be able to highlight the specific features in the medical image or patient data that led to that conclusion. Furthermore, the AI must be transparent about what it *cannot* do, or where its performance might be degraded. An autonomous vehicle's AI, for example, should clearly signal when it is entering a mode of operation where human supervision is required, perhaps due to adverse weather conditions or encountering an unusual road scenario. This requires developing sophisticated explanation mechanisms, moving beyond simple "black box" outputs to provide actionable insights. Techniques from explainable AI (XAI), such as feature attribution methods (e.g., SHAP, LIME) or rule extraction from learned models, can be adapted to generate human-understandable explanations. The challenge lies in tailoring these explanations to the specific user and context, ensuring they are informative without being overwhelming or misleading. Over-promising the AI's capabilities or masking its uncertainties can create a false sense of security, leading to situations where humans over-rely on the AI or fail to intervene when necessary. Conversely, an AI that is overly cautious and constantly signals uncertainty may lead to operator fatigue and distrust, diminishing its utility and potentially leading to its disengagement. Therefore, finding the right balance in communicating intent and limitations is an ongoing engineering challenge. This communication must also be robust to noise and errors in the AI's own perception or reasoning; an AI that incorrectly believes it has full capability when it does not is a significant safety hazard.

Effective
oversight mechanisms are another cornerstone of human-AI safety engineering. While AI can augment human capabilities and automate certain tasks, the ultimate responsibility for system safety often rests with a human operator. This necessitates designing systems that allow for continuous and effective monitoring of the AI's performance and decision-making. The human operator must have the ability to observe the AI's actions, assess their appropriateness, and intervene when necessary. This requires well-defined monitoring tools, alert systems, and clear protocols for escalation and intervention. In an industrial setting, for

instance, a human supervisor overseeing a fleet of autonomous robots on a factory floor needs to be able to quickly identify if a robot is deviating from its task, entering a hazardous area, or exhibiting abnormal behavior. This might involve a dashboard displaying the status of each robot, their operational parameters, and any anomalies detected. The alert system should be designed to distinguish between minor deviations and critical safety concerns, avoiding alarm fatigue. The intervention mechanisms must be equally well-thought-out. This could range from a simple "pause" or "abort" command to more nuanced controls for adjusting the AI's parameters or guiding its actions. The speed and clarity of these mechanisms are critical, especially in time-sensitive situations. For example, in a surgical robot application, the human surgeon must have immediate and intuitive control to override the AI if an unintended movement occurs. The design of these oversight and intervention capabilities must consider the human operator's workload, attention span, and stress levels. An operator who is overloaded or constantly distracted by irrelevant alerts will be less effective in providing oversight. Therefore, the design of these mechanisms must be integrated into the overall user-centered design process, ensuring they are practical, efficient, and minimize the risk of human error. Furthermore, the system should provide feedback on the outcome of human interventions, allowing the operator to understand the impact of their actions and for the AI to potentially learn from these adjustments.

A particularly critical aspect of human-AI interaction safety arises in scenarios requiring a
safe handover of control. These are moments where responsibility for a task or system shifts between the human and the AI. This handover can occur in either direction: from AI to human, or from human to AI. In autonomous driving, for instance, a vehicle's AI might need to hand over control to the human driver when it encounters a situation beyond its capabilities, such as a complex construction zone or a sudden, unmapped obstacle. Conversely, a human driver might engage the autonomous driving system, handing over control to the AI. Both scenarios present

significant safety challenges. For an AI-to-human handover, the AI must clearly signal its intention to relinquish control well in advance, providing sufficient time for the human to regain situational awareness and take over safely. This requires not only an alert but also context-setting information that helps the human understand *why* the handover is occurring and what actions they need to take. The AI should not simply "drop" control; it should transition smoothly, providing a clear description of the current state and any immediate hazards. In the case of a human-to-AI handover, the human operator needs assurance that the AI is capable of safely assuming control and that it has correctly understood the current situation. This might involve the AI confirming its understanding of the environment and its intended course of action. For example, before an autonomous drone initiates a complex flight maneuver, it might confirm its understanding of the flight path and airspace clearance with the human operator. The handover process must be unambiguous, leaving no room for misinterpretation about who is in control. This can be achieved through standardized protocols, clear visual and auditory cues, and confirmation steps. Research in this area often involves studying human factors, particularly the phenomenon of "mode confusion," where users misunderstand which mode a system is operating in, leading to errors. Designing for safe handover requires careful consideration of these human psychological aspects, ensuring that the transition is predictable, understandable, and provides adequate time and information for the human operator to react appropriately. The engineering of these handover protocols must account for potential delays in human perception or reaction time, ensuring that the handover is initiated with a sufficient buffer. Furthermore, the system should have safeguards against accidental or premature handovers, and mechanisms to handle situations where the human is unable to take control when required. This might involve the AI executing a safe fallback maneuver, such as bringing the vehicle to a controlled stop, or alerting external safety personnel.

Beyond these core principles, the safety of human-AI interaction is further enhanced by fostering **situational awareness and shared understanding**. The AI should strive to maintain a model of the human operator's state – their attention, their likely intentions, and their current understanding of the situation. This allows the AI to adapt its behavior accordingly, providing information proactively when the human seems to be struggling to grasp the situation, or offering assistance when the human appears to be overloaded. Conversely, the human operator should have access to information that clarifies the AI's understanding of the world and its operational goals. This shared understanding creates a more robust and collaborative system. For example, in a collaborative robotics scenario, if a human is working alongside a robot arm, the robot's visual system might highlight the area of the workspace it is currently monitoring or controlling. This immediate visual feedback reinforces the human's understanding of the robot's scope of action, preventing accidental collisions or interference.

Moreover, the concept of **trust calibration** is paramount. Humans tend to develop a level of trust in AI systems. This trust can be inappropriately low (under-trust), leading to underutilization of beneficial AI capabilities, or inappropriately high (over-trust), leading to complacency and a failure to intervene when necessary. The goal of AI safety engineering in this context is to calibrate trust appropriately. This is achieved through consistent, reliable performance, transparent communication of capabilities and limitations, and clear feedback on system behavior. When an AI performs as expected, and its limitations are well-understood, users are more likely to develop a calibrated level of trust. Conversely, unexpected behaviors or failures erode trust. Therefore, the design of the human-AI interface and the AI's overall behavior must be geared towards building and maintaining appropriate levels of trust. This involves not just the functional correctness of the AI, but also its predictability and understandability. If an AI system consistently behaves in a manner that aligns with its stated purpose and limitations, users will develop a more accurate and reliable sense of its capabilities.

Finally, the continuous **evaluation and refinement** of human-AI interfaces is essential. As AI capabilities evolve and new interaction paradigms emerge, the safety of human-AI systems must be continuously reassessed and improved. This involves collecting feedback from users, analyzing operational data for incidents or near-misses related to human-AI interaction, and conducting periodic safety reviews. The development of rigorous testing methodologies for human-AI interaction, including usability testing, stress testing of handover scenarios, and evaluating the effectiveness of oversight mechanisms, is crucial. This iterative process ensures that as AI becomes more integrated into our lives and work, the safety of our interactions with these powerful technologies keeps pace, fostering a future where AI augments human capabilities in a secure and trustworthy manner. The ultimate goal is to engineer AI systems that are not just intelligent, but also inherently safe and beneficial collaborators within the human ecosystem.

Chapter 3: Privacy Engineering in the Age of AI

The proliferation of artificial intelligence (AI) across virtually every sector of society has ushered in an era of unprecedented technological capability, but it has also amplified existing concerns and introduced novel challenges regarding personal privacy. As AI systems become more sophisticated, their insatiable appetite for data, coupled with their remarkable ability to discern intricate patterns and infer sensitive attributes, necessitates a fundamental re-evaluation of how we approach privacy protection. This re-evaluation is not merely an extension of established data protection regimes; it requires a proactive and pervasive integration of privacy principles into the very fabric of AI design, development, and deployment. The following sections will delve into the foundational privacy principles that must guide our endeavors in this new landscape, exploring their inherent complexities and their critical importance in building trustworthy AI.

At the very core of responsible data stewardship lies the principle of **data minimization**. In traditional data processing, this concept dictates that organizations should collect and retain only the data that is strictly necessary for a specific, legitimate purpose. However, for AI systems, this principle presents a formidable challenge. Many AI models, particularly those based on deep learning, thrive on vast datasets. The performance and accuracy of these models often improve with the quantity and diversity of data they are trained on. This creates a tension: the desire for highly performant AI versus the imperative to collect minimal personal data. Consider, for instance, an AI system designed to predict crop yields based on satellite imagery, weather patterns, and soil data. While the primary goal is agricultural optimization, the AI might inadvertently ingest data points that, when correlated, could reveal information about land ownership, irrigation practices, or even the presence of specific crops that might be sensitive or proprietary. A strict application of data minimization would require identifying precisely which pixels, which weather readings, and which soil compositions are absolutely indispensable for the predictive task, and discarding all extraneous information. This often involves sophisticated data preprocessing and feature engineering techniques to distill the essence of the data relevant to the AI's objective, without retaining auxiliary information that could pose privacy risks. Furthermore, the continuous learning nature of some AI systems can mean that the definition of "necessary" data evolves over time, requiring ongoing scrutiny of data collection practices. The challenge intensifies when considering AI systems that learn from real-time user interactions, such as recommendation engines or personalized assistants. Here, every user query, every click, and every interaction can potentially be data that refines the AI's model. Implementing data minimization effectively means establishing clear boundaries on what constitutes essential interaction data versus what is merely incidental and potentially privacy-infringing. This might involve anonymizing or pseudonymizing data at the point of collection, employing differential privacy techniques that inject noise to obscure individual contributions, or designing AI architectures that can learn effectively from aggregated or synthetic data.

Complementary to data minimization is the principle of **purpose limitation**. This principle asserts that data collected for one specific purpose should not be used for another incompatible purpose without further consent or legal basis. AI systems, by their very nature, can be highly versatile and can often discover novel insights and correlations that were not anticipated at the time of data collection. This inherent exploratory power of AI can lead to "purpose creep," where data initially gathered for one reason is later repurposed for entirely different applications, potentially without the knowledge or consent of the individuals concerned. Imagine a dataset collected to train an AI for medical image analysis, identifying specific diseases. If this same dataset, containing sensitive health information, were later used to train an AI for marketing personalized health products or even for risk assessment by insurance companies, it would represent a significant breach of purpose limitation. The challenge with AI is that its ability to generate new insights can reveal previously unknown connections. An AI trained on public social media data to understand general sentiment might, through sophisticated correlation, infer an individual's political affiliation, sexual orientation, or health status – attributes that were never explicitly shared and certainly not intended to be discovered. Enforcing purpose limitation in the AI context requires robust governance frameworks that clearly define and document the intended purposes for data use in AI development and deployment. This involves rigorous oversight of data pipelines, ensuring that data flows are restricted to authorized AI models and for approved objectives. It also means developing mechanisms to audit AI model outputs and data usage patterns to detect and prevent unauthorized repurposing. For instance, a company developing an AI for fraud detection might have legitimate access to transaction data. However, using that same data to build a profiling system for targeted advertising would likely violate purpose limitation, even if the AI could technically perform both tasks. The legal and ethical obligation here is to maintain a clear demarcation between the initial, consented purpose and any subsequent, potentially divergent applications. This requires transparency with individuals about how their data might be used by AI systems and providing avenues for them to control or object to such repurposing.

The cornerstone of modern data protection, particularly in consumer-facing applications, is **consent**. Consent-based privacy frameworks stipulate that individuals must be informed and freely give their permission before their personal data is collected, processed, or shared. However, the opacity and complexity of AI systems render obtaining meaningful consent a significant hurdle. Traditional consent mechanisms, often buried in lengthy privacy policies or presented as all-or-nothing checkboxes, are increasingly inadequate for AI. Individuals may not understand the full implications of consenting to data collection for an AI that might perform complex inferences or continuous learning. For example, consenting to the use of voice data for a smart home assistant might seem innocuous, but the AI could be continuously learning vocal patterns, inferring emotional states, or even identifying other individuals in the household. True consent requires a granular understanding of what data is being collected, how it will be used by the AI, the potential inferences that might be drawn, and the duration for which the data will be retained. This level of detailed disclosure is often impractical to convey in a user-friendly manner, leading to what is known as "informed consent fatigue." As a result, many individuals provide blanket consent without truly comprehending the privacy implications. Furthermore, the dynamic nature of AI means that the uses of data can evolve, potentially rendering initial consent obsolete or insufficient. A more effective approach to consent in the age of AI might involve tiered consent models, where individuals can opt-in or opt-out of specific data uses or AI functionalities. It also necessitates the development of privacy dashboards and control panels that provide individuals with ongoing visibility and control over their data and the AI systems that process it. Moreover, the concept of "revocable consent" becomes paramount; individuals should have the clear and straightforward ability to withdraw their consent at any time, and for the AI system to cease processing their data accordingly. This requires robust mechanisms for managing consent preferences and ensuring that data processing ceases promptly upon revocation.

The principle of the
right to be forgotten, also known as the right to erasure, empowers individuals to request the deletion of their personal data under certain circumstances. This right is particularly complex to implement for AI systems, especially those that have been trained on vast amounts of historical data. Once an AI model has learned from a particular data point, that knowledge is often embedded within the model's parameters in a distributed and non-linear fashion. Simply deleting the original data point from the training set might not be sufficient to "unlearn" the information it imparted. The AI might still retain the learned patterns or associations derived from that data. For instance, if an AI was trained on news articles that mentioned an individual in a particular context, and that individual later wishes for that information to be forgotten, it becomes technically

challenging to remove the influence of that historical mention from the AI's knowledge base. While techniques like "model unlearning" are an active area of research, they are often computationally intensive and may not guarantee complete erasure of the learned information without degrading overall model performance. This means that companies deploying AI systems need to consider the "forgettability" of data from the outset. This might involve employing AI architectures that are more amenable to unlearning, or carefully curating training datasets to exclude data that might later be subject to erasure requests. In practice, fulfilling the right to be forgotten for AI might involve a multi-pronged approach: deleting the individual's data from any associated databases, purging their information from future training datasets, and, where technically feasible, attempting to retrain or modify the AI model to mitigate the influence of the erased data. However, in many cases, complete erasure of the learned representation might be practically impossible without significant effort or impact on the AI's utility. This necessitates a pragmatic approach that prioritizes transparency with individuals about the limitations of "forgetting" in AI contexts and focusing on preventing the collection and retention of data that is likely to be subject to such requests.

The inferential power of AI introduces a new dimension to privacy concerns. AI systems possess a remarkable capacity to infer sensitive information about individuals from seemingly innocuous data. This is often referred to as

inferential privacy. For example, an AI analyzing purchasing habits might infer an individual's dietary restrictions, health conditions, or even their socio-economic status. Similarly, analyzing browsing history could reveal political leanings or religious beliefs. This inferential capability means that data not explicitly considered sensitive can become so when processed by AI. A person's location history, for instance, when combined with public records or social media activity, could reveal patterns of association, routines, and even sensitive personal circumstances. This presents a significant challenge to traditional privacy frameworks that often categorize data based on its explicit content. With AI, the privacy risk is not just in what is directly provided, but in what can be deduced. This necessitates a shift towards a more proactive and pervasive approach to privacy protection. Instead of solely focusing on protecting explicitly sensitive data, privacy engineering for AI must anticipate and mitigate the risks associated with inferred data. This involves conducting comprehensive privacy risk assessments that consider not only the data being collected but also the potential inferences that AI models might draw from it. Techniques such as differential privacy can be employed not only to protect training data but also to mask the outputs of AI models, making it harder to infer individual attributes from query results. Furthermore, privacy-enhancing technologies (PETs) are becoming increasingly crucial. These technologies, including homomorphic encryption, secure multi-party computation, and federated learning, allow AI models to be trained and operated on data without exposing the raw data itself. Federated learning, for instance, enables AI models to learn from decentralized datasets residing on user devices, with only model updates being shared, rather than the data itself. This approach inherently enhances privacy by keeping sensitive data localized. The challenge with inferential privacy is that it can be difficult to predict all possible inferences an AI might make, especially with complex, data-driven models. This underscores the need for ongoing monitoring, auditing, and a culture of privacy-by-design that embeds privacy considerations into every stage of the AI lifecycle, from conceptualization to deployment and decommissioning. The ethical imperative is to ensure that AI's power to reveal is matched by a commensurate commitment to safeguard what should remain private.

Data governance forms the bedrock upon which effective privacy engineering in AI is built. It's not merely a set of bureaucratic procedures, but a dynamic framework that governs how data is handled, protected, and utilized throughout its entire existence, a journey that mirrors the lifecycle of AI systems themselves. Without a meticulously crafted and rigorously enforced data governance strategy, the privacy risks inherent in AI data pipelines, no matter how sophisticated the privacy-enhancing technologies employed, can become unmanageable. This necessitates a comprehensive approach to managing data from its inception—collection—through its active phases of storage and processing, its controlled dissemination through sharing, and its eventual, inevitable retirement through deletion.

At the heart of any robust data governance program lies the unambiguous establishment of
data ownership. In the context of AI, where datasets can be vast, complex, and sourced from myriad origins, defining who is accountable for specific data assets is paramount. Data ownership extends beyond simple custodianship; it encompasses the responsibility for ensuring data quality, security, and, crucially, compliance with privacy regulations. For AI development, this means identifying not only the business units or teams that manage particular datasets but also the individuals or roles that have the ultimate authority and accountability for their use in AI models. For instance, a dataset comprising customer transaction histories might be owned by the marketing department, but its use in an AI fraud detection model might necessitate collaboration with the security and data science teams, with clear delineation of responsibilities. Ownership dictates who can authorize access, who is responsible for implementing data minimization principles for that specific dataset, and who must ensure that its use aligns with purpose limitations. Without this clarity, data can become orphaned, its handling falling into a grey area where privacy controls are neglected, and risks escalate. This can lead to situations where sensitive customer information, initially collected for one purpose, might be inadvertently fed into an AI model for a different, unauthorized application because no single entity felt the direct responsibility to monitor and control its flow. Clear ownership fosters accountability and ensures that there is always a point person or team responsible for safeguarding the privacy of the data under their purview.

Crucially intertwined with ownership are

access controls. These are the gatekeepers of data, dictating who can see, modify, or utilize specific data assets. For AI systems, which often require broad access to large datasets for training and validation, implementing granular and context-aware access controls is a significant challenge. The principle of least privilege—granting users and systems only the minimum access necessary to perform their functions—must be meticulously applied. This means that not every data scientist working on an AI project needs unfettered access to all raw customer data. Instead, access should be role-based and task-specific. A data scientist might need access to anonymized or pseudonymized versions of the data for model training, while a data engineer might require access to the raw data for pipeline construction and cleaning, but only for a defined period and within secure environments. Furthermore, access controls must extend to the AI models themselves. Once trained, AI models can encapsulate sensitive information derived from their training data. Therefore, access to these models, their parameters, and their outputs must also be carefully managed to prevent unauthorized inference of private information. For example, an AI model that predicts customer churn based on usage patterns and demographic data should not be accessible to marketing personnel who might then use this information for discriminatory practices. Implementing robust access controls involves leveraging technologies such as identity and access management (IAM) systems, role-based access control (RBAC), and attribute-based access control (ABAC). It also requires a continuous process of review and auditing to ensure that access permissions remain appropriate as roles change and projects evolve. The goal is to create a secure environment where data is accessible to those who *need* it for legitimate AI purposes, but strictly protected from those who do not, thereby minimizing the potential for data breaches and misuse.

A fundamental pillar of data governance, particularly concerning privacy, is the establishment and enforcement of **data retention policies**. AI systems are often designed for continuous learning and improvement, which can lead to a natural inclination to accumulate and retain data indefinitely. However, from a privacy perspective, this "data hoarding" is a significant risk. The longer data is retained, the greater the potential for it to be exposed in a breach, misused, or to become outdated and inaccurate, leading to flawed AI outputs. Data retention policies define how long specific categories of data should be kept, based on legal requirements, business needs, and the sensitivity of the data. For AI, this means carefully considering the lifecycle of the data used for training and operationalizing models. For instance, data used for training a predictive maintenance AI for industrial machinery might have a different retention period than sensitive personal health information used to train a diagnostic AI. The policy should clearly specify not only the retention period but also the secure methods for data deletion or anonymization at the end of that period. Implementing these policies effectively requires automated systems that can track data age and trigger deletion processes, alongside human oversight to ensure that sensitive data is not prematurely purged or unnecessarily retained. The challenge with AI models is that the "data" can become embedded within the model's parameters. Therefore, retention policies must also consider the model's operational lifespan and the data used for its ongoing monitoring and retraining. If a model is decommissioned, the associated training data should also be subject to deletion or anonymization according to the established policy. This proactive approach to data lifecycle management not only reduces privacy risks but also contributes to operational efficiency by managing storage costs and reducing the complexity of data management.

Furthermore, ensuring
auditability is critical for any effective data governance framework, especially in the context of AI. Auditability refers to the ability to trace and verify all actions taken with respect to data. This means having a clear, immutable record of who accessed what data, when, why, and what actions were performed. For AI data pipelines, this is indispensable for demonstrating compliance with privacy regulations such as GDPR or CCPA, and for investigating any suspected privacy incidents. Audit logs

should capture details about data ingestion, transformations, model training, inference requests, and data deletions. This comprehensive logging allows organizations to reconstruct the data journey, understand how a particular AI model was trained, and identify any anomalies or unauthorized activities. For example, if a privacy complaint arises regarding an AI system's output, audit logs can help determine if the input data was handled appropriately, if the model was trained on compliant data, and if any unauthorized access occurred. The challenge in the AI domain lies in the sheer volume and velocity of data processing, which can generate an overwhelming amount of audit information. Therefore, robust logging mechanisms need to be coupled with effective log management and analysis tools. This might involve using Security Information and Event Management (SIEM) systems to aggregate and analyze logs, and employing AI-powered tools to detect suspicious patterns or potential privacy violations within the audit trails. The principle of immutability is also key; audit logs should be protected from tampering to ensure their integrity. By maintaining a transparent and verifiable record of data handling, organizations can build trust with individuals and regulators, and proactively identify and address potential privacy vulnerabilities in their AI systems.

The complexity of AI data pipelines often necessitates a tiered approach to data access and governance. For instance, raw, sensitive data might be housed in highly restricted environments, accessible only to a minimal set of personnel for specific, approved tasks like initial data cleaning or anonymization. From this secure zone, processed, pseudonymized, or aggregated datasets can be made available to a broader group of data scientists for model development. Finally, inference APIs or specific model outputs might be exposed to end-user applications, with access tightly controlled and monitored. This segmentation ensures that sensitive information is protected at its most vulnerable points, while still enabling the necessary data flows for AI innovation.

Beyond internal controls, external factors also heavily influence data governance for AI. Regulatory landscapes are constantly evolving, with new privacy laws and guidelines emerging globally. A robust data governance framework must be agile enough to adapt to these changes. This involves continuous monitoring of legal and regulatory developments, performing gap analyses against current practices, and updating policies and procedures accordingly. For example, the advent of new regulations regarding AI bias detection might necessitate new data governance protocols for auditing training data for representational fairness and ensuring that the data used for bias mitigation is appropriately managed.

Moreover, the ethical implications of data use in AI cannot be overlooked within data governance. While compliance focuses on legal adherence, ethical considerations delve into broader societal impacts and the moral responsibility of organizations. Data governance, therefore, should also incorporate mechanisms for ethical review of data usage in AI projects, particularly for applications that have a significant impact on individuals or society, such as in healthcare, finance, or criminal justice. This might involve establishing ethics committees or review boards to assess potential harms and ensure that data is used in a way that respects human dignity and promotes well-being.

In essence, data governance for AI is not a one-time setup but an ongoing commitment. It requires a blend of technological solutions, policy development, organizational culture, and continuous vigilance. By meticulously managing data throughout its lifecycle – from clear ownership and stringent access controls to well-defined retention policies and comprehensive auditability – organizations can build a strong foundation for privacy engineering, enabling them to harness the power of AI responsibly and ethically, while safeguarding the fundamental right to privacy for individuals. This rigorous approach to data governance is not merely a compliance burden; it is a strategic imperative that fosters trust, mitigates risks, and ultimately, drives sustainable innovation in the age of artificial intelligence.

The preceding discussion has underscored the foundational role of robust data governance in establishing a secure and privacy-conscious environment for AI development. However, governance alone, while essential, is often insufficient to address the complex privacy challenges inherent in AI's data-intensive nature. The sheer volume, variety, and sensitivity of data processed by AI systems demand proactive, technologically driven solutions that can actively shield individual privacy. This is where the critical domain of Privacy-Preserving Technologies (PPTs) comes to the fore. These are not merely add-ons but rather integral components that can be woven into the fabric of AI development and deployment, offering powerful mechanisms to minimize privacy risks at their source.

At its core, privacy engineering in the age of AI necessitates a proactive stance—anticipating potential harms and building safeguards into systems from the outset. PPTs provide the sophisticated tools to achieve this. Instead of relying solely on post-hoc anonymization or access controls, these technologies enable the processing and analysis of sensitive data in ways that fundamentally protect individual identities. They offer a spectrum of solutions, each with its own strengths, weaknesses, and ideal applications, collectively forming a vital toolkit for engineers seeking to build AI systems that are both innovative and respectful of privacy. Understanding and strategically deploying these technologies is no longer a niche concern; it is a central tenet of responsible AI development.

One of the most prominent and widely discussed PPTs is

Differential Privacy (DP). At its heart, differential privacy is a mathematical guarantee that the output of an algorithm is unlikely to change significantly whether or not any single individual's data is included in the input dataset. This might sound abstract, but its implications are profound. Imagine a census being conducted, and an algorithm is used to calculate the average income of a particular demographic. If this algorithm is differentially private, then an attacker who knows everything about the dataset *except* for one person's income would still learn very little about that specific individual's income by observing the algorithm's output. The presence or absence of any single data point has a statistically negligible impact.

The mechanism by which differential privacy achieves this is through the controlled injection of noise. When data is analyzed or an algorithm is run, a carefully calibrated amount of random noise is added to the results. This noise is sufficient to obscure the contribution of any single individual, thus protecting their privacy, but it is not so great that it renders the overall analysis useless for aggregate insights. The "privacy budget," often denoted by the Greek letter epsilon (ϵ), quantifies the level of privacy. A smaller epsilon signifies stronger privacy guarantees, meaning more noise is added and the output is less sensitive to individual data points. Conversely, a larger epsilon allows for more accurate results but offers weaker privacy protection. The choice of epsilon is a critical trade-off that depends heavily on the sensitivity of the data and the acceptable level of utility.

Differential privacy can be applied in two main ways: **local differential privacy** and **global differential privacy**. In local differential privacy, noise is added to each individual data point *before* it is collected or sent to a central server. This offers the strongest privacy protection, as the data owner never relinquishes their raw, sensitive information. For example, a mobile app might use local DP to collect user browsing habits; each user's device adds noise to their data before transmitting it. This means the central server never sees the original, precise data from any user. The downside is that this often requires a significant amount of data to overcome the aggregated noise for meaningful analysis.

Global differential privacy, on the other hand, involves adding noise to the *output* of a computation performed on an aggregate dataset. Here, the raw data is collected and processed centrally, and then noise is added to the final results or intermediate statistics. This generally leads to more accurate results for a given privacy budget compared to local DP, as the noise is applied once to the aggregate. However, it relies on trusting the entity collecting and processing the data not to misuse the raw, un-noised information before the privacy mechanism is applied. Many large tech companies, like Apple and Google, have employed differential privacy techniques to gather insights from user data while attempting to preserve individual privacy. For instance, they might use it to understand popular features or identify emerging trends without compromising the specific activities of individual users.

The strengths of differential privacy are its strong, mathematically provable privacy guarantees and its adaptability to various data analysis tasks. It is a robust defense against many privacy attacks. However, it's not a panacea. The primary limitation is the inherent utility-privacy trade-off. As privacy guarantees strengthen (lower epsilon), the accuracy and utility of the resulting analysis can degrade, potentially making the insights less valuable. This is particularly challenging for complex AI models that often require high-fidelity data for optimal performance. Another challenge is the complexity of implementing DP correctly, especially in dynamic AI training pipelines where data is constantly being updated. Accurately managing the privacy budget over multiple queries or model updates is crucial and technically demanding.

Another powerful paradigm in the PPT landscape is

Federated Learning (FL). Instead of bringing vast amounts of sensitive data to a central server for model training, federated learning brings the model *to the data*. In a typical FL setup, a global model is initialized on a central server. This model is then sent to multiple distributed devices or clients (e.g., smartphones, hospitals, different branches of a bank) that hold local datasets. Each client trains the model on its local data, producing an updated model. These local model updates, which are typically gradients or parameter changes, are then sent back to the central server. The server aggregates these updates (often using techniques like federated averaging) to improve the global model. Crucially, the raw data itself *never leaves the client device.*

This distributed approach offers significant privacy advantages. Since raw personal data remains on the user's device, the risk of a central data breach is significantly reduced. It allows for training AI models on diverse, real-world datasets that might be too sensitive or voluminous to centralize. Consider a healthcare scenario: multiple hospitals could collaborate to train a diagnostic AI model without sharing their patient records with each other or a third party. Each hospital trains the model on its local patient data, and only the model updates are shared. This respects patient privacy and complies with regulations like HIPAA. Similarly, financial institutions could collaborate on fraud detection models without exposing their proprietary customer transaction data.

While federated learning fundamentally enhances privacy by keeping data local, it's important to note that it's not inherently fully private on its own. The model updates sent back to the server, while not raw data, can potentially still leak information about the local training data through sophisticated inference attacks. Therefore, federated learning is often combined with other privacy-enhancing techniques, such as differential privacy or secure aggregation, to further bolster privacy. For example, adding differential privacy to the model updates before they are sent to the server can provide stronger guarantees against inferential attacks.

Secure aggregation protocols ensure that the central server can only see the sum of all updates, not individual client updates, further obscuring information.

The strengths of federated learning lie in its ability to train models on decentralized data, preserving privacy by design and enabling collaboration across data silos. It's particularly well-suited for applications where data is naturally distributed and sensitive, such as on mobile devices or within different organizations. However, FL also presents challenges. Communication overhead can be significant, especially with a large number of clients. Clients may have varying computational capabilities and network connectivity, leading to issues with training convergence. Furthermore, dealing with non-IID (non-independently and identically distributed) data across clients—where data distributions vary significantly—can degrade model performance. Ensuring the security and integrity of the aggregation process is also paramount.

Moving into the realm of cryptographic solutions, **Homomorphic Encryption (HE)** stands out as a transformative technology. In essence, homomorphic encryption allows computations to be performed directly on encrypted data without decrypting it first. Imagine having a locked box containing sensitive numbers. With homomorphic encryption, you could perform calculations like addition or multiplication on the numbers inside the box *while they remain locked*. Only after the computations are complete would you unlock the box to reveal the encrypted result, which can then be decrypted to yield the final answer.

There are different types of homomorphic encryption, each with varying capabilities:

Partially Homomorphic Encryption (PHE) supports only one type of operation, either addition or multiplication, an unlimited number of times.
Somewhat Homomorphic Encryption (SHE) supports a limited number of both addition and multiplication operations.
Fully Homomorphic Encryption (FHE) supports an unlimited number of both addition and multiplication operations. FHE is the most powerful but also the most computationally intensive.

The implications for AI are enormous. With HE, sensitive data can be encrypted by its owner and sent to a cloud provider or AI service. The AI model can then process this encrypted data, perform training or inference, and return the encrypted result. The service provider never gets access to the raw, unencrypted data, thus preserving privacy. For instance, a user could encrypt their personal medical records and send them to a cloud-based AI for diagnosis. The AI could process the encrypted data and return an encrypted diagnosis, which only the user with the decryption key could read. This eliminates the need for trust in the data processor regarding data confidentiality.

HE is particularly promising for privacy-preserving AI inference, where a pre-trained model is used to make predictions on new data. It also opens doors for secure outsourcing of AI computations. However, the primary hurdle for widespread adoption of homomorphic encryption, especially FHE, is its significant computational overhead. Operations on encrypted data are orders of magnitude slower than operations on plaintext data. This makes training large, complex AI models using FHE currently impractical for most real-world scenarios. Research is actively progressing to improve efficiency, and PHE and SHE are finding more practical applications for specific, less computationally intensive tasks. The development of specialized hardware and optimized libraries is crucial for unlocking the full potential of HE in AI.

Closely related to homomorphic encryption, and offering complementary capabilities, is

Secure Multi-Party Computation (SMPC), also known as Secure Multiparty Computing. SMPC allows multiple parties to jointly compute a function over their private inputs while keeping those inputs private from each other. Unlike HE, where one party encrypts data and another computes on it, SMPC involves a protocol where each participant contributes their private data, and through a series of interactive communication rounds, they collectively arrive at a result without revealing their individual inputs.

Consider a scenario where several companies want to train a machine learning model on their combined datasets, but they are unwilling to share their proprietary data with each other. Using SMPC, they can collaboratively train the model. Each company's data remains private, and the SMPC protocol ensures that only the final trained model or specific aggregated statistics are revealed, not the individual data used in the process. This is invaluable for collaborative AI development, competitive analysis, and any situation where data is distributed across entities that do not fully trust each other.

SMPC can be used for various AI tasks, including training models, performing privacy-preserving inference, and enabling secure data analysis. For example, it can be used to compute private set intersection (finding common elements between two datasets without revealing the non-common elements), which is a fundamental building block for many data-sharing and analytics tasks. It can also be employed in conjunction with federated learning to add an extra layer of privacy by ensuring that the aggregation of model updates is done securely, so no single party or observer can infer information from individual updates.

The strengths of SMPC lie in its ability to enable secure collaboration on private data among multiple distrusting parties. It offers strong privacy guarantees and can be more efficient than FHE for certain types of computations, especially those involving a moderate number of parties. However, SMPC protocols often require multiple rounds of communication between participants, which can lead to latency issues, especially in networks with high latency or a large number of participants. The complexity of implementing SMPC correctly can also be a barrier, and the computational cost can still be significant, though often less so than FHE for specific tasks. The performance of SMPC can be sensitive to the network topology and the number of participating parties.

Beyond these core technologies, other techniques contribute to the privacy-preserving arsenal for AI.
Anonymization and Pseudonymization, while often considered data governance tools, are also technologies that can be applied at various stages. Anonymization aims to remove or obscure personally identifiable information (PII) so that individuals cannot be identified. Pseudonymization replaces PII with artificial identifiers (pseudonyms), allowing for data linkage and analysis while reducing direct identification. However, simple anonymization can be brittle, as re-identification risks remain, especially when combined with external datasets. More advanced anonymization techniques, often incorporating elements of differential privacy, aim to provide stronger guarantees.

Data Synthesis is another emerging technique where synthetic datasets are generated that mimic the statistical properties of real data but do not contain any actual individual records. These synthetic datasets can be used for training AI models, testing systems, or sharing data for research without exposing real individuals. The challenge with synthetic data is ensuring that it is representative enough to train effective models and that it doesn't inadvertently encode biases or leak sensitive information from the original data generation process.

The choice of which PPT to employ, or what combination of technologies to use, depends heavily on the specific AI application, the nature of the data, the desired privacy guarantees, and the acceptable trade-offs in terms of utility and performance. For instance:

A company analyzing user behavior on its website might use **differential privacy** to aggregate clickstream data for insights into user engagement, ensuring that no single user's browsing pattern can be identified.
A mobile operating system provider might use **federated learning** to train predictive text models across millions of devices, keeping user typing data on the device while improving the global model. This could be augmented with **differential privacy** applied to model updates for enhanced protection.
A financial institution wanting to detect sophisticated fraud patterns by analyzing encrypted transaction data from multiple banks could explore **homomorphic encryption** for secure inference or **secure multi-party computation** for collaborative model training, where each bank's transaction data remains confidential.
A healthcare research consortium aiming to build a predictive model for rare diseases could use **federated learning** to train models across different hospital systems, potentially employing **SMPC** to securely aggregate model parameters, and utilizing **advanced anonymization** or **data synthesis** for sharing derived datasets for further study.

In practice, a layered approach is often the most effective. Combining different PPTs can create a more robust privacy posture than relying on a single technology. For example, federated learning can be paired with differential privacy to protect against inference attacks on model updates, while secure aggregation can be used to ensure that the server only sees aggregated updates. Homomorphic encryption might be used for specific parts of an AI pipeline, like secure inference, while other parts rely on differential privacy.

The development and adoption of these technologies are crucial for building trust in AI systems. As AI becomes more pervasive, its ability to process and derive insights from sensitive information will only increase. Without sophisticated privacy-preserving measures, the potential for misuse, breaches, and erosion of public trust is significant. Engineers and policymakers must therefore invest in understanding, developing, and deploying these PPTs, recognizing them not as optional extras but as fundamental enablers of responsible and ethical AI innovation. The journey from data governance to privacy-preserving technologies represents a continuum of efforts to ensure that the power of AI is harnessed for the benefit of humanity without compromising the fundamental right to privacy.

The preceding discussion has illuminated the indispensable role of Privacy-Preserving Technologies (PPTs) in fortifying AI systems against privacy vulnerabilities. However, the mere selection and implementation of these sophisticated tools, while crucial, represent only a part of the comprehensive privacy engineering lifecycle. A truly robust approach demands a systematic and proactive process of identifying, analyzing, and mitigating potential privacy risks *before* they can manifest as harms. This is the essence of a Privacy Risk Assessment, a foundational practice that guides the application of PPTs and other privacy controls throughout the AI development and deployment continuum.

A privacy risk assessment is not a static, one-time event. Instead, it should be an iterative and adaptive process, integrated into every stage of an AI system's lifecycle, from initial design and data collection to model training, deployment, and ongoing maintenance. The objective is to anticipate how an AI system, by its very nature and the data it processes, could inadvertently or intentionally compromise individual privacy. This involves a multi-faceted examination of potential threats, the likelihood of those threats occurring, and the severity of the impact should they materialize. Without such an assessment, even the most advanced PPTs might be misapplied, overlooked, or insufficient to address the unique privacy landscape of a given AI application.

The process typically begins with a thorough understanding of the AI system itself. What kind of data does it process? Where does this data come from? What are the characteristics of the individuals whose data is involved – are they particularly vulnerable populations? What is the intended purpose of the AI system, and what are its potential secondary uses? Answering these questions provides the essential context for identifying potential privacy risks. For instance, an AI system designed to analyze medical images for disease detection will inherently handle highly sensitive personal health information (PHI). The risks associated with this system will be far greater than, say, an AI that analyzes public weather data.

Once the system and its data context are understood, the next step is to identify potential privacy threats. These threats can arise from various sources.

Data breaches are perhaps the most obvious, where unauthorized parties gain access to sensitive datasets. This could be due to external cyberattacks, insider threats, or accidental exposure. However, privacy risks extend beyond outright breaches. **Inference attacks** are a significant concern in AI. These attacks leverage the outputs or behaviors of an AI model to infer sensitive information about the individuals in the training data, even if the model itself doesn't directly reveal PII. For example, an attacker might be able to infer a person's medical condition by querying a diagnostic AI model with specific inputs.

Another category of threats relates to

data misuse. This can occur when data collected for one purpose is used for another, unauthorized purpose without consent. For instance, customer service chat logs collected to improve support might be repurposed for targeted advertising or behavioral profiling. Similarly, **function creep**, where a system's capabilities expand over time to encompass new functionalities that involve greater privacy intrusion, is a prevalent risk. The aggregation of data from multiple sources can also exacerbate privacy risks, as seemingly innocuous datasets can become highly revealing when combined.

Beyond these more direct threats,
bias and discrimination embedded within AI systems can also lead to privacy harms. If an AI system exhibits bias against certain demographic groups, it could result in unfair outcomes, such as discriminatory loan application rejections or biased surveillance, which can be considered a form of privacy violation by imposing unwarranted scrutiny or limitations on individuals. The lack of transparency and explainability in many AI models also contributes to risk, making it difficult to ascertain *how* decisions are made and *whether* privacy has been compromised in the process.

After identifying potential threats, the assessment must evaluate their **likelihood** and **impact**. Likelihood refers to how probable it is that a specific threat will occur. This can be assessed based on factors like the security of the infrastructure, the sensitivity of the data, the potential motivation of attackers, and the known vulnerabilities of the technologies used. Impact, on the other hand, measures the severity of the consequences if the threat is realized. This includes the financial costs of a breach, reputational damage, regulatory penalties, and, crucially, the harm to individuals, such as identity theft, discrimination, emotional distress, or loss of autonomy.

To facilitate this evaluation, various methodologies can be employed.

Threat modeling is a structured approach that involves systematically identifying potential threats and vulnerabilities. Techniques like STRIDE (Spoofing, Tampering, Repudiation, Information Disclosure, Denial of Service, Elevation of Privilege) can be adapted to identify AI-specific threats. For example, "Information Disclosure" in STRIDE maps directly to risks of sensitive data leakage from AI models or datasets. "Tampering" could relate to malicious manipulation of training data or model parameters.

Another critical aspect of risk assessment is understanding the sensitivity and characteristics of the data itself. This involves **data classification**, where data is categorized based on its PII content, sensitivity level, and regulatory requirements (e.g., GDPR, HIPAA). For AI, it's not just about identifying PII but also understanding **inferential sensitivity**. This means recognizing that even non-PII data, when processed by AI, could lead to the inference of sensitive attributes. For example, purchase history, browsing patterns, and location data, when analyzed by an AI, could reveal information about an individual's health, political leanings, or sexual orientation.

Data flow mapping is another essential tool. This involves visually representing how data moves through the AI system, from collection to processing, storage, and eventual deletion. This mapping helps to pinpoint critical junctures where privacy risks might be amplified, such as data aggregation points, API integrations, or third-party data sharing mechanisms. By tracing the data's journey, assessors can identify opportunities for unauthorized access, modification, or disclosure.

Re-identification risk assessment is particularly relevant for AI, especially when working with anonymized or pseudonymized data. While anonymization aims to protect privacy by removing or obscuring direct identifiers, it's rarely foolproof. Techniques like k-anonymity, l-diversity, and t-closeness aim to quantify and mitigate re-identification risks. However, with the power of AI and the availability of auxiliary datasets, even seemingly well-anonymized data can be vulnerable. A thorough assessment would involve attempting to re-identify individuals from the dataset using various inference techniques, often simulating potential attacker capabilities. This involves understanding the "quasi-identifiers" – attributes that, when combined, can uniquely identify an individual (e.g., zip code, date of birth, gender). AI models can be particularly adept at finding complex correlations between quasi-identifiers and sensitive information.

Once risks are identified and assessed, the focus shifts to **mitigation strategies**. The goal is to reduce the likelihood and/or impact of identified risks to an acceptable level. This is where the previously discussed PPTs, alongside other privacy engineering practices, play a crucial role. The selection of mitigation strategies should be tailored to the specific risks identified.

Data Minimization is a fundamental principle. It involves collecting and processing only the data that is strictly necessary for the intended purpose. For AI, this means carefully considering what features are truly required for model training and inference. Over-collection of data increases the attack surface and the potential for privacy violations.

Anonymization and Pseudonymization techniques, when applied with a clear understanding of their limitations and re-identification risks, can be effective mitigation measures. For instance, if an AI model needs to be trained on a large dataset of user interactions but the specific identities of users are not required, pseudonymization can replace direct identifiers with unique tokens. Further anonymization techniques, such as k-anonymity or differential privacy, can then be applied to the pseudonymized data to provide stronger privacy guarantees. The key is to implement these techniques not as a one-off process but as an integral part of the data pipeline, with continuous monitoring for effectiveness. For example, a system might periodically re-evaluate its anonymization methods as new datasets or attack vectors emerge.

When privacy risks are particularly high, and data cannot be fully anonymized,
Differential Privacy (DP) offers a mathematically rigorous approach to privacy protection during data analysis and model training. As discussed earlier, DP adds carefully calibrated noise to query results or model parameters, ensuring that the output does not reveal whether any single individual's data was included. Integrating DP into the AI training process, for instance, can significantly reduce the risk of inferring individual data points from the trained model. The choice of the privacy budget (ϵ) becomes a critical decision point during risk mitigation, balancing the strength of privacy guarantees against the utility of the AI model.

Federated Learning (FL) acts as a powerful mitigation strategy for risks associated with centralizing sensitive data. By training models on distributed devices, FL keeps raw data local, significantly reducing the risk of large-scale data breaches at a central repository. The risk assessment here would focus on the privacy of the model updates themselves, leading to the incorporation of techniques like secure aggregation or DP applied to these updates.

Homomorphic Encryption (HE) and **Secure Multi-Party Computation (SMPC)** offer robust solutions for scenarios where data must be processed collaboratively or by third parties without revealing the underlying sensitive information. If a risk assessment reveals that sharing raw data with a cloud AI provider is unacceptable, HE allows the data owner to encrypt their data, and the provider can perform computations on the encrypted data. SMPC is ideal for collaborative training among multiple parties who do not trust each other, mitigating the risk of data leakage between participants. The risk assessment would guide the selection between HE and SMPC based on the specific computational needs, the number of parties involved, and communication constraints.

Beyond these PPTs,
access controls and robust security measures are paramount. Implementing the principle of least privilege, ensuring that users and systems only have access to the data and functionalities they absolutely need, is a fundamental mitigation strategy. This involves strong authentication, authorization mechanisms, and regular audits of access logs. Encryption of data at rest and in transit, even for non-sensitive data, adds an additional layer of defense against breaches.

Data retention and deletion policies are also critical mitigation elements. Retaining sensitive data for longer than necessary increases the window of opportunity for it to be compromised. Implementing strict policies for data retention, based on legal and business requirements, and ensuring secure deletion of data when it is no longer needed, are essential steps in minimizing privacy risk. For AI, this might involve developing strategies for model "forgetting," where specific data points can be removed from a trained model without retraining from scratch, though this is an area of active research.

Transparency and explainability in AI systems, while often discussed as ethical imperatives, also serve as vital risk mitigation strategies. When individuals understand how an AI system uses their data and makes decisions, they can better identify and report potential privacy violations or unfair outcomes. For developers and auditors, explainable AI (XAI) techniques can help uncover potential privacy leaks or biases within the model that might otherwise go unnoticed. A risk assessment might identify a lack of transparency as a significant risk factor and mandate the incorporation of XAI methods.

The process of privacy risk assessment and mitigation is iterative. As AI systems evolve, new data is collected, and new threats emerge, the assessment needs to be revisited and updated. This requires establishing a continuous monitoring framework. For deployed AI systems, this could involve monitoring for anomalous data access patterns, unusual model behavior, or external reports of vulnerabilities. Regular privacy audits, both internal and external, can help ensure that mitigation strategies remain effective and that the system continues to comply with privacy regulations and ethical standards.

In essence, privacy risk assessment and mitigation transform privacy from a reactive compliance exercise into a proactive engineering discipline. It provides the framework for strategically applying privacy-preserving technologies and best practices, ensuring that the development and deployment of AI systems are not only innovative but also fundamentally respectful of individual privacy rights. Without this systematic approach, the promise of AI risks being overshadowed by the potential for significant and widespread privacy harms. It is the bridge that connects the theoretical possibilities of privacy-enhancing technologies to their practical, real-world application in building trustworthy AI.

Ensuring that AI systems operate within the bounds of established privacy laws is not merely a matter of ethical consideration; it is a fundamental legal requirement. The rapid advancement and widespread adoption of AI have outpaced the development of specific legislation in many areas, yet existing data protection frameworks provide a robust, albeit sometimes challenging, foundation for governing AI's privacy implications. Navigating this complex regulatory landscape, which is increasingly global in scope with frameworks like the General Data

Protection Regulation (GDPR) in Europe, the California Consumer Privacy Act (CCPA) and its successor, the California Privacy Rights Act (CPRA), in the United States, and numerous other national and regional laws, is paramount. Compliance with these regulations translates directly into actionable privacy engineering tasks, shaping the design, development, and deployment of AI systems.

The core of regulatory compliance for AI lies in understanding and adhering to a set of fundamental principles and obligations. At the forefront is the principle of
lawfulness, fairness, and transparency. For AI systems, this means that any processing of personal data must have a legal basis, be conducted in a manner that individuals would reasonably expect, and be communicated clearly to them. This translates into engineering requirements for clear data use policies, accessible privacy notices, and mechanisms to ensure that data processing aligns with the stated purposes. Transparency, in particular, is a significant challenge for many AI models, especially complex neural networks. Privacy engineering efforts must therefore focus on developing methods to explain, to the extent possible, how AI systems use personal data and how they arrive at their decisions, even if a full technical explanation is beyond the grasp of the average data subject. This might involve generating high-level summaries of data usage, providing justifications for algorithmic outputs when feasible, or clearly delineating the scope and limitations of the AI's data processing capabilities.

Another critical pillar is
purpose limitation. Personal data collected for specific, explicit, and legitimate purposes should not be further processed in a manner incompatible with those purposes. For AI, this principle demands rigorous control over the intended use cases of the data and the models trained on it. Engineering teams must design systems that prevent or detect unauthorized "function creep," where data collected for one AI application might be inadvertently or intentionally used for another, more

intrusive purpose. This requires robust data governance frameworks that track data provenance and intended use throughout the AI lifecycle. It also necessitates careful consideration during the design phase to ensure that the AI architecture itself does not facilitate or encourage the repurposing of data. For instance, if an AI is developed to analyze customer sentiment for product feedback, its design should actively preclude its use for, say, sensitive demographic profiling or credit scoring without explicit new consent and a new legal basis.

The principle of
data minimization is equally vital. AI systems, often fueled by vast datasets, must be engineered to collect and process only the personal data that is strictly necessary for the specified purpose. This is a direct challenge to the "more data is better" mentality prevalent in some AI development circles. Privacy engineers must work closely with data scientists to identify the minimal set of features and data points required for the AI to achieve its objectives effectively. This might involve exploratory data analysis focused on identifying redundant or non-essential data attributes, developing feature selection techniques that prioritize privacy, and implementing automated checks to ensure that only approved datasets and variables are used in training and inference. For example, if an AI model for image recognition can achieve acceptable accuracy using grayscale images, then color data, which might contain more identifying information or be more sensitive, should be excluded from processing unless absolutely necessary and justified.

Furthermore, regulations emphasize the importance of
accuracy and **storage limitation**. Personal data must be accurate and, where necessary, kept up to date, with reasonable steps taken to correct or delete inaccurate data. AI systems that continuously learn or operate on dynamic datasets must have mechanisms to ensure data accuracy over time. Storage limitation means that personal data should not be kept longer than necessary for the purposes for which it is processed. This requires implementing and enforcing clear data retention and deletion

policies. For AI, this extends to model data; if an AI model is trained on specific data, and that data is later deleted or becomes obsolete, mechanisms should exist to update or retrain the model accordingly, or to ensure that the model itself does not retain inferential capabilities that depend on the now-deleted data. This can be particularly challenging for models that embed learned patterns from vast historical datasets.

A cornerstone of many privacy regulations, particularly the GDPR, is the requirement for
accountability. Organizations must not only comply with privacy principles but also be able to demonstrate their compliance. This principle mandates a proactive approach to privacy, moving beyond mere box-ticking. For AI systems, demonstrating accountability involves several key practices.

One of the most significant practical obligations is the
Record of Processing Activities (RoPA). Under GDPR, organizations must maintain detailed records of all data processing activities. For AI, this translates into an even more complex undertaking. A RoPA for an AI system needs to document not just the raw data collected and its sources, but also the specific AI models used, their training methodologies, the parameters and algorithms employed, the purposes for which the AI is used, how data flows into and out of the AI system, and the security measures in place. It should also detail the legal basis for processing, data retention periods, and any data transfers. Maintaining an up-to-date and accurate RoPA for multiple AI systems requires robust data governance tools and processes, potentially leveraging automated data cataloging and lineage tracking systems that can integrate with AI development workflows. The challenge lies in keeping these records dynamic, reflecting the iterative nature of AI development and deployment. For example, each significant model update, retraining event, or change in data input for an AI system should ideally trigger an update to the relevant RoPA entries.

Another critical component of demonstrating accountability, especially for AI systems that are likely to result in a
high risk to the rights and freedoms of natural persons, is the **Data Protection Impact Assessment (DPIA)**, also known as a Privacy Impact Assessment (PIA) under other frameworks. A DPIA is a process designed to systematically analyze, evaluate, and mitigate the privacy risks associated with a project, system, or technology. For AI, conducting a DPIA is often not just advisable but legally mandated. This assessment should be initiated early in the AI development lifecycle, ideally during the design phase, and revisited at key stages of deployment and operation.

The process of conducting a DPIA for an AI system involves several steps. First, it requires a clear description of the processing operation, including the nature, scope, context, and purposes of the AI system. This involves detailing the types of personal data involved, the volume of data, the characteristics of the data subjects, and the intended outcomes of the AI. Second, the DPIA must assess the necessity and proportionality of the processing in relation to the purposes. Are there less privacy-intrusive ways to achieve the same objectives? Can the AI achieve its goals with less data, or with anonymized or pseudonymized data? Third, and critically, the DPIA must identify and assess the risks to individuals' privacy. This goes beyond standard IT security risks to encompass a broader range of potential harms, such as:

Increased surveillance and profiling: AI systems can create detailed profiles of individuals based on their online activities, interactions, and even physical movements, leading to a chilling effect on freedom of expression and association.
Bias and discrimination: If an AI system is trained on biased data or uses biased algorithms, it can perpetuate and amplify existing societal inequalities, leading to discriminatory outcomes in areas like hiring, lending, or criminal justice, which constitutes a significant privacy harm.

Re-identification risks: Even "anonymized" datasets can potentially be de-anonymized using AI techniques when combined with other available data, revealing sensitive information about individuals.
Automated decision-making with significant effects: AI-powered decisions, such as loan rejections, job application screenings, or access to essential services, can have profound impacts on individuals' lives. A lack of transparency or recourse in these automated decisions can be a serious privacy concern.
Security vulnerabilities leading to disclosure of sensitive inferences: Beyond direct data breaches, sophisticated attacks could potentially infer sensitive personal characteristics from the AI model's behavior or outputs.

The DPIA process must also identify measures envisioned to mitigate these identified risks. This is where the principles of privacy engineering, including the application of privacy-preserving technologies (PPTs) like differential privacy, federated learning, homomorphic encryption, and robust anonymization techniques, come into play. It also includes organizational measures such as implementing clear data governance policies, establishing oversight committees, ensuring human review for critical automated decisions, and providing channels for individuals to challenge AI-driven outcomes. The DPIA should conclude with a decision on whether the residual risks, after mitigation, are acceptable or if the processing should be prohibited or modified. Crucially, the DPIA is not a one-off document but a living assessment that should be reviewed and updated, particularly if there are significant changes to the AI system or the data it processes.

Another vital aspect of regulatory compliance, directly impacting privacy engineering, is the handling of
Data Subject Rights (DSRs). Privacy regulations grant individuals a set of rights concerning their personal data. For AI systems, fulfilling these rights presents unique technical and operational challenges.

The
right of access allows individuals to obtain confirmation from an organization as to whether their personal data is being processed and, if so, to access that data and related information. For an AI system, this means not only providing access to the raw data that an individual has provided but also potentially explaining what inferences have been made about them, how their data has contributed to model training, and what outputs have been generated concerning them. Privacy engineers may need to develop tools that can query AI models to retrieve specific data points or aggregated information related to a particular individual, while ensuring that such access does not inadvertently reveal information about other data subjects.

The
right to rectification empowers individuals to have inaccurate personal data corrected. If an AI system learns from or uses inaccurate data, and this leads to incorrect outputs or profiles, mechanisms must be in place to identify and correct these inaccuracies. This could involve updating the underlying datasets, retraining the AI model with corrected data, or implementing post-processing adjustments to compensate for inaccuracies.

The
right to erasure, often referred to as the "right to be forgotten," allows individuals to request the deletion of their personal data. This is particularly complex for AI systems. If an individual's data has been incorporated into a trained AI model, simply deleting the original data point may not be sufficient if the model retains a learned representation of that data. Privacy engineering research is actively exploring techniques for "unlearning" specific data from trained models, but these are often computationally intensive and may degrade model performance. In the interim, organizations must have strategies to manage this, perhaps by ensuring data is not retained indefinitely in training sets, or by developing

methods to mitigate the impact of removed data. In some cases, it might require retraining the model from scratch without the problematic data, a significant engineering undertaking.

The
right to restrict processing allows individuals to request that the processing of their data be limited under certain circumstances. This could mean that an AI system, while still operational, is prevented from using an individual's data for specific purposes or from making certain types of inferences about them. Implementing such restrictions requires granular control over data flow and processing within the AI pipeline.

The
right to data portability enables individuals to receive their personal data in a structured, commonly used, and machine-readable format and to transmit it to another data controller. For AI, this could involve providing the individual with access to the data they have contributed, as well as potentially a representation of how their data has been used or transformed by the AI, in a usable format.

Finally, the
right to object and rights related to **automated decision-making and profiling** are particularly pertinent to AI. Individuals have the right to object to the processing of their personal data under certain conditions, and they have specific rights concerning decisions made solely by automated means that produce legal or similarly significant effects. For AI systems that make such decisions, regulations often require that individuals have the right to obtain human intervention, to express their point of view, and to contest the decision. Privacy engineers must ensure that AI systems are designed with such human oversight mechanisms built-in, and that there are clear pathways for individuals to exercise these rights. This often involves developing interfaces that allow for human review of high-stakes AI decisions and providing clear explanations for the automated outcomes.

Compliance with global privacy regulations is not a static achievement but an ongoing process that requires continuous vigilance, adaptation, and integration into the very fabric of AI development and operations. It demands a culture of privacy-by-design and privacy-by-default, where privacy considerations are not an afterthought but a primary driver from the initial conceptualization of an AI project through to its eventual decommissioning. This involves not only technical solutions but also robust organizational policies, comprehensive training for personnel, and a commitment to ongoing monitoring and auditing of AI systems' adherence to legal and ethical standards. The increasing complexity of AI and the evolving regulatory landscape necessitate a sophisticated and proactive approach to privacy engineering, ensuring that innovation in AI does not come at the expense of fundamental human rights to privacy.

Chapter 4: Ensuring Fairness and Mitigating Bias

The aspiration to build artificial intelligence systems that are not only powerful but also equitable and just is a core challenge in contemporary AI development. Yet, the very concept of "fairness" in this context is far from monolithic. It is a fluid, context-dependent notion, deeply intertwined with societal values, ethical principles, and the specific application domain of the AI. Attempting to impose a single, universal definition of fairness onto all AI systems would be akin to trying to fit a square peg into a round hole – a futile endeavor that risks misunderstanding and misapplication. Instead, we must embrace the inherent complexity and strive for context-specific fairness definitions that are rigorously debated and clearly articulated for each system.

One of the earliest and most intuitive mathematical formulations of fairness, particularly in the context of classification tasks (where an AI predicts a category, such as loan approval or criminal recidivism), is **demographic parity**. This metric seeks to ensure that the proportion of individuals receiving a positive outcome (e.g., loan approval) is the same across different demographic groups, typically defined by protected attributes like race, gender, or age. In essence, it aims for parity in the *prediction rates*. For instance, if an AI system is used to determine who receives a job interview, demographic parity would mandate that the percentage of Black applicants invited for an interview is the same as the percentage of White applicants, and so on for other racial groups. The appeal of demographic parity lies in its simplicity and its direct address of potential disparities in outcomes. However, its limitations become apparent quickly. It does not consider whether the individuals receiving the positive outcome are actually qualified or deserving of it. A system could achieve demographic parity by approving an equal percentage of both qualified and unqualified individuals from different groups, thus failing to achieve substantive fairness. This is particularly problematic if the underlying base rates of qualification differ significantly between groups, a situation that can arise due to historical or systemic inequities. Applying demographic parity without considering true qualifications can lead to the approval of less qualified candidates in one group over more qualified candidates in another, which itself could be perceived as unfair.

Moving beyond simple outcome parity,
equalized odds offers a more nuanced approach. This definition requires that the true positive rates (the proportion of correctly predicted positive instances) and the false positive rates (the proportion of incorrectly predicted positive instances) are equal across different demographic groups. For an AI used in a hiring context, this would mean that an AI correctly identifies qualified candidates at the same rate for all demographic groups, and it incorrectly flags unqualified candidates at the same rate for all groups. This approach attempts to ensure that the AI is equally reliable in its predictions, regardless of group membership. However, equalized odds still has its own set of challenges. It assumes that the underlying probability of being qualified is the same across groups, or at least that any differences are not systematically related to the AI's predictions. If, for example, there are systemic factors that make it harder for women to acquire certain credentials recognized by the AI, equalized odds might still lead to disparities in the actual number of women hired, even if the *rates* of correct and incorrect predictions are equal. Furthermore, achieving equalized odds can be computationally very difficult, often requiring complex trade-offs with overall accuracy.

A related concept,
predictive parity, focuses on the precision of the predictions. It requires that among individuals who are predicted to receive a positive outcome, the proportion who are actually deserving of that outcome (the precision) is the same across all groups. In the loan application scenario, this means that if the AI predicts a loan will be approved, the probability that the applicant is creditworthy should be the same whether they are male or female, or belong to any other demographic group. Predictive parity is concerned with the trustworthiness of a positive prediction for any given individual, regardless of their group. While important for ensuring that individuals who are given a positive prediction can rely on it, predictive

parity does not necessarily address disparities in the *number* of people who receive positive outcomes or in the rates of correctly identifying deserving individuals. For instance, a system could have perfect predictive parity but still disproportionately deny loans to a particular group if its underlying assessment of creditworthiness for that group is systematically lower, even if the predicted approvals are accurate.

The inherent tension and trade-offs between these and other fairness metrics are a central concern. It has been mathematically demonstrated that, under certain conditions (specifically, if base rates of the outcome differ between groups), it is impossible to satisfy demographic parity, equalized odds, and predictive parity simultaneously. This implies that developers and deployers of AI systems must make deliberate choices about which definition of fairness to prioritize, or how to balance competing definitions. This is not a technical problem that can be solved by a single algorithm; it is an ethical and societal decision that must be informed by the specific context and the potential harms of the AI system. For example, in a high-stakes medical diagnosis system, ensuring equalized odds might be paramount to guarantee that diagnostic accuracy is consistent across populations, even if it leads to slightly different overall rates of diagnosis. Conversely, in a system for allocating scarce resources where equity of access is the primary goal, demographic parity might be a more appropriate starting point, with careful attention paid to mitigating any negative consequences arising from potentially different qualification rates.

The critical takeaway is that "fairness" is not a one-size-fits-all solution. The appropriate definition of fairness for an AI system must be determined by its intended use, the societal impact it is expected to have, and the values of the community it serves. This requires a deep understanding of the domain in which the AI will operate. For instance, fairness considerations in an AI designed for autonomous vehicles might differ significantly from those in an AI used for personalized education, or for predicting which areas might be most susceptible to a public health crisis.

In the realm of hiring, a system that screens resumes for entry-level positions might prioritize demographic parity to ensure a diverse pool of candidates is considered, while a system used for advanced medical training selection might prioritize equalized odds to ensure that all qualified candidates have an equal chance of being identified, even if the overall pool of qualified candidates is smaller for certain groups due to historical educational access issues. The choice of fairness definition must be a deliberate, transparent, and justifiable decision, not an accidental byproduct of the development process. This necessitates close collaboration between AI developers, ethicists, domain experts, policymakers, and crucially, the communities that will be affected by the AI system. Without this interdisciplinary and stakeholder-inclusive approach, efforts to achieve fairness in AI risk being superficial, misguided, or even counterproductive, potentially exacerbating existing inequalities under the guise of technological advancement.

Furthermore, the pursuit of fairness in AI cannot be divorced from the broader goal of building trustworthy and reliable systems. A system that is deemed "fair" by one metric but performs poorly overall, or is easily gamed, is unlikely to be adopted or to achieve its intended beneficial purpose. Therefore, fairness must be considered alongside other crucial performance metrics, such as accuracy, robustness, and interpretability. The challenge often lies in finding an optimal balance, a compromise that acknowledges the inherent trade-offs and aims for the most equitable and beneficial outcome given the constraints.

This nuanced understanding of fairness also highlights the limitations of purely automated solutions. While algorithms can be developed to optimize for specific fairness metrics, the fundamental decisions about which metrics to prioritize and how to weigh them involve human judgment and ethical reasoning. This underscores the importance of human oversight and continuous evaluation. As AI systems are deployed and interact with the real world, their impact on different groups must be constantly monitored. Feedback mechanisms should be established to identify any emergent unfairness, and processes must be in place to adapt and retrain models or adjust their deployment strategies accordingly. The journey towards fair AI is an ongoing process of learning, adaptation, and continuous improvement, rather than a static destination.

The discussion around fairness also intersects with the concept of algorithmic accountability. If an AI system is found to be unfair, who is responsible? The developers who built the model? The organization that deployed it? The data scientists who curated the training data? Establishing clear lines of accountability is essential, and this requires transparency not only in the fairness metrics being used but also in the entire development and deployment lifecycle of the AI system. This transparency can help identify where biases may have been introduced and facilitate the remediation of unfair outcomes.

In conclusion, defining and achieving fairness in AI is a complex, iterative, and deeply contextual endeavor. It requires moving beyond simplistic, universal definitions and embracing a multifaceted approach that considers various mathematical formulations of fairness, their inherent trade-offs, and the specific application domain. It demands interdisciplinary collaboration, robust evaluation, continuous monitoring, and a commitment to ethical decision-making. Only through such rigorous and thoughtful engagement can we hope to build AI systems that not only perform effectively but also serve to advance equity and justice in society.

The journey to equitable artificial intelligence is paved with a critical understanding of its origins and manifestations. Before we can effectively build AI systems that are fair, we must first meticulously examine the root causes and the insidious ways in which bias can infiltrate these technologies. This exploration is not merely an academic exercise; it is a foundational step towards developing AI that serves humanity justly and equitably, rather than perpetuating or amplifying existing societal inequalities. The very essence of AI's potential for good is undermined if its underlying mechanisms are skewed, leading to discriminatory outcomes. Therefore, a deep dive into the sources and manifestations of AI bias is paramount for anyone involved in the design, development, deployment, or governance of these powerful tools.

At its core, artificial intelligence learns from data. This fundamental dependency means that if the data fed into an AI system reflects existing societal biases, the AI will, in turn, learn and perpetuate those biases. This is perhaps the most pervasive and well-documented source of AI bias: **biased training data**. Imagine an AI system being trained on historical hiring data from a company that, for decades, predominantly hired men for engineering roles. Even if the company's stated policy is now to hire the most qualified candidate regardless of gender, the historical data itself encodes a strong preference for male applicants. The AI, diligently learning patterns from this data, might inadvertently develop a bias towards male candidates, perceiving them as more suitable for engineering positions, simply because the historical record shows a higher proportion of men in those roles. This is not a malicious act by the AI; it is a direct consequence of the information it was given. The data, in this instance, is not a neutral reflection of reality but a historical artifact shaped by human decisions and societal norms that may have been discriminatory.

The origins of biased training data are multifaceted. One significant contributor is

historical bias, where past discriminatory practices are embedded in the data. This can manifest in numerous domains. In loan applications, historical data might show lower approval rates for certain minority groups, not necessarily due to their creditworthiness, but due to past discriminatory lending practices. An AI trained on this data might learn to associate these groups with higher risk, even if current economic conditions and individual financial profiles suggest otherwise. Similarly, in the criminal justice system, recidivism prediction models trained on arrest and conviction data can reflect systemic biases in policing and prosecution, disproportionately impacting marginalized communities. If certain communities are policed more heavily, leading to higher arrest rates for similar offenses, the data will reflect this disparity, and an AI might learn to associate individuals from those communities with a higher likelihood of reoffending, regardless of individual circumstances.

Another critical source is
sampling bias. This occurs when the data collected does not accurately represent the population to which the AI system will be applied. For instance, if a facial recognition system is primarily trained on images of individuals with lighter skin tones, it is likely to perform poorly when identifying individuals with darker skin tones. This is not because the AI is inherently racist, but because its training set was not representative. The system simply has less experience with, and therefore less accurate models for, the underrepresented group. This can have serious consequences, from misidentification in security contexts to biased outcomes in applications that use facial analysis for demographic estimation. Similarly, if a language model is trained predominantly on text from Western cultures, it may struggle to understand or accurately represent nuances, idioms, or cultural references from other parts of the world.

Selection bias, closely related to sampling bias, arises when the process of selecting data for training introduces a systematic error. This can happen in various ways. Consider an AI designed to predict customer churn. If the dataset only includes customers who have already left, and does not include active customers, the AI may fail to identify the early warning signs that lead to churn. In a medical context, if a dataset for training a diagnostic AI is primarily composed of patients from a specific geographic region or socioeconomic background, it may not generalize well to patients from different backgrounds who may present with different symptoms or have different underlying health conditions. This is particularly concerning when dealing with diseases that disproportionately affect certain populations or when healthcare access varies significantly.

Beyond the data itself,
algorithmic design choices can also introduce or amplify bias. While algorithms are often perceived as purely mathematical constructs, the decisions made by engineers in selecting, weighting, and configuring these algorithms can have profound ethical implications. For example, when developing a recommendation system for online content, engineers might choose to optimize for engagement metrics, such as click-through rates or time spent on page. If the existing content library or user behavior data contains biases, an engagement-maximizing algorithm might inadvertently amplify polarizing or extremist content, simply because it generates more clicks and engagement, thereby creating echo chambers and potentially contributing to radicalization. The algorithm, in this case, is not inherently biased, but its objective function and the parameters it optimizes for can lead to biased outcomes by prioritizing engagement over other values like diversity of thought or factual accuracy.

The choice of model architecture itself can also play a role. Some models, particularly deep learning networks with millions of parameters, can be highly effective at capturing complex patterns in data. However, they can also be prone to "memorizing" spurious correlations present in the training data, which may be proxies for protected attributes. For instance, a model might learn to associate a particular zip code with a certain loan default rate. If that zip code is also disproportionately inhabited by a minority group due to historical housing segregation, the AI may inadvertently penalize individuals from that group, even if their individual financial profiles are strong. The algorithm is not explicitly told to discriminate based on race, but it learns to use a proxy for it, leading to a similar discriminatory outcome.

Furthermore, the very process of **feature engineering** – the selection and transformation of variables used by an AI model – can introduce bias. If developers choose to include features that are highly correlated with protected attributes, even if those attributes are not directly used, the model might learn to discriminate. For instance, in an AI used for credit scoring, using features like "time at current address" or "type of neighborhood" could indirectly capture and reinforce historical biases related to housing discrimination and socioeconomic status.

The human element in the AI lifecycle extends beyond algorithmic design to encompass **human biases in data labeling and interpretation**. AI systems often rely on human annotators to label data, providing the ground truth that the AI learns from. These annotators, being human, bring their own conscious and unconscious biases to the task. For example, if annotators are asked to label images for sentiment, their personal interpretations of an expression or context can vary based on their own cultural background, personal experiences, and implicit associations. In content moderation, human moderators tasked with identifying hate speech or misinformation may interpret the same content differently based on their own biases, leading to inconsistent and potentially unfair outcomes. This is especially problematic in subjective tasks where there is no single "correct" label.

Interpretation of AI outputs can also be a site of bias. Even if an AI system produces outputs that are statistically equitable across different groups, the way humans interpret and act upon these outputs can introduce bias. For instance, a hiring AI might provide a list of candidates ranked by predicted success. If a human recruiter consistently overrules the AI's recommendation for candidates from a particular demographic group, or consistently places more scrutiny on their applications, then human bias, rather than algorithmic bias, becomes the primary driver of unfairness. This highlights the crucial interaction between AI systems and the humans who use them, and the need for training and awareness among users of AI.

These sources of bias – biased data, algorithmic design, and human interpretation – do not operate in isolation. They often interact and amplify each other in a complex feedback loop. For example, historical biases in data can lead to algorithmic choices that further entrench those biases, and human annotators trained on biased data or using biased interpretations can further contaminate the datasets and models. This interconnectedness makes identifying and mitigating bias a challenging but essential task.

The
manifestations of AI bias are as diverse as the AI systems themselves and can have profound real-world consequences. One of the most widely discussed areas is **bias in hiring**. AI tools are increasingly used to screen resumes, conduct initial interviews, and even predict candidate success. If these tools are biased, they can systematically disadvantage certain groups. For instance, an AI that penalizes resumes with gaps in employment history might unfairly impact women who have taken time off for childcare. An AI that learns from past hiring decisions in a male-dominated industry might incorrectly flag female candidates as less

suitable for technical roles. This can perpetuate gender inequality and limit opportunities for qualified individuals.

In the realm of
lending and finance, AI is used for credit scoring, loan approval, and fraud detection. Biased AI systems can lead to discriminatory access to financial services. If an AI unfairly assigns higher risk scores to individuals from certain racial or ethnic groups, it can result in higher interest rates, lower credit limits, or outright denial of loans, hindering their ability to buy homes, start businesses, or manage financial emergencies. This exacerbates economic inequality and limits upward mobility for already marginalized communities. The historical redlining practices, which denied financial services to certain neighborhoods primarily inhabited by minority groups, can be inadvertently replicated by AI systems that use proxy variables like zip codes or even linguistic patterns in loan applications.

The
criminal justice system is another area where AI bias can have severe consequences. Predictive policing algorithms, designed to forecast where and when crimes are likely to occur, can lead to over-policing of certain neighborhoods, often those with higher minority populations, creating a self-fulfilling prophecy. Similarly, risk assessment tools used in sentencing and parole decisions can disproportionately assign higher risk scores to individuals from minority groups, even when controlling for other factors. This can lead to longer sentences and reduced opportunities for parole, perpetuating a cycle of incarceration for already overrepresented groups. The inherent biases in historical crime data, reflecting societal inequities in policing and judicial practices, are directly translated into these AI systems.

In
healthcare, AI is being deployed for diagnostics, treatment recommendations, and drug discovery. Biases in these systems can lead

to disparities in care. For example, an AI trained on medical data that primarily includes men might be less accurate in diagnosing heart conditions in women, who often present with different symptoms. An AI used to predict patient outcomes might underestimate the severity of illness in certain minority groups if the training data does not adequately represent their health profiles or if it is influenced by socioeconomic factors that affect access to care. This can result in delayed diagnoses, inappropriate treatments, and poorer health outcomes for specific populations.

Even in seemingly benign applications like **online content recommendation**, bias can manifest in harmful ways. Algorithms that personalize news feeds or suggest videos can create filter bubbles and echo chambers, reinforcing existing beliefs and limiting exposure to diverse perspectives. If the underlying data or the algorithm's optimization goals are biased, this can lead to the amplification of misinformation, hate speech, or extremist ideologies, particularly for vulnerable individuals who may be more susceptible to such content. The system, designed to keep users engaged, can inadvertently steer them towards more extreme or harmful content if that content happens to be highly engaging.

Natural language processing (NLP) models, which power chatbots, translation services, and sentiment analysis tools, are also susceptible to bias. If trained on text data that reflects societal stereotypes, these models can perpetuate those stereotypes. For instance, a language model might associate certain professions with specific genders (e.g., "doctor" with "he," "nurse" with "she") or exhibit negative sentiment towards particular demographic groups. This can manifest in biased translations, offensive chatbot responses, or inaccurate sentiment analysis that misrepresents the views of marginalized communities.

The insidious nature of AI bias lies in its ability to appear objective and data-driven, masking the underlying human decisions and societal inequities that shaped it. Unlike overt discrimination, which can be challenged directly, algorithmic bias can be more difficult to detect and address because it is embedded within complex technological systems. This makes understanding the sources and manifestations of AI bias not just an ethical imperative, but a practical necessity for building a more just and equitable future. The challenge ahead is to move from awareness to action, developing robust methodologies and ethical frameworks to identify, measure, and mitigate these biases, ensuring that AI serves as a tool for empowerment and progress, not for oppression and discrimination.

The preceding discussion has illuminated the pervasive origins and concerning manifestations of bias within artificial intelligence systems. Having established a foundational understanding of *why* and *how* AI can become biased, our attention now shifts to the crucial practicalities of **bias detection and measurement techniques**. This is where theoretical concerns crystallize into actionable insights, allowing us to move beyond qualitative observations of unfairness to quantifiable evidence of bias. The ability to accurately detect and measure bias is not merely an academic exercise; it is a fundamental prerequisite for building trustworthy and equitable AI. Without robust methods for identification, any attempts at mitigation would be akin to treating symptoms without understanding the disease.

To effectively address bias, we must first be able to recognize its presence and quantify its extent. This involves employing a suite of statistical measures and systematic auditing processes. These techniques enable us to scrutinize both the datasets used to train AI models and the models themselves, looking for disparities in their performance or outcomes across different demographic groups or other relevant subgroups. The goal is to transform our understanding of bias from a general concern into a specific, measurable problem that can be tracked, understood, and ultimately, corrected. This quantitative approach allows us to establish clear benchmarks, understand the magnitude of the bias, and monitor progress as mitigation strategies are implemented.

One of the primary avenues for bias detection involves scrutinizing the training data. Before any model is even built, the data itself can reveal significant predispositions. For instance, examining the distribution of labels or features across different demographic groups is a crucial first step. If a dataset intended for training a medical diagnostic tool shows a disproportionately low number of diagnoses for a particular condition within a specific racial group, this immediately signals a potential issue with data representation. This initial data audit can employ simple descriptive statistics, such as counts, proportions, and averages, broken down by sensitive attributes like race, gender, age, or socioeconomic status. For example, if we are building a system to predict loan default risk, we would want to examine the historical default rates and loan approval rates for different racial and gender groups within the dataset. A statistically significant difference in these rates, even when controlling for relevant financial factors, might indicate historical bias embedded in the data collection or decision-making processes that generated it.

Beyond simple distributions, more sophisticated statistical tests can be employed to detect subtle imbalances. For example, if a dataset for training a facial recognition system has a significantly higher error rate for images of individuals with darker skin tones compared to lighter skin tones, this is a direct indicator of bias. Measuring this would involve segmenting the dataset by skin tone and then calculating performance metrics like accuracy, precision, recall, or false positive/negative rates for each segment. Techniques like chi-squared tests can be used to determine if observed differences in categorical variables (e.g., number of fraudulent transactions flagged per demographic group) are statistically significant or likely due to random chance. Understanding these initial data characteristics is vital, as a model trained on biased data is almost guaranteed to exhibit biased behavior.

Once a model is trained, the focus shifts to evaluating its performance across different subgroups. This is where the concept of **fairness metrics** becomes paramount. Fairness in AI is not a monolithic concept; it encompasses various definitions, and the appropriate metric often depends on the specific application and its societal implications. Different fairness definitions can even be mathematically incompatible, meaning that optimizing for one might inadvertently worsen another. Therefore, selecting and understanding these metrics is a critical part of bias detection.

One common category of fairness metrics focuses on **equality of outcomes**. This approach seeks to ensure that the model's predictions or decisions are distributed similarly across different groups. For example, in a loan approval system, an outcome-based fairness metric might aim for parity in the approval rates between male and female applicants, assuming they have similar creditworthiness profiles. Metrics like **demographic parity** (also known as statistical parity) aim for this, requiring that the probability of a positive outcome (e.g., loan approval) is the same for all groups. Mathematically, this is expressed as $P(\hat{Y} = 1 \mid A = a) = P(\hat{Y} = 1 \mid A = b)$ for any two groups 'a' and 'b', where $\hat{Y}$ is the predicted outcome and A is the sensitive attribute. While intuitive, demographic parity can be problematic if there are genuine differences in underlying base rates between groups that are relevant to the outcome. For instance, if men, on average, have demonstrably different risk profiles for a certain investment than women, enforcing strict demographic parity might lead to suboptimal or unfair decisions.

Another important class of metrics focuses on **equality of opportunity**. These metrics are concerned with ensuring that individuals who are truly similar in terms of their underlying characteristics (i.e., their true potential for a positive outcome) receive similar treatment, regardless of their group affiliation. This is particularly relevant when the outcome is conditional on some unobserved ground truth. For example, in a hiring context, we might care about ensuring that equally qualified candidates from different demographic groups have an equal chance of being hired. Metrics like **equalized odds** aim to achieve this by requiring that the true positive rates (sensitivity) and false positive rates are equal across groups. Mathematically, this means $P(\hat{Y} = 1 \mid Y = 1, A = a) = P(\hat{Y} = 1 \mid Y = 1, A = b)$ and $P(\hat{Y} = 1 \mid Y = 0, A = a) = P(\hat{Y} = 1 \mid Y = 0, A = b)$, where Y is the true outcome. A related metric is **equal opportunity**, which relaxes the requirement for equal false positive rates and only enforces equal true positive rates, focusing on ensuring that those who *should* receive a positive outcome are equally likely to do so. This is often preferred in situations where the cost of a false negative (failing to identify someone who deserves a positive outcome) is higher than the cost of a false positive.

Beyond these outcome-based metrics, we can also assess bias by examining the
performance disparity of the model. This involves calculating standard machine learning performance metrics (accuracy, precision, recall, F1-score, AUC) separately for each subgroup and then comparing them. For instance, if a facial recognition system has an overall accuracy of 99%, but its accuracy for identifying women is only 85%, this is a significant performance disparity that indicates bias. The **difference** or **ratio** between these group-specific metrics can serve as a measure of bias. For example, a large difference in accuracy between the majority and minority groups is a clear sign of a problem.

The
confusion matrix is a fundamental tool for this analysis. By breaking down predictions into true positives, true negatives, false positives, and false negatives for each subgroup, we can derive a rich set of performance indicators and compare them. For example, a higher false positive rate for

a particular group in a recidivism prediction tool could mean that individuals from that group are more likely to be wrongly flagged as high-risk, leading to harsher sentencing or denial of parole. Conversely, a higher false negative rate could mean that individuals from that group are more likely to be wrongly classified as low-risk, potentially leading to insufficient supervision or treatment.

Auditing techniques provide a structured approach to systematically evaluate AI systems for bias. These audits can be conducted internally by development teams or externally by independent third parties. A comprehensive audit typically involves several stages: defining the scope and objectives, identifying sensitive attributes and relevant subgroups, selecting appropriate fairness metrics, collecting or generating test data, performing the analysis, and reporting the findings.

One powerful auditing technique is **counterfactual fairness testing**. This involves making minimal changes to an input instance (specifically, altering only the sensitive attribute) and observing whether the model's output changes. For example, if we have an application for a mortgage and the system approves it when the applicant is listed as 'male' but denies it when the applicant is listed as 'female' (all other details being identical), this demonstrates bias. This method helps to isolate the impact of the sensitive attribute on the model's decision. However, it is important to note that counterfactual fairness can be complex to implement and interpret, especially in models that learn intricate, non-linear relationships where multiple features might be correlated with the sensitive attribute.

Another crucial aspect of bias detection is understanding **model interpretability**. While not a direct measurement metric, interpretability methods can help *explainwhy* a model is making biased decisions. Techniques like SHAP (SHapley Additive exPlanations) or LIME (Local Interpretable Model-agnostic Explanations) can reveal which features are most influential in a model's prediction for a specific instance or for the model overall. If interpretability analyses consistently show that a model is relying heavily on features that are proxies for sensitive attributes (e.g., zip code as a proxy for race, or certain linguistic patterns that correlate with gender), this can pinpoint the source of bias. For example, if a model predicts a higher likelihood of loan default and SHAP values indicate that "neighborhood" is a highly influential feature, and that neighborhood feature is strongly correlated with a particular racial group due to historical segregation, it reveals a bias pathway.

The development of specialized **bias detection tools and libraries** has greatly facilitated this process. Open-source projects like AI Fairness 360 (from IBM), Fairlearn (from Microsoft), and What-If Tool (from Google) offer implementations of various fairness metrics, bias detection algorithms, and visualization capabilities. These tools allow developers and auditors to easily test their models against multiple fairness criteria and to explore the impact of different mitigation strategies. They provide a common language and a set of reproducible methods for engaging with AI fairness.

The process of bias detection is not a one-time event but an ongoing one. AI systems operate in dynamic environments, and their performance can drift over time. Therefore, continuous monitoring and re-evaluation are essential. This involves setting up systems to regularly re-run bias detection metrics on new data or on models that have been retrained or updated. For example, a recommendation system that was deemed fair at launch might become biased over time as user engagement patterns evolve and the system learns new, potentially biased, associations. Regular audits and monitoring help to catch these issues before they cause significant harm.

Furthermore, the selection of sensitive attributes to monitor is critical. While common attributes like race, gender, and age are often prioritized, it is important to consider intersectionality—how multiple sensitive attributes can combine to create unique forms of disadvantage. For instance, the experience of a Black woman may differ significantly from that of a white woman or a Black man. Bias detection techniques should ideally be able to account for intersectional groups to provide a more nuanced understanding of fairness.

Finally, it is crucial to acknowledge that quantitative measures alone do not tell the whole story. They provide the evidence and the benchmarks, but the interpretation of these metrics and the determination of what constitutes "fair enough" often require human judgment, ethical reasoning, and stakeholder consultation. The goal of bias detection and measurement is not to achieve perfect mathematical equality across all conceivable metrics—which may be impossible—but to identify and quantify unfair disparities so that they can be understood, debated, and mitigated to the greatest extent possible, aligning technological performance with societal values of justice and equity. By embracing these diverse techniques, we equip ourselves with the necessary tools to shine a light on the often-hidden biases within AI, paving the way for more responsible and equitable AI development and deployment.

Having established the critical importance of identifying and quantifying bias within AI systems, our focus now necessarily pivots to the practical and indispensable task of **strategies for bias mitigation**. It is one thing to detect the presence of unfairness, to measure its scope and its impact across different demographic groups, but it is an entirely different, yet equally vital, challenge to actively correct it. This phase represents the tangible application of our understanding, moving from diagnosis to treatment. The goal is not merely to point out where AI systems fall short of equitable ideals, but to implement robust, systematic, and effective interventions that steer these powerful technologies towards fairness. This is where the theoretical underpinnings of AI ethics and the practical engineering of safe AI converge, demanding thoughtful consideration of techniques that can be applied throughout the entire lifecycle of an AI system, from the initial stages of data collection and preparation to the final deployment and ongoing monitoring.

The journey of mitigating bias is inherently multifaceted, and the most effective approaches often involve a combination of strategies tailored to the specific context of the AI system. Broadly, these strategies can be categorized based on when they are applied within the AI development pipeline: pre-processing, in-processing, and post-processing. Each of these stages offers unique opportunities and challenges for intervention.

Pre-processing Strategies: Reimagining the Foundations

The pre-processing stage deals with the data *before* it is used to train an AI model. Given that much of the bias in AI systems originates from biased data, intervening at this earliest point can be incredibly impactful. The principle here is to "cleanse" or "rectify" the data so that the model learns from a more equitable representation of reality.

One of the most direct pre-processing techniques is **data re-sampling**. If a dataset is found to be imbalanced in terms of representation of certain groups, re-sampling can help to correct this. There are two primary forms of re-sampling: **undersampling** and **oversampling**.

Undersampling involves randomly removing instances from the majority group(s) until the class distribution is more balanced. For example, if a dataset for credit scoring has 90% approvals and 10% rejections, and analysis shows that rejections are disproportionately concentrated among a particular demographic, undersampling could involve removing a portion of the approved loans from the majority group to create a more balanced ratio of approvals to rejections for all groups. While effective in balancing class representation, undersampling has a significant drawback: it discards potentially valuable data from the majority group, which might lead to a loss of information and a reduction in overall model performance if not done carefully.

Oversampling, conversely, involves increasing the representation of the minority group(s). This can be achieved by duplicating existing instances from the minority class or, more sophisticatedly, by generating synthetic data points. A well-known technique for synthetic oversampling is the **Synthetic Minority Over-sampling Technique (SMOTE)**. SMOTE works by selecting a minority class instance and then finding its nearest neighbors within the minority class. It then creates a new synthetic instance along the line segment connecting the original instance and its chosen neighbor. This approach helps to create a more diverse set of minority class examples, rather than just simple duplicates, which can lead to better generalization by the model. For example, in a medical diagnosis system where rare diseases are underrepresented in the dataset, SMOTE could generate synthetic patient records exhibiting these rare conditions, thereby improving the model's ability to detect them. However, oversampling, particularly with simple duplication, can also lead to overfitting, where the model becomes too specialized to the repeated or synthetic examples and performs poorly on unseen data. SMOTE, by generating new instances, aims to mitigate this risk, but careful validation is still crucial.

Beyond simple re-sampling,
data augmentation is another powerful pre-processing strategy, especially for tasks involving unstructured data like images, text, or audio. Data augmentation artificially increases the size and diversity of the training dataset by creating modified copies of existing data. For instance, in image recognition, data augmentation might involve applying

transformations such as rotations, flips, zooms, or changes in brightness and contrast to existing images. If a facial recognition dataset has fewer images of women in different lighting conditions, augmentation can create artificial variations of existing images of women to better represent these scenarios. Similarly, for text data, techniques like synonym replacement, random insertion or deletion of words, or back-translation (translating a sentence to another language and then back) can increase linguistic diversity. The key benefit of data augmentation is that it can help to make models more robust to variations in input data and can improve performance, particularly when the original dataset is small or lacks diversity. When used with fairness in mind, augmentation can be specifically applied to underrepresented groups to artificially bolster their presence and variety in the training set.

Another pre-processing approach involves **feature engineering and selection**. This entails carefully examining the features used to train the model. If certain features are found to be highly correlated with sensitive attributes and are also strong predictors of the outcome, they might be removed or transformed. For example, a zip code might be a proxy for race due to historical residential segregation. If a model uses zip code to predict loan default risk, and this leads to disparate outcomes for different racial groups, engineers might consider removing the zip code feature or engineering it in a way that reduces its racial correlation, perhaps by grouping zip codes into broader, less racially homogenous economic regions. This process requires a deep understanding of the data and its potential for encoding societal biases.

In-processing Strategies: Building Fairness into the Model

In-processing strategies aim to modify the learning algorithm itself to incorporate fairness constraints during the model training phase. The idea is to guide the model's learning process so that it simultaneously optimizes for predictive accuracy *and* fairness.

One prominent family of in-processing techniques involves **fairness-aware algorithms**. These algorithms are designed with fairness metrics embedded into their objective functions. For example, a classification algorithm could be modified to include a regularization term that penalizes the model for exhibiting disparities in outcomes across different groups. This regularization term would be directly related to a chosen fairness metric, such as demographic parity or equalized odds. By adding this penalty, the optimization process is nudged towards solutions that are not only accurate but also fair. For instance, if the goal is to achieve demographic parity in loan approvals, the regularization term would penalize the model if the approval rates for different racial groups deviate significantly from each other.

Another in-processing strategy is **adversarial debiasing**. This technique involves training two models simultaneously: a predictor model that tries to predict the desired outcome (e.g., loan approval), and an adversary model that tries to predict the sensitive attribute (e.g., race) from the predictor's output. The predictor model is trained to minimize its prediction error while simultaneously trying to "fool" the adversary. If the adversary cannot accurately predict the sensitive attribute from the predictor's output, it implies that the predictor's decisions are independent of that sensitive attribute, thus achieving a form of fairness. The adversary model is trained to maximize its prediction error, thereby pushing the predictor to learn representations that are less indicative of sensitive attributes. This approach can be very effective but is also computationally intensive and can be challenging to tune.

Constraint-based optimization is another in-processing method. Here, fairness constraints are explicitly stated as mathematical inequalities or equalities that must be satisfied by the model's predictions. The training process then becomes an optimization problem subject to these fairness constraints. For example, one might specify that the difference in false positive rates between two groups must not exceed a certain threshold. The optimization algorithm then seeks the best possible model that adheres to this constraint. This approach offers a high degree of control over specific fairness criteria but requires expertise in optimization techniques and a clear definition of the desired constraints.

The choice of which fairness metric to optimize for in-processing is crucial and depends heavily on the application context. For instance, in a hiring context, where the goal is to ensure equally qualified candidates have an equal chance of being selected, metrics like equal opportunity or equalized odds might be more appropriate than demographic parity. If the true positive rate (i.e., the rate at which qualified candidates are selected) is unequal across groups, it indicates a failure to provide equal opportunities, even if the overall selection rates are balanced.

It is important to note that in-processing methods, while powerful, can sometimes lead to a
fairness-accuracy trade-off. By enforcing fairness constraints, the model might sacrifice some degree of predictive accuracy. The challenge lies in finding an optimal balance that respects both performance and equity. This trade-off is not always inherent; in some cases, debiasing can even improve overall accuracy by forcing the model to learn more robust and generalizable patterns. However, it is a critical consideration during development and requires careful evaluation.

Post-processing Strategies: Refining the Output

Post-processing techniques involve adjusting the model's predictions *after* they have been generated, without retraining the model or modifying the underlying algorithm. These methods are often simpler to implement as they do not require access to the training data or the original model architecture.

One common post-processing technique is
threshold calibration. For binary classification problems, models typically output a probability score, and a threshold is used to convert this score into a class prediction (e.g., if the probability is above 0.5, classify as positive). Different thresholds can be applied to different subgroups to achieve fairness. For instance, if a model has a higher false positive rate for group A than for group B, one could set a higher threshold for group A and a lower threshold for group B. This would mean that individuals in group A would need a higher probability score to be classified as positive, thereby reducing the false positive rate for that group and bringing it closer to the rate for group B.

The
Equalized Odds Post-processing (EOP) algorithm is a well-known method for threshold calibration. It aims to equalize both true positive rates and false positive rates across groups by adjusting the decision thresholds. Suppose a model outputs a score s. EOP finds thresholds $\tau{a,TP}, \tau{a,FP}, \tau{b,TP}, \tau{b,FP}$ for groups a and b such that $P(\hat{Y}=1|Y=1, A=a) = P(\hat{Y}=1|Y=1, A=b)$ and $P(\hat{Y}=1|Y=0, A=a) = P(\hat{Y}=1|Y=0, A=b)$, where $\hat{Y}$ is the predicted label and Y is the true label. This is achieved by partitioning the score space based on the true label and applying group-specific thresholds.

Another post-processing technique is

rejection option classification. This approach allows the model to abstain from making a prediction when it is uncertain or when making a prediction might lead to unfair outcomes. For example, if a loan application score falls within a range where the model is known to be less accurate for a particular demographic, the system might be programmed to refer such applications for human review rather than making an automated decision. This strategy can be particularly useful when the cost of an unfair decision is very high.

Predictive parity adjustment is another method that focuses on ensuring that the predicted outcome is reflective of the true outcome probability for all groups. This means that for individuals classified as positive, the probability that they are truly positive should be the same across all groups. This is often achieved by adjusting the predicted probabilities themselves, rather than just the decision thresholds.

A crucial consideration for post-processing methods is that they typically require access to the ground truth labels for the training or validation data to determine the optimal adjustments. They also operate under the assumption that the underlying bias stems primarily from how the model's scores translate into decisions, rather than from fundamental flaws in the model's learned representations. If the model has learned deeply flawed representations, post-processing might only offer a superficial fix.

Practical Implications and Trade-offs

Each of these mitigation strategies—pre-processing, in-processing, and post-processing—comes with its own set of practical implications and potential trade-offs.

Pre-processing strategies, such as re-sampling and data augmentation, are powerful because they address bias at its source: the data. However, they can be data-intensive, require careful handling to avoid introducing new biases or degrading performance, and may not be feasible if access to raw data is restricted. Undersampling can lead to loss of valuable information, while oversampling, especially simple duplication, can lead to overfitting. SMOTE and its variants aim to improve generalization but require careful tuning. Data augmentation, while useful, needs to be applied thoughtfully to ensure the generated data is realistic and relevant.

In-processing strategies offer the advantage of building fairness directly into the model's learning process. Fairness-aware algorithms and adversarial debiasing can achieve strong fairness guarantees by optimizing for both accuracy and equity simultaneously. However, these methods can be computationally expensive, require significant expertise to implement and tune, and may involve a discernible trade-off between fairness and predictive accuracy. The choice of fairness metric to optimize for is critical and can have profound implications for the model's behavior. Furthermore, these methods often require access to the model architecture and the training pipeline, making them less suitable for black-box systems.

Post-processing strategies are often the easiest to implement, as they can be applied to pre-trained models without the need for retraining or access to the training data. Threshold calibration and rejection option classification can effectively mitigate certain types of bias, especially when the primary issue is the interpretation of model scores. However, these methods operate on the model's output and may not address deeper, systemic biases learned by the model. They also typically require access to validation data with ground truth labels to calibrate the adjustments. Moreover, post-processing might mask the underlying bias rather than fundamentally correcting it, and it can be challenging to ensure that fairness is maintained across a wide range of scenarios and contexts.

The selection of the most appropriate mitigation strategy, or combination of strategies, is highly context-dependent. It requires a thorough understanding of:

1. **The specific application and its potential harms**: What are the consequences of biased decisions in this particular domain? For example, bias in a criminal justice system has far more severe implications than bias in a movie recommendation system.
2. **The nature of the bias**: Where does the bias originate? Is it predominantly in the data, or in the model's architecture and learning process?
3. **The available data and resources**: Do we have access to raw data for pre-processing? Is there computational power for in-processing methods?
4. **The definition of fairness being prioritized**: Which fairness metric or metrics are most relevant and important for this application? As we've seen, different metrics can lead to different optimal solutions.
5. **The acceptable trade-offs**: What level of accuracy is acceptable in exchange for increased fairness? Who decides this, and based on what criteria?

Often, a hybrid approach combining techniques from different stages of the AI lifecycle yields the best results. For instance, one might start with data cleaning and augmentation (pre-processing), then employ a fairness-aware algorithm during training (in-processing), and finally fine-tune the decision thresholds for specific subgroups (post-processing).

Moreover, the process of bias mitigation is not a static, one-time event. It is an iterative and ongoing endeavor. As AI systems are deployed and interact with the real world, new data is generated, user behaviors evolve, and societal contexts shift. This means that biases can re-emerge or new ones can develop. Therefore, continuous monitoring, re-evaluation, and adaptation of mitigation strategies are essential. Regular audits, feedback loops from users and stakeholders, and mechanisms for flagging and addressing emergent biases are crucial components of a robust AI fairness lifecycle.

In conclusion, while detecting and measuring bias are foundational steps, the true challenge lies in effectively mitigating it. The strategies available—spanning pre-processing, in-processing, and post-processing—offer a diverse toolkit for developers and policymakers. Each approach presents its own strengths, weaknesses, and trade-offs, demanding careful consideration of the specific context, ethical objectives, and technical constraints. The ultimate goal is to move beyond merely acknowledging bias to actively and systematically reducing its presence, striving for AI systems that are not only intelligent but also equitable and just. This requires a commitment to responsible innovation, continuous learning, and a deep understanding of the complex interplay between technology, data, and society.

Ensuring that AI systems remain fair and unbiased throughout their operational life is not a one-time fix but a continuous process. Having explored various strategies for mitigating bias, from data manipulation to algorithm modification and output adjustment, we now turn our attention to the critical mechanisms that ensure these efforts are sustained and effective over time. This requires establishing robust processes for **fairness audits and continuous monitoring**. Just as organizations conduct regular security audits to protect against evolving threats and vulnerabilities, they must implement analogous procedures to safeguard against the insidious creep of bias into their AI systems.

The landscape of AI deployment is dynamic. Models that were deemed fair at the time of their initial training and deployment can, and often do, drift into unfairness as they encounter new data distributions, user behaviors, or evolving societal norms. This drift can be subtle, manifesting as a gradual increase in disparate impact on certain demographic groups, or it can be more pronounced, triggered by unforeseen edge cases or changes in the operational environment. Therefore, proactive and systematic auditing is paramount. These audits are not merely technical checks; they are integral to responsible AI governance, providing a structured approach to identifying, quantifying, and rectifying emergent unfairness.

The foundation of effective continuous monitoring lies in the meticulous **documentation of fairness assessments**. Every audit, every test, and every intervention should be thoroughly recorded. This documentation should detail the methodology employed, the specific fairness metrics used, the datasets tested, the results obtained, and any mitigation steps taken. For instance, when auditing a recidivism prediction tool, documentation would include the specific definition of fairness prioritized (e.g., equal false positive rates across racial groups), the dataset used for evaluation (e.g., a hold-out set representative of current operational conditions), the statistical tests performed, and the observed disparities, if any. This detailed record-keeping serves multiple purposes: it provides a historical account of the system's fairness performance, enables comparison of results over time, aids in troubleshooting, and forms the basis for accountability and transparency. Without comprehensive documentation, it becomes exceedingly difficult to track progress, understand the root causes of any detected bias, or demonstrate due diligence to regulators and stakeholders. This archival function is crucial for demonstrating a commitment to ongoing fairness and for learning from past interventions.

Establishing clear **governance processes for addressing identified issues** is the next essential step. When a fairness audit reveals problematic biases, a defined workflow must be in place to manage the response. This governance structure should outline who is responsible for reviewing audit findings, who makes decisions about mitigation strategies, and who oversees their implementation. For example, a cross-functional AI ethics committee, comprising members from engineering, legal, compliance, and business units, might be tasked with reviewing audit reports. This committee would then convene experts to diagnose the root cause of the bias—whether it stems from data drift, changes in feature importance, or unforeseen model interactions—and recommend appropriate interventions. The decision-making process should be transparent and auditable, ensuring that biases are addressed systematically and not overlooked. This might involve a tiered approach: minor deviations might be handled by the engineering team, while significant biases with potential for large-scale harm could trigger a more comprehensive review and remediation process involving senior leadership and potentially external consultants. The governance framework should also specify timelines for remediation and require re-auditing to confirm the effectiveness of implemented solutions.

A crucial element of these governance processes is the establishment of **feedback loops**. AI systems do not operate in a vacuum; they are deployed in complex, real-world environments that are constantly evolving. User feedback, operational metrics, and external societal shifts can all provide invaluable signals about the system's fairness performance. Implementing mechanisms to capture and act on this feedback is vital for adapting mitigation strategies. For a customer service chatbot, for instance, feedback loops could include analyzing user complaints about the bot's responses to specific demographic queries, monitoring sentiment analysis of user interactions, or conducting periodic user surveys on perceived fairness. If users from a particular background report consistently unhelpful or biased responses, this direct feedback should trigger an investigation and potential retraining or adjustment of the chatbot's parameters. Similarly, in a financial lending context, if the system's default prediction rates for a newly emerging economic segment begin to diverge significantly from initial expectations, this necessitates a review and potential recalibration of the model. These feedback channels ensure that the system remains aligned with its fairness objectives, even as its operational context changes.

Moreover,
continuous monitoring extends beyond periodic audits to encompass real-time or near-real-time tracking of key fairness indicators. This involves deploying monitoring tools that continuously assess model performance against defined fairness metrics in live production environments. For example, a system used for content moderation might continuously track the rate at which content from different linguistic communities is flagged for review. If this rate begins to disproportionately increase for one community without a corresponding increase in policy violations, it signals an emergent bias. Such real-time monitoring allows for immediate detection and potential intervention before a bias can cause significant harm. This might involve triggering an alert to the operations team, temporarily rolling back the model to a previous stable version, or initiating an automated retraining process with updated data.

The technical implementation of continuous monitoring can involve several components.
Data drift detection algorithms can identify shifts in the distribution of input data compared to the training data, which is a common precursor to bias. **Model performance monitoring** tools can track accuracy, precision, recall, and other performance metrics across different demographic subgroups. **Fairness dashboards** can provide a

consolidated view of various fairness metrics, allowing stakeholders to quickly assess the system's equity status. These dashboards should be designed for clarity, enabling non-technical users to understand the system's fairness posture and the potential implications of any observed deviations. The choice of which metrics to monitor should be guided by the established fairness objectives and the potential harms associated with bias in the specific application domain.

Adapting mitigation strategies as the system evolves or operates in new environments is a cornerstone of this continuous process. This adaptation might involve several actions. First, it could mean **revisiting and refining the initial mitigation techniques**. If a particular pre-processing technique, like oversampling, proves insufficient to counter emergent biases in production, engineers might explore more advanced in-processing methods or more sophisticated data augmentation strategies. Second, it might necessitate **adjusting the fairness thresholds or constraints**. As the context shifts or new demographic groups become relevant, the acceptable levels of disparity might need to be recalibrated, always with a focus on minimizing harm. For example, if a facial recognition system is deployed in a new geographical region where facial features differ significantly from the training data, its performance might degrade for certain local populations, requiring adjustments to its decision thresholds or even retraining on more representative data. Third, it could involve **retraining or re-evaluating the model entirely**. In cases where bias is deeply entrenched or significant shifts occur, a full retraining of the model with updated data and potentially a revised architecture might be the most effective course of action. This retraining should be followed by a rigorous re-auditing process to confirm that the new model meets fairness standards.

Furthermore, the concept of **"drift in fairness"** itself needs to be understood and monitored. Fairness metrics can drift independently of predictive accuracy. A model might maintain its overall accuracy but become significantly less fair to a particular group over time due to subtle changes in data distribution or user interaction patterns. For example, a loan application model might continue to approve loans at a high overall rate, but if the proportion of loans approved for a historically underserved community declines, this represents a drift in fairness that requires attention. Continuous monitoring systems should be specifically designed to detect such divergences in fairness metrics.

The process of auditing and monitoring also necessitates a robust approach to
change management. When mitigation strategies are updated or new ones are introduced, these changes must be carefully managed to avoid unintended consequences. This involves rigorous testing of any modified model or system component in a staging environment before deploying it to production. The impact of the changes on both fairness and overall performance should be thoroughly assessed. This cautious approach helps to prevent the introduction of new biases or the degradation of existing fairness guarantees during the remediation process.

Crucially, the responsibility for fairness audits and continuous monitoring cannot be solely confined to the technical teams. It requires a broader organizational commitment.
Establishing clear lines of accountability across different departments—from product development and data science to legal and compliance—is essential. This ensures that fairness is treated as a shared responsibility, rather than an afterthought or the burden of a single team. Regular reporting to senior leadership on the fairness status of AI systems, along with transparent communication about any challenges and remediation efforts, fosters a culture of accountability. This organizational buy-in is critical for allocating the necessary resources—both human and financial—to sustain these ongoing efforts. Without it, even the most sophisticated monitoring systems are likely to fall into disrepair or be deprioritized.

Finally, the evolution of AI systems means that the very definition of fairness and the metrics used to assess it may also need to be revisited. As our understanding of AI's societal impact deepens and ethical discourse progresses, what is considered "fair" today may be viewed differently tomorrow. Therefore, a commitment to continuous learning and adaptation extends to the frameworks and definitions of fairness themselves. This implies regular reviews of the chosen fairness metrics and goals in light of evolving ethical standards, societal expectations, and regulatory guidance. It's an iterative journey of refinement, ensuring that AI systems not only perform their intended functions but do so in a manner that upholds human values and promotes equity, not just at deployment, but for the entire duration of their operational life.

Chapter 5: Developing AI Safety Cases

The rigorous pursuit of safety in complex technological systems has long necessitated a structured and evidence-based approach. As artificial intelligence moves from the realm of theoretical research into critical applications—infrastructure, healthcare, autonomous transportation, and more—the demand for equivalent, if not more robust, assurances of safety becomes paramount. This is where the concept of a **safety case** emerges as a foundational element in demonstrating and maintaining the acceptable safety of AI systems. At its core, a safety case is not simply a collection of documents or a checklist; it is a reasoned argument, meticulously constructed and rigorously supported by evidence, asserting that a system is acceptably safe for its intended use under specified operating conditions. This argument is directed towards a diverse set of stakeholders, including developers, operators, regulators, and the public, all of whom have a vested interest in the system's safe operation.

The primary purpose of a safety case is to provide **assurance**. For developers and operators, it serves as an internal validation tool, forcing a deep examination of potential hazards and the effectiveness of implemented safety measures. For regulators, it is an indispensable artifact for oversight, enabling them to assess whether a system meets established safety standards and legal requirements before deployment, and to monitor its ongoing safety. For end-users and the broader public, the safety case, or summaries derived from it, can foster trust by demonstrating that significant effort has been invested in understanding and mitigating risks. It transforms the abstract notion of "safety" into a concrete, demonstrable achievement, grounded in evidence and logical reasoning. Without such a structured argument, claims of AI safety remain unsubstantiated and open to doubt, particularly in domains where failures can have catastrophic consequences.

To understand the weight and structure of an AI safety case, it is beneficial to draw upon the legacy of safety cases in other high-risk industries. For decades, sectors such as aviation, nuclear power, and offshore oil and gas have relied on comprehensive safety case methodologies. These industries, operating at the frontiers of technological possibility and facing inherent, significant dangers, developed sophisticated frameworks for managing risk. Early approaches to safety often involved simply reacting to incidents and implementing fixes. However, the increasing complexity of these systems and the scale of potential failures necessitated a more proactive and systematic approach. This led to the formalization of safety cases as a requirement for obtaining operating licenses and maintaining public trust.

In the nuclear industry, for instance, the development of a safety case for a new power plant is an exhaustive undertaking. It involves identifying all credible hazards, analyzing the probability and severity of potential accidents, and detailing the engineered safety features, operational procedures, and emergency plans designed to prevent or mitigate these events. The case must demonstrate that the risks to workers, the public, and the environment are As Low As Reasonably Practicable (ALARP). Similarly, in aviation, the safety case for a new aircraft design involves extensive analysis of structural integrity, flight control systems, engine reliability, and human factors, supported by vast amounts of testing and simulation data. The principle is consistent: present a compelling, evidence-based argument that the system's residual risks are acceptable.

The evolution of these safety case methodologies has been driven by a continuous learning process, often spurred by significant accidents. Events like the Challenger space shuttle disaster, the Chernobyl nuclear accident, and major railway or aviation incidents have provided harsh lessons, emphasizing the need for comprehensive hazard identification, robust risk assessment, and stringent verification and validation processes. They highlighted the dangers of complacency, the importance of considering human factors, and the necessity of ensuring that safety arguments are not just technically sound but also clearly communicated and understood by all relevant parties. These historical precedents underscore why a similar structured approach is not merely advisable but essential for AI systems deployed in safety-critical contexts. The potential for emergent behaviors, the opacity of certain AI models (the "black box" problem), and the rapid pace of AI development introduce unique challenges that a well-structured safety case must address.

A modern AI safety case, therefore, builds upon this rich history while adapting to the specific characteristics of AI. It must not only cover the traditional engineering aspects of a system but also grapple with the unique challenges posed by learning, adaptation, and the potential for unpredictable behavior in AI. The argument for safety needs to encompass the entire lifecycle of the AI system, from data acquisition and model training to deployment, operation, and eventual decommissioning. The evidence supporting the safety argument will draw from diverse sources, including formal verification, rigorous testing (both simulated and real-world), expert judgment, and operational monitoring data. The goal is to create a holistic and convincing demonstration that the AI system can perform its intended function reliably and safely, minimizing the risk of harm to individuals and society. The credibility and effectiveness of the safety case hinge on its completeness, its transparency, and the robustness of the evidence it presents. It is a living document, intended to evolve as the system itself, its operating environment, or our understanding of AI risks changes.

The transition from established safety engineering practices to the nascent field of AI safety necessitates a critical re-evaluation and adaptation of the safety case paradigm. Traditional safety cases, born from the structured, predictable worlds of mechanical and electrical engineering, often rely on deterministic models and exhaustive analysis of known failure modes. AI systems, however, operate within a fundamentally different landscape, characterized by probabilistic reasoning, emergent behaviors, and continuous learning. Consequently, framing a compelling safety argument for an AI system demands a nuanced approach that acknowledges and addresses these unique characteristics head-on. This involves moving beyond simply documenting existing safety measures to actively constructing a reasoned argument that accounts for the inherent uncertainties and adaptive nature of AI. The core challenge lies in translating the abstract assurance of "safety" into a concrete, evidence-backed assertion that is relevant and comprehensible to all stakeholders, despite the complex and often opaque internal workings of AI models.

One of the most significant divergences from traditional safety cases arises from the learned and probabilistic nature of AI. Unlike a mechanical component that fails in predictable ways based on material fatigue or stress, an AI model's "failure" might manifest as a statistically improbable or unexpected output, a deviation from desired behavior under novel circumstances, or a degradation in performance over time due to data drift. The safety argument must therefore shift from demonstrating the absence of specific, known failure modes to articulating a high degree of confidence in the system's ability to perform within acceptable bounds across a vast, often unspecifiable, range of operating conditions. This requires a probabilistic framing of risk, where safety is understood not as an absolute state but as a quantifiable likelihood of undesirable outcomes falling below a defined threshold. The safety case must therefore clearly define what constitutes an "undesirable outcome" for the specific AI application and establish the acceptable probability for such events occurring. This definition will be highly context-dependent, with much lower tolerance for error in a medical diagnosis AI compared to a recommendation engine. The argument needs to demonstrate, with sufficient evidence, that these acceptable probability thresholds are met and will continue to be met throughout the system's operational life.

The integration of evidence from diverse sources is paramount in constructing a robust AI safety case. Traditional safety cases often rely heavily on formal verification, design reviews, and exhaustive physical testing of components. For AI, this spectrum of evidence must be broadened considerably. This includes, but is not limited to:

Model Testing and Validation: This forms a cornerstone of AI safety evidence. It goes beyond simple accuracy metrics to encompass a comprehensive evaluation of the model's performance under a wide array of scenarios, including those that are expected to be rare or challenging. Techniques such as adversarial testing, where inputs are deliberately crafted to provoke erroneous outputs, are crucial for uncovering vulnerabilities that might not be apparent in standard validation datasets. Testing must also assess the model's performance across different demographic groups to identify potential biases that could lead to discriminatory or unsafe outcomes. The safety case must detail the methodologies used for testing, the coverage achieved, and the statistical significance of the results. It should also explicitly state any limitations of the testing protocols and the resulting inferences. For instance, an autonomous vehicle's perception system might perform exceptionally well in clear weather and daylight but its safety case would need to demonstrate how its performance in fog, heavy rain, or at night has been rigorously tested and deemed acceptable. The evidence here could include extensive simulations of various weather conditions, real-world testing in controlled environments, and documented safety metrics demonstrating performance degradation within acceptable limits.

Robustness Analysis: This specifically addresses the AI system's resilience to perturbations in its input data or environment. For example, how does a medical imaging AI perform if the image quality is slightly degraded due to a scanner malfunction? How does a natural language processing (NLP) system used for customer service handle misspellings or grammatical errors? Robustness analysis seeks to quantify and demonstrate the system's ability to maintain its safety-critical functions even when faced with imperfect or unexpected inputs. Evidence here might include quantifiable measures of performance degradation under varying degrees of input noise, sensitivity analysis to identify critical input features, and documented procedures for detecting and responding to significant input anomalies. The safety case would need to explain the acceptable thresholds for performance degradation and how these are monitored in operation. A self-driving car's LiDAR system, for example, might be subject to environmental factors like dust or heavy rain; its safety case would need to provide evidence on how it maintains reliable object detection under such conditions, perhaps through sensor fusion with other modalities like cameras or radar, and how the system would gracefully degrade or initiate a safe stop if sensor reliability drops below a critical threshold.

Explainability and Interpretability (XAI): While not always directly a measure of safety, the ability to understand why an AI system makes a particular decision is crucial for debugging, auditing, and building trust. For safety-critical systems, opaque "black box" models present a significant challenge. The safety case should articulate the level of explainability achieved and how it contributes to safety assurance. This might involve using inherently interpretable models where possible, or employing XAI techniques to provide insights into the decision-making process of more complex models. Evidence could include the results of human studies evaluating the clarity and usefulness of explanations, documentation of the XAI methods employed, and a reasoned argument for why the level of interpretability is sufficient for the intended safety assurance. For instance, a loan application AI flagged for denial might need to provide an explanation for the denial that is understandable to the applicant and regulators, demonstrating that the decision was based on objective, non-discriminatory criteria rather than arbitrary or biased factors.

Formal Verification and Assurance Techniques: Where applicable, formal methods can provide mathematical guarantees about certain properties of the AI system, particularly for algorithmic components or decision logic. This can be invaluable for proving that the system adheres to specific safety constraints under defined conditions. The safety case would present the formal models, the verification proofs, and a clear argument about the scope and limitations of these guarantees. For example, certain control logic within an autonomous system might be formally verified to ensure it never commands a state that would lead to an immediate, unrecoverable failure. The evidence would comprise the formal specification, the verification tools and processes used, and the resulting proofs of correctness for those specific properties.

Operational Monitoring and Feedback Loops: AI systems operate in dynamic environments, and their performance can change over time due to evolving data distributions (data drift) or changes in the operational context. A crucial aspect of the AI safety case is demonstrating that mechanisms are in place to monitor the system's performance in real-time, detect deviations from expected behavior, and trigger appropriate responses, which could include retraining, human intervention, or system shutdown. The safety case needs to detail these monitoring strategies, the metrics used, the thresholds for triggering alerts or interventions, and the procedures for handling such events. Evidence here includes the design of the monitoring infrastructure, simulation or test results of anomaly detection capabilities, and documented incident response protocols. The safety case for a predictive maintenance AI in a factory, for instance, would need to detail how it continuously monitors sensor data, how it flags anomalies that might indicate an impending equipment failure, and what automated actions or human alerts are triggered to prevent such a failure.

Data Governance and Quality Assurance: The performance and safety of AI systems are fundamentally dependent on the data used for training and operation. The safety case must provide strong evidence of robust data governance practices, including clear data provenance, rigorous data quality checks, mechanisms for identifying and mitigating bias in datasets, and secure data handling procedures. This evidence could include data dictionaries, audit logs of data processing, documented procedures for data validation and cleaning, and reports on bias detection and mitigation strategies. For an AI used in criminal justice, for example, the provenance and quality of the data used to train its risk assessment models would be a critical component of its safety case, demonstrating that it doesn't perpetuate historical biases present in policing or judicial data.

The construction of a cohesive and convincing safety argument from this diverse array of evidence requires a structured approach that links each piece of evidence back to the overarching safety claims. This is where the argumentative structure of the safety case becomes critical. It's not enough to present a repository of test results and monitoring data; these must be woven into a logical narrative that demonstrates, for each identified hazard or risk, how the evidence collectively shows that the risk is acceptably managed. This typically involves a hierarchical structure, starting with high-level safety goals and progressively decomposing them into more specific requirements and safety properties, with each property supported by specific evidence.

For instance, a safety goal might be "prevent unintended acceleration in an autonomous vehicle." This could be decomposed into requirements such as "maintain accurate speed estimation," "ensure reliable braking actuation," and "prevent erroneous throttle commands." The evidence for "maintain accurate speed estimation" might include a combination of sensor validation reports, real-world testing data showing minimal deviation across various speeds and conditions, and robustness analysis demonstrating resilience to minor sensor noise. The safety case must explicitly draw these connections, arguing that the evidence presented for speed estimation directly contributes to the overall safety goal of preventing unintended acceleration.

Furthermore, the safety case must explicitly address the limitations of the evidence presented and the assumptions made. No AI system, particularly a complex one, can be proven "perfectly" safe. The safety case should therefore articulate the residual risks and provide a compelling argument for why these are acceptable given the context of use, the benefits provided by the system, and the established risk tolerance levels for that domain. This transparency about limitations is crucial for building credibility with regulators and other stakeholders. It acknowledges the inherent uncertainties in AI and demonstrates a mature understanding of the system's capabilities and boundaries. For example, a weather forecasting AI might have excellent accuracy for short-term predictions but its safety case for critical infrastructure management would need to clearly state its limitations in predicting extreme, low-probability weather events and detail contingency plans for when the AI's confidence in its forecast falls below a certain threshold.

The adaptive nature of AI also presents a unique challenge for the temporal aspect of safety cases. Traditional safety cases often focus on a static system at a particular point in time. AI systems, however, can learn and adapt, potentially changing their behavior in ways that were not anticipated during their initial design and validation. This necessitates a "living" safety case, one that is continuously updated and re-evaluated as the system evolves and new data becomes available. The safety case must therefore include robust processes for managing changes, re-validating safety claims after updates or retraining, and incorporating feedback from operational deployment. Evidence in this regard would include the change management procedures, the protocols for re-testing and re-verification after modifications, and the system for tracking and analyzing operational performance over time to identify any emergent safety concerns.

In essence, tailoring safety cases for AI systems is an exercise in bridging the gap between deterministic engineering and probabilistic intelligence. It requires a shift in mindset from proving the absence of failures to demonstrating a high degree of confidence in acceptable performance under uncertainty. This involves embracing a broader spectrum of evidence, from rigorous testing and robustness analysis to explainability and operational monitoring, and then meticulously weaving this evidence into a clear, reasoned argument. The goal is to provide stakeholders with a compelling and transparent assertion that the AI system, despite its complexity and adaptive nature, has been developed and is operated in a manner that renders its risks acceptably managed for its intended purpose. This adaptive and evidence-rich approach is fundamental to fostering trust and enabling the responsible deployment of AI in critical applications.

The construction of a comprehensive AI safety case is a multi-faceted endeavor, requiring a systematic and well-organized approach to effectively communicate the safety assurances of an AI system. A meticulously structured document is not merely a formality; it is the bedrock upon which trust and confidence in the.AI's safe operation are built. Without a logical and coherent framework, even the most robust evidence can become disjointed and unconvincing. This section delves into the typical architecture of an AI safety case, outlining its essential components and emphasizing the importance of a clear, argumentative flow that seamlessly integrates evidence with safety claims. The primary objective is to create a document that is accessible and comprehensible to a diverse audience, including engineers, domain experts, regulators, and even the public, who may not possess deep technical expertise in artificial intelligence.

At its core, an AI safety case document serves as a reasoned argument, supported by evidence, that the AI system in question is acceptably safe for its intended use. This argument must be transparent, traceable, and verifiable. To achieve this, a standard structure is often adopted, though the specifics may vary depending on the application domain, regulatory requirements, and the complexity of the AI system. Typically, the document begins with a thorough
System Description. This section provides a high-level overview of the AI system, its purpose, its operational environment, and its intended users. It should clearly define the scope of the safety case – what aspects of the AI system's behavior and lifecycle are being addressed. For instance, an autonomous vehicle's safety case would detail its sensing capabilities, decision-making algorithms, actuation mechanisms, and the operational design domain (ODD), which specifies the conditions under which the vehicle is designed to operate safely. Similarly, a medical diagnostic AI's description would cover the types of medical images it analyzes, the diagnostic tasks it performs, and its intended role within a clinical workflow, perhaps as a decision support tool for physicians. Crucially, this section should also outline the system's architecture, including the interplay between different AI models, software components, hardware, and any human-in-the-loop mechanisms. Understanding the system's context and boundaries is the foundational step for any subsequent safety analysis.

Following the system description, a critical component is the
Hazard Identification and Risk Analysis. This is where the potential sources of harm associated with the AI system are systematically identified, and the likelihood and severity of the resulting risks are assessed. Unlike traditional safety engineering, where hazards might be well-understood through historical data and physical principles, AI systems introduce novel and sometimes emergent hazards. These can

arise from model inaccuracies, unexpected behavior under novel conditions, biases in training data, adversarial attacks, or even unintended interactions between different AI components. The process of hazard identification should be comprehensive, drawing upon domain knowledge, expert judgment, failure mode and effects analysis (FMEA), and any available historical data, including that from similar AI systems or related technologies. For an AI system controlling industrial robots, hazards might include unintended movements, collisions with personnel or equipment, or failure to detect safety barriers. For an AI-powered financial trading system, hazards could involve generating erroneous trades, experiencing cascading failures in volatile markets, or being susceptible to manipulation.

The risk analysis then quantifies these identified hazards. This involves estimating the probability of a hazardous event occurring and the potential severity of its consequences. The nature of AI means that this analysis often leans heavily on probabilistic methods. Instead of stating a risk is "impossible," the safety case might argue that the probability of a specific unsafe event is "acceptably low," defined by a quantifiable threshold. This requires defining what constitutes an "unacceptable outcome" for the specific application. For a chatbot providing mental health support, an unacceptable outcome could be providing advice that exacerbates a user's distress, while for a drone used for agricultural surveying, it might be crashing due to navigational errors. The risk analysis section must clearly articulate the methodologies used for probability estimation and impact assessment, acknowledging any uncertainties inherent in these estimations. This might involve Monte Carlo simulations, Bayesian networks, or statistical modeling based on testing data. The output of this phase is a prioritized list of risks, guiding the subsequent definition of safety requirements.

The next logical step is the articulation of

Safety Requirements. These are the specific, measurable, achievable, relevant, and time-bound (SMART) criteria that the AI system must meet to mitigate the identified risks to an acceptable level. Safety requirements are derived directly from the risk analysis and serve as the targets that the design and development process must achieve. They should be clear, unambiguous, and verifiable. For an AI system in healthcare, a safety requirement might be: "The AI shall achieve a sensitivity of at least 95% and a specificity of at least 90% in detecting malignant tumors from MRI scans, with a false positive rate not exceeding 5% for benign lesions." This requirement directly addresses the risk of misdiagnosis. Another example, for an autonomous driving system, could be: "The system shall maintain a minimum safe following distance of 2 seconds at all operational speeds under clear weather conditions, and shall adapt this distance to a minimum of 4 seconds in rain or fog."

Safety requirements can be functional (what the system *must do* or *not do*) or non-functional (how the system *must perform*). Functional requirements might include specific decision-making logic or error handling protocols. Non-functional requirements often relate to performance, robustness, reliability, security, and ethical considerations. For an AI system used in content moderation, a non-functional requirement might specify that the system must process content within a certain latency to ensure timely removal of harmful material, or that it must be auditable to ensure fairness. The safety case document should clearly link each safety requirement back to the specific hazards and risks it is intended to mitigate, demonstrating a clear chain of reasoning.

The bedrock of any safety case is the **Verification and Validation (V&V) Evidence**. This is where the actual proof lies that the AI system meets its safety requirements. This section is typically the most extensive and data-rich part of the document, detailing the rigorous testing, analysis, and review processes undertaken. As discussed previously, the nature of AI necessitates a broad spectrum of V&V activities beyond traditional software testing. This includes:

Model Performance Testing: This encompasses not only accuracy metrics but also evaluations under diverse and challenging conditions. Standard test sets are insufficient; the safety case must detail performance on out-of-distribution data, edge cases, and adversarial examples. The methodologies for generating these test cases, the specific metrics used (e.g., precision, recall, F1-score, AUC, mean squared error), and the statistical significance of the results must be clearly presented. For instance, the safety case for a facial recognition AI used for security access control would need to demonstrate its accuracy across various lighting conditions, angles, and the presence of disguises or accessories, supported by quantitative data from extensive testing.

Robustness and Resilience Testing: Evidence here demonstrates the system's ability to withstand perturbations, noise, or unexpected inputs without failing in a safety-critical manner. This could involve injecting noise into sensor data, altering input parameters slightly, or simulating environmental variations. The safety case should provide quantifiable measures of performance degradation under these conditions and demonstrate that any degradation remains within acceptable safety margins. For a navigation AI in a delivery drone, this would include testing its performance when GPS signals are intermittent or when wind gusts affect its flight path, with data showing its ability to maintain course or execute a safe landing.

Bias and Fairness Evaluation: For AI systems that interact with or make decisions about people, demonstrating fairness and the absence of harmful biases is a critical safety concern. This section would present the results of tests designed to detect and quantify biases related to protected attributes such as race, gender, or age. Evidence might include demographic parity metrics, equalized odds, or counterfactual fairness analyses. The safety case should detail the datasets used for bias testing and the mitigation strategies employed if biases are detected. An AI used for loan application processing, for example, would need to present evidence that its decision-making is not systematically prejudiced against certain demographic groups, backed by audits and statistical analyses.

Explainability and Interpretability Evidence: While not a direct measure of safety, the ability to understand an AI's decision-making process is vital for debugging, auditing, and building trust, especially when something goes wrong. This section would detail the XAI techniques employed and the insights they provide. For safety-critical systems, the argument might be that explainability enables human oversight, facilitates incident investigation, or helps identify emergent unsafe behaviors. For an AI assisting in critical care patient monitoring, evidence might include sample explanations for alarm triggers, demonstrating to medical staff why a particular alert was raised, thereby enabling them to assess its validity and respond appropriately.

Formal Methods and Assurance: Where applicable, evidence from formal verification of critical algorithms or properties should be included. This provides mathematical guarantees of certain behaviors under specified conditions. The safety case would present the formal models, the verification results, and a clear explanation of the scope of these guarantees. For a safety-critical control system within an autonomous system, formal verification might prove that certain undesirable states can never be reached, providing a very high level of assurance for that specific aspect.

Operational Monitoring and Anomaly Detection: Since AI systems can evolve, evidence of their ongoing monitoring in deployment is essential. This includes details of performance monitoring, anomaly detection mechanisms, and incident response protocols. The safety case should present data or simulations demonstrating the effectiveness of these monitoring systems in identifying deviations from expected behavior, data drift, or performance degradation that could impact safety. For an AI system predicting equipment failure in a manufacturing plant, this would include logs and analysis showing how it detects subtle changes in sensor readings that precede a breakdown and triggers timely maintenance alerts.

Data Quality and Governance Evidence: The integrity of the data used to train and operate the AI is fundamental to its safety. This section would provide evidence of robust data management practices, including data provenance, quality control checks, bias mitigation in datasets, and secure data handling. For instance, an AI used in legal contexts, such as predictive policing, would need to demonstrate the chain of custody for all data used, the rigorousness of its cleaning and validation processes, and how any historical biases within the data were identified and addressed.

A crucial element that often underpins the credibility of the V&V evidence is the clarity and completeness of the
Assumptions made throughout the safety case development. No AI system operates in a vacuum, and certain assumptions are always made about its operating environment, the reliability of its components, and the behavior of external entities. These assumptions must be explicitly stated and justified. This might include assumptions about the range of environmental conditions the AI will encounter, the trustworthiness of input data from other systems, or the availability of external resources like power or network connectivity. The safety case needs to argue why these assumptions are reasonable and what the implications are if they are violated. For an AI system operating in a smart city infrastructure, an assumption might be the continuous availability of reliable power and network connectivity. The safety case would need to detail contingency

plans for power outages or network disruptions, and if these are not feasible, it must acknowledge the resulting limitations on safe operation.

The **Argument Structure** is perhaps the most critical, yet often overlooked, component of a robust AI safety case. It is not enough to simply present a collection of descriptions, analyses, and evidence. The safety case must weave these elements into a coherent and compelling narrative that logically demonstrates how the evidence supports the overall safety claims. This typically involves a hierarchical structure, starting with high-level safety goals and progressively decomposing them into more specific requirements, properties, and then linking each of these to concrete evidence. For instance, a high-level goal might be "prevent harm to humans." This could be decomposed into requirements like "avoid collisions," "maintain operational stability," and "respond appropriately to emergencies." Each of these requirements would then be supported by evidence from the V&V activities.

The argument structure should clearly articulate the logic connecting each piece of evidence to the safety claim it supports. This might involve using diagrams, traceability matrices, or a structured argumentation framework. The goal is to make the reasoning explicit and transparent, allowing reviewers to follow the logic and assess its validity. For example, if a safety requirement is to ensure the AI's outputs are within a certain acceptable range, the argument structure would present this requirement, then point to specific testing data (e.g., from robustness analysis or operational monitoring) that demonstrates this behavior, and finally explain *how* this data confirms the requirement is met.

Furthermore, the argument structure must explicitly address the **Limitations and Residual Risks**. No AI system can be proven to be perfectly safe, especially given the inherent uncertainties and the dynamic nature of AI. The safety case should candidly acknowledge the limitations of the analyses, the assumptions made, and the remaining risks that, despite all mitigation efforts, still exist. The crucial part of this section is to provide a compelling argument for *why* these residual risks are acceptable, considering the benefits the AI system provides, the context of its deployment, and the established risk tolerance of the domain. This transparency is vital for building trust with regulators and stakeholders. It demonstrates a mature understanding of the technology's capabilities and limitations. For an AI system designed for scientific discovery, where experiments are inherently uncertain, the safety case might acknowledge the risk of pursuing unproductive research avenues, but argue that this is an acceptable risk given the potential for groundbreaking discoveries and the minimal direct harm it poses.

Finally, a forward-looking aspect that is increasingly vital for AI safety cases is the consideration of
Lifecycle and Evolution. AI systems are not static entities; they learn, adapt, and are subject to updates and retraining. The safety case must therefore address how safety will be maintained throughout the system's lifecycle. This includes processes for managing changes, re-evaluating safety claims after updates, and incorporating feedback from operational deployment. Evidence in this area might include detailed change management protocols, procedures for re-verification and re-validation after model retraining, and mechanisms for continuous learning about potential safety issues in the field. The safety case for a self-driving car's perception system, for instance, must outline how new data gathered from deployed vehicles will be used to identify potential blind spots or performance degradations, and what the process is for updating the model and re-certifying its safety. This perspective acknowledges that safety is not a one-time achievement but an ongoing commitment.

In summary, structuring an AI safety case is about creating a persuasive and auditable document. It requires a systematic progression from understanding the system and its context, through rigorous identification and analysis of hazards, to the definition of clear safety requirements, and finally, the presentation of comprehensive evidence that demonstrates compliance with these requirements. The argument must be logically structured, transparent about assumptions and limitations, and forward-looking in its consideration of the system's lifecycle. By adhering to such a framework, developers can build confidence in their AI systems and enable their responsible deployment in an increasingly AI-driven world.

The efficacy of any AI safety case is intrinsically tied to the quality, relevance, and comprehensiveness of the evidence presented. This evidence forms the empirical foundation upon which all safety claims are built. Without it, the most sophisticated argumentation and meticulously defined requirements remain speculative. Consequently, the gathering and presentation of this evidence are paramount, demanding a systematic approach that ensures both thoroughness and clarity.

A fundamental category of evidence pertains to the data underpinning the AI system. This begins with
dataset provenance and quality. For any AI model, the data used for training, validation, and testing is the source of its learned behaviors. Therefore, detailed information about the origin of this data, its collection methodologies, and the steps taken to ensure its quality are critical. This includes documentation of:

Source Identification: Clearly stating where the data originated (e.g., specific sensors, public datasets, proprietary databases, human annotations). For a medical imaging AI, this might involve detailing the hospitals from which anonymized scans were obtained, the imaging modalities used (MRI, CT, X-ray), and the consent mechanisms employed.
Data Collection Procedures: Describing the protocols followed during data acquisition. This is especially important if the data was collected in a controlled environment or through specific experimental setups. For an AI system controlling robotic manipulation, documenting the precise

movements, environmental conditions, and object properties during training data collection would be essential.

Data Preprocessing and Cleaning: Outlining the steps taken to clean the data, handle missing values, normalize or standardize features, and remove outliers or erroneous entries. The rationale behind each cleaning step should be clear. For an AI designed to predict stock market trends, detailing how historical price anomalies or data entry errors were identified and addressed is crucial.

Labeling and Annotation Accuracy: For supervised learning, the accuracy and consistency of the labels or annotations are paramount. This section should detail the annotation guidelines, the qualifications of the annotators, inter-annotator agreement metrics, and any quality control mechanisms implemented to ensure label fidelity. For an object detection AI used in autonomous driving, the precision with which bounding boxes are drawn around pedestrians, vehicles, and traffic signs directly impacts the model's ability to recognize these objects safely.

Data Representativeness: Evidence that the dataset adequately represents the diversity of scenarios, environments, and conditions the AI system is expected to encounter in its operational domain. This includes demographic diversity for AI systems making decisions about people, or environmental variations (lighting, weather, terrain) for autonomous systems.

Data Security and Privacy: Documenting measures taken to protect sensitive data, comply with privacy regulations (e.g., GDPR, HIPAA), and ensure anonymization or de-identification where appropriate.

Beyond the raw data, evidence of the **model training process** provides insight into how the AI system learned. This typically includes:

Training Environment and Parameters: A clear record of the hardware used (e.g., specific GPUs), software frameworks (e.g., TensorFlow, PyTorch), and hyperparameter settings (learning rate, batch size,

optimizer choice, regularization techniques). This allows for reproducibility and debugging.
Training Logs and Checkpoints: Detailed logs capturing the progress of training, including epoch-by-epoch or step-by-step performance metrics on validation sets, loss curves, and saved model checkpoints at various stages of training. These logs can reveal issues like overfitting or underfitting.
Model Architecture: A precise description of the neural network architecture or algorithm used, including the number of layers, types of layers, activation functions, and connections. This is crucial for understanding the model's inductive biases and potential failure modes.
Resource Utilization: Information on the computational resources consumed during training, which can be an indicator of model complexity and potentially training time requirements for retraining.

The core of the empirical evidence lies in **performance metrics across diverse scenarios**. This goes beyond simple accuracy on a standard test set. A robust safety case requires demonstrating performance under a wide range of conditions, particularly those that are challenging or atypical. This includes:

Standard Performance Metrics: Reporting well-established metrics relevant to the task, such as accuracy, precision, recall, F1-score, AUC for classification tasks, or Mean Squared Error (MSE), R-squared for regression tasks. These should be reported for representative test sets.
Out-of-Distribution (OOD) Performance: Crucially, evidence of how the AI performs when presented with data that differs from its training distribution. This is where many AI systems fail unsafely. Test cases should be designed to probe OOD scenarios relevant to the operational domain. For a facial recognition system, OOD data might include images with unusual angles, poor lighting, or novel accessories.
Edge Case Performance: Demonstrating performance on rare but potentially high-impact scenarios. This requires careful identification and

generation of such edge cases. For an AI controlling a drone, edge cases might include sudden changes in wind speed, encountering unexpected obstacles, or operating in areas with poor GPS signals.

Adversarial Robustness: For AI systems susceptible to adversarial attacks, presenting evidence of their resilience against intentionally crafted perturbations designed to fool the model. This might involve reporting performance under various types of adversarial attacks (e.g., FGSM, PGD) and detailing any defensive mechanisms employed.

Performance Degradation Analysis: Quantifying how performance degrades as inputs deviate from nominal conditions or as noise levels increase. This helps understand the system's operating envelope and limits.

Fairness and Bias Metrics: Reporting metrics that evaluate the system's performance across different demographic groups or sensitive attributes to ensure it does not exhibit unfair biases. Examples include demographic parity, equalized odds, and disparate impact analyses. Evidence of mitigation strategies employed to address identified biases should also be provided.

Operational Contextualization: Presenting performance metrics not just in isolation, but within the context of the system's intended operational environment. This might involve simulations or real-world data that mimics the deployment scenario.

Robustness test results are a distinct but related category, focusing on the AI's resilience to perturbations and unexpected events. This evidence demonstrates that the system can tolerate deviations from ideal conditions without catastrophic failure. Key aspects include:

Noise Injection: Testing the AI's performance when sensor data or input features are corrupted with various types and levels of noise (e.g., Gaussian noise, salt-and-pepper noise).

Sensor Degradation Simulation: For systems relying on physical sensors, evidence of how the AI performs when sensor readings are imprecise, intermittently unavailable, or biased. This could involve simulating camera blur, lidar noise, or GPS drift.
Stress Testing: Pushing the system to its limits by exposing it to high loads, rapid changes in input, or extreme environmental conditions.
Fault Injection: Simulating component failures (e.g., communication drops, actuator malfunctions) and observing how the AI system responds. This is crucial for understanding graceful degradation and fail-safe mechanisms.
Sensitivity Analysis: Quantifying how sensitive the AI's output is to small changes in input parameters. High sensitivity in critical areas can indicate potential instability.

Explainability reports provide evidence of the AI's interpretability, which is vital for debugging, auditing, and building trust. While not always directly proving safety, it aids in understanding *why* a certain decision was made, especially when it is incorrect or unexpected. Evidence here can take several forms:

Feature Importance Analysis: Techniques like SHAP (SHapley Additive exPlanations) or LIME (Local Interpretable Model-agnostic Explanations) can highlight which input features most influenced a particular decision. For a loan application AI, this could show that income and credit score were the primary drivers of a denial.
Concept Activation Vectors (CAVs): For image recognition tasks, demonstrating which high-level concepts the model has learned and how they contribute to classification.
Decision Tree/Rule Extraction: If applicable, presenting simplified models or rules that approximate the AI's behavior, making it more transparent.

Counterfactual Explanations: Demonstrating what minimal changes to the input would have resulted in a different outcome. For a medical diagnosis AI, a counterfactual might show that a slight alteration in an image feature would have changed a "malignant" prediction to "benign."
Visualization of Internal States: For deep learning models, visualizing activation patterns in intermediate layers can offer clues about the model's internal processing.
Human-AI Interaction Logs: In systems involving human oversight, logs of how humans interact with the AI's explanations and whether they accept or override its suggestions can be informative.

Incident response data forms critical evidence of how the system behaves when things go wrong and how effectively the organization handles failures. This is particularly important for systems that have already been deployed, even in limited trials.

Failure Logs: Detailed records of all detected anomalies, errors, crashes, or deviations from expected behavior. This should include timestamps, system states, input data leading to the failure, and any error codes generated.
Root Cause Analysis (RCA) Reports: For significant incidents, thorough RCA reports are essential. These documents explain the underlying causes of failures, distinguishing between software bugs, data issues, environmental factors, or emergent AI behaviors.
Incident Response Actions: Documented actions taken in response to an incident, including immediate mitigation steps, corrective actions, and preventative measures implemented to avoid recurrence.
Performance Monitoring Alerts: Evidence from continuous monitoring systems that detected deviations from normal operating parameters or performance thresholds. This shows the effectiveness of proactive safety mechanisms.

Feedback Loops: Records of how feedback from users, operators, or post-incident reviews are incorporated into system improvements and safety case updates.
Metrics on Response Time and Resolution: Quantifiable data on how quickly incidents were detected, responded to, and resolved.

Presenting this often complex and voluminous data effectively is as crucial as gathering it. The goal is to make the evidence accessible, understandable, and clearly linked to the safety claims.

Structured Data Repositories: Establishing a well-organized system for storing and accessing all evidence, ideally with clear version control and audit trails. This might involve dedicated databases, cloud storage with robust indexing, or specialized safety case management tools.
Traceability: Ensuring that every safety claim and requirement can be traced back to the specific evidence that supports it, and vice versa. Traceability matrices, diagrams, and clear referencing are key. For example, a requirement to "maintain vehicle stability in crosswinds" should be linked to specific wind tunnel test data, simulation results, and real-world driving logs exhibiting crosswind conditions.
Visualizations: Employing graphs, charts, heatmaps, and other visual aids to present performance data, robustness analyses, and explainability insights in an easily digestible format. For instance, a plot showing performance degradation versus increasing levels of sensor noise can be far more impactful than a table of numbers.
Summaries and Executive Overviews: Providing high-level summaries of the evidence for stakeholders who may not need to delve into the granular details. These summaries should distill the most critical findings and their implications for safety.
Contextualization: Always presenting evidence within its relevant context. Simply stating a model achieved 99% accuracy is meaningless without specifying the dataset, the task, and the definition of accuracy.

Similarly, explaining the operational context in which robustness tests were conducted is vital.
Quantification and Benchmarking: Whenever possible, quantifying the evidence and comparing it against predefined safety thresholds or benchmarks. If a specific risk has a quantitative acceptable probability, the evidence should demonstrate that the AI system meets or exceeds that threshold.
Clarity in Reporting Uncertainty: Acknowledging and clearly articulating any uncertainties associated with the evidence, such as confidence intervals for performance metrics, limitations of simulation environments, or assumptions made during data collection or analysis.
Narrative Flow: Integrating the evidence into the overall safety argument. Each piece of evidence should serve to bolster a specific safety claim, and the presentation should guide the reader through this logical progression.
Peer Review and Independent Audits: Evidence of independent review or auditing of the data collection, analysis, and testing processes can significantly enhance credibility. This demonstrates that the evidence has been scrutinized by parties external to the development team.
Reproducibility: Where possible, providing sufficient detail and access to methodologies (e.g., code, scripts, configurations) to allow for the reproduction of key results. This fosters transparency and allows for verification by third parties.

In essence, gathering and presenting evidence for AI safety is a discipline in itself. It requires meticulous record-keeping, rigorous analysis, creative visualization, and a deep understanding of how to communicate complex technical information to diverse audiences. The goal is not just to collect data, but to transform that data into compelling, verifiable proof that the AI system is acceptably safe for its intended purpose.

The development of AI safety cases is not merely an academic exercise; it is a critical engineering discipline that underpins the responsible deployment of artificial intelligence. To bridge the gap between theoretical frameworks and practical implementation, we will now explore a comprehensive case study: an AI-powered subway control system. This examination will not just highlight the abstract principles of safety case development but will vividly illustrate their application in a high-stakes environment where system failures can have severe consequences.

The operational domain for an AI-powered subway control system is inherently complex and safety-critical. These systems are responsible for managing train movements, ensuring optimal scheduling, and most importantly, preventing collisions. The introduction of AI into such a system promises enhanced efficiency, improved passenger experience through more reliable service, and potentially greater safety by augmenting or even replacing human operators in certain functions. However, it also introduces novel failure modes and hazards that must be rigorously analyzed and mitigated.

Our case study focuses on an AI system designed to manage train departures, speed regulation, and inter-train spacing within a specific section of a metropolitan subway network. This system integrates data from various sources, including track sensors, onboard train equipment (such as speedometers and GPS), station arrival/departure monitors, and potentially, visual perception systems for obstacle detection. The AI's primary objective is to maintain safe headways between trains, adhere to schedules, and respond dynamically to real-time network conditions, such as unexpected delays or track obstructions.

The first crucial step in developing the safety case for this AI-powered subway control system is
hazard identification. This process involves a systematic review of potential events or conditions that could lead to harm. For a subway control system, these hazards are numerous and can be broadly

categorized. A primary concern is the risk of **collision**, which could arise from various AI-related failures. For instance, if the AI's perception module misinterprets sensor data, it might fail to detect an adjacent train or an obstruction on the track, leading to a collision. Similarly, errors in the AI's decision-making logic could result in inappropriate speed commands, causing a train to overshoot its stopping point or to accelerate into a hazardous situation.

Another significant hazard is **derailment**. While direct AI causation of derailment is less common than collision, indirect links exist. For example, an AI commanding excessive speed around a curve, perhaps due to erroneous track geometry data or a miscalculation of safe operating limits, could lead to a derailment. Unexpected and abrupt braking or acceleration, if not properly managed, can also induce forces on the train that, under certain conditions (e.g., track defects), could contribute to derailment.

Beyond physical safety, the AI system's failures could lead to significant **service disruptions**. While not a direct safety hazard in the immediate sense, prolonged or widespread disruptions can have cascading negative effects, impacting public trust, emergency response capabilities (if a subway line is a critical transport artery), and even economic activity. For instance, an AI system that repeatedly fails to manage train movements efficiently could lead to systemic delays, rendering the subway line unreliable.

Furthermore, **human-AI interaction hazards** are a growing concern. If the AI system is designed to work in conjunction with human supervisors or operators, misunderstandings or over-reliance on the AI could lead to errors. This could manifest as a human operator failing to intervene when the AI makes an incorrect decision, or conversely, a human overriding a correct AI decision due to a lack of trust or understanding. The "automation surprise" phenomenon, where an operator is suddenly required to take control in an unexpected situation, is a classic example.

Cybersecurity vulnerabilities represent another class of hazards. If the AI system's integrity is compromised by malicious actors, it could be manipulated to cause intentional harm, such as orchestrating collisions or bringing the entire network to a standstill. The data inputs to the AI are also susceptible to manipulation, which could feed erroneous information into the system, leading to unsafe decisions.

Once hazards are identified, the next step is to establish **safety requirements**. These requirements define the acceptable risk levels and the conditions under which the AI system must operate safely. For our subway control system, these requirements would be derived from existing railway safety standards, regulatory mandates, and the outcomes of the hazard analysis.

A fundamental safety requirement would be to **prevent collisions**. This translates into specific, quantifiable requirements for the AI system. For instance, the AI must maintain a minimum safe headway between trains, defined as a specific time interval (e.g., 90 seconds) or a minimum distance (e.g., 150 meters), under all foreseeable operational conditions. This requirement would be further decomposed: the perception system must detect other trains and obstacles with a specified probability of detection and a low rate of false negatives within a defined range. The AI's control algorithms must ensure that if a detected hazard necessitates an emergency stop, the train can decelerate from its maximum operational speed to a complete stop within a safe distance, without causing undue passenger discomfort or risk of secondary incidents.

Another critical requirement concerns

speed control. The AI must ensure that train speeds never exceed the maximum safe speed for the current track segment, considering factors like curvature, gradient, and track condition. This requires precise knowledge of the train's location and the track geometry, and the AI's decision-making must incorporate a sufficient safety margin.

Reliability and availability are paramount. The AI system must be available for operation during peak hours with a very high degree of certainty. This translates into requirements for fault tolerance and graceful degradation. If a component of the AI system fails, it must either continue to operate safely in a degraded mode or transition to a safe state (e.g., bring the train to a controlled stop) without compromising overall network safety. The Mean Time Between Failures (MTBF) for critical AI functions would be specified, along with the maximum allowable downtime.

Requirements for **predictability and controllability** are also essential. The AI's behavior should be understandable to human supervisors, and its actions should be controllable. This means that operators must be able to override AI commands if necessary, and the system should provide clear indications of its current state, intent, and any deviations from planned operations. This might involve requirements for specific levels of transparency or explainability in the AI's decision-making process.

For the perception components of the AI, **robustness to environmental conditions** is a key requirement. For example, the system must maintain its detection capabilities in varying lighting conditions (day, night, twilight), adverse weather (rain, fog, snow), and potentially, in the presence of visual noise or occlusions. Specific performance metrics for detection rates and false alarm rates under these varied conditions would be defined.

Cybersecurity requirements would mandate the implementation of specific security protocols, encryption standards, intrusion detection systems, and secure update mechanisms to protect the AI system from unauthorized access and manipulation.

With hazards and requirements defined, the next phase involves **selecting and designing the AI models**. For an AI-powered subway control system, a hybrid approach is often employed, combining traditional control algorithms with machine learning components.

The core train control functions, such as maintaining a target speed or executing a braking profile, might still rely on well-established, deterministic control laws (e.g., PID controllers). These systems are highly predictable and their behavior is well-understood. However, AI, particularly machine learning, can enhance these systems in several ways.

For
perception, deep learning models, such as Convolutional Neural Networks (CNNs), are often used for analyzing sensor data. If the system incorporates visual sensors for obstacle detection, CNNs trained on vast datasets of images of subway environments would be employed. These models would be designed to identify specific objects like other trains, personnel on the tracks, fallen debris, or signal malfunctions. The choice of network architecture (e.g., ResNet, EfficientNet) would depend on the trade-off between accuracy, computational efficiency, and robustness.

For
predictive tasks, such as forecasting potential delays or estimating arrival times, Recurrent Neural Networks (RNNs) or Long Short-Term Memory (LSTM) networks might be utilized. These models can learn

temporal patterns from historical operational data to predict future states of the network.

Decision-making and planning for optimal train movements, especially in dynamic scenarios, could involve Reinforcement Learning (RL) agents. An RL agent could be trained in a simulated environment to learn optimal strategies for adjusting speeds, managing headways, and responding to unforeseen events, maximizing objectives like punctuality and energy efficiency while adhering to safety constraints. However, the application of RL in safety-critical systems requires extreme caution due to its potential for unexpected emergent behaviors. Therefore, extensive verification and validation of RL policies are paramount.

The AI models chosen must not only be performant but also align with the established safety requirements. This implies a rigorous selection process that considers factors beyond raw accuracy. For instance, a perception model might be preferred not for achieving the absolute highest detection rate, but for its consistency and low false positive rate across a wide range of conditions, especially those that could lead to unnecessary emergency braking.

A critical aspect of the safety case is providing **evidence that the system is acceptably safe**. This involves a multifaceted approach, generating and presenting various forms of evidence to demonstrate compliance with the safety requirements and the mitigation of identified hazards.

Data evidence is foundational. The AI models for perception and prediction are trained on large datasets. For our subway AI, this would include:

Sensor data logs: Recordings from actual subway operations, capturing images from onboard cameras, track sensor readings, GPS coordinates, and train telemetry (speed, acceleration, braking). This data must be meticulously curated, labelled, and documented, including its source, collection methodology, and any preprocessing steps.
Simulated data: Given the safety-critical nature, real-world data alone is often insufficient. Extensive use of high-fidelity simulations is essential. These simulations must accurately model track geometry, train dynamics, sensor characteristics, environmental conditions (lighting, weather), and the behavior of other trains. The AI models would be trained and tested on datasets generated from these simulations, allowing for exploration of a vast range of scenarios, including rare and dangerous ones that are impractical or impossible to collect in the real world.
Augmented data: Techniques like data augmentation (e.g., adding noise to images, varying lighting conditions) would be used to increase the diversity of the training data and improve model robustness.
Ground truth: For supervised learning, accurate labelling of data is critical. This includes precise identification of objects in images, accurate annotation of track conditions, and correct labelling of train positions and speeds. Evidence of the annotation process, including the qualifications of annotators, inter-annotator agreement, and quality control procedures, would be part of the safety case.

Model development and training evidence would detail:

Model architecture and parameters: Clear documentation of the chosen AI architectures, their hyperparameters, and the rationale behind their selection.

Training procedures: Detailed logs of the training process, including the computational resources used, learning curves, convergence criteria, and the specific optimization techniques employed.
Version control: Rigorous version control for all model code, training scripts, and trained model weights.

Performance testing evidence is perhaps the most extensive. This would go far beyond a simple test set accuracy.

Standard operational scenarios: Testing the AI's performance in nominal conditions, ensuring it meets performance targets for punctuality, speed regulation, and headway maintenance. Metrics would include on-time performance rates, average headway, and adherence to speed limits.
Edge case testing: This is paramount for safety. The AI must be tested on a wide array of challenging and rare scenarios identified during hazard analysis. Examples include:
Sudden obstacle detection: A scenario where an object suddenly appears on the track and the AI must react within the required braking distance.
Sensor degradation: Testing the AI's performance when sensor data is noisy, incomplete, or biased (e.g., a camera lens is partially obscured, GPS signal is weak).
System failures in other trains: Simulating scenarios where another train behaves erratically, requiring the AI to maintain safe separation.
Extreme environmental conditions: Performance under heavy fog, snow, or during power fluctuations.
Rapidly changing network conditions: Testing how the AI responds to sudden service disruptions or unexpected track closures.
Adversarial testing: For critical perception or prediction models, evidence of their resilience against potential adversarial attacks, even if the attack surface in a closed subway network is limited.

Out-of-distribution (OOD) performance: Evaluating how the AI performs on data that is significantly different from its training distribution. This might include unexpected track configurations, unusual maintenance vehicles, or novel types of debris.
Human-AI interaction testing: Scenarios designed to evaluate how well human operators understand and interact with the AI system, including testing override mechanisms and alarm systems. This would involve user studies and simulations of human supervisory roles.
Fail-safe mechanism validation: Demonstrating that when the AI system encounters conditions beyond its safe operating envelope, it reliably transitions to a safe state, such as activating emergency brakes or alerting a human supervisor.

Robustness and resilience evidence would focus on the AI's ability to withstand perturbations:

Noise injection: Quantifying performance degradation as noise is added to sensor inputs.
Fault injection: Simulating failures in critical AI components or supporting systems (e.g., communication links, sensor hardware) and verifying that the system responds appropriately and safely.
Stress testing: Pushing the system to its limits under high load conditions, such as during peak hours with maximum train density, to ensure it does not exhibit unexpected behaviors or performance collapses.

Explainability and transparency evidence would be crucial for building trust and enabling effective oversight. While complex deep learning models can be black boxes, efforts must be made to provide insights:

Feature importance analysis: For critical decisions, demonstrating which sensor inputs or internal states most strongly influenced the AI's output. For example, if the AI decides to brake, showing that this decision was primarily driven by detecting an object on the track or receiving a red signal.
Counterfactual explanations: Showing what minimal changes to the input data would have led to a different decision. This helps in understanding the sensitivity of the AI to specific conditions.
Visualization of learned concepts: For perception models, visualizing the features or patterns the AI has learned to recognize (e.g., what constitutes a "train" in its internal representation).
Decision logic transparency: For any rule-based or hybrid components of the AI, clearly documenting the logic and decision trees.

Verification and validation (V&V) evidence plays a critical role in substantiating the safety claims. This includes:

Formal verification: Where applicable, using mathematical methods to prove that certain AI properties hold true under specific assumptions. This is often challenging for complex, data-driven AI models but can be applied to specific modules or properties.
Model checking: Similar to formal verification, this involves systematically exploring the state space of the system to check for violations of safety properties.
Simulation-based V&V: As mentioned earlier, extensive simulations are used not just for testing but for rigorous validation of the AI's behavior against safety requirements. This involves creating a large number of test cases, systematically varying parameters, and statistically analyzing the results.
Independent testing: Having the AI system tested by an independent third party to provide an unbiased assessment of its safety.

Operational evidence gathered during pilot deployments or phased rollouts is invaluable.

Performance monitoring logs: Continuous monitoring of the AI system in a live environment, tracking key performance indicators and detecting any anomalies or deviations from expected behavior.
Incident reports: Detailed documentation of any safety-relevant incidents, near misses, or unexpected events that occurred during operation, including thorough root cause analyses and the corrective actions taken.
Maintenance and update logs: Records of all software updates, model retraining, and hardware maintenance, ensuring that the system remains in a known safe state.

The presentation of this evidence in the safety case must be structured and coherent. A traceability matrix linking each hazard to the safety requirements that mitigate it, and then linking those requirements to the specific pieces of evidence that demonstrate their fulfillment, is essential. Visualizations, such as graphs of performance under varying conditions, heatmaps of error probabilities, and flowcharts of decision processes, will make the evidence more accessible and impactful.

In conclusion, the development of an AI safety case for a system as critical as a subway control network is an intricate, multi-disciplinary undertaking. It requires a deep understanding of AI capabilities and limitations, a rigorous hazard analysis process, the formulation of precise safety requirements, and the generation of comprehensive, verifiable evidence. This case study illustrates that the journey from AI model development to safe deployment hinges on meticulously building and presenting a robust safety case, ensuring that the promise of AI in enhancing public transportation is realized without compromising the safety of passengers and the public. The evidence collected must not only satisfy technical requirements but also build confidence among regulators, operators, and the public that the AI system can be trusted with the responsibility of managing our vital transit networks.

Chapter 6: Implementing Robust Data Governance

Establishing a robust data governance framework is foundational to the responsible and effective management of any AI infrastructure. Without clear structures, policies, and defined responsibilities, data assets can become unmanageable, leading to inconsistencies, inaccuracies, security risks, and ultimately, a compromised ability to build trustworthy AI systems. This framework acts as the architectural blueprint for how data is acquired, stored, processed, used, and ultimately retired within an organization, ensuring it aligns with both business objectives and ethical considerations. It is not a one-time setup but an ongoing process of refinement and adaptation as data sources evolve, AI models advance, and regulatory landscapes shift.

The cornerstone of any data governance framework is the **definition of roles and responsibilities**. This ensures accountability and clarity on who is responsible for what aspects of data management. At the highest level, **Data Owners** are typically senior executives or business unit leaders who have ultimate accountability for specific data domains (e.g., customer data, product data, operational data). They are responsible for approving data policies and standards for their domain, ensuring data quality, and making strategic decisions regarding data usage and access. They are the ultimate custodians of the data's value and integrity.

Working closely with Data Owners are **Data Stewards**. These individuals are subject matter experts within their respective data domains. They are the operational linchpins of data governance, responsible for the day-to-day management and implementation of data policies and standards. Their duties often include defining data elements, documenting metadata, ensuring data quality, resolving data-related issues, and managing data access requests within their domain. Data Stewards act as the bridge between the strategic directives of Data Owners and the practical realities of data handling by various teams, including AI development teams. For instance, in an AI context, a Data Steward for sensor data might be responsible for cataloging all available sensor streams, defining their accuracy metrics, and ensuring that any new sensor integration adheres to established quality standards. They would also work with AI engineers to ensure that the data used for training is representative and free from systematic biases.

Beyond these core roles, a comprehensive framework also includes **Data Custodians**, who are typically IT professionals responsible for the technical infrastructure and systems that store, move, and secure data. They implement the policies set by Data Owners and Stewards, manage databases, ensure data backup and recovery, and enforce security controls. While they manage the physical and digital aspects of data, they do so under the guidance of the data governance policies. Finally, **Data Users** are all individuals and systems that access and utilize data. Their responsibility lies in adhering to the established data policies and using data ethically and appropriately for authorized purposes. This includes AI developers, data scientists, analysts, and any other personnel interacting with the data.

Crucially, the framework must define
data policies and standards. These are the rules of engagement for data. **Data Policies** are high-level principles that guide data management and usage. They might cover aspects like data privacy, data security, data retention, data sharing, and data ethics. For AI systems, specific policies are needed to address the unique challenges, such as policies on algorithmic bias, the use of sensitive data in training, and the transparency of AI decision-making. For example, a policy on 'Fairness in AI' might dictate acceptable thresholds for demographic parity or equalized odds in model predictions.

Data Standards are more specific, prescriptive guidelines that ensure consistency and interoperability. This includes:

Data Naming Conventions: Standardized ways to name data files, tables, columns, and fields to avoid ambiguity and facilitate discovery.
Data Formatting Standards: Guidelines for how data should be structured and formatted (e.g., date formats, units of measurement, encoding standards) to ensure consistency across different systems and datasets.
Metadata Standards: Rules for documenting data, including its origin, definitions, transformations, lineage, and quality metrics. This is vital for AI systems, as understanding the provenance and characteristics of training data is essential for debugging and validation. A standard might specify that all datasets used for AI model training must include information on their collection date, geographical source, preprocessing steps, and any known limitations.
Data Quality Standards: Defining what constitutes "good" data for specific purposes, including acceptable levels of accuracy, completeness, consistency, timeliness, and validity.

The implementation of these policies and standards is supported by robust
Data Quality Management processes. This is an ongoing cycle of assessment, monitoring, and improvement. It begins with establishing **data quality metrics** tailored to the specific data domains and their intended uses. For AI, these metrics are particularly critical for the data used in model training and validation. For instance, for an image recognition AI, metrics might include pixel-level accuracy, object detection precision and recall, and consistency of annotations. For a predictive maintenance AI, metrics might focus on the accuracy of sensor readings, the completeness of historical failure logs, and the timeliness of data updates.

The next step is

data profiling, which involves analyzing datasets to understand their content, structure, and quality. This includes identifying anomalies, outliers, missing values, and inconsistencies. Tools can automate much of this process, providing reports on data distributions, value frequencies, and potential quality issues. Following profiling, **data cleansing and enrichment** activities are undertaken. Cleansing involves correcting or removing inaccurate, incomplete, or duplicate data. Enrichment might involve adding supplementary data from external sources to improve the context and utility of existing data. For an AI system, this stage is crucial for ensuring that the training data is as clean and representative as possible. For example, if a dataset used for training a financial fraud detection AI contains many duplicate entries or misclassified transactions, the resulting AI model will be less effective and potentially biased.

Data quality monitoring is then put in place to continuously track data quality against defined standards and metrics. This involves setting up automated checks and alerts that notify relevant stakeholders (often Data Stewards) when data quality degrades. This proactive approach helps prevent issues from escalating and impacting AI model performance or causing erroneous decisions. Finally, **root cause analysis and remediation** are essential when quality issues are detected. Instead of just fixing the symptom, the goal is to understand why the data quality problem occurred and implement measures to prevent its recurrence. This might involve improving data entry processes, enhancing data validation rules, or refining data integration pipelines.

Finally, and perhaps most critically in the context of AI, the data governance framework must encompass rigorous **data security and compliance** measures. **Data Security** aims to protect data from unauthorized access, corruption, or theft. This involves implementing a multi-layered approach:

Access Control: Implementing granular access controls based on the principle of least privilege. This means users (including AI systems) only have access to the data they absolutely need to perform their designated functions. Role-based access control (RBAC) and attribute-based access control (ABAC) are common mechanisms. For AI model training, this might involve creating specific service accounts with limited permissions to access only the required training datasets, and ensuring these accounts cannot exfiltrate data.
Encryption: Encrypting data both at rest (when stored) and in transit (when being transferred between systems). This ensures that even if data is intercepted or accessed improperly, it remains unintelligible without the decryption key. For sensitive AI training data, such as personal identifiable information (PII) or proprietary business information, end-to-end encryption is a critical safeguard.
Data Masking and Anonymization: For training AI models on sensitive data, techniques like data masking (replacing sensitive values with realistic but artificial ones) and anonymization (removing direct and indirect identifiers) are crucial for privacy protection. Differential privacy techniques, which add statistical noise to data or query results, can further enhance privacy guarantees, especially when dealing with aggregated data or model outputs.
Auditing and Monitoring: Maintaining comprehensive audit logs of all data access and modification activities. These logs are essential for detecting suspicious behavior, investigating security incidents, and ensuring accountability. Real-time monitoring of these logs can help identify potential breaches or policy violations as they occur.
Secure Data Lifecycle Management: Ensuring that data is securely handled throughout its entire lifecycle, from collection and processing to storage, use, and eventual secure disposal. This includes secure deletion practices to prevent data recovery.

Compliance refers to adhering to relevant laws, regulations, and industry standards governing data privacy and usage. This is particularly complex in the AI domain, where regulations like GDPR, CCPA, and various sector-specific laws (e.g., HIPAA for healthcare) have significant implications. Key compliance considerations include:

Consent Management: For any personal data used in AI systems, ensuring that appropriate consent has been obtained from individuals, and that this consent is managed and respected throughout the data lifecycle. This means understanding how consent applies to data used for training, inference, and model improvement.
Data Minimization: Collecting and processing only the data that is strictly necessary for the intended purpose of the AI system. This aligns with privacy principles and reduces the risk associated with handling large amounts of data.
Purpose Limitation: Ensuring that data collected for a specific purpose is not used for other incompatible purposes without explicit consent or legal basis. This is crucial for AI systems that might be repurposed or whose outputs could lead to new applications.
Data Subject Rights: Establishing processes to fulfill data subject rights, such as the right to access, rectify, erase, or port their personal data. This applies to data used in AI systems, and it can be challenging to implement for complex models where data is deeply embedded.
Regulatory Reporting and Audits: Being prepared to demonstrate compliance to regulatory bodies through documentation, audits, and reporting. This requires meticulous record-keeping of data governance practices, data lineage, and AI model development processes.

By establishing a comprehensive data governance framework encompassing clearly defined roles, robust policies and standards, diligent data quality management, and stringent security and compliance measures, organizations can lay a solid foundation for developing and deploying AI systems that are not only effective but also trustworthy, ethical, and resilient. This framework ensures that data, the lifeblood of AI, is managed as a strategic asset, safeguarding both the organization and the individuals whose data it processes.

The lifeblood of any sophisticated AI system is the data that fuels its learning and decision-making processes. However, simply having access to vast quantities of data is insufficient for building trustworthy, reliable, and ethically sound AI. A fundamental question arises: where did this data come from, and what has happened to it along its journey? This is where the concepts of **data provenance** and **data lineage tracking** become paramount. Without a clear understanding of a dataset's origin and transformation history, it becomes exceptionally difficult to ascertain its quality, identify potential biases, ensure its compliance with regulations, and troubleshoot errors when they inevitably arise within an AI system.

Data provenance refers to the origin and history of data. It encompasses the entire lifecycle of a data asset, from its initial creation or acquisition through all subsequent modifications, movements, and uses. Think of it as the genealogical record of your data. Knowing that a piece of data originates from a trusted, verified source, such as a sensor in a controlled laboratory environment, is fundamentally different from data scraped from an unverified website. The provenance of data directly impacts its credibility and suitability for various AI applications. For an AI model designed to predict equipment failures, data originating from authenticated sensor readings on a specific machine has much higher provenance than anecdotal reports from maintenance staff, even if the latter are more readily available. Understanding provenance is the first step in establishing trust in the data.

Complementary to provenance, data lineage tracking provides a dynamic, auditable record of how data has flowed and been transformed over time. It maps the journey of data through various systems, processes, and transformations. This includes detailing the specific operations performed on the data, such as aggregations, filtering, cleaning, feature engineering, or any other manipulation that alters its structure or content. Data lineage answers the question: "How did the data get to be the way it is now?" For example, if an AI model is exhibiting unexpected behavior, tracing its lineage might reveal that a particular data transformation step introduced a subtle but significant alteration, or that data from a previously trusted source was, for a period, being fed through a faulty processing pipeline. This granular understanding is indispensable for debugging, auditing, and ensuring the integrity of AI outputs.

The importance of data provenance and lineage tracking cannot be overstated, particularly in the context of AI development and deployment. In AI, where models learn patterns from data, any imperfections or biases in the training data can be amplified and propagated by the model.

Firstly,
ensuring data quality and integrity is directly dependent on understanding provenance and lineage. If the source of the data is known to be unreliable or if the transformations applied introduced errors, this information can be used to assess the data's quality and, if necessary, flag it for revalidation or exclusion from critical AI tasks. For instance, if a dataset used for training a medical diagnostic AI has its lineage traced back to manual data entry prone to transcription errors, this raises a red flag. A data steward can then investigate the transformation steps and identify specific records or subsets that require correction or re-verification. Without this tracking, such errors might go unnoticed, leading to an AI that makes incorrect diagnoses.

Secondly,
debugging AI models becomes significantly more manageable. When an AI model produces erroneous or unexpected results, the first step in diagnosing the problem is often to examine the data it was trained on or

the data it is currently processing. With robust lineage tracking, developers can pinpoint the exact data sources and transformations that led to the problematic output. Imagine an AI-powered customer service chatbot suddenly providing nonsensical responses. By examining the lineage, one might discover that an update to the natural language processing (NLP) pipeline, which was intended to improve sentiment analysis, inadvertently corrupted the tokenization process for a specific subset of user queries. This detailed trail allows for targeted fixes rather than broad, potentially disruptive, system-wide adjustments.

Thirdly,
regulatory compliance and auditability are critically dependent on provenance and lineage. Many regulations, such as GDPR, CCPA, and industry-specific mandates like HIPAA, require organizations to demonstrate how personal or sensitive data is collected, processed, and used. Knowing the origin of data and its entire transformation path is essential for proving adherence to privacy policies, consent management, and data minimization principles. For example, if a user requests the deletion of their data under GDPR, an organization must be able to confidently identify and remove all instances of that user's data across all systems and model training sets. Data lineage provides the map to achieve this. Furthermore, in highly regulated fields, audits may require verifiable proof of data integrity and the absence of manipulation. A clear, immutable record of data provenance and lineage serves as this proof.

Fourthly,
ethical AI development and bias mitigation are deeply intertwined with data lineage. Biases in AI systems often originate from biased data. By meticulously tracking the provenance of data used for training, organizations can identify datasets that may have inherent biases due to their collection methods, demographic representation, or historical context. For example, if facial recognition AI exhibits lower accuracy for certain ethnic groups, tracing the lineage of the training data might reveal that it was predominantly sourced from images of individuals of a

particular ethnicity. This understanding allows for proactive measures, such as seeking out more diverse datasets or applying debiasing techniques during data preprocessing, guided by the knowledge of the data's origin and composition.

Finally,
building trust and transparency with stakeholders, including customers, partners, and regulators, requires the ability to explain the origins and journey of data. When AI systems are deployed in sensitive areas like finance, healthcare, or criminal justice, the black box nature of some models can be a source of apprehension. Demonstrating a clear and auditable trail for the data used to train and operate these systems can significantly enhance confidence and acceptance. It shows a commitment to responsible data handling and a willingness to be accountable for the inputs that shape AI behavior.

To effectively implement data provenance and lineage tracking, several key technical and organizational strategies are employed. At the core of these strategies is
metadata management. Metadata, essentially "data about data," is crucial for capturing and storing information about data's origin, characteristics, and transformations. This includes:

Source Metadata: Information about where the data was first generated or acquired. This can include the name of the original system, the date and time of creation, the user or process that created it, and any unique identifiers assigned at the source. For example, for sensor data, this would include sensor ID, location, calibration information, and timestamp of reading.
Transformation Metadata: Details about every operation performed on the data. This includes the type of transformation (e.g., aggregation, filtering, normalization, imputation), the parameters used, the software or script version that performed the transformation, the date and time of the

transformation, and the input and output identifiers for the data. A transformation might be described as "Applied Z-score normalization to feature 'income' using Python script v2.1 on 2023-10-27."
Usage Metadata: Information about how and by whom the data has been accessed or utilized. This includes user IDs, application names, timestamps of access, and the purpose of access. For AI models, this would include which models were trained on specific data versions, and which datasets were used for validation or inference.
Quality Metadata: Details about the data's quality at various stages, including quality metrics, profiling results, and any identified issues.

Effective metadata management is not a passive activity; it requires a structured approach to capture, store, and access this information consistently. This often involves the use of
data catalogs. A data catalog acts as a centralized inventory of an organization's data assets. It goes beyond a simple list by providing rich metadata, including data descriptions, ownership, usage policies, and crucially, data lineage information. When integrated with data processing pipelines, a data catalog can automatically ingest and display lineage details, making it easier for users to discover and understand data.

For example, a data scientist looking for customer demographic data can query the data catalog. The results would not only show available datasets but also present their lineage: where the customer data was initially collected (e.g., CRM system), how it was cleaned and anonymized (e.g., script run by the data engineering team), and which features were engineered for specific AI models. This transparency is invaluable. Modern data catalogs often provide visual representations of data lineage, allowing users to explore data flow through interactive graphs, highlighting dependencies and transformations.

Beyond traditional metadata management and data catalogs, organizations are exploring more advanced techniques for robust provenance and lineage tracking, especially in distributed and dynamic AI environments.

One such approach involves leveraging **log analysis and event-driven architectures**. Every significant action within a data processing system—data ingestion, transformation execution, model training, inference—can be logged as an event. By aggregating and analyzing these logs, a comprehensive picture of data flow and transformations can be reconstructed. Event-driven architectures, where systems communicate through events, naturally lend themselves to lineage tracking, as each event can carry metadata about its origin and context. For instance, an Apache Kafka stream can log messages indicating a new batch of data being processed, along with identifiers linking it to previous stages and subsequent processing jobs.

Another increasingly relevant technology for ensuring immutable and auditable provenance is **blockchain**. While not suitable for tracking every single data point's transformation due to scalability limitations, blockchain can be used to record critical "checkpoints" or hash values of datasets at various stages of their lifecycle. By storing cryptographic hashes of datasets on a blockchain, organizations can create an tamper-evident record of their existence and integrity at specific points in time. Any subsequent modification to the dataset would result in a different hash, making unauthorized alterations immediately detectable.

Consider an AI model being used for financial auditing. The integrity of the financial data used for training and auditing is paramount. A blockchain could be used to record hashes of the raw financial data upon ingestion, after anonymization, after feature engineering, and after the final training dataset is compiled. Auditors could then verify the integrity of the data by comparing the hashes on the blockchain with the hashes of the data they are provided, ensuring that no data has been altered since it was officially recorded. This provides an unprecedented level of assurance for sensitive applications.

Furthermore, specialized **data lineage tools and platforms** are emerging that are specifically designed to automatically capture, visualize, and manage data lineage across complex data ecosystems, including cloud environments and various data processing engines (e.g., Spark, SQL databases, ETL tools). These tools often integrate with data processing frameworks and orchestrators to parse execution logs and query plans, automatically inferring and mapping data flows. They provide sophisticated visualization capabilities, allowing users to trace data from its source to its consumption by AI models, and vice versa. Some platforms also offer lineage-aware impact analysis, helping organizations understand which downstream AI models or reports would be affected by a change in a particular data source or transformation.

The implementation of comprehensive data provenance and lineage tracking is not without its challenges.

One significant challenge is the **complexity and scale of modern data infrastructures**. Organizations often operate with a multitude of data sources, processing engines, and applications, making it difficult to achieve end-to-end lineage coverage. Integrating lineage capture across diverse, heterogeneous systems requires significant effort and often relies on custom connectors or agents.

Another challenge is **performance overhead**. Capturing detailed lineage information for every data operation can introduce performance bottlenecks. Organizations must strike a balance between the granularity of lineage tracking and its impact on processing times, often prioritizing the capture of lineage for critical data assets and transformations.

Cultural and organizational inertia can also be a barrier. Data provenance and lineage are not always seen as a priority by development teams focused on delivering features rapidly. Fostering a culture where data governance, including lineage tracking, is considered an integral part of the development lifecycle requires strong leadership buy-in and continuous education.

Finally, **maintaining the accuracy and completeness of lineage information** over time is an ongoing task. As data pipelines evolve, systems are updated, and new data sources are introduced, lineage tracking mechanisms must be continuously maintained and adapted to reflect these changes. Without proper governance, lineage information can quickly become outdated and unreliable.

Despite these challenges, the benefits of investing in robust data provenance and lineage tracking are substantial and far-reaching. As AI systems become more pervasive and influential, the ability to trust, understand, and control the data that underpins them is no longer a luxury but a necessity. It is the bedrock upon which responsible, ethical, and effective AI is built. By meticulously documenting where data comes from and how it travels, organizations can unlock greater confidence in their AI deployments, navigate complex regulatory landscapes with greater ease, and ultimately, build AI systems that serve humanity reliably and equitably. The investment in these capabilities is an investment in the long-term viability and trustworthiness of an organization's AI initiatives.

The integrity and reliability of any AI system are intrinsically linked to the quality of the data it consumes. Flawed data, tainted by inaccuracies, inconsistencies, or biases, can lead to AI models that are not only ineffective but potentially harmful. This section delves into the critical practices and methodologies for implementing robust data quality assurance and continuous monitoring, ensuring that the data fueling AI decision-making is sound, trustworthy, and fit for purpose.

At the heart of data quality assurance lies
data profiling. This is the process of examining data to understand its structure, content, and the relationships between data elements. Data profiling provides a foundational understanding of a dataset's characteristics, uncovering potential issues before they manifest as problems in AI models. Comprehensive data profiling involves several key activities. Firstly, **statistical analysis** is employed to derive metrics such as mean, median, mode, standard deviation, and range for numerical features. This helps in understanding the distribution of values and identifying extreme outliers. For categorical data, frequency distributions, cardinality (the number of unique values), and the presence of null or empty values are examined. For instance, profiling a customer age dataset might reveal a mean age of 45, but a standard deviation of 20, along with values like 200 or -10, immediately flagging these as anomalies requiring investigation.

Secondly,
data type and format validation ensures that data conforms to expected types (e.g., integers, strings, dates) and formats (e.g., YYYY-MM-DD for dates, specific currency formats). Inconsistent formatting can disrupt data processing pipelines and lead to misinterpretations by AI algorithms. Imagine a dataset intended for financial forecasting where transaction dates are sometimes recorded as "2023-10-27," sometimes as "Oct 27, 2023," and occasionally as "27/10/2023." Without validation, attempting to sort or perform time-series analysis on this data would be impossible or erroneous.

Thirdly,

completeness checks assess the extent to which data is present. This involves identifying missing values across columns and rows and understanding their prevalence. High rates of missing data can significantly reduce the utility of a dataset and may necessitate imputation strategies or, in severe cases, lead to the exclusion of the data altogether. For a predictive maintenance AI, if critical sensor readings for temperature or pressure are missing for a substantial percentage of operational hours, the model's ability to accurately predict equipment failure will be severely compromised.

Fourthly,
uniqueness checks verify that data elements that should be unique, such as primary keys or customer IDs, are indeed unique. Duplicate records can lead to overrepresentation of certain entities or events, skewing analytical results and model training. Profiling a customer database might reveal multiple entries for the same individual due to variations in name spelling or address, requiring a de-duplication process.

Finally,
dependency and relationship analysis explores the logical connections between different data elements. This might involve checking referential integrity in relational databases or identifying unexpected correlations between seemingly unrelated variables in unstructured data. For example, profiling a dataset for an e-commerce AI might reveal an inverse correlation between the number of items added to a cart and the final purchase amount, which could indicate a data entry error or a faulty pricing logic.

Once data has been profiled and its characteristics understood, the next step is to establish
data validation rules. These rules are explicit criteria that data must meet to be considered of acceptable quality for its intended use. They act as automated gatekeepers, flagging or rejecting data that deviates from predefined standards. Developing effective validation rules requires a

deep understanding of the data's domain, the business context, and the requirements of the AI applications.

Validation rules can be categorized into several types. **Format and type rules** are straightforward checks to ensure data adheres to expected data types and formatting conventions, as identified during profiling. For instance, a rule might state that all phone numbers must conform to a specific international format. **Range and value rules** ensure that numerical or categorical data falls within acceptable bounds. For a medical AI, a rule might dictate that a patient's body temperature must be within a physiologically plausible range (e.g., 35°C to 42°C), and any value outside this range would be flagged. Similarly, a categorical feature like "customer segment" might only be allowed to contain predefined values such as "new," "loyal," or "vip."

Consistency rules ensure that related data points do not contradict each other. For example, in a sales dataset, a rule could enforce that the "order*date" must always be before or the same as the "ship*date." If a record violates this rule, it suggests an error in data entry or a flaw in the upstream data capture process. **Uniqueness rules** reinforce the findings from profiling by ensuring that fields designated as unique (like email addresses or product SKUs) do not contain duplicate entries. **Referential integrity rules** are particularly important in relational databases, ensuring that foreign key values in one table correspond to valid primary key values in another table, thereby maintaining the logical structure of the data.

The implementation of these rules can occur at various points in the data lifecycle: during data ingestion, as part of data transformation pipelines, or before data is fed into AI models. When a validation rule is violated, the system can be configured to take different actions: reject the erroneous record, flag it for manual review, or attempt automatic correction if the error is minor and predictable. For instance, a rule enforcing uppercase for a country code could automatically convert "us" to "US" if the country code is otherwise valid.

Beyond predefined rules,
anomaly detection plays a crucial role in identifying unusual patterns or outliers that may not be explicitly covered by validation rules. Anomalies can be indicative of errors, fraud, system malfunctions, or novel events that an AI might need to learn about. Machine learning techniques are often employed for anomaly detection. Unsupervised learning algorithms, such as clustering (e.g., K-Means) or density-based methods (e.g., DBSCAN), can group normal data points together and identify points that fall far outside these clusters as anomalies. For example, in a fraud detection AI, a transaction that is orders of magnitude larger than a user's typical spending pattern, or occurring at an unusual time or location, would be flagged as an anomaly.

Supervised or semi-supervised methods can also be used if historical data containing labeled anomalies is available. Techniques like Isolation Forests or One-Class SVMs are effective in identifying deviations from established normal behavior. For an AI system monitoring industrial equipment, an anomaly might be a sudden spike in vibration or temperature that doesn't correspond to any known operational condition, potentially signaling an impending failure. Detecting such anomalies proactively allows for timely intervention, preventing costly breakdowns and ensuring operational safety.

The dynamic nature of data, especially in real-time AI applications, necessitates
continuous monitoring of data quality. Data quality is not a one-time fix; it's an ongoing process. This involves establishing systems that constantly track key data quality metrics and alert stakeholders when issues arise. This continuous monitoring can be achieved through several mechanisms.

Scheduled data quality checks can be performed at regular intervals (e.g., hourly, daily, weekly) on incoming data streams or existing datasets. These checks execute the predefined validation rules and profiling analyses, generating reports on the data's quality status.

Real-time monitoring is essential for applications requiring immediate data quality insights, such as fraud detection or algorithmic trading. This involves integrating data quality checks directly into the data pipelines, often using streaming analytics platforms. As data flows through the system, quality metrics are calculated and analyzed on the fly. If a metric breaches a predefined threshold—for example, if the percentage of null values in a critical feature exceeds 5%—an alert can be triggered immediately. This allows for rapid response to prevent the propagation of poor-quality data into downstream systems or AI models.

Data quality dashboards are vital for visualizing the results of monitoring efforts. These dashboards provide a centralized, up-to-date view of the data quality landscape, often using color-coding to indicate the severity of issues. Key metrics such as data completeness, accuracy, consistency, and timeliness can be tracked over time, allowing teams to identify trends and assess the effectiveness of their data quality initiatives. A well-designed dashboard can quickly highlight a sudden drop in data accuracy for a specific data source, prompting an investigation into the source system or data ingestion process.

Furthermore,
feedback loops are crucial for addressing data quality issues at their root. When data quality problems are detected, whether through validation rules, anomaly detection, or monitoring, this information should be channeled back to the source systems or processes responsible for data generation or transformation. This feedback loop enables data stewards, engineers, and even business users to understand the impact of

data quality issues and implement corrective actions. For example, if consistent errors are found in customer address data, the feedback loop can inform the team responsible for the customer onboarding portal to improve the address validation mechanisms during data entry.

These corrective actions might involve **data cleansing**, the process of detecting and correcting or removing inaccuracies, inconsistencies, and corrupt data. Cleansing can range from simple tasks like correcting typos and standardizing formats to more complex operations like imputing missing values or resolving conflicting records. **Data enrichment** is another strategy, where missing or incomplete data is supplemented with information from external or internal authoritative sources. For instance, if a customer record is missing demographic information, it could be enriched by linking it to a verified third-party demographic dataset, provided privacy and legal considerations are met.

Addressing data quality issues systematically requires a clear understanding of the **data lifecycle and ownership**. Assigning clear ownership for data domains and datasets ensures accountability for data quality. Data stewards, acting as subject matter experts, play a pivotal role in defining data quality standards, overseeing validation rule development, and managing data quality issue resolution. Their involvement is crucial in bridging the gap between technical data quality metrics and the business context that defines "good quality."

The process of establishing and maintaining high data quality is iterative. It begins with understanding the data (profiling), defining what constitutes good quality (validation rules), identifying deviations (anomaly detection), ensuring continuous adherence (monitoring), and finally, creating mechanisms for improvement (feedback loops and cleansing/enrichment). This multifaceted approach is not merely a technical exercise; it is a fundamental pillar of responsible AI development, ensuring that the insights and decisions derived from AI systems are grounded in truth, fairness, and reliability. Without these rigorous data quality assurance and monitoring practices, AI systems risk perpetuating errors, generating biased outcomes, and undermining the very trust they are intended to build. The investment in robust data quality frameworks is therefore an indispensable component of any organization's AI strategy, safeguarding against the downstream consequences of compromised data and paving the way for AI that truly delivers on its promise.

Ensuring the integrity and trustworthiness of AI systems extends critically to how the data they rely upon is protected throughout its lifecycle. Once data quality is established through rigorous profiling and validation, the next fundamental pillar of robust data governance is the implementation of **Secure Data Storage and Access Control**. This involves safeguarding data against unauthorized access, modification, or deletion, thereby preserving its confidentiality, integrity, and availability. Protecting sensitive information is not merely a technical challenge; it is a prerequisite for maintaining user trust, complying with regulatory mandates, and preventing malicious actors from exploiting vulnerabilities.

At the core of secure data storage lies the concept of **encryption**. Encryption is the process of encoding data into a secret code to prevent unauthorized access. It is a vital layer of defense, transforming readable data into an unintelligible format that can only be deciphered with the correct decryption key. Encryption is applied in two primary contexts: **encryption at rest** and **encryption in transit**.

Encryption at rest refers to the protection of data stored on physical media, such as hard drives, solid-state drives, databases, or cloud storage. When data is encrypted at rest, even if an unauthorized party gains physical access to the storage medium, the data remains unreadable without the decryption key. This is crucial for protecting sensitive information against theft or loss of devices. For instance, a company storing customer personally identifiable information (PII) on its servers must ensure that this data is encrypted. Modern operating systems and database management systems offer robust options for full-disk encryption or transparent data encryption (TDE), which automatically encrypts data as it is written to disk and decrypts it upon retrieval, with minimal impact on performance. Cloud providers also offer encryption services for data stored in their object storage, block storage, and databases, often managed through key management services (KMS) that allow organizations to control their own encryption keys. The choice of encryption algorithms is critical; industry-standard algorithms like AES (Advanced Encryption Standard) with key lengths of 128, 192, or 256 bits are widely recommended for their strong security and proven track record. The management of encryption keys is equally paramount. Compromised keys render the encryption useless, so robust key management practices, including secure generation, storage, rotation, and destruction of keys, are essential. Hardware Security Modules (HSMs) are often employed to provide a dedicated, tamper-resistant hardware device for securely storing and managing cryptographic keys.

Encryption in transit protects data as it moves across networks, whether it be between an application and a database, between different microservices, or between a user and a web server. Without encryption in transit, data can be intercepted and read by malicious actors monitoring network traffic, a technique known as a "man-in-the-middle" attack. Secure communication protocols, such as TLS/SSL (Transport Layer Security/Secure Sockets Layer), are the standard for encrypting data in transit. When you see "https" in your browser's address bar, it signifies that the connection between your browser and the website is secured using TLS/SSL. This protocol ensures that any data exchanged, such as login credentials or payment information, is encrypted before it leaves your device and decrypted only upon reaching its intended destination. In enterprise environments, ensuring that all internal and external network communications are encrypted is a fundamental security practice. This includes encrypting database connections, API calls, and file transfers. For example, when an AI model running on a cloud server needs to access data from a data lake also hosted in the cloud, the connection between the model and the data lake must be encrypted using TLS. Similarly, if sensitive data is being streamed to an AI model for real-time analysis, the streaming channel should be secured with encryption. The implementation of strong cipher suites and up-to-date TLS versions is critical to prevent vulnerabilities associated with older or weaker encryption configurations.

Beyond the technical measures of encryption, a robust data governance framework mandates stringent
Access Control Mechanisms. These mechanisms dictate who can access what data, under what circumstances, and with what permissions. The goal is to ensure that access is granted on a "need-to-know" basis, minimizing the attack surface and the potential for misuse or accidental exposure of sensitive information. Two primary models for access control are widely adopted: Role-Based Access Control (RBAC) and Attribute-Based Access Control (ABAC).

Role-Based Access Control (RBAC) simplifies access management by assigning permissions to roles rather than directly to individual users. Users are then assigned to one or more roles, inheriting the permissions associated with those roles. This hierarchical approach streamlines administration, especially in large organizations with many users and resources. For instance, in an organization developing an AI for medical diagnostics, roles could be defined such as "Data Scientist," "AI Engineer," "Medical Reviewer," and "Administrator." The "Data Scientist" role might have read and write access to anonymized patient datasets for model training, while the "Medical Reviewer" role would have read-only access to specific patient records for validation purposes. An "Administrator" role would have broad permissions to manage users, roles, and system configurations. RBAC is effective for managing access to common datasets and functionalities where permissions can be logically grouped. However, it can become complex to manage in highly dynamic environments or when granular, context-specific access is required, potentially leading to "role explosion" where the number of roles becomes unwieldy.

A more sophisticated and flexible approach is **Attribute-Based Access Control (ABAC)**. ABAC grants access based on a set of attributes associated with the user, the resource, and the environment. These attributes can be anything from user roles, departments, security clearances, and project assignments to resource sensitivity levels, data classifications, time of day, geographical location, and device security posture. ABAC allows for highly dynamic and context-aware access decisions. For example, an ABAC policy might state that a user can access patient X-ray images (the resource) only if they are a "Radiologist" (user attribute), the images are from a specific hospital network (environment attribute), and the access attempt occurs during working hours (environment attribute). Furthermore, the policy could specify that access is only permitted for diagnostic purposes (action attribute) and that the data cannot be downloaded (access type attribute). This level of granularity is particularly valuable when dealing with highly sensitive data or when compliance regulations require fine-grained control. ABAC systems typically rely on policies written in a declarative language, which are evaluated in real-time when an access request is made. While ABAC offers superior flexibility and expressiveness, it can also be more complex to design, implement, and manage due to the multitude of attributes and policies involved. Organizations often use a hybrid approach, combining RBAC for broad access controls and ABAC for more specific, context-dependent permissions.

To effectively implement and manage secure data storage and access control, establishing

secure data environments is crucial. This involves creating a controlled and isolated space where sensitive data is stored and processed, minimizing the risk of external compromise. For AI development, this often translates to utilizing secure cloud environments or on-premises data centers that are hardened against threats. These environments incorporate multiple layers of security, including network segmentation, firewalls, intrusion detection and prevention systems (IDPS), and secure configuration management. For instance, data used for training AI models might be stored in an isolated virtual private cloud (VPC) or a dedicated network segment within an on-premises data center, with access strictly controlled and monitored. Sensitive data might be further segregated within this environment, with different datasets residing in different storage tiers or access zones, each with its own set of security controls. The principle of least privilege is fundamental here: systems and users should only be granted the minimum level of access necessary to perform their intended functions.

Finally, a critical component of any robust security posture is **Auditing Access Logs**. Auditing is the process of systematically examining records to determine whether they are accurate, complete, and authorized. In the context of data security, this means meticulously recording and reviewing all access attempts, data modifications, and system activities related to sensitive data. Secure access logs provide an invaluable trail of who did what, when, and where. These logs are essential for several reasons. Firstly, they serve as a deterrent against unauthorized access, as individuals are aware that their actions are being recorded. Secondly, they are crucial for detecting and investigating security incidents. If a data breach occurs, access logs can help investigators determine the scope of the breach, identify the compromised data, and understand the methods used by attackers. For example, by analyzing logs, an organization might discover that an unauthorized user repeatedly attempted to access a particular dataset outside of business hours, or that a specific user account was used to exfiltrate a large volume of data.

Effective auditing requires more than just collecting logs; it demands proper management and analysis. Logs should be collected from all relevant sources, including operating systems, databases, applications, and network devices. They should be stored securely, protected against tampering, and retained for a sufficient period to comply with legal and regulatory requirements. Automated tools for log analysis and anomaly detection can help sift through vast amounts of log data to identify suspicious patterns or events that might indicate a security threat. Regularly reviewing these logs, either manually or through automated systems, is a proactive measure that can help identify and address security vulnerabilities before they are exploited. Establishing clear policies and procedures for log review, incident response, and evidence preservation is also vital. By diligently implementing secure data storage solutions, granular access control mechanisms, secure environments, and comprehensive auditing, organizations can build a strong foundation for protecting their valuable data assets, thereby fostering trust and enabling the responsible development and deployment of AI technologies. This multilayered approach is not a one-time setup but an ongoing commitment to vigilance and adaptation in the face of evolving threats.

The journey of data within an AI system, and indeed any digital ecosystem, is not a static one. It is a dynamic process that necessitates meticulous management from its inception through to its eventual cessation. Building upon the foundational principles of secure storage and access control, the subsequent, indispensable stages of data governance revolve around defining and implementing robust **Data Retention, Archiving, and Deletion Policies**. These policies are not mere administrative formalities; they are strategic imperatives that dictate the lifespan of data, ensuring compliance with a complex web of legal mandates, aligning with evolving business objectives, and upholding fundamental privacy principles. Failing to establish and adhere to these policies can expose an organization to significant legal liabilities, operational inefficiencies, and reputational damage.

At the heart of this lifecycle management lies the concept of **Data Retention**. This refers to the defined period for which data is kept active and accessible within operational systems. Establishing appropriate retention periods requires a delicate balance. On one hand, retaining data for too short a period can hinder future analysis, model retraining, or regulatory audits, leading to lost opportunities or compliance failures. Conversely, retaining data for excessively long durations incurs escalating storage costs, increases the attack surface for potential data breaches, and can lead to the accumulation of outdated, irrelevant, or even legally encumbered information. The process of defining these periods must be informed by a comprehensive understanding of the data's purpose, its potential future utility, and, critically, legal and regulatory obligations. For instance, financial transaction data might be subject to specific legal retention requirements for several years to comply with auditing and fraud detection mandates. Similarly, employee data often has defined retention periods post-employment, dictated by labor laws and contractual agreements.

A crucial element in defining retention policies is the consultation with legal counsel and relevant compliance officers. Regulatory frameworks such as the General Data Protection Regulation (GDPR) in Europe, the California Consumer Privacy Act (CCPA) in the United States, and industry-specific regulations like HIPAA (Health Insurance Portability and Accountability Act) for healthcare data, often prescribe minimum or maximum retention periods for certain types of personal information. These regulations emphasize data minimization, advocating for the deletion of data once it is no longer necessary for the purpose for which it was collected. Therefore, a well-defined retention policy will map data types to their permissible retention durations, considering both business value and legal compliance. For AI systems, this is particularly pertinent. Models trained on historical data may require access to that data for a specified period to enable auditing of model decisions, to understand shifts in data patterns over time, or to facilitate the retraining and improvement of the model with updated information. The policy should clearly articulate what data is retained, where it is stored, and for how long, with automated mechanisms to flag or initiate deletion processes as these periods approach.

Beyond active operational use, organizations frequently need to preserve historical data for extended periods. This is where
Data Archiving becomes paramount. Archiving involves the process of moving data from active, high-performance storage systems to a separate, lower-cost, long-term storage solution. Archived data is typically less frequently accessed than operational data but remains important for various strategic reasons, including legal discovery, historical analysis, compliance auditing, and potential future model retraining if unforeseen needs arise. The key distinction between archiving and simple backup is purpose. Backups are primarily for disaster recovery and restoring systems to a previous state, while archives are designed for long-term preservation and retrieval of specific historical records.

When designing archiving strategies, several factors must be considered. Firstly, the
format and integrity of archived data are critical. Data must be stored in a format that is accessible and readable for the foreseeable future, often requiring migration to newer storage formats over time as technology evolves. Tools and techniques should be employed to ensure that the integrity of the archived data is maintained, preventing corruption or loss. This might involve checksums, digital signatures, or periodic integrity checks. Secondly, **accessibility and retrieval** mechanisms for archived data are essential. While archived data is not accessed daily, there must be a clear, documented process for retrieving specific datasets when required. This process should be efficient enough to meet potential legal discovery deadlines or business analysis needs, without incurring prohibitive costs or delays. For AI applications, archived datasets can be invaluable. Imagine an AI system used for fraud detection that was

deployed five years ago. If a legal dispute arises concerning a transaction from that period, the archived data used to train and operate that model might be crucial for establishing the model's decision-making process. Furthermore, if the organization wishes to understand how the fraud landscape has evolved, accessing historical datasets from archives can provide invaluable insights for retraining or developing new detection models.

The selection of archiving solutions is also a strategic decision. This can range from tape libraries and specialized archival storage appliances to cloud-based archival services like Amazon S3 Glacier, Google Cloud Archive Storage, or Azure Archive Storage. These cloud solutions offer significant advantages in terms of scalability, cost-effectiveness, and durability, though they necessitate careful consideration of retrieval times and costs, which can be higher than for operational storage. The policy should specify the criteria for what data qualifies for archiving, the chosen archival technology, the expected duration of archival, and the procedures for accessing and retrieving archived data. It is also vital to ensure that archived data remains subject to appropriate security controls, even though it is less actively accessed. This includes encryption and access logging, to prevent unauthorized access to potentially sensitive historical information.

Perhaps the most sensitive and legally fraught aspect of data lifecycle management is
Data Deletion. This refers to the permanent and irreversible removal of data from all systems, archives, and backups. In an era increasingly defined by privacy regulations and the imperative to minimize risk, defensible data deletion is not an optional extra; it is a fundamental requirement. The concept of "defensible deletion" implies that an organization can demonstrate, with clear evidence, that data has been deleted in accordance with its policies and legal obligations. This is particularly important in legal discovery processes, where parties may

need to certify that all relevant data has been preserved or, conversely, that data subject to deletion requests has been appropriately purged.

Implementing effective deletion policies requires a multi-pronged approach. Firstly, data should be deleted as soon as it is no longer necessary for its intended purpose or for legal/regulatory compliance. This aligns with the principle of data minimization and reduces the potential for exposure. Secondly, a clear understanding of where all copies of the data reside is essential. Data often exists in multiple locations: production databases, backups, archives, logs, temporary files, and even end-user devices. A comprehensive deletion policy must account for all these locations. For instance, simply deleting a record from a production database does not remove it from historical backups or transaction logs. A robust data governance framework will include procedures for identifying and purging data from all relevant repositories.

For AI systems, this can be particularly challenging. Models themselves can be considered data, and their components, such as trained weights and parameters, may need to be deleted if they were trained on data that is subject to a deletion request. Furthermore, training datasets, intermediate data artifacts, and model outputs all fall under the purview of deletion policies. The policy should define the triggers for deletion – for example, the expiration of a retention period, a specific user request (under regulations like GDPR's "right to erasure"), or a legal mandate. It should also specify the methods of deletion. For digital data, this typically involves overwriting data with random patterns or cryptographic erasure, rendering the original data irrecoverable. For physical media, it involves secure shredding or degaussing.

A critical aspect of defensible deletion is maintaining **auditable records** of the deletion process. When data is deleted, a record should be created documenting what was deleted, when, by whom, and using what method. This audit trail is crucial for demonstrating compliance during legal proceedings or regulatory audits. For example, if an individual requests the deletion of their personal data, the organization must be able to provide proof that this request was fulfilled, specifying the data that was purged and confirming its irreversible removal. In the context of AI, if a user requests their data be deleted, any data used to train a model that is directly attributable to that user must also be purged. This can be a complex technical challenge if the data has been deeply integrated into the model's parameters, potentially requiring model retraining or careful data anonymization techniques. The policy must therefore address these nuances and establish clear procedures for handling such requests.

Integrating these three pillars – retention, archiving, and deletion – into a cohesive data governance strategy is essential. This integration ensures that data is managed proactively throughout its entire lifecycle, minimizing risks, maximizing value, and maintaining trust. A well-defined policy framework, supported by appropriate technology and clear operational procedures, transforms data management from a reactive necessity into a strategic advantage. The ongoing evolution of AI, coupled with increasingly stringent global data privacy regulations, makes these lifecycle management policies not just a best practice, but an absolute requirement for any organization aiming to operate responsibly and sustainably in the digital age. Organizations must invest in the tools and expertise necessary to implement and maintain these policies, recognizing that robust data governance, encompassing retention, archiving, and deletion, is a continuous process of vigilance, adaptation, and demonstrable accountability. This systematic approach safeguards the organization, its users, and the integrity of the AI systems it deploys.

Chapter 7: Navigating Standards and Compliance

The expansive landscape of Artificial Intelligence (AI), while brimming with transformative potential, also presents a complex web of challenges concerning its responsible development, deployment, and societal integration. As AI systems become increasingly sophisticated and pervasive, the need for a shared understanding, common methodologies, and agreed-upon benchmarks becomes not just desirable, but critical. This is where the role of **standards and best practices** emerges as a cornerstone for effective AI governance. Standards act as the essential scaffolding upon which robust AI ecosystems can be built, fostering consistency, predictability, and a baseline level of trustworthiness across diverse applications and organizations.

At their core, standards are formalized agreements that specify requirements, guidelines, or characteristics for products, processes, or services. In the context of AI, these standards aim to address a myriad of concerns, ranging from the technical underpinnings of AI models to their ethical implications and societal impact. One of the most significant contributions of standards is their ability to foster **interoperability**. AI systems rarely operate in isolation. They are often integrated into larger software architectures, interact with other AI components, or exchange data with various platforms. Without standardized protocols, data formats, and API specifications, achieving seamless integration would be a Herculean task, leading to fragmented ecosystems and inhibited innovation. Imagine different AI models developed by disparate teams or organizations; if they cannot communicate effectively due to proprietary or incompatible data structures and communication methods, the potential for synergistic advancements is severely curtailed. Standards provide a common language, enabling different AI components to understand and process information from one another, thereby accelerating the development of complex, interconnected AI solutions. For instance, standards for data labeling, feature representation, or model exchange formats can dramatically simplify the process of sharing and integrating AI models, allowing for quicker iteration and broader application of AI technologies.

Beyond technical interoperability, standards play a vital role in establishing **benchmarks for quality and safety**. Developing AI systems that are reliable, robust, and secure is paramount, especially in safety-critical applications such as autonomous vehicles, medical diagnostics, or financial fraud detection. Standards can define acceptable levels of performance, accuracy, and resilience against adversarial attacks or unexpected inputs. They can also outline best practices for rigorous testing, validation, and verification processes. For example, a standard might specify the types of testing that an AI system must undergo before being deployed in a healthcare setting, such as evaluating its diagnostic accuracy against diverse patient populations or its robustness to noisy sensor data. Similarly, standards can address the security of AI models themselves, defining requirements for protecting them from intellectual property theft, tampering, or data poisoning. By providing clear, measurable criteria, standards empower developers to build better AI and enable regulators and end-users to assess the quality and safety of AI systems with a greater degree of confidence. This, in turn, contributes to the responsible adoption of AI technologies, mitigating the risks associated with deploying unproven or inadequately tested systems.

Furthermore, standards are instrumental in **building public trust and fostering societal acceptance of AI**. As AI systems become more autonomous and make decisions that affect individuals' lives, public apprehension is a natural consequence. Concerns about bias, fairness, transparency, accountability, and potential misuse can erode confidence. Standards that promote ethical AI development, such as those addressing fairness in algorithmic decision-making, explainability of AI outputs, or privacy-preserving AI techniques, can help alleviate these anxieties. When an AI system is developed in adherence to recognized ethical standards, it signals a commitment to responsible innovation. For example, standards related to bias mitigation can provide developers with methodologies to identify and correct for discriminatory patterns in training data or model outputs. Similarly, standards for AI explainability can guide the development of techniques that make AI decision-making processes more understandable to humans, enabling scrutiny and recourse. This transparency and commitment to ethical principles are crucial for gaining and maintaining public trust, which is essential for the widespread and beneficial integration of AI into society. Without such trust, the full potential of AI may remain unrealized due to societal resistance or regulatory hurdles.

The development of AI standards is a dynamic and evolving process, reflecting the rapid pace of AI research and its diverse applications. International bodies, national standardization organizations, and industry consortia are all actively engaged in this endeavor. Organizations like the International Organization for Standardization (ISO) and the International Electrotechnical Commission (IEC) are working on broad AI standards that cover areas such as terminology, risk management, and AI lifecycle processes. National bodies, such as the National Institute of Standards and Technology (NIST) in the United States, are developing frameworks and guidelines for AI risk management and trustworthy AI. Industry groups and open-source communities are also playing a crucial rolc by developing practical standards and best practices for specific AI technologies and applications. For instance, consortia focused on areas like natural language processing or computer vision may establish standards for benchmark datasets or model evaluation metrics.

However, the current landscape of AI standards is not without its limitations. One significant challenge is the **nascent stage of many AI technologies**. AI is a rapidly evolving field, and formal standards often lag behind the cutting edge of innovation. By the time a standard is developed and ratified, the technology it aims to govern may have already advanced, rendering the standard outdated or incomplete. This necessitates a continuous and agile approach to standardization, requiring regular updates and the development of flexible frameworks that can adapt to emerging AI capabilities.

Another challenge lies in the
inherent complexity and multifaceted nature of AI. AI systems are not monolithic entities; they encompass a wide range of technologies, algorithms, and applications, each with its unique set of challenges and ethical considerations. Developing a one-size-fits-all standard for all AI is therefore impractical. Instead, a more nuanced approach is required, with standards tailored to specific AI domains, use cases, or risk levels. This means that a standard for an AI system used in entertainment recommendation engines might differ significantly from one designed for autonomous weapon systems, reflecting the vastly different potential impacts and safety requirements. This also leads to the challenge of **fragmentation and potential conflicts** between standards developed by different bodies. Without effective coordination, the proliferation of diverse and potentially conflicting standards could create confusion for developers and hinder global interoperability.

The
difficulty in standardizing abstract concepts like "fairness" or "explainability" is also a considerable hurdle. These concepts are often subjective, context-dependent, and can be interpreted differently across cultures and ethical frameworks. While standards can provide methodologies for measuring and mitigating bias, or for generating explanations, achieving universal consensus on what constitutes "fair" or "explainable" AI remains a complex undertaking. This often necessitates the development of principles and guidelines rather than prescriptive, rigid rules.

Furthermore, the
enforcement and adoption of AI standards present their own set of challenges. Standards are often voluntary, and their effectiveness depends

on widespread adoption by industry stakeholders. Encouraging compliance, particularly for smaller organizations or those operating in less regulated sectors, can be difficult. Regulatory bodies play a crucial role in driving the adoption of standards, often by referencing them in legislation or mandating their use for certain applications. However, the regulatory landscape for AI is still developing, and the mechanisms for ensuring compliance are not yet fully established globally.

In response to these challenges, ongoing efforts are focused on developing more comprehensive and adaptive AI standards. There is a growing recognition of the need for
risk-based approaches to AI standardization, where the stringency and scope of standards are proportional to the potential risks posed by an AI system. This involves categorizing AI systems based on their intended use, potential impact, and the level of autonomy they possess, and then applying appropriate sets of standards accordingly. Frameworks like NIST's AI Risk Management Framework are examples of this trend, offering a flexible approach to identifying, assessing, and managing AI risks.

There is also a significant push towards developing standards that address the
entire AI lifecycle, from data collection and model training to deployment, monitoring, and decommissioning. This holistic approach ensures that considerations for quality, safety, fairness, and transparency are integrated at every stage of AI development and operation, rather than being an afterthought. Standards related to MLOps (Machine Learning Operations), for instance, are emerging to provide best practices for managing the deployment and ongoing operation of machine learning models.

Moreover, there is increasing emphasis on fostering
international collaboration and harmonization of AI standards. Organizations like ISO/IEC and regional bodies are working to align their

efforts and develop globally recognized standards that can facilitate cross-border trade and innovation. This also involves engaging a diverse range of stakeholders, including researchers, industry practitioners, policymakers, and civil society representatives, to ensure that standards reflect a broad spectrum of perspectives and concerns.

The development of standards specifically for **responsible and ethical AI** is also a priority. This includes work on standards for AI ethics frameworks, bias detection and mitigation, explainable AI (XAI), privacy-preserving AI, and AI security. These efforts aim to translate ethical principles into practical, implementable guidelines and technical specifications, making it easier for organizations to build AI systems that are not only functional but also trustworthy and aligned with societal values. For example, efforts are underway to develop standards for auditing AI systems for bias, or for documenting the data used to train AI models to ensure transparency.

The integration of AI standards into broader regulatory frameworks is also a key area of development. As governments grapple with how to regulate AI, many are looking to existing and emerging standards as a foundation for policy. This can help to ensure that regulations are technically feasible, adaptable, and aligned with international best practices. The European Union's AI Act, for example, references the importance of standards in defining requirements for certain categories of AI systems.

In conclusion, standards and best practices are indispensable tools for navigating the complex landscape of AI governance. They provide the essential common ground for interoperability, establish vital benchmarks for quality and safety, and are critical for building the public trust necessary for AI's widespread and beneficial integration. While the challenges of standardizing such a rapidly evolving and multifaceted technology are significant, ongoing efforts towards risk-based approaches, lifecycle coverage, international collaboration, and a focus on ethical AI are paving the way for a more robust and trustworthy AI ecosystem. The continuous evolution and adoption of these standards will be a defining factor in our ability to harness the transformative power of AI responsibly and equitably.

The burgeoning field of Artificial Intelligence, while offering unparalleled opportunities for innovation and societal advancement, also necessitates a robust structure of governance. This structure is increasingly being built upon a foundation of standards and frameworks that aim to guide the development, deployment, and ethical considerations of AI systems. These benchmarks are not merely technical specifications; they represent a collective effort to ensure AI is developed and used in ways that are safe, reliable, fair, and beneficial to humanity. Navigating this evolving landscape requires an understanding of the key standards and frameworks that are shaping the AI ecosystem.

Among the most significant contributors to AI standardization is the **International Organization for Standardization (ISO)**, often in conjunction with the **International Electrotechnical Commission (IEC)**. These bodies are at the forefront of developing a comprehensive suite of standards that span the entire AI lifecycle. For instance, the **ISO/IEC JTC 1/SC 42** committee is dedicated to Artificial Intelligence, and its work is foundational. This subcommittee is actively producing standards that address fundamental aspects of AI, such as terminology and concepts, to ensure a common language across different regions and industries. Beyond establishing a shared vocabulary, they are developing standards for AI risk management, outlining processes for identifying, assessing, and mitigating risks associated with AI systems throughout their lifecycle. This includes considerations for data quality, model robustness, and the potential for unintended consequences. Furthermore, SC 42 is addressing the critical need for standards related to AI trustworthiness, encompassing areas like AI governance, ethical considerations, and the assurance of AI systems. The objective is to provide organizations with a structured approach to building and deploying AI systems that are not only functional but also inherently trustworthy, fostering confidence among users and regulators alike. These ISO/IEC standards aim to create a global consensus on best practices, facilitating international trade and collaboration in AI technologies. Their broad scope means they are intended to be applicable across a wide range of AI applications, from foundational AI research to specific AI applications in various sectors.

Another crucial development in the realm of AI governance is the **National Institute of Standards and Technology (NIST) AI Risk Management Framework**. Developed in the United States, this framework offers a flexible and adaptable approach to managing the risks associated with AI. Unlike prescriptive standards that might dictate specific technical solutions, the NIST framework provides a structured process for organizations to identify, assess, manage, and govern AI risks. It is designed to be sector-agnostic, meaning it can be applied by organizations of all sizes and across various industries. The framework is built around four core functions: Govern, Map, Measure, and Manage. The "Govern" function emphasizes establishing a culture of AI risk management, with clear roles, responsibilities, and policies. "Map" involves understanding the AI systems in use, their context, and their potential impacts. "Measure" focuses on analyzing and assessing AI risks, including technical performance, bias, and security vulnerabilities. Finally, "Manage" is about implementing processes to mitigate and respond to identified risks. A key strength of the NIST framework is its emphasis on a socio-technical approach, recognizing that AI risks arise not only from technical limitations but also from human factors, organizational processes, and societal contexts. It encourages continuous improvement and adaptation, acknowledging that the AI landscape is constantly evolving. The framework also promotes transparency by encouraging organizations to document their AI systems and their risk management practices, fostering accountability and enabling external scrutiny. Its voluntary nature allows organizations to adopt it at their own pace, integrating it into their existing risk management practices rather than imposing entirely new systems. The NIST AI Risk Management Framework is a testament to the ongoing effort to translate ethical principles and safety concerns into actionable guidance for practitioners.

The
Institute of Electrical and Electronics Engineers (IEEE) is another significant player in the development of AI standards and best practices. IEEE, a global organization with a vast network of members, is actively engaged in creating standards that address various aspects of AI, from ethical considerations to technical performance and safety. Their initiatives often focus on specific technical domains and practical implementation. For example, IEEE has been instrumental in developing standards related to machine learning, data ethics, and AI for specific applications such as autonomous systems. One notable effort is the **IEEE P7000™ series**, which focuses on ethical considerations in the design of autonomous systems. This series aims to provide guidance on how to build systems that are transparent, fair, and accountable, addressing issues such as algorithmic bias, privacy, and the impact of AI on society. IEEE's approach often involves extensive stakeholder engagement, bringing together researchers, engineers, policymakers, and ethicists to ensure that standards are comprehensive and widely applicable. They also emphasize the importance of education and awareness, recognizing that effective AI governance requires not only robust standards but also a skilled workforce capable of implementing them. IEEE's work often complements that of ISO/IEC by delving into more specific technical details and practical applications, providing developers with actionable guidance for building responsible AI. Their focus on the IEEE Standards Association (IEEE SA) ensures a structured process for developing and publishing these important benchmarks.

Beyond these overarching bodies, various industry consortia, research institutions, and national agencies are contributing to the development of AI standards and frameworks. For instance, the

Partnership on AI (PAI), a multi-stakeholder organization, brings together companies, academics, and civil society organizations to develop best practices and recommendations for responsible AI. PAI's work often focuses on specific use cases and societal impacts, providing practical guidance for companies on topics such as fairness, transparency, and safety. Their reports and frameworks serve as valuable resources for organizations grappling with the real-world implications of AI.

In the domain of AI safety and reliability, efforts are also underway to develop standards for
AI testing and validation. This includes developing methodologies and metrics for assessing the performance, robustness, and security of AI models. For example, standards may specify requirements for adversarial testing, which involves evaluating how AI systems perform when subjected to malicious or unexpected inputs. Similarly, standards are being developed for **AI explainability (XAI)**, aiming to provide methods for understanding how AI models make decisions. This is crucial for building trust and enabling accountability, particularly in high-stakes applications. Standards in this area often focus on the types of explanations required, the target audience for these explanations, and the technical methods that can be used to generate them.

The development of standards for
AI lifecycle management is also a growing area of focus. This recognizes that responsible AI development and deployment extend beyond the initial training of a model. Standards are emerging to address best practices for data management, model versioning, deployment, monitoring, and even the decommissioning of AI systems. This holistic approach, often referred to as MLOps (Machine Learning Operations), aims to ensure that AI systems are managed effectively and responsibly throughout their entire existence. This includes aspects like ensuring data privacy and security at each stage, managing model drift, and having mechanisms for auditing and retraining models as needed.

The importance of these standards and frameworks cannot be overstated. They provide organizations with a roadmap for navigating the complex ethical and technical challenges of AI. By adhering to these benchmarks, companies can:

Enhance Trust and Credibility: Demonstrating a commitment to recognized standards signals to customers, partners, and regulators that an organization is serious about responsible AI development and deployment. This can build significant trust and enhance brand reputation.
Mitigate Risks: Standards provide systematic approaches to identifying and mitigating potential risks, such as bias, security vulnerabilities, and performance issues. This proactive approach can prevent costly mistakes, legal liabilities, and reputational damage.
Improve Interoperability and Efficiency: Standardized approaches to data formats, APIs, and model development can improve interoperability between different AI systems and components, leading to more efficient development cycles and easier integration into existing infrastructure.
Facilitate Compliance: As regulatory landscapes for AI continue to evolve, adherence to established standards can help organizations meet compliance requirements and avoid penalties. Standards often serve as a basis for future regulations.
Drive Innovation: By providing a common ground and clear guidelines, standards can free up resources that would otherwise be spent on reinventing basic safety and ethical considerations. This allows teams to focus on more innovative aspects of AI development.
Promote Ethical AI Practices: Standards that emphasize fairness, transparency, and accountability embed ethical considerations into the AI development process, helping to ensure that AI systems are aligned with societal values and human rights.

In conclusion, the landscape of AI standards and frameworks is diverse and rapidly evolving. From the comprehensive, lifecycle-oriented standards from ISO/IEC to the flexible, risk-management-focused approach of NIST, and the practical, ethically-driven guidance from IEEE and other organizations, there is a growing ecosystem of resources available. Understanding and engaging with these key standards and frameworks is no longer optional for organizations involved in AI; it is a fundamental requirement for responsible innovation, risk mitigation, and building a future where AI serves humanity effectively and equitably. These benchmarks are not static pronouncements but living guides that are continually updated to reflect the dynamic nature of AI technology and its societal implications.

The adoption of standards and frameworks, as discussed previously, lays the groundwork for responsible AI development and deployment. However, simply adhering to these guidelines is often insufficient to instil the necessary confidence in the safety, reliability, and ethical integrity of AI systems. This is where certification and assurance mechanisms come into play, serving as crucial tools for verifying compliance and providing tangible evidence of due diligence. These mechanisms act as a stamp of approval, signaling to stakeholders—be they end-users, regulators, or business partners—that an AI system has undergone rigorous evaluation and meets predefined benchmarks.

Certification, in essence, is a formal process by which an independent body attests that a product, system, or service conforms to specific standards or requirements. For AI, this translates into evaluating whether an AI model, its underlying data, or its operational environment meets established criteria for aspects such as fairness, robustness, security, privacy, and explainability. The landscape of AI certification is still in its nascent stages, but several models and approaches are emerging. One prominent model involves third-party certification, where specialized organizations, accredited for their expertise in AI and related domains, conduct assessments. These auditors play a critical role in providing an unbiased evaluation, free from the potential conflicts of interest that might arise if a developer self-certified their own systems. The process typically involves a detailed review of documentation, testing of the AI system under various conditions, and an examination of the development and deployment lifecycle.

There are various forms of certification that can be envisioned for AI. We might see product-specific certifications, where a particular AI-powered application (e.g., a medical diagnostic tool or an autonomous vehicle control system) is certified for its safety and performance. Alternatively, there could be process-based certifications, focusing on the methodologies and governance structures employed by organizations in developing and managing their AI systems, aligning with frameworks like the NIST AI Risk Management Framework. Furthermore, we could anticipate data-centric certifications, verifying the quality, provenance, and ethical handling of the data used to train AI models, which is a critical component of AI trustworthiness. The development of these certification schemes requires careful consideration of the specific risks and benefits associated with different AI applications. A certification for an AI system used in a low-stakes environment, such as a content recommendation engine, would naturally differ in its rigor and scope from one intended for a high-stakes application like clinical decision support or critical infrastructure management.

The role of third-party auditors is paramount in establishing credible assurance. These auditors must possess a deep understanding of AI technologies, statistical methods, ethical principles, and relevant regulatory requirements. Their expertise allows them to go beyond superficial checks and perform in-depth analyses to identify potential flaws or vulnerabilities that might not be apparent to the developers themselves. This might involve conducting penetration testing on AI systems to identify security weaknesses, performing bias audits to detect and quantify unfair treatment of different demographic groups, or stress-testing models to assess their resilience to unexpected or adversarial inputs. The methodologies employed by these auditors are crucial. They need to be robust, reproducible, and adaptable to the rapidly evolving nature of AI. This often means drawing upon a combination of established auditing practices from other fields and developing novel techniques specifically tailored for AI. For instance, techniques for verifying the explainability of deep learning models, which are notoriously opaque, are a subject of ongoing research and development within the auditing community.

Assurance mechanisms extend beyond formal certification to encompass a broader spectrum of activities that provide confidence in AI systems. This includes mechanisms like conformity assessments, where organizations demonstrate that their AI systems meet specified requirements, often through self-declaration supported by evidence, or through market surveillance by regulatory bodies. Another important aspect is the development of standardized testing protocols and benchmarks. These provide a common ground for evaluating AI performance across different systems and organizations, enabling comparative analysis and fostering a competitive environment for AI safety and reliability. For example, initiatives to create standardized datasets and evaluation metrics for specific AI tasks, such as image recognition or natural language understanding, help in objectively assessing the progress and maturity of AI models.

However, the verification of complex AI behaviors presents significant challenges. Unlike traditional software, where behavior can often be exhaustively tested, the emergent and often unpredictable nature of AI, particularly machine learning models, makes complete verification exceptionally difficult. AI systems can learn and adapt, meaning their behavior can change over time in response to new data, making static certifications potentially obsolete. This necessitates continuous monitoring and re-evaluation. The problem of "brittleness" in AI, where systems perform well within their training data distribution but fail catastrophically when encountering out-of-distribution data, is a prime example of a challenge that standard testing might miss. Auditors must therefore employ sophisticated methods to probe the boundaries of an AI's operational domain and assess its graceful degradation or failure modes.

Furthermore, the complexity of AI models, especially deep neural networks, can make it challenging to provide clear and comprehensive explanations for their decisions. While explainability is a key tenet of trustworthy AI, certifying the "explainability" of a system is not straightforward. What constitutes a sufficient explanation can vary greatly depending on the context and the audience. For a user interacting with a chatbot, a simple, human-readable explanation might suffice. For a regulator auditing a financial AI system, a more detailed, technical audit trail might be required. Developing standards and certification processes that can accommodate these varying needs is an ongoing endeavor.

Another significant hurdle is the potential for "gaming" the certification process. As with any system that can be audited, there is a risk that developers might optimize their AI systems not for genuine safety and ethical compliance, but for passing specific certification tests. This highlights the need for dynamic, adaptive, and comprehensive assurance mechanisms that are difficult to circumvent. This could involve incorporating techniques that test for robustness against adversarial attacks designed to trick the AI into failing, or requiring evidence of ongoing monitoring and incident response capabilities. The concept of "assurance cases," which are structured arguments supported by evidence to demonstrate that a system is acceptably safe for a specific purpose, is gaining traction as a more holistic approach to AI assurance. These cases aim to build a compelling narrative of safety, encompassing design, testing, operational data, and risk management.

The ethical dimension of AI assurance is equally critical. Certifying that an AI system is "fair" or "unbiased" is fraught with complexity, as defining and measuring these concepts can be context-dependent and involve trade-offs. Different notions of fairness (e.g., demographic parity, equalized odds, predictive parity) can be mutually exclusive, meaning a system cannot satisfy all of them simultaneously. Assurance mechanisms must therefore be transparent about which definition of fairness is being used and why, and provide clear justification for any trade-offs made. This underscores the importance of societal input and multi-stakeholder consensus in defining the criteria for AI certification.

The establishment of credible assurance mechanisms is vital for demonstrating due diligence and building confidence in AI-enabled infrastructure. When an organization can present evidence that its AI systems have undergone rigorous certification by reputable third parties, or have met specific, auditable assurance criteria, it significantly reduces perceived risk for all stakeholders. This can accelerate the adoption of beneficial AI technologies, particularly in sectors where safety and trust are paramount, such as healthcare, finance, and transportation. It also provides a mechanism for accountability, allowing for recourse if an AI system fails to perform as expected or causes harm. In the absence of robust assurance mechanisms, the widespread deployment of advanced AI systems risks being hampered by public apprehension and regulatory uncertainty, ultimately hindering the realization of AI's full potential. Therefore, the ongoing development and refinement of AI certification and assurance methodologies represent a critical frontier in ensuring that AI is developed and deployed in a manner that is both innovative and responsible. The journey towards truly trustworthy AI is one that relies heavily on the ability to verify and validate claims of safety, fairness, and reliability through well-defined and rigorously applied assurance processes. This involves not just technical validation but also ethical and societal considerations, ensuring that AI systems align with human values and contribute positively to society.

The journey from abstract ethical principles and technical standards to tangible, legally enforceable obligations is complex. It requires a nuanced understanding of how existing legal frameworks can be, and are being, adapted to govern artificial intelligence, as well as the emergence of new legislation specifically designed for this rapidly evolving technology. For engineers, product managers, and legal teams alike, interpreting these legal frameworks is not merely an academic exercise; it is a critical step in ensuring that AI development and deployment are not only technically sound but also legally compliant and ethically responsible. This involves a proactive approach to identifying potential legal risks and embedding compliance considerations throughout the AI lifecycle, from initial design and data sourcing to deployment and ongoing monitoring.

One of the most significant legal challenges posed by AI revolves around liability. When an AI system causes harm – whether it's a self-driving car involved in an accident, a medical diagnostic tool that misinterprets an image, or a credit scoring algorithm that unfairly denies a loan – determining who is responsible is far from straightforward. Traditional legal doctrines often struggle to accommodate the distributed nature of AI development and the autonomous decision-making capabilities of these systems. Consider the principle of
res ipsa loquitur ("the thing speaks for itself"), which can apply when an accident occurs due to an obviously defective product. However, with AI, identifying the exact defect can be incredibly difficult. Was the harm caused by faulty code, biased training data, unforeseen environmental factors, or a combination thereof? Assigning blame might fall on the developers who wrote the algorithm, the company that deployed it, the

user who interacted with it, or even the manufacturer of the hardware on which it runs.

Legal frameworks are grappling with these questions through various approaches. Some jurisdictions are exploring strict liability, where a party can be held liable for harm regardless of fault, particularly in high-risk AI applications. Others are focusing on negligence, requiring plaintiffs to prove that a party failed to exercise reasonable care in the design, development, testing, or deployment of the AI system. This raises further questions about what constitutes "reasonable care" in the context of AI. Is it adherence to industry best practices? Compliance with emerging AI standards? The presence of robust risk management frameworks? For companies developing AI, this means meticulously documenting every stage of the AI lifecycle, from the initial conception and data collection to model training, validation, and post-deployment monitoring. This documentation serves as crucial evidence in demonstrating due diligence and rebutting claims of negligence.

The concept of the "legal personhood" of AI, while largely theoretical for now, also complicates liability. If an AI were to achieve a sufficient degree of autonomy, could it be held responsible for its actions? Current legal systems are not equipped for such a scenario. Instead, the focus remains on human or corporate responsibility. This underscores the importance of implementing strong governance structures and oversight mechanisms within organizations developing and deploying AI. Appointing dedicated AI ethics officers, establishing internal review boards, and ensuring clear lines of accountability are practical steps that can help mitigate liability risks. Furthermore, sophisticated insurance products are emerging to cover AI-specific risks, acknowledging the unique challenges in predicting and preventing AI-caused harm.

Intellectual property (IP) law presents another complex area where AI intersects with legal frameworks. For decades, IP law has been built around the concept of human authorship and inventorship. Copyright protects original works of authorship fixed in a tangible medium, and patents protect new and useful inventions. The question now is: who owns the copyright or patent for content or inventions created by AI? If an AI algorithm generates a piece of music, a novel, or a design, does the copyright belong to the AI itself, its developer, or the user who prompted its creation?

Current interpretations in many jurisdictions lean towards AI not being capable of holding IP rights. For instance, copyright law typically requires a human author. This means that AI-generated works might not be eligible for copyright protection, or the rights might vest with the human who directed or supervised the AI's creation process. This can have significant implications for businesses that rely on AI for content generation or innovation. Companies need to carefully review their IP strategies, potentially focusing on protecting the underlying AI models, algorithms, and datasets as trade secrets or through patents where human inventorship can be demonstrated. The legal landscape here is dynamic, with ongoing court cases and legislative proposals attempting to clarify these ambiguities. For example, the U.S. Copyright Office has issued guidance stating that works created solely by AI without human creative input are not registrable. This necessitates a careful balance, ensuring that human creativity remains a central element in any AI-assisted creation seeking IP protection.

The patentability of AI inventions also faces scrutiny. While AI can accelerate the discovery and invention process, the threshold for patentability – namely, human inventorship – remains a hurdle. In cases where AI has played a substantial role in an invention, legal teams must be adept at identifying and articulating the human contribution to demonstrate inventorship. This often involves detailed technical analysis and careful drafting of patent applications to highlight the innovative steps taken by human researchers or engineers, even if those steps were informed or guided by AI.

Anti-discrimination laws, designed to prevent unfair treatment based on protected characteristics such as race, gender, religion, or disability, are also being critically examined in the context of AI. Algorithms, particularly those used in hiring, lending, or criminal justice, can inadvertently perpetuate or even amplify existing societal biases present in the data they are trained on. If an AI hiring tool is trained on historical data where a particular demographic group was underrepresented in certain roles, the AI may learn to discriminate against candidates from that group, even if no explicit discriminatory intent was programmed.

Interpreting and applying anti-discrimination laws to AI requires a deep understanding of both the legal statutes and the technical mechanisms by which AI systems can produce discriminatory outcomes. This involves proactive measures to audit algorithms for bias. Such audits go beyond simply checking for explicit discriminatory features in the code. They involve rigorous statistical analysis of the AI's outputs across different demographic groups to identify disparities. Techniques like disparate impact analysis, commonly used in employment law, are being adapted for AI. This analysis examines whether a seemingly neutral AI policy or practice has a disproportionately negative effect on a protected group.

For engineers and product managers, this translates into a responsibility to implement "fairness-aware" AI development practices. This might involve using debiasing techniques during data preprocessing or model training, or employing fairness metrics to evaluate and mitigate bias in AI outputs. However, it's crucial to recognize that defining and achieving "fairness" in AI is not a simple technical problem. Different mathematical definitions of fairness (e.g., demographic parity, equal opportunity, predictive parity) can be mutually exclusive, meaning a single AI system cannot satisfy all of them simultaneously. Legal teams must work closely with technical teams to understand these trade-offs and make informed decisions about which fairness objectives are most appropriate for a given application, often guided by regulatory guidance and societal expectations.

Furthermore, transparency and explainability become critical legal and ethical imperatives when dealing with anti-discrimination laws. If an AI system's decision leads to an adverse outcome for an individual, they have a right to understand the basis for that decision, particularly if they suspect discrimination. While many advanced AI models, such as deep neural networks, operate as "black boxes," making their decision-making processes opaque, legal frameworks are increasingly demanding a level of explainability. This is driving the development of explainable AI (XAI) techniques. For example, methods like LIME (Local Interpretable Model-agnostic Explanations) or SHAP (SHapley Additive exPlanations) can provide insights into which features contributed most to a particular AI decision.

Regulatory bodies are also stepping in with specific guidance and, in some cases, new legislation. The European Union's proposed AI Act, for instance, categorizes AI systems based on risk levels and imposes different requirements accordingly. High-risk AI systems, such as those used in critical infrastructure, employment, or law enforcement, face stringent obligations regarding data governance, transparency, human oversight, and accuracy, including specific provisions related to non-discrimination. Similar legislative efforts are underway in other regions.

For organizations operating internationally, navigating this patchwork of evolving legal frameworks is a significant challenge. It necessitates a robust compliance strategy that accounts for the most stringent requirements across all relevant jurisdictions. This often involves establishing a centralized AI governance function that can monitor legal developments, conduct risk assessments, and implement appropriate technical and organizational measures. The role of legal counsel is paramount in this process, providing expertise in interpreting legal nuances, advising on risk mitigation strategies, and ensuring that internal policies and procedures align with legal obligations.

Translating these legal frameworks into concrete actions requires a multidisciplinary approach. Engineers need to be trained not only on the technical aspects of AI but also on the legal implications of their work. Product managers must integrate legal risk assessment into their product development roadmaps, considering potential liabilities, IP issues, and anti-discrimination concerns from the outset. Legal teams, in turn, need to develop a deeper understanding of AI technologies to effectively advise their organizations. This might involve investing in ongoing training, engaging external AI ethics and legal experts, and fostering a culture of collaboration between technical, legal, and business units.

Ultimately, interpreting and applying legal frameworks to AI is not a static endeavor. It is an ongoing process of adaptation, learning, and proactive engagement with an evolving legal and technological landscape. The goal is not simply to avoid legal penalties but to build AI systems that are trustworthy, fair, and beneficial to society, thereby fostering public confidence and enabling the responsible advancement of this transformative technology. This requires a commitment to continuous monitoring of legal precedents, regulatory guidance, and emerging legislation, ensuring that compliance efforts remain agile and responsive to the dynamic nature of AI.

Compliance, as we have established, is not a static endpoint but a dynamic and ongoing commitment. While robust policies, legal interpretations, and technical safeguards are indispensable components, their effectiveness hinges on a deeper, more pervasive element: a culture of compliance embedded within the very fabric of an organization. This section delves into the strategies and principles required to cultivate such a culture, transforming adherence from a procedural obligation into an intrinsic organizational value. Without this fundamental shift, even the most meticulously crafted compliance framework risks becoming a superficial exercise, prone to circumvention or accidental neglect.

The bedrock of any strong compliance culture is comprehensive and continuous education. This extends far beyond a one-time onboarding session or a perfunctory annual review. It necessitates a multi-pronged approach that caters to different roles and levels within the organization. For engineers and data scientists, training must illuminate the ethical and legal ramifications of their algorithmic designs, data handling practices, and model development choices. This includes understanding how seemingly neutral technical decisions can lead to disparate impacts, the importance of data provenance, and the legal implications of bias detection and mitigation techniques. For product managers, education should focus on integrating compliance considerations into the product lifecycle management process, from initial ideation and requirements gathering through to deployment and post-market surveillance. This means understanding risk assessment frameworks, the evolving landscape of AI regulations, and the ethical considerations pertinent to their specific product domains. For those in legal and governance roles, ongoing education is crucial to keep pace with the rapid advancements in AI technology and the equally swift evolution of regulatory and legal precedents. This might involve specialized courses, attendance at industry conferences, and deep dives into technical literature to foster a shared understanding between legal and technical teams. The aim is not to turn every engineer into a lawyer or every lawyer into an engineer, but to build bridges of comprehension, enabling informed dialogue and effective collaboration.

Beyond formal training, the clear and consistent communication of policies and expectations is paramount. These are not merely documents to be filed away, but living guidelines that should inform daily decision-making. This requires a multi-channel communication strategy. Internal memos, company-wide town halls, dedicated intranet portals, and regular team meetings can all serve as vehicles for disseminating and reinforcing compliance mandates. Crucially, communication must be tailored to the audience. Technical guidelines for engineers will differ in detail and emphasis from overarching ethical principles communicated to the entire workforce. Leaders at all levels have a critical role to play in this communication cascade. Their visible commitment to compliance, their willingness to champion ethical practices, and their consistent reinforcement of these values in their interactions with their teams send a powerful message. When leaders not only preach compliance but visibly practice it, it signals to the entire organization that these principles are not negotiable. This also involves articulating *why* compliance matters – connecting it to the company's mission, its reputation, its long-term viability, and its positive impact on society. Understanding the 'why' can significantly enhance buy-in and foster a genuine desire to adhere to these principles.

Establishing formal oversight mechanisms, such as internal review boards or ethics committees, provides a structured avenue for scrutinizing AI projects and ensuring compliance. These bodies can act as gatekeepers, reviewing proposals for new AI systems, assessing potential risks and ethical challenges, and recommending mitigation strategies before development even commences. The composition of these boards is critical. They should comprise individuals with diverse expertise, including technical specialists, legal counsel, ethicists, and representatives from different business units. This multidisciplinary approach ensures that a wide range of perspectives are considered, from the technical feasibility and legal soundness to the societal impact and ethical implications. The review process itself should be transparent and well-documented, with clear criteria for approval, rejection, or revision of projects. Furthermore, these boards should not be static entities; their mandates and compositions may need to evolve as the field of AI and its regulatory landscape change. In some cases, these boards might be empowered to halt projects that pose unacceptable risks, demonstrating a tangible commitment to prioritizing compliance and ethical conduct over expediency.

Incentivizing responsible practices is another vital lever in cultivating a culture of compliance. This involves more than just penalizing non-compliance; it means actively rewarding and recognizing adherence and proactive engagement with compliance principles. Performance reviews can incorporate metrics related to ethical AI development, risk mitigation efforts, and contributions to the company's compliance initiatives. Innovation awards could be established for teams that develop particularly novel or effective approaches to bias mitigation, privacy protection, or explainability. Recognition programs, whether formal or informal, can highlight individuals and teams who consistently demonstrate a commitment to responsible AI practices. This reinforces the idea that compliance is not just a duty, but a source of positive organizational recognition and advancement. Moreover, creating psychological safety is crucial. Employees must feel empowered to raise concerns about potential compliance issues or ethical dilemmas without fear of reprisal. This might involve establishing anonymous reporting channels, implementing robust whistle-blower protection policies, and fostering an environment where open discussion of challenges is encouraged. When employees know they can voice concerns and that these concerns will be taken seriously and addressed constructively, they are more likely to be vigilant and proactive in upholding compliance standards.

The challenge of building a compliance culture is amplified by the inherent complexity and rapid evolution of AI. The "black box" nature of some AI models, the constantly shifting legal terrain, and the global reach of AI deployments all add layers of difficulty. However, these challenges also underscore the necessity of a strong, ingrained culture. When laws are ambiguous or regulations are still in their nascent stages, a well-established culture of ethical responsibility and proactive risk assessment becomes the organization's most reliable compass. It enables teams to make sound judgments even in the absence of explicit directives, guided by a shared understanding of what constitutes responsible AI development and deployment.

Consider the practical application of these principles. A software engineering team developing a new AI-powered recruitment tool might be trained on anti-discrimination laws and the specific biases that can manifest in hiring algorithms. Their product manager ensures that bias detection and mitigation are key requirements in the product roadmap, allocating resources for fairness audits. An internal AI ethics review board scrutinizes the proposed algorithms and training data, demanding robust validation across diverse demographic groups. If the team discovers a potential for bias during development, they are encouraged to flag it immediately, knowing that their transparency will be valued and that the company will support their efforts to address it, rather than punish them for encountering a common challenge. The engineers who develop effective debiasing techniques are recognized and rewarded. The legal team proactively monitors emerging regulations in key markets, advising on necessary adjustments to the tool's features and documentation. This integrated approach, driven by a cultural commitment to compliance and ethics, ensures that the tool is not only technically sound but also legally defensible and socially responsible.

Another critical aspect of fostering a compliance culture is ensuring that compliance is not viewed as an impediment to innovation, but as an enabler of sustainable innovation. When AI systems are built with compliance and ethical considerations integrated from the outset, they are less likely to face costly redesigns, legal challenges, or reputational damage down the line. This foresight allows for more predictable development cycles and builds greater trust with customers, regulators, and the public. Organizations that prioritize responsible AI are often better positioned to attract talent, secure investment, and maintain a competitive edge in the long run.

The role of leadership in embedding this culture cannot be overstated. Senior executives must not only champion compliance verbally but demonstrate it through their actions and strategic decisions. This includes allocating sufficient resources for compliance initiatives, empowering compliance officers and ethics committees, and holding individuals accountable for breaches, regardless of their seniority or contribution to other business metrics. When leadership consistently prioritizes compliance, it creates a ripple effect throughout the organization, signaling that adherence to standards and regulations is a core business imperative. This involves fostering an environment where difficult conversations about AI's potential harms are welcomed, and where lessons learned from mistakes or near-misses are systematically captured and disseminated to prevent future occurrences.

Furthermore, the integration of compliance considerations into performance management systems is a powerful tool. When employees' performance reviews and compensation are tied, in part, to their adherence to compliance policies, their commitment to these principles is significantly reinforced. This could manifest as specific objectives related to data privacy, algorithmic fairness, or transparent documentation. For example, an engineer might have a performance objective to successfully implement and validate a privacy-preserving technique in a new AI model. A product manager might be evaluated on their ability to demonstrate that their AI product meets specific regulatory requirements. This direct link between compliance and personal or team success transforms compliance from an abstract ideal into a tangible professional goal.

The external landscape also plays a role in shaping internal culture. As regulatory bodies release more specific guidance and as legal precedents are established, organizations must be agile in adapting their internal policies and practices. This requires a proactive monitoring system and a willingness to invest in updating training programs and compliance frameworks. However, relying solely on external pressures is insufficient. A truly robust culture of compliance originates from within, driven by a shared understanding of the importance of ethical AI and a commitment to building trustworthy systems. This internal drive ensures that an organization is not just reacting to regulations but is actively striving to set and maintain the highest standards of responsible AI development and deployment.

The continuous feedback loop is also essential. Regularly soliciting feedback from employees on the effectiveness of compliance training, the clarity of policies, and the accessibility of reporting channels can identify areas for improvement. Post-deployment reviews of AI systems should not only assess performance metrics but also scrutinize compliance adherence, data drift, and any unexpected ethical outcomes. The lessons learned from these reviews must be fed back into the development process and the training programs, creating a virtuous cycle of continuous improvement. This iterative process ensures that the compliance framework remains relevant, effective, and responsive to the dynamic nature of AI and its societal implications.

Ultimately, building a culture of compliance is a marathon, not a sprint. It requires sustained effort, consistent reinforcement, and a genuine commitment from all levels of an organization. It is about fostering an environment where ethical considerations are as integral to the design and development of AI as technical performance. When this culture takes root, compliance becomes less of a burden and more of a competitive advantage, enabling organizations to navigate the complexities of AI with confidence, integrity, and a clear conscience, building systems that are not only innovative but also trustworthy and beneficial to all. This deep-seated adherence is the true differentiator between organizations that merely react to compliance demands and those that proactively lead in the responsible advancement of artificial intelligence.

Chapter 8: Auditing AI Systems for Safety and Ethics

The advent of artificial intelligence systems has brought about a paradigm shift in how we design, develop, and deploy technology. While the potential benefits are immense, so too are the risks. AI, by its very nature, can operate in ways that are opaque, unpredictable, and capable of generating profound societal impacts. This inherent complexity necessitates a rigorous and systematic approach to ensure that these systems are not only functional and efficient but also safe, ethical, and compliant with the myriad of evolving standards and regulations. This is where the crucial discipline of AI auditing comes into play.

AI auditing, in essence, is a systematic and independent examination of an artificial intelligence system, its development process, its underlying data, and its deployment environment. Its primary purpose is to provide an objective assessment of an AI system's adherence to a predefined set of criteria. These criteria can encompass a wide spectrum, ranging from functional requirements and performance metrics to more abstract, yet equally vital, considerations of safety, fairness, privacy, security, and ethical alignment. Unlike traditional software audits, which might primarily focus on code quality, security vulnerabilities, or adherence to specific functional specifications, AI audits delve deeper, probing the probabilistic nature of AI, the potential for emergent behaviors, and the subtle yet significant impacts that data, algorithms, and deployment contexts can have on outcomes.

The fundamental objective of an AI audit is to verify compliance. This compliance can be with a variety of mandates: industry-specific safety standards, established ethical principles, legal requirements, and internal organizational policies. For instance, an AI system used in autonomous vehicles must comply with stringent automotive safety standards. An AI-powered loan application system must adhere to fair lending laws and avoid discriminatory practices. An AI diagnostic tool in healthcare must meet regulatory requirements for medical devices and uphold patient privacy. Audits serve as the mechanism to rigorously check whether these systems meet these critical benchmarks, providing assurance to stakeholders that the AI is functioning as intended and within acceptable risk parameters.

Beyond mere verification, AI audits are indispensable for identifying potential risks and areas for improvement. The development of AI is often an iterative process, and even meticulously designed systems can harbor unforeseen weaknesses or unintended consequences. Audits can uncover these vulnerabilities before they manifest in the real world, preventing potential harm. This might involve identifying biases in training data that could lead to discriminatory outcomes, detecting weaknesses in a model's robustness that could be exploited by adversaries, or revealing instances where the AI's decision-making process lacks sufficient transparency to be trusted in high-stakes scenarios. By proactively identifying these risks, audits enable organizations to implement necessary mitigations, refine algorithms, augment datasets, or even reconsider the deployment of a system altogether. This foresight is invaluable in preventing costly failures, reputational damage, and, most importantly, harm to individuals and society.

The scope of an AI audit is consequently broad, encompassing not just the final deployed model but the entire AI lifecycle. This includes an examination of:

Data Governance and Management: The audit scrutinizes the sourcing, collection, labeling, storage, and pre-processing of data used to train and operate the AI system. This involves assessing data quality, representativeness, provenance, and adherence to privacy regulations

like GDPR or CCPA. Ensuring that the data is free from significant biases and accurately reflects the intended operational domain is paramount.
Model Development and Training: This phase involves reviewing the algorithms, model architectures, training methodologies, hyperparameter tuning, and validation strategies. The audit will assess the chosen techniques for their suitability, potential for bias, and alignment with ethical principles. It also examines the computational resources used and the reproducibility of the training process.
Testing and Validation: A comprehensive audit will delve into the testing protocols employed to evaluate the AI system's performance, accuracy, robustness, fairness, and safety. This includes evaluating the test datasets, the metrics used for evaluation, and the rigor of stress testing and adversarial testing.
Deployment and Operations: The audit extends to how the AI system is deployed, monitored, and maintained in its operational environment. This involves assessing its integration with existing systems, its real-time performance, mechanisms for detecting data drift or model degradation, and procedures for handling errors or unexpected behaviors.
Explainability and Transparency: For many AI systems, particularly those in sensitive domains, the audit will assess the level of explainability and transparency provided. This includes evaluating whether the system's decisions can be understood, whether the reasoning behind predictions or actions can be traced, and whether appropriate documentation exists to inform users and stakeholders.
Security and Privacy: The audit will examine the system's susceptibility to cyber-attacks, unauthorized access, and data breaches. It will also verify that privacy-preserving techniques are appropriately implemented and that the system complies with relevant data protection laws.
Ethical Considerations: This is an increasingly critical component. Audits will assess whether the AI system aligns with ethical frameworks, societal values, and principles of human-centric AI. This may involve evaluating the system for fairness, accountability, non-maleficence, and beneficence.

Documentation and Governance: The audit reviews all documentation related to the AI system, including design documents, training logs, testing reports, risk assessments, and any internal governance policies. This ensures that there is a clear, auditable trail of decisions and processes.

The critical role of independent audits in building trust and accountability cannot be overstated. As AI systems become more integrated into critical infrastructure, from power grids and transportation networks to financial markets and healthcare, public trust is an essential commodity. When AI systems malfunction or exhibit biased behavior, the consequences can be severe, leading to economic disruption, physical harm, or erosion of public confidence. Independent audits, conducted by third-party entities with no vested interest in the system's success, provide an unbiased and objective assessment of an AI system's reliability and integrity. This independence lends credibility to the audit findings, assuring regulators, consumers, and the public that the system has been evaluated impartially.

For safety-critical infrastructure, the imperative for independent AI audits is even more pronounced. Consider AI systems governing the operation of a nuclear power plant, managing air traffic control, or making life-or-death medical diagnoses. In these contexts, any failure or ethical lapse could have catastrophic consequences. Traditional methods of quality assurance and regulatory oversight, while important, may not be sufficient to address the unique challenges posed by advanced AI. Independent audits provide an additional layer of scrutiny, bringing specialized expertise and an objective perspective to bear on complex AI systems. They act as a crucial mechanism for accountability, ensuring that the organizations responsible for these systems are held to the highest standards of safety, reliability, and ethical conduct. Without such independent verification, the widespread adoption of AI in critical domains would remain a fraught and potentially perilous endeavor, undermining the very progress it promises to deliver. The trust that underpins societal acceptance and technological advancement is, therefore, deeply intertwined with the robustness and independence of AI auditing processes.

The very fabric of a robust AI audit process is woven from the threads of comprehensive audit trails. These trails are not mere records of activity; they are the indispensable narrative that allows us to rewind, replay, and dissect the lifecycle of an AI system, especially when things go awry or when we seek to understand the nuances of its operation. For AI, characterized by its dynamic nature, probabilistic outputs, and potential for emergent behaviors, the requirement for detailed and meticulously maintained audit trails becomes not just important, but paramount. Without them, diagnosing anomalies, verifying performance, ensuring fairness, and ultimately establishing accountability become Herculean, if not impossible, tasks.

At its core, an audit trail for an AI system must capture a granular view of its journey from inception to deployment and ongoing operation. This begins with the data. Every piece of data that flows into an AI system, whether for training, validation, or inference, must be logged. This includes not only the raw input but also any pre-processing steps applied. For instance, if a natural language processing model is fed a user query, the audit trail should record the original query, any tokenization performed, stemming or lemmatization applied, and any feature engineering that transforms the text into a format the model can understand. Similarly, for an image recognition system, the original image, along with any resizing, normalization, or augmentation applied during the pipeline, should be logged. This detailed record of data input is crucial for several reasons. Firstly, it allows for the reconstruction of specific events. If a model produces an incorrect prediction, tracing back the exact data that led to that prediction is the first step in debugging. Secondly, it enables the verification of data provenance and integrity. Were the correct datasets used? Was the data corrupted or altered in transit or during processing? A thorough data audit trail provides the answers. Furthermore, in scenarios involving sensitive data, such as personal health information or financial records, the audit trail serves as a critical tool for demonstrating compliance with privacy regulations, showing precisely what data was accessed, processed, and used. The granularity here is key; simply logging that "data was processed" is insufficient. The log must specify the data's origin, its content (or a hashed representation if privacy is a concern), and the transformations applied.

Beyond the raw data inputs, the audit trail must meticulously log the AI model's outputs and predictions. This encompasses the actual prediction or classification made by the model, along with any associated confidence scores or probabilities. For complex models that might output multiple potential results, all relevant outputs should be recorded. For instance, a recommendation engine might generate a ranked list of items; the audit trail should capture this entire list and the specific ranking. This level of detail is vital for evaluating the model's performance over time and across different input scenarios. It allows auditors to identify patterns in errors or unexpected behaviors. If a system consistently misclassifies a particular type of input, or if its confidence scores are systematically misaligned with actual accuracy, the audit trail of predictions will be instrumental in uncovering these issues. Moreover, for systems operating under regulatory scrutiny, such as in finance or healthcare, the recorded predictions form the basis for compliance checks. Auditors can compare the AI's decisions against established benchmarks or against decisions made by human experts. The temporal aspect of these logs is also critical, allowing for the reconstruction of sequences of predictions and the analysis of how the system's behavior evolves over time, especially in response to new data or environmental changes.

Key operational parameters and system states during the AI's operation also demand inclusion in the audit trail. This might include information such as the version of the model being used for a particular inference, the specific configurations or settings active at the time of the operation, and any hardware or software environment details that could influence performance. For instance, if an AI system is deployed across multiple servers or instances, logging which specific instance handled a particular request is important for troubleshooting. Similarly, if the system's behavior is sensitive to resource availability (e.g., CPU load, memory usage), these metrics should be captured. In distributed AI systems, tracking communication patterns and latency between different components can be essential for diagnosing performance bottlenecks. This operational context is particularly important for AI systems that exhibit dynamic behavior or are subject to external influences. Understanding the conditions under which a particular prediction was made can be as important as understanding the input data itself. This includes logging parameters like the 'temperature' setting in a generative AI model, which influences the randomness of its output, or the specific hyperparameters that were dynamically adjusted based on real-time conditions. Without these operational details, it becomes exceedingly difficult to reproduce a specific outcome or to determine whether observed anomalies stem from the model itself, the data, or the environment in which it is operating.

The configurations of the AI system, including any changes made to its architecture, parameters, or underlying software, must be meticulously documented within the audit trail. This requires a version control system for models and code, and the audit trail should reference specific versions. When updates or modifications are made to the AI system—whether it's a new model version, a change in the pre-processing pipeline, or an update to the inference engine—this event must be logged. The log should specify what changed, when it changed, and by whom. This is crucial for understanding how system updates might have impacted performance or introduced new behaviors, both positive and negative. For example, if a sudden drop in accuracy is observed after a scheduled deployment, the audit trail of configuration changes can quickly pinpoint the suspect update. This also supports the principle of reproducibility; if a specific behavior or outcome needs to be replicated, knowing the exact configuration under which it occurred is fundamental. This extends to external dependencies as well; if the AI system relies on external APIs or databases, changes in those dependencies might also need to be logged if they have a demonstrable impact. The rigor applied to logging these configurations should mirror that applied to code repositories, ensuring a complete history of the system's evolution.

Perhaps one of the most critical, and often overlooked, aspects of AI audit trails is the logging of human interventions. AI systems, even highly automated ones, often involve human oversight, manual adjustments, or override mechanisms. Every instance where a human interacts with the system—whether it's to correct a prediction, provide feedback, manually label data, adjust parameters, or even trigger an emergency stop—must be logged. This log should detail who intervened, when they intervened, what action they took, and the context for that intervention. For instance, if a human operator overrides an autonomous vehicle's decision, the audit trail should record the vehicle's intended action, the operator's intervention, and potentially the operator's reasoning if the system allows for such input. This is vital for understanding the human-AI interaction, identifying areas where the AI is consistently requiring human correction, and ensuring that human overrides are used appropriately and not to mask systemic flaws. In safety-critical applications, the ability to audit human decisions and their impact on the AI's behavior is as important as auditing the AI's own actions. This also serves as a crucial check against potential misuse or unauthorized manipulation of the system. If a system's behavior deviates unexpectedly, and that deviation coincides with a series of unlogged human adjustments, it raises a significant red flag.

The integrity and immutability of these audit trails are non-negotiable requirements. If an audit trail can be tampered with, altered, or deleted, it loses its value as a reliable source of truth. Therefore, robust mechanisms must be in place to ensure that logs are protected from unauthorized modification. This often involves implementing write-once, read-many (WORM) storage solutions, employing cryptographic hashing to verify the integrity of log entries, and establishing strict access controls over who can view or manage the logs. Blockchain technology, with its inherent immutability and distributed ledger capabilities, is increasingly being explored as a robust solution for ensuring the integrity of critical audit trails, particularly in high-stakes environments. The immutability requirement means that once an event is logged, it cannot be changed or deleted. This creates a permanent, tamper-evident record. For forensic analysis, this is paramount. Imagine a situation where an AI system causes significant financial loss or physical harm. Investigators need to be able to trust that the logs they are examining accurately reflect what happened, without any possibility of exculpatory evidence being removed or incriminating evidence being fabricated. This focus on integrity transforms the audit trail from a simple record-keeping function into a foundational element of trust and accountability within the AI ecosystem. Without immutable audit trails, the very concept of auditing AI systems for safety and ethics is severely undermined, leaving organizations vulnerable to undetected failures and a lack of recourse when harm occurs. The investment in secure and immutable logging infrastructure is therefore not an optional add-on, but a fundamental prerequisite for responsible AI deployment.

The practical execution of an AI audit hinges on a diverse toolkit of methodologies, each designed to probe different facets of an AI system's behavior and underlying construction. These methodologies are not mutually exclusive; rather, they form a synergistic ecosystem, where the insights gained from one technique can inform and refine the application of another. At the foundational level, the audit must scrutinize the very ingredients that bring an AI to life: its training data. This involves a rigorous examination to uncover potential biases that, if left unchecked, can propagate into discriminatory outputs. Techniques here range from statistical analysis of demographic distributions within the dataset to more sophisticated methods for detecting subtle correlations that might disadvantage specific subgroups. For instance, an audit of a hiring AI might involve calculating the representation of different gender and ethnic groups in the training data, identifying any significant underrepresentation or overrepresentation that could skew the model's predictions. Furthermore, auditors might employ natural language processing (NLP) techniques to scan text data for stereotypical language or associations that could implicitly teach the model prejudiced views. Beyond simple counts, advanced methods can identify proxy variables—attributes that might seem neutral but are highly correlated with protected characteristics—and assess their influence. The goal is to ensure that the data accurately and equitably reflects the reality it is intended to model, or at least, that any inherent societal biases within the data are consciously identified and accounted for. This might involve data augmentation strategies to artificially balance underrepresented groups, or the application of re-weighting techniques during training to give more importance to data points from minority groups. It also necessitates a deep understanding of the data collection process itself, questioning the provenance, collection methods, and potential for sampling errors or historical injustices to be encoded within the dataset. For example, if historical loan approval data is used, and that data reflects past discriminatory lending practices, an AI trained on it will likely perpetuate those same biases unless specific mitigation steps are taken. Therefore, data auditing is not just about analyzing what's present, but also understanding what's missing and why.

Once the training data has been assessed, the methodologies shift to evaluating the AI model's performance and behavior. A critical component of this is the assessment of fairness, moving beyond raw accuracy to measure how equitably the model treats different demographic groups. This involves defining and applying a suite of fairness metrics. Common metrics include demographic parity, which checks if the proportion of positive outcomes is the same across different groups; equalized odds, which ensures that the true positive rates and false positive rates are equal across groups; and equal opportunity, which focuses on ensuring equal true positive rates. The choice of metric depends heavily on the application and the societal values being upheld. For instance, in a loan application system, equal opportunity might be prioritized to ensure that individuals with similar creditworthiness have an equal chance of approval, regardless of their race or gender. Auditing involves testing the model on carefully constructed datasets designed to highlight potential disparities. This could involve creating synthetic datasets where all attributes are identical except for a protected characteristic, and observing if the model's predictions change. Alternatively, real-world data can be segmented by demographic groups, and performance metrics calculated for each segment. Discrepancies in these metrics then signal potential fairness issues. The interpretation of these metrics is crucial; a model might satisfy one fairness criterion while violating another, highlighting the complex trade-offs inherent in AI fairness. Therefore, a comprehensive audit will typically report on multiple fairness metrics, providing a nuanced picture of the model's equitable performance. This evaluation often requires access to ground truth labels for specific subgroups, which can be challenging to obtain without privacy concerns. When direct group membership is not available or permissible, proxy variables might be used, albeit with caution due to the inherent risks of misclassification and error. The goal is to provide stakeholders with the information needed to make informed decisions about the model's deployment, understanding its potential societal impact.

Beyond fairness, the robustness of an AI system is paramount, particularly in safety-critical applications. This involves testing the model's resilience to unexpected or malicious inputs. One of the most prominent methodologies in this domain is adversarial testing. Adversarial examples are inputs that have been subtly perturbed in a way that is imperceptible to humans but causes the AI model to make an incorrect prediction. For instance, a self-driving car's vision system might be tricked by a few strategically placed stickers on a stop sign, causing it to misclassify it as a speed limit sign. Auditing for robustness involves generating and testing against such adversarial examples. This can be done through various techniques, including gradient-based attacks (where attackers use the model's gradients to find optimal perturbations) or optimization-based attacks. Automated tools are widely used to generate a diverse range of adversarial examples, covering different attack types and perturbation magnitudes. The audit assesses how the model's performance degrades under these attacks, and whether the outputs become nonsensical or dangerous. For a medical imaging AI, for example, an adversarial attack might cause it to miss a critical tumor or to generate a false positive, leading to unnecessary anxiety or a missed diagnosis. Auditors would measure the model's accuracy on a clean dataset versus an adversarially perturbed dataset, and report on the 'adversarial robustness' score. Furthermore, robustness testing extends to other forms of input variations, such as noisy data, out-of-distribution samples (data that differs significantly from the training data), and even environmental changes (e.g., variations in lighting for computer vision systems, or background noise for speech recognition). The aim is to understand the boundaries of the AI's reliable operation and to identify scenarios where it is most vulnerable. This often leads to the development of defense mechanisms, such as adversarial training (where adversarial examples are included in the training data to make the model more resilient) or input sanitization techniques.

The implementation of safety controls and mechanisms designed to prevent harm is another critical area of AI auditing. This involves verifying that the intended safeguards are correctly implemented and are effective in practice. This can include reviewing the design specifications of safety features, such as emergency stop mechanisms in robotics, or fail-safe protocols in financial trading algorithms. For AI systems that have explicit safety constraints programmed into them (e.g., an autonomous vehicle programmed not to exceed a certain speed in residential areas), auditors will test these constraints rigorously. This might involve simulations where the AI is placed in scenarios designed to trigger these safety limitations. For instance, an auditor might simulate a situation where the autonomous vehicle approaches a school zone and verify that its speed automatically reduces to the safe limit. Beyond explicit programming, AI systems often incorporate monitoring mechanisms to detect anomalous behavior. Auditing these monitoring systems involves testing their sensitivity and accuracy in identifying deviations from expected performance. Are the alert thresholds set appropriately? Do they correctly distinguish between normal operational variations and genuine safety risks? This often involves injecting simulated anomalies or failures into the system and observing whether the monitoring system detects them within an acceptable timeframe. For instance, if a manufacturing robot's safety system is designed to detect unusual vibrations that might indicate a mechanical failure, auditors would introduce controlled vibrations and ensure the system triggers an alert. This aspect of auditing often requires a deep understanding of the system's operational environment and the potential failure modes specific to that context. It's not just about whether a safety control exists, but whether it functions reliably when needed. This can involve not only functional testing but also stress testing and longevity testing to ensure that safety mechanisms do not degrade over time or under heavy load.

A comprehensive AI audit rarely relies on a single approach. Instead, it typically employs a combination of automated tools and manual expert review, recognizing the strengths and limitations of each. Automated tools are invaluable for systematically examining large datasets, running extensive test suites, and performing repetitive checks efficiently. This includes statistical analysis packages for bias detection, fairness metric calculators, and frameworks for generating and evaluating adversarial examples. These tools can provide quantitative measures of performance, fairness, and robustness, offering a scalable way to audit AI systems, especially at scale. They can also automate the process of logging and reporting, ensuring consistency and reproducibility. However, automated tools are often limited by the scope of their programming and the specific metrics they are designed to measure. They may struggle with nuanced ethical considerations, contextual understanding, or emergent behaviors that fall outside predefined parameters. This is where manual expert review becomes indispensable. Human auditors, with their domain expertise, critical thinking skills, and understanding of ethical principles, can provide a qualitative assessment that complements the quantitative data from automated tools. Experts can interpret the results of automated tests within the broader context of the AI system's intended use and its potential societal impact. They can identify subtle biases that automated tools might miss, assess the plausibility of model outputs, and evaluate the ethical implications of fairness trade-offs. For example, while an automated tool can flag that a model has a slightly higher false positive rate for one demographic group, a human expert can assess whether this difference is ethically acceptable given the application, or if it indicates a more serious problem. Expert review is also crucial for evaluating AI systems that involve complex decision-making processes, subjective criteria, or significant ethical dilemmas. This might involve domain specialists (e.g., medical doctors reviewing a diagnostic AI), ethicists, legal scholars, or social scientists. Their insights are vital for identifying risks that are not easily quantifiable or predictable by algorithms alone. The interplay between automated tools and human expertise is therefore central to a robust AI auditing process, creating a multi-layered approach that increases the thoroughness and trustworthiness of the audit findings. The goal is to leverage the speed and scale of automation while retaining the depth and critical judgment of human oversight.

Furthermore, the auditing methodologies must consider the specific lifecycle stage of the AI system. Auditing is not a one-time event but an ongoing process that adapts to the system's evolution. During the development phase, auditing might focus on data quality, model architecture choices, and initial performance evaluations. This includes ensuring that the chosen algorithms are appropriate for the task, that the hyperparameter tuning is systematic, and that early bias assessments are conducted. As the model moves towards deployment, the focus shifts to more rigorous testing of fairness, robustness, and safety in simulated or controlled environments. This phase often involves extensive validation against benchmark datasets and the development of initial operational guidelines. Once the AI system is deployed, continuous monitoring and auditing become paramount. This involves tracking key performance indicators (KPIs), fairness metrics, and system stability in real-world conditions. Unexpected drifts in model performance, increases in error rates, or the emergence of new biases need to be detected and addressed promptly. This continuous auditing might involve periodic re-audits using the full suite of methodologies, or it might be integrated into the system's operational feedback loops through automated monitoring and anomaly detection systems. The audit methodologies must also be tailored to the specific risks associated with the AI's application domain. A facial recognition system used for security purposes will require different auditing methodologies than an AI used for generating creative text or providing personalized educational content. High-stakes domains such as healthcare, finance, and autonomous systems demand more stringent and frequent auditing, often involving regulatory compliance checks. For instance, auditing a medical AI might involve verifying its adherence to HIPAA regulations in the US or GDPR in Europe, in addition to assessing its clinical accuracy and patient safety. This lifecycle-aware and domain-specific approach ensures that auditing remains relevant and effective throughout the AI system's existence, from conception to retirement.

The methodologies for AI auditing are not static; they are constantly evolving in response to advancements in AI technology and our growing understanding of its potential impacts. As AI systems become more complex, sophisticated, and integrated into societal functions, the need for comprehensive, rigorous, and adaptable auditing methodologies will only intensify. The development of new adversarial attack techniques necessitates the creation of new defense and detection mechanisms, which in turn require new auditing approaches to verify their effectiveness. Similarly, emerging ethical concerns, such as those related to AI's impact on employment, democratic processes, or mental well-being, will drive the development of new audit frameworks and metrics. This ongoing evolution underscores the importance of a proactive and adaptive stance in AI auditing, anticipating future challenges and developing the necessary tools and techniques to address them. This includes fostering interdisciplinary collaboration, where computer scientists work alongside social scientists, ethicists, legal experts, and policymakers to develop holistic auditing frameworks. The goal is to move beyond purely technical assessments to encompass a broader understanding of AI's societal, ethical, and legal implications. The development and application of these methodologies are not merely technical exercises; they are fundamental to building trust, ensuring accountability, and realizing the beneficial potential of artificial intelligence while mitigating its risks.

The integrity and effectiveness of any AI audit are inextricably linked to the caliber and suitability of the individuals or organizations tasked with conducting it. Selecting the right AI auditors is therefore not merely a procedural step but a foundational element that underpins the entire credibility and value of the auditing process. This selection demands a meticulous approach, ensuring that the chosen auditors possess a potent combination of technical acumen, unwavering independence, and a profound comprehension of the specific domain in which the AI system operates. Without these core attributes, even the most sophisticated auditing methodologies can yield superficial or misleading results, failing to uncover critical risks or provide actionable insights.

Technical expertise forms the bedrock of an effective AI audit. Auditors must possess a deep understanding of AI principles, machine learning algorithms, data science methodologies, and the various techniques used in AI development. This includes familiarity with different model architectures, training processes, evaluation metrics, and common pitfalls such as overfitting, underfitting, and data leakage. Furthermore, they need proficiency in the tools and frameworks commonly used in AI development and auditing, such as Python libraries (e.g., TensorFlow, PyTorch, scikit-learn), data analysis platforms, and specialized auditing software. Beyond the theoretical underpinnings, auditors must be adept at interpreting the outputs of these tools and methodologies. For instance, when presented with fairness metrics, they need to understand the nuances of different fairness definitions (e.g., demographic parity, equalized odds) and be able to articulate what specific metrics reveal about the AI's behavior in relation to protected groups. Similarly, when examining the results of adversarial robustness tests, auditors must be able to gauge the severity of vulnerabilities identified and assess the practical implications of these weaknesses for the AI's intended use. This technical depth allows auditors to not only identify deviations from expected performance but also to diagnose potential root causes within the model or its training data, and to recommend appropriate remediation strategies. It is this technical mastery that enables auditors to move beyond a superficial check of compliance and delve into the underlying mechanisms that govern an AI's performance and potential for harm.

However, technical prowess alone is insufficient. Independence is a paramount requirement for AI auditors to ensure impartiality and objectivity. The auditors should not have any vested interest in the AI system being audited, nor should they be unduly influenced by the organization developing or deploying the system. This independence can be achieved through several avenues. Organizations can engage third-party auditing firms that specialize in AI ethics and safety, providing an external and unbiased perspective. Alternatively, if an internal audit team is established, it must be structurally independent from the AI development teams, reporting directly to a high-level oversight committee or the board of directors, thereby mitigating the risk of internal pressures compromising audit findings. The appearance of independence is almost as crucial as actual independence; stakeholders need to trust that the audit process is free from conflicts of interest. This might involve clearly defined protocols for auditor selection, disclosure of any potential conflicts, and strict guidelines on post-audit engagement that could compromise future objectivity. An independent auditor is empowered to ask difficult questions, challenge assumptions, and deliver findings without fear of retribution or favoritous treatment, which is essential for uncovering the most significant risks.

Crucially, AI auditors must possess a deep understanding of the specific domain in which the AI system is intended to operate. An AI system designed for medical diagnostics, for instance, carries vastly different ethical and safety implications than one used for content moderation on social media or for optimizing supply chain logistics. Domain expertise allows auditors to contextualize the AI's behavior and assess its risks within the framework of the relevant industry standards, regulatory requirements, and societal expectations. For a healthcare AI, auditors would need to be familiar with medical ethics, patient privacy regulations (like HIPAA), clinical trial methodologies, and the potential consequences of misdiagnosis or treatment recommendation errors. For a financial AI, knowledge of financial regulations, market dynamics, and the impact of algorithmic trading on market stability would be essential. This domain-specific knowledge helps auditors identify risks that might not be apparent to a purely technical expert, such as subtle biases that could lead to discriminatory lending practices, or the potential for an AI-driven trading algorithm to trigger a market crash. It also enables auditors to ask more insightful questions about the intended use case, the impact on different user groups, and the acceptable thresholds for error or bias within that specific context. Without this contextual understanding, auditors risk applying generic standards that are either too stringent or too lenient for the particular application, thus failing to provide a truly meaningful assessment.

The process of defining the audit scope is another critical antecedent to engaging auditors. A well-defined scope ensures that the audit is focused, efficient, and covers all relevant aspects of the AI system. This involves clearly articulating what the audit aims to achieve, which components of the AI system will be examined (e.g., data pipeline, model itself, deployment infrastructure, user interface), and what criteria will be used for evaluation. The scope should be determined collaboratively between the organization and the chosen auditors, leveraging the auditors' expertise to refine the scope and ensure it is comprehensive yet manageable. This collaboration helps to avoid scope creep and ensures that both parties have a shared understanding of the audit's objectives and boundaries. Key elements to define within the scope include: the specific AI models and versions under review; the data sources and their associated preprocessing steps; the intended operational environment and any associated constraints; the key performance indicators (KPIs) and ethical metrics that will be assessed; the types of risks to be prioritized (e.g., bias, safety, privacy, security); and the specific regulatory frameworks or industry standards that must be adhered to. A clear scope document serves as a roadmap for the audit, guiding the auditors' work and providing a benchmark for measuring the audit's completion and success. It also helps in managing expectations, ensuring that stakeholders understand what will and will not be covered by the audit.

Once the scope is established, the organization must commit to providing auditors with the necessary access and documentation. This is often a significant undertaking, requiring a willingness to be transparent and open throughout the process. Auditors will typically require access to a comprehensive set of information, including: detailed documentation of the AI system's architecture, algorithms, and design principles;

information about the training, validation, and testing datasets, including their provenance, collection methods, and any preprocessing steps; access to the AI model itself, potentially including model weights and parameters, or at least the ability to interact with a deployed version; information on the system's deployment environment, including hardware and software configurations; logs and performance metrics from the system's operation; documentation of any safety protocols, ethical guidelines, and risk assessments that have been conducted; and details of any previous audits or internal reviews. The level of access required will vary depending on the audit's objectives and the nature of the AI system. For instance, auditing proprietary algorithms might necessitate non-disclosure agreements (NDAs) to protect intellectual property while still allowing for thorough examination. The organization must facilitate this access in a timely and organized manner, ensuring that the auditors have the resources they need to conduct their work effectively. This might involve setting up secure environments for data access, providing access to code repositories, or arranging for demonstrations and walkthroughs of the system's functionality. A lack of transparency or deliberate withholding of information can significantly undermine the audit's findings and raise suspicions about the organization's commitment to responsible AI development.

Ensuring constructive collaboration between the audit team and the organization being audited is paramount to achieving a successful outcome. Auditing should not be perceived as an adversarial process, but rather as a partnership aimed at improving the AI system's safety, ethics, and overall reliability. This requires fostering an environment of mutual respect and open communication. The organization should view the auditors not as external critics, but as expert advisors providing valuable insights. Likewise, auditors must approach their work with a constructive mindset, focusing on identifying risks and offering practical, actionable recommendations for mitigation. Regular communication channels should be established, allowing for prompt clarification of questions, discussion of emerging findings, and feedback on the audit process itself. This might involve regular progress meetings, dedicated points of contact within both the audit team and the organization, and a clear protocol for reporting and escalating issues. The organization's technical teams should be prepared to collaborate closely with the auditors, providing explanations, performing requested tests, and working together to troubleshoot any issues that arise. This collaborative spirit not only facilitates the audit process but also helps to build internal capacity within the organization, fostering a culture of continuous improvement and responsible AI development. When collaboration is strong, auditors are more likely to gain a holistic understanding of the AI system and its operational context, leading to more accurate and impactful findings. Conversely, a confrontational or uncooperative relationship can create barriers to information flow, increase resistance to change, and ultimately diminish the value of the audit. The goal is to transform the audit from a compliance exercise into an opportunity for learning and enhancement.

The selection process itself should be formalized, with clear criteria for evaluating potential auditors. This might involve reviewing their credentials, experience with similar AI systems and domains, track record, and proposed methodology. In some cases, a request for proposal (RFP) process can be used to solicit proposals from multiple auditing firms, allowing for a comparative evaluation of their capabilities and costs. The organization should also consider the auditors' approach to reporting and their ability to communicate complex technical and ethical issues clearly to various stakeholders, including technical teams, management, and potentially the public. The final choice of auditors should be based on a holistic assessment of their technical competence, independence, domain expertise, and their proposed approach to conducting the audit in a collaborative and constructive manner. This rigorous selection process sets the stage for an effective and valuable AI audit, ensuring that the insights gained will contribute meaningfully to the responsible development and deployment of artificial intelligence.

The true measure of an AI audit's efficacy lies not in the thoroughness of its execution, but in its capacity to catalyze meaningful change. Once the meticulous process of examination and evaluation has concluded, the resulting audit findings become the focal point for transformation. This stage is where potential risks are translated into actionable insights, and where the abstract principles of AI ethics and safety are grounded in concrete improvements. Interpreting these findings is a critical juncture, demanding careful consideration and a commitment to addressing identified shortcomings. It is the gateway to remediation, the process by which an AI system is brought into closer alignment with its intended safety and ethical standards.

The initial step in interpreting audit findings involves a systematic review of the audit report. This document, typically a comprehensive output from the auditing team, details their observations, the evidence gathered, and their conclusions regarding the AI system's performance against predefined criteria. It is imperative that all relevant stakeholders within the organization, including development teams, product managers, legal counsel, and senior leadership, engage with this report. The interpretation process should not be a superficial skim but a deep dive into each finding. Auditors often categorize their findings based on severity and impact, and understanding these categorizations is crucial. This might involve distinguishing between critical failures that pose immediate risks to users or the organization, significant issues that could lead to substantial problems if unaddressed, and minor observations that represent opportunities for optimization or marginal improvements. For instance, a finding that an AI model exhibits discriminatory bias against a protected demographic in a loan application system would undoubtedly be classified as a critical failure, potentially leading to legal repercussions and severe reputational damage. Conversely, a finding that the model's prediction confidence scores could be presented to users in a more understandable format might be deemed a minor observation, an opportunity for enhanced user experience.

A pivotal aspect of interpretation is risk prioritization. Not all findings carry the same weight, and resources for remediation are invariably finite. Therefore, a robust framework for prioritizing issues is essential. This prioritization should be driven by a comprehensive risk assessment, considering factors such as the likelihood of an adverse event occurring, the potential severity of its impact, and the urgency with which it needs to be addressed. Likelihood can be estimated based on historical data, the nature of the AI system's deployment, and the robustness of existing safeguards. Severity can be evaluated across various dimensions: financial loss, reputational damage, legal or regulatory penalties, harm to individuals or groups (including psychological harm, discrimination, or physical injury), and operational disruption. The urgency of remediation is often linked to the immediate threat posed by the finding. For example, a security vulnerability that could allow unauthorized access to sensitive user data demands immediate attention, whereas a subtle bias that might only manifest under very specific and rare conditions could be scheduled for a later remediation cycle. This prioritization exercise often involves a collaborative workshop where auditors and the audited organization discuss each finding, share perspectives on its implications, and jointly agree on a tiered order of importance. This ensures that remediation efforts are strategically focused on the most critical areas first, maximizing the impact of available resources and safeguarding against the most significant potential harms.

Following prioritization, the next critical phase is the assignment of responsibility for corrective actions. Vague accountability is a common pitfall that can render even the best-laid remediation plans ineffective. Each prioritized finding must be assigned to a specific individual, team, or department within the organization. This assignment should be based on the nature of the finding and the expertise required to address it. For a technical issue, such as bias in the model's algorithms or data, responsibility might fall to the AI development team or data science unit. If the finding relates to the deployment infrastructure or data governance policies, the IT operations or data governance teams would be the appropriate assignees. Issues pertaining to user interface design or communication of AI outputs might be handled by the product management or user experience teams. Crucially, the assigned party must have the authority, resources, and expertise to implement the necessary changes. Simply assigning a task without ensuring these prerequisites are met is a recipe for failure. Clear ownership not only ensures that tasks are completed but also fosters a sense of accountability throughout the organization, promoting a culture where responsibility for AI safety and ethics is broadly shared.

Equally important as assigning responsibility is establishing clear timelines for implementation. Without deadlines, remediation efforts can languish indefinitely, especially when competing priorities arise. Each corrective action should have a defined start date, milestones, and a target completion date. These timelines should be realistic, taking into account the complexity of the required changes, the availability of resources, and any necessary testing and validation procedures. For critical findings, these timelines will be aggressive, potentially involving expedited development sprints or immediate hotfixes. For less urgent issues, more extended timelines might be appropriate, integrating them into regular development cycles. The establishment of these timelines should be a collaborative process, ideally agreed upon by the assigned responsibility owner and senior management, ensuring buy-in and commitment. Furthermore, it is beneficial to define intermediate milestones for longer-term remediation projects. These milestones allow for progress tracking and provide opportunities to identify and address any emerging roadblocks early in the process, preventing them from derailing the entire remediation effort. The transparency of these timelines is also key, making them visible to relevant stakeholders so that progress can be monitored and managed effectively.

The remediation process itself often involves a multi-faceted approach. It is rarely a simple fix; more often, it requires iterative adjustments to the AI system. For instance, addressing algorithmic bias might involve re-training the model with more diverse and representative data, implementing fairness-aware algorithms during the training phase, or applying post-processing techniques to adjust model outputs. If the issue lies in the data pipeline, it might require changes to data collection methods, improvements in data cleaning and preprocessing, or the implementation of more robust data validation checks. For issues related to model interpretability, it could involve developing better explanation mechanisms, generating more detailed model cards, or redesigning the user interface to provide clearer insights into the AI's decision-making process. Security vulnerabilities might necessitate code patches, strengthened access controls, or the implementation of enhanced monitoring systems. The process should always include thorough testing and validation to ensure that the implemented changes have effectively addressed the original finding without introducing new issues or unintended consequences. This validation phase is critical and should be as rigorous as the initial audit, potentially involving re-running specific audit tests or performing targeted stress tests.

A fundamental aspect of ensuring the long-term efficacy of remediation is the establishment of a robust follow-up mechanism. The audit and remediation cycle should not be a one-off event. To confirm that the implemented changes have indeed resolved the identified issues and that the AI system remains compliant with safety and ethical standards, follow-up audits or assessments are indispensable. These follow-up activities can take several forms. They might involve a full re-audit of the system, focusing specifically on the areas that were remediated. Alternatively, they could be targeted assessments conducted by internal teams or a subset of the external auditors, designed to verify the effectiveness of specific corrective actions. The timing of these follow-up audits is also important. For critical issues, a follow-up might be scheduled relatively soon after the remediation is complete, perhaps within a few weeks or months, to quickly confirm the fix. For less critical issues, the follow-up might be integrated into the regular audit cycle. The objective is to create a continuous loop of assessment, remediation, and re-assessment, ensuring that the AI system evolves responsibly over time.

This follow-up process serves multiple purposes. Firstly, it verifies the effectiveness of the remediation efforts. Did the changes actually fix the problem? Are the new controls working as intended? Secondly, it can identify any new risks or issues that may have emerged as a consequence of the remediation. Sometimes, attempting to fix one problem can inadvertently create another, and a follow-up audit helps to catch these unforeseen side effects. Thirdly, it reinforces the organization's commitment to ongoing AI safety and ethics. Knowing that their work will be subject to subsequent review encourages teams to implement robust and sustainable solutions rather than quick fixes. Finally, it provides valuable feedback for improving the auditing and remediation processes themselves. What worked well? What were the bottlenecks? How can future audits be more effective?

The documentation of the entire remediation journey is also paramount. This includes meticulous records of the original audit findings, the remediation plan, the assigned responsibilities, the timelines, the changes implemented, and the results of testing and validation. This documentation serves several crucial functions. It provides a clear audit trail, demonstrating due diligence and accountability. It is invaluable for future audits, allowing auditors to quickly understand the system's history and track record. It also supports knowledge management within the organization, ensuring that lessons learned from the remediation process are captured and disseminated. For regulatory compliance, such documentation is often a mandatory requirement. Without thorough documentation, the entire remediation process risks being perceived as ad-hoc or incomplete, undermining the credibility of the organization's commitment to responsible AI.

The interpretation of audit findings and subsequent remediation is not merely a technical or procedural exercise; it is a strategic imperative. It requires a culture that embraces transparency, accountability, and a commitment to continuous improvement. Organizations that treat audit findings as opportunities for growth, rather than as punitive assessments, are far more likely to develop AI systems that are not only effective but also trustworthy and beneficial to society. The journey from identifying a risk to implementing a sustainable solution is often complex, but it is an essential part of building responsible AI. It is through this diligent and ongoing process of interpretation and remediation that the true value of an AI audit is realized, ensuring that AI systems are developed and deployed in a manner that aligns with human values and societal well-being. The ability to effectively interpret complex findings, prioritize them based on a nuanced understanding of risk, and execute timely and effective remediation plans is a hallmark of mature and responsible AI governance. This iterative cycle of assessment and improvement is what separates superficial compliance from genuine commitment to AI safety and ethics.

Chapter 9: Incident Response and Management for AI

The landscape of incident response is fundamentally altered when AI systems are involved. Unlike conventional software or hardware failures, incidents stemming from AI-driven infrastructure present a unique set of challenges that demand specialized approaches. These aren't merely an escalation of existing problems; they are qualitative shifts in how incidents manifest, propagate, and are diagnosed. The complexity, autonomy, and learning capabilities inherent in AI introduce a layer of unpredictability that makes traditional incident response playbooks insufficient.

One of the most significant challenges is the phenomenon of emergent behavior. AI models, particularly deep learning systems, can develop capabilities or exhibit responses that were not explicitly programmed or even foreseen by their creators. These emergent behaviors can arise from intricate interactions between the model's architecture, its training data, and novel input it encounters in deployment. When such emergent behavior leads to an incident – perhaps a financial trading algorithm executing a series of erroneous trades, or a recommendation system pushing harmful content – the root cause is often deeply embedded within the model's learned patterns, making it exceedingly difficult to isolate. Traditional debugging methods, which rely on tracing code execution paths or examining configuration files, often fall short. The "logic" of an AI, derived from vast datasets and complex neural network layers, is not always transparent or easily interpretable, transforming an incident investigation into a detective mission where the suspect's thought process is largely opaque.

This opacity is directly linked to the challenge of pinpointing root causes. For complex AI models, especially those with millions or billions of parameters, understanding precisely *why* a specific output or action was generated is a monumental task. The concept of "explainability" or "interpretability" in AI is an active area of research precisely because of this difficulty. In an incident scenario, where rapid diagnosis is critical, the inability to clearly identify the contributing factors – whether it's a specific feature in the input data, a subtle interaction within a neural network layer, or an unforeseen consequence of a recent model update – can paralyze response efforts. Instead of a clear line of code to patch or a faulty component to replace, responders might face a complex web of interconnected learned associations, making it hard to distinguish between a true root cause and a mere symptom. This is compounded by the fact that the model itself may have evolved since its last audit or deployment, making historical data less reliable for diagnosing current issues.

Furthermore, the interconnectedness of modern AI systems often leads to cascading failures. AI is rarely deployed in isolation. Instead, it forms part of complex ecosystems where multiple AI models, traditional software, and human workflows interact. An anomaly or failure in one AI component can trigger a chain reaction throughout the system. For example, a defect in an AI-powered fraud detection system might lead to legitimate transactions being incorrectly flagged, which then overwhelms a customer service AI designed to handle disputes. This could, in turn, trigger an automated process to reduce service capacity, impacting other AI-driven customer interactions. The interconnected nature means that an incident originating in one corner of the system can rapidly propagate, escalating in scope and complexity. Tracing the lineage of such a failure through multiple AI components and their interactions requires a sophisticated understanding of the entire AI ecosystem, not just the individual parts. This is especially true for AI systems that are continuously learning and adapting; the failure might be caused by an interaction that only occurs when the systems have reached a certain state of adaptation, making it a moving target for diagnosis.

The potential for rapid, large-scale impact is another defining characteristic of AI incidents. Because AI systems are often deployed to automate tasks at scale or to make decisions impacting vast numbers of users, a single failure can have immediate and widespread consequences. Consider an AI-powered content moderation system that malfunctions and incorrectly flags a significant volume of legitimate user-generated content as violating policy. This could lead to a sudden and massive disruption for users, a surge in support requests, and significant reputational damage. Similarly, a flaw in an AI-driven logistics or supply chain optimization system could lead to widespread delivery delays, stockouts, or misrouted goods, impacting an entire region or even a global network. The speed at which AI can operate and influence these systems means that incidents can escalate from a minor anomaly to a major crisis in a matter of minutes or hours, leaving little time for traditional, measured response protocols to be effective. The sheer velocity of potential damage necessitates pre-emptive strategies and extremely agile response capabilities.

The very nature of AI as a "learning" system introduces a temporal dimension to incidents that is absent in static software. An AI model's performance can drift over time as it encounters new data that differs from its training distribution – a phenomenon known as "data drift" or "concept drift." This drift can subtly degrade performance, leading to a gradual increase in errors or biases, which may only be recognized as an "incident" when a threshold of unacceptable performance is crossed. By the time it's identified as an incident, the model may have been operating sub-optimally for an extended period, meaning that understanding the root cause might involve analyzing historical data that spans months or even years, looking for the subtle shifts that led to the current failure. This temporal complexity makes it challenging to attribute blame or identify a single "point of failure" in the way one might with a traditional software bug. The incident might not be a sudden event, but the culmination of a series of subtle, evolving changes.

Moreover, the reliance on vast datasets for training and operation means that data integrity and security are paramount, and failures in these areas can be particularly insidious. An incident might not stem from a flaw in the AI algorithm itself, but from corrupted, poisoned, or manipulated training data that subtly (or not so subtly) alters the model's behavior. For instance, an adversary could deliberately introduce mislabeled data into a self-driving car's training set, causing it to misinterpret stop signs under specific conditions. Or, malicious actors might inject adversarial examples into the live data stream of an image recognition system, causing it to make critical errors. Diagnosing such data-related incidents requires not only inspecting the AI model but also a deep dive into the entire data pipeline, from collection and storage to preprocessing and labeling. This adds layers of complexity to the incident response process, as it involves not just code and algorithms, but also data governance, integrity checks, and potentially forensic analysis of data sources.

The automation inherent in AI-driven systems also presents a double-edged sword during incidents. While automation can accelerate response, it can also amplify errors. If an automated response mechanism is triggered incorrectly by a faulty AI signal, it might perform actions that exacerbate the incident. For example, an AI-powered automated trading system that detects a perceived market anomaly might trigger a massive sell-off, which, if based on flawed reasoning, could destabilize markets. The speed and scale of automated actions mean that responders must be able to rapidly override or control automated responses that are contributing to the problem, demanding a high level of vigilance and precise control over autonomous systems. This requires developing response playbooks that explicitly address how to manage and, if necessary, disengage automated response actions initiated by AI.

Finally, the regulatory and ethical implications of AI incidents are often more profound and far-reaching than those of traditional IT incidents. AI systems can make decisions that directly impact human lives, civil liberties, and societal well-being. An incident involving biased hiring AI, discriminatory loan application AI, or an AI that incorrectly identifies individuals in law enforcement scenarios carries immense ethical and legal weight. The response must not only address the technical failure but also the potential for harm caused to individuals and communities, and the potential for legal liability and reputational damage. This adds significant pressure to the incident response process, requiring close coordination with legal, compliance, and public relations teams, and demanding a level of transparency and accountability that may not be required for less impactful incidents. The very definition of "damage" extends beyond system downtime or data loss to encompass social and ethical harms, making the incident response framework for AI inherently more complex and demanding.

The advent of artificial intelligence in our technological infrastructure necessitates a paradigm shift in how we approach unforeseen disruptions. Gone are the days when a well-worn incident response playbook, designed for predictable software bugs and hardware failures, could suffice. AI systems, with their inherent complexity, emergent behaviors, and capacity for continuous learning, introduce a spectrum of vulnerabilities and failure modes that demand a more sophisticated, proactive, and adaptable strategy. At the heart of this evolution lies the imperative to develop a robust AI Incident Response Plan (AIRP). This isn't merely an addendum to existing IT security protocols; it is a foundational element for the responsible deployment and management of AI, designed to mitigate harm, ensure rapid recovery, and maintain trust in the systems we increasingly rely upon.

Developing an effective AIRP begins with the fundamental understanding that AI incidents are not uniform. They can range from subtle performance degradations and biases creeping into decision-making processes, to outright system failures, unintended consequences of autonomous actions, and even data integrity breaches that corrupt the very foundation of AI models. Each type of incident requires a tailored response, and the plan must be granular enough to address this diversity. The process of creating such a plan is iterative and multidisciplinary, requiring input from AI researchers, data scientists, software engineers, cybersecurity professionals, legal and compliance experts, and business stakeholders.

Establishing the AI Incident Response Team

The cornerstone of any effective incident response plan is a well-defined team with clear roles and responsibilities. For AI systems, this team, often referred to as the AI Incident Response Team (AIRT), needs to be augmented and specialized compared to traditional IT incident response units. Membership should draw from a diverse pool of expertise to tackle the unique challenges AI presents.

Key Roles within the AIRT:

Incident Commander (AI Focus): This individual, analogous to the traditional Incident Commander, holds ultimate authority during an incident. Their role is amplified by the need to understand the potential cascading effects and ethical implications of AI failures. They must be adept at making rapid decisions under pressure, coordinating complex technical and non-technical responses, and ensuring alignment with organizational objectives and risk appetite. Crucially, they need to have a foundational understanding of AI principles, or at least a strong capacity to quickly grasp the technical nuances presented by the AI specialists on the team.

AI Technical Lead: This is a critical new role. The AI Technical Lead is the foremost expert on the AI system(s) involved in the incident. They are responsible for deep technical analysis, understanding the AI model's architecture, training data, inference mechanisms, and any associated machine learning operations (MLOps) pipelines. They will guide the diagnostic process, identify potential root causes related to model behavior, data drift, or algorithmic flaws, and evaluate proposed technical remediation steps. This role often requires a deep background in machine learning engineering, data science, or AI research.

Data Scientist/ML Engineer: These team members are instrumental in analyzing the AI model's performance and behavior. They will be tasked with examining model outputs, evaluating data quality and integrity, performing root cause analysis on algorithmic failures, and potentially re-training or fine-tuning models as part of the recovery phase. Their expertise is vital for understanding subtle biases, performance degradation, and emergent behaviors.

AI Systems Engineer/MLOps Specialist: This role focuses on the infrastructure and deployment of the AI system. They understand the MLOps pipelines, deployment environments, model monitoring tools, and the interactions between the AI model and its surrounding software and hardware. They are crucial for understanding how the incident might have manifested due to infrastructure issues, deployment errors, or failures in the automated workflows that manage the AI lifecycle.

Cybersecurity Analyst (AI Threat Specialization): While traditional cybersecurity skills are essential, this role requires a specific focus on AI-related threats. This includes understanding adversarial attacks against AI (e.g., data poisoning, model evasion, privacy attacks), vulnerabilities in AI frameworks and libraries, and the potential for AI systems to be exploited or to exhibit malicious behavior. They will work to detect and prevent AI-specific compromises.

Legal and Compliance Liaison: Given the ethical and regulatory implications of AI, this role is paramount. This individual will provide guidance on legal obligations, privacy regulations (e.g., GDPR, CCPA), ethical guidelines, and potential liabilities. They will advise on communication strategies, ensure compliance during the incident response process, and help assess the downstream legal and reputational risks associated with the incident.

Communications Lead: Responsible for managing all internal and external communications related to the incident. This includes stakeholder updates, customer notifications, and managing public relations. For AI incidents, this role must be particularly adept at explaining complex technical issues in an understandable manner, while also addressing concerns about AI safety, fairness, and trustworthiness.

Domain Expert: Depending on the AI application, a domain expert who understands the business context or the specific area where the AI is deployed (e.g., finance, healthcare, transportation) is invaluable. They can help interpret the impact of the incident within the operational context and assess the real-world consequences of AI failures.

The AIRT should be structured with clear reporting lines. The Incident Commander typically oversees the entire response, delegating tasks to specific sub-teams or individuals. Regular, scheduled briefings are essential to maintain situational awareness and ensure coordinated action. Crucially, the AIRT must have the authority to access necessary systems, data, and personnel.

Defining Clear Roles and Responsibilities

Beyond the specific roles, the AIRP must clearly delineate responsibilities for various stages of incident management:

Detection and Alerting: Who is responsible for monitoring AI systems for anomalous behavior? This typically involves a combination of automated AI monitoring tools (detecting performance degradation, bias shifts, unexpected outputs) and human oversight. Clearly defined thresholds for alerts and escalation paths are critical. For instance, a slight increase in prediction error might trigger a low-level alert for a data scientist to investigate, while a sudden output of harmful content by a generative AI would trigger a high-priority, immediate response from the full AIRT.

Triage and Prioritization: Once an alert is received, who assesses its severity and impact? This requires a framework for categorizing incidents based on factors like the affected system's criticality, the number of users impacted, the potential for financial loss, reputational damage, ethical breaches, and safety risks. Prioritization ensures that the most critical incidents receive immediate attention. For example, an AI failure in a medical diagnostic tool would be prioritized above an AI-driven marketing personalization engine experiencing minor drift.

Investigation and Diagnosis: The AIRT members, particularly the AI Technical Lead, AI Systems Engineer, and Data Scientists, are responsible for delving into the root cause. This involves log analysis, model introspection (where possible), data pipeline audits, performance metric evaluation, and potentially controlled experimentation to reproduce the incident. The plan should outline the tools and techniques available for this phase, acknowledging the specialized nature of AI diagnostics.

Containment: This phase focuses on limiting the spread and impact of the incident. For AI systems, containment might involve disabling specific AI features, isolating the affected model, reverting to a previous stable version, or restricting user access. The decision to contain must balance the need to stop damage against the potential disruption to legitimate operations. For example, if a trading AI begins to execute irrational trades, immediate containment might involve shutting down its trading capabilities, even if it means missing out on potential profitable trades.

Eradication: Once the root cause is identified, eradication involves removing the threat or flaw. For AI, this could mean patching faulty code, re-training a model with corrected data, implementing new validation checks, or removing malicious data. The AIRP must specify procedures for verifying that the eradication was successful.

Recovery: This phase is about restoring affected systems and services to normal operation. For AI, this might involve redeploying a corrected model, re-enabling features, and performing post-incident validation to ensure stability and performance. It also includes restoring any impacted data and ensuring user confidence.

Post-Incident Review (PIR) and Lessons Learned: A comprehensive PIR is crucial. This is where the team analyzes what happened, why it happened, how the response was executed, and what can be improved for future incidents. For AI, PIRs must specifically examine the effectiveness of AI-specific detection mechanisms, the accuracy of diagnostic tools, the agility of containment strategies for autonomous systems, and the adequacy of the team's AI expertise. Lessons learned should feed directly back into refining the AIRP, updating training, and improving AI development and deployment practices.

Establishing Communication Protocols

Effective communication is the lifeblood of incident response, and for AI, its importance is magnified by the potential for widespread impact and public scrutiny. A well-defined communication plan ensures that all relevant parties are informed promptly, accurately, and consistently.

Key Elements of AI Incident Communication:

Internal Stakeholder Communication: This includes regular updates to senior management, relevant department heads (e.g., product, engineering, legal, PR), and the broader technical teams. The AIRP should specify the frequency and format of these updates, as well as the escalation triggers for notifying different levels of management. For AI incidents, it's crucial that technical details are translated into business impact and risk assessments for leadership.

External Stakeholder Communication: For incidents impacting customers, partners, or the public, a clear and transparent communication strategy is vital. This includes:

Notification Channels: How will affected parties be informed? (e.g., email, in-app messages, website banners, social media).

Content of Communications: What information needs to be conveyed? This typically includes acknowledging the issue, explaining the impact (in user-friendly terms), what steps are being taken to resolve it, and when users can expect resolution. For AI incidents, careful wording is needed to avoid causing undue alarm or revealing proprietary information while still being informative. Transparency about the type of AI involved and its function can build trust.

Spokesperson Designation: Who is authorized to speak on behalf of the organization? This ensures a consistent message.

Crisis Communication Integration: The AIRT must coordinate closely with the organization's crisis communication team to ensure a unified and strategic approach.

Information Flow within the AIRT: Establishing clear channels for real-time communication among AIRT members is essential. This could involve dedicated incident management platforms, secure chat channels, or regular virtual huddles. The goal is to ensure everyone involved has access to the latest information and can contribute effectively.

Escalation Procedures: The plan must clearly define how and when to escalate an incident to higher levels of management or external agencies. This includes defining the criteria for escalation (e.g., severity, duration, impact, regulatory requirement).

Post-Incident Communication: Following resolution, a summary of the incident and the response should be communicated internally, often as part of the PIR findings. Externally, a follow-up communication might be necessary to confirm resolution and outline any preventative measures taken.

AI-Specific Communication Considerations:

Explaining AI to Non-Experts: A significant challenge in communicating AI incidents is translating complex technical jargon into understandable terms for diverse audiences, including executives, customers, and the media. The AIRP should encourage the development of "incident communication templates" or "talking points" that can be adapted, and ensure team members have training in communicating technical concepts clearly and empathetically.

Addressing Ethical and Societal Concerns: If an AI incident involves bias, fairness, or potential harm to individuals or groups, communication must be handled with extreme sensitivity. Transparency about the nature of the bias, the steps taken to rectify it, and the commitment to ethical AI development is paramount. This often requires close collaboration with legal, ethics, and public relations departments.

Data Privacy and Security: When an AI incident may involve data breaches or misuse of personal information, communication must adhere strictly to data protection regulations and legal counsel.

Developing Specific Incident Response Steps for AI

The core of the AIRP lies in detailing the procedures for each phase of incident management, tailored to the nuances of AI systems.

Detection and Alerting for AI Systems

Proactive detection is far more effective than reactive response. For AI, this involves:

Robust Monitoring Frameworks: Implementing comprehensive monitoring systems that track not only system health (CPU, memory, network) but also AI-specific metrics. This includes:
Performance Metrics: Accuracy, precision, recall, F1-score, latency, throughput. Drift detection algorithms can flag subtle changes over time.
Data Drift and Concept Drift: Monitoring input data distributions and the relationship between inputs and outputs to detect deviations from training data or underlying concepts. Statistical tests (e.g., Kolmogorov-Smirnov, Jensen-Shannon divergence) can be employed.
Output Anomaly Detection: Identifying outputs that fall outside expected ranges or patterns. This is crucial for generative AI where unexpected or harmful content can be produced.
Bias and Fairness Metrics: Regularly assessing model predictions and outputs for demographic disparities or unfair treatment across different groups. Tools can be integrated to flag emerging biases.
Resource Utilization: Unusual spikes or drops in computational resource usage might indicate an issue, such as an AI model stuck in a loop or an inefficient inference process.

Human Oversight and Feedback Loops: While automation is key, human intuition and domain expertise are irreplaceable. Establishing channels for users and internal teams to report unexpected AI behavior or results is vital. This feedback loop should directly inform the monitoring systems and the AIRT.
Adversarial Threat Detection: Implementing systems to detect potential adversarial attacks, such as unusual patterns in input data that might suggest evasion attempts, or anomalies in model confidence scores that could indicate manipulation.
Alert Prioritization and Routing: As mentioned, alerts must be categorized based on severity and impact, with clear escalation paths to the appropriate AIRT members or teams. For example, an alert indicating a significant drop in classification accuracy for a critical system should be routed immediately to the AI Technical Lead and Incident Commander.

Containment Strategies for AI Incidents

Containment aims to stop the spread of damage and prevent further harm. For AI, this can be more complex than simply shutting down a service.

Selective Disablement: Instead of disabling an entire system, it may be possible to disable specific AI components or functionalities. For example, if an AI-powered recommendation engine starts suggesting inappropriate content, the recommendation module can be temporarily disabled while the core service remains available.
Rollback to Previous Versions: Reverting the AI model or its underlying software to a known stable version is a common containment strategy. This requires robust version control and an efficient rollback mechanism within the MLOps pipeline.

Quarantining Data: If data integrity is compromised or malicious data is suspected, the affected data pipelines or storage locations may need to be quarantined to prevent further corruption.
Traffic Rerouting or Throttling: In some cases, reducing or rerouting traffic to the affected AI system can limit the volume of erroneous transactions or inferences, thereby mitigating widespread impact. This might involve directing a portion of requests to a fallback system or a manual process.
Isolating AI Models: For complex AI architectures, it might be necessary to isolate a specific model or a cluster of models that are exhibiting problematic behavior, preventing them from interacting with other parts of the system.
Automated Response Override: If an AI system is triggering automated response actions that are exacerbating the incident, the AIRT must have the capability to quickly override or disable these autonomous responses. This highlights the need for "fail-safe" mechanisms in automated AI responses.

Eradication and Recovery Processes for AI

Eradication focuses on removing the root cause, while recovery restores normal operations.

Root Cause Analysis (AI Specific): This is often the most challenging step. It may involve:
Model Debugging and Introspection: Utilizing techniques like LIME, SHAP, or attention visualization to understand why a model made a particular decision or produced a certain output.

Data Forensics: Examining training and inference data for anomalies, corruption, or signs of adversarial manipulation. This can involve tracing data lineage.

Code and Configuration Audits: Reviewing the AI model's code, hyperparameter configurations, and the surrounding software infrastructure.

Simulation and Reproducibility: Attempting to reproduce the incident under controlled conditions to validate hypotheses about the root cause.

Remediation Steps:

Model Re-training/Fine-tuning: Correcting biases, updating performance, or addressing vulnerabilities by re-training the model with curated datasets or fine-tuning its parameters.

Data Cleansing and Validation: Identifying and removing or correcting erroneous data points from training or inference datasets. Implementing stricter data validation checks.

Algorithm Patching: Modifying the AI algorithm itself to address logical flaws or security vulnerabilities.

Infrastructure Fixes: Addressing any underlying hardware or software infrastructure issues that contributed to the AI's failure.

Implementing Safeguards: Developing and deploying new validation rules, monitoring checks, or human oversight points to prevent recurrence.

Recovery and Validation:

Phased Redeployment: Reintroducing the corrected AI model or system gradually, perhaps starting with a subset of users or a limited scope of functionality.

Intensive Monitoring: Closely monitoring the system after recovery to ensure stability, performance, and the absence of recurring issues. This phase requires a heightened level of vigilance.

User Acceptance Testing (UAT): Involving end-users or domain experts to validate that the recovered system meets requirements and functions as expected.

Performance Benchmarking: Comparing the performance of the recovered system against pre-incident benchmarks and established KPIs.

Post-Incident Review (PIR) and Continuous Improvement

The PIR is not a formality; it is a critical learning opportunity. For AI incidents, PIRs must delve deeply into:

Effectiveness of AI-Specific Detection: How well did the AI monitoring tools and human oversight identify the incident? Were the alerts timely and accurate?
Diagnostic Success: How effective were the AI-specific investigation techniques? Was the root cause identified efficiently?
Containment and Eradication Agility: How quickly and effectively were containment and eradication measures implemented? Were there any challenges in controlling autonomous AI actions?
Team Performance: How effectively did the AIRT members collaborate? Was there sufficient expertise available?
Lessons Learned: What specific technical, procedural, or organizational changes are needed to prevent similar incidents? This includes updating training programs for AI expertise, refining MLOps pipelines, enhancing AI model validation processes, and potentially revising AI development best practices.
AIRP Updates: The PIR findings should directly inform updates to the AIRP, ensuring it remains a living document that evolves with the organization's AI landscape.

By meticulously developing and regularly refining an AI Incident Response Plan, organizations can move from a state of reactive damage control to proactive risk mitigation. This systematic approach, grounded in a deep understanding of AI's unique characteristics, is essential for building resilience, fostering trust, and ensuring the responsible advancement and deployment of artificial intelligence. It requires a commitment to continuous learning, cross-functional collaboration, and a clear understanding that in the age of AI, preparedness is not an option, but a necessity. The investment in a robust AIRP is an investment in the future reliability and ethical integrity of an organization's AI-driven operations.

The fundamental principle underpinning any effective incident response framework, whether for traditional IT systems or sophisticated AI deployments, is the adage: "The sooner you know, the sooner you can fix." This holds particularly true for artificial intelligence, where the interconnectedness of components, the inherent opacity of some models, and the potential for emergent behaviors can lead to rapid escalation of issues. Therefore, establishing robust mechanisms for the early detection and rapid triage of AI incidents is not merely a best practice; it is a critical prerequisite for maintaining operational integrity, safeguarding user trust, and mitigating potential harm. The process begins with a comprehensive understanding of *what* to look for and *how* to detect it within the unique operational context of AI systems.

Leveraging Advanced Monitoring Systems for AI

Traditional infrastructure monitoring, which focuses on hardware health, network traffic, and application availability, forms the baseline for AI system surveillance. However, AI systems introduce a new layer of complexity that necessitates specialized monitoring tools and techniques. These systems need to go beyond simply tracking uptime and resource utilization to actively scrutinize the AI's behavior and outputs. At the forefront of this are sophisticated AI monitoring platforms. These platforms are designed to continuously collect and analyze a wide array of metrics, providing real-time insights into the AI's performance and operational state.

A crucial aspect of AI monitoring is the tracking of **performance metrics**. This includes standard measures like accuracy, precision, recall, and F1-score for classification tasks, or Mean Squared Error (MSE) and R-squared for regression models. However, the real power comes from observing these metrics *over time*. AI systems are not static; they operate in dynamic environments where the underlying data distributions and the relationships between variables can shift. Therefore, detecting subtle drifts in these performance metrics is paramount. This involves implementing **drift detection algorithms**, which act as early warning systems. For instance, if an AI model trained to detect fraudulent transactions starts showing a gradual decrease in its precision, it might indicate that new, previously unseen fraud patterns are emerging, or that legitimate transactions are being misclassified. Detecting this drift early allows for intervention *before* a significant number of fraudulent transactions go unnoticed or legitimate users are unfairly flagged.

Beyond direct performance metrics, monitoring the **data itself** is equally vital. AI models are highly dependent on the quality and characteristics of their training and inference data. **Data drift** refers to changes in the input data distribution compared to the training data, while **concept drift** signifies changes in the relationship between input variables and the target variable. Monitoring these drifts requires statistical analysis of incoming data streams. Tools can compare the statistical properties of live data (e.g., mean, variance, distribution type) against historical data or a baseline distribution. Significant deviations trigger alerts, prompting investigation into whether the model's performance is likely to degrade due to these shifts. For example, a natural language processing (NLP) model used for customer sentiment analysis might experience data drift if the language used in customer reviews suddenly shifts due to a new product launch or a marketing campaign. Without monitoring, the model might continue to interpret the new linguistic patterns with its old understanding, leading to inaccurate sentiment scores.

Furthermore, the outputs generated by AI systems, especially generative AI, must be closely scrutinized.
Output anomaly detection involves identifying predictions, classifications, or generated content that fall outside expected norms or predefined safety parameters. For a generative AI creating text, this could mean flagging outputs that are nonsensical, repetitive, factually incorrect, or contain harmful content (e.g., hate speech, misinformation). For AI systems making automated decisions, anomaly detection might focus on outputs that are statistically improbable, excessively confident in erroneous predictions, or fall outside acceptable operational ranges. This often involves setting up thresholds, statistical bounds, or employing outlier detection algorithms on the model's outputs.

Finally, monitoring
resource utilization can provide indirect but critical clues. Unusual spikes or sustained high usage of CPU, GPU, or memory by an AI service might indicate inefficiencies, unexpected computational complexity in processing certain inputs, or even a system stuck in an infinite loop or an uncontrolled recursive process. Conversely, a sudden drop in resource usage might suggest that the AI has become unresponsive or is no longer processing requests. These anomalies, while not direct indicators of flawed AI logic, can point to underlying infrastructure issues or system malfunctions that are impacting the AI's ability to perform correctly.

Harnessing Anomaly Detection Algorithms

At the heart of proactive AI incident detection lie sophisticated anomaly detection algorithms. These algorithms are designed to identify patterns in data that deviate from expected behavior, flagging them as potential incidents. While the specific algorithms employed will vary based on the type of AI system and the data it processes, several categories are commonly utilized.

Statistical Methods form a foundational approach. Techniques such as z-scores, Modified Z-scores, or Grubbs' test can identify data points that are statistically improbable given a known distribution. For time-series data, moving averages, Exponential Smoothing, and more advanced methods like ARIMA (AutoRegressive Integrated Moving Average) can be used to model expected behavior and flag deviations. When monitoring performance metrics over time, statistical process control (SPC) charts can be invaluable for detecting shifts or trends that indicate a system is moving out of its stable operational state.

Machine Learning-Based Anomaly Detection offers more sophisticated capabilities, especially when dealing with complex, high-dimensional data where statistical assumptions might not hold. **Clustering algorithms** (e.g., K-Means, DBSCAN) can group similar data points, and points that fall outside any cluster or are far from cluster centroids can be identified as anomalies. **Density-based methods**, such as Local Outlier Factor (LOF), measure the local density deviation of a data point with respect to its neighbors, identifying points that are in sparser regions as outliers.

Tree-based algorithms, like Isolation Forests, are particularly efficient for anomaly detection. They work by randomly partitioning the data, isolating anomalies in fewer steps than normal data points. This makes them scalable and effective for large datasets.

Deep Learning approaches are increasingly employed for anomaly detection, especially for complex data types like images, audio, or sequences. **Autoencoders**, a type of neural network trained to reconstruct its input, can learn a compressed representation of normal data. When presented with anomalous data, the autoencoder will struggle to reconstruct it accurately, resulting in a high reconstruction error that signals an anomaly. Other deep learning architectures, such as Recurrent Neural Networks (RNNs) or Transformers, can be trained to predict the next element in a sequence; deviations from the predicted sequence can indicate anomalies.

Crucially, the effectiveness of these algorithms depends on careful tuning. **False positives** (flagging normal behavior as anomalous) can lead to alert fatigue, causing valuable alerts to be ignored. **False negatives** (failing to detect actual anomalies) can allow incidents to escalate unnoticed. Therefore, continuous refinement of anomaly detection models, including periodic re-training and adjustment of thresholds based on feedback from incident response activities, is essential. The AI incident response team (AIRT) must have access to the outputs of these algorithms and the expertise to interpret them correctly.

Integrating User Feedback and Human Oversight

While automated monitoring and anomaly detection are indispensable, they are not infallible. The nuanced understanding of context, the ability to discern subtle issues that elude algorithms, and the capacity for creative problem-solving remain uniquely human strengths. Therefore, integrating robust
user feedback mechanisms and ensuring consistent **human oversight** are critical components of an effective AI incident detection strategy.

Users, whether they are end-customers interacting with a public-facing AI application or internal employees relying on an AI-powered tool, often have the first-hand experience of when something is not right. Unexpectedly poor results, confusing interactions, or outright errors in an AI system's output are frequently noticed by those who are actively using it. Establishing clear, accessible, and responsive channels for users to report these issues is paramount. This could involve:

In-app feedback forms or reporting tools: Allowing users to provide immediate feedback directly within the application where the AI is deployed.
Dedicated customer support channels: Training support staff to recognize and escalate AI-related issues reported by users.
Internal reporting dashboards or communication channels: For internal users, providing easy ways to flag AI system malfunctions or unexpected behaviors.
"Report an issue" buttons: Strategically placed within AI-generated outputs or interfaces that prompt users to report problems.

When a user reports an issue, it should not be treated as a mere bug report; it should be seen as a potential incident alert. The AIRT must have a defined process for receiving, acknowledging, and triaging these user-submitted alerts. This involves quickly assessing the severity and scope of the reported issue and determining if it warrants a full incident response. For example, if multiple users report that an AI-powered chatbot is providing nonsensical answers or refusing to perform basic functions, this should trigger an immediate investigation by the AIRT.

Human oversight extends beyond just receiving user feedback. It involves having subject matter experts and AI practitioners regularly review AI system performance and outputs, even when automated systems don't flag any anomalies. This is particularly important for AI systems that operate in safety-critical domains or make decisions with significant ethical implications. Regular manual audits, where experts examine a sample of AI decisions or outputs, can uncover subtle biases, systemic errors, or emergent behaviors that might not trigger algorithmic alerts. This is where the **domain expert** role within the AIRT becomes invaluable, as they can often spot contextual anomalies that a purely technical observer might miss.

Furthermore, a culture of continuous learning and proactive engagement from the technical teams is vital. Data scientists and ML engineers should not just build and deploy models; they should also actively participate in monitoring their performance in the real world. This includes engaging with MLOps teams, reviewing monitoring dashboards, and staying abreast of user feedback. This proactive engagement fosters a sense of ownership and responsibility, making teams more attuned to potential issues before they escalate into full-blown incidents.

The Crucial Role of Triage and Prioritization

Once a potential AI incident has been detected through any of the aforementioned mechanisms – automated alerts, user feedback, or human observation – the immediate next step is **triage**. Triage is the process of rapidly assessing the nature, severity, and potential impact of the detected issue to determine its priority and the appropriate response. For AI incidents, triage requires a nuanced approach that considers factors unique to AI systems.

The primary goal of triage is to answer several critical questions: Is this a genuine incident? How severe is it? What is its immediate and potential future impact? Who needs to be involved in the response? Based on the answers, the incident is then assigned a priority level, dictating the urgency and resources allocated to its resolution.

A robust triage process for AI incidents typically involves the following steps and considerations:

1.
Initial Assessment and Verification: The first step is to verify if the alert or report represents a genuine problem. This might involve quickly reproducing the reported issue, checking system logs for related errors, or confirming the anomaly with a quick glance at monitoring dashboards. For instance, an alert from a drift detection algorithm might be verified by examining the statistical properties of the current data against the baseline. If the alert is confirmed, the incident proceeds to the next stage.

2.
Defining the Scope and Impact: This is where the unique characteristics of AI come into play. The AIRT must assess:
Affected System(s) and Functionality: Which AI model, service, or feature is malfunctioning? Is it a core component or a peripheral one?
User Impact: How many users or customers are affected? Is it a specific segment or the entire user base?
Business Impact: What is the potential financial loss (e.g., lost revenue, increased operational costs)? What is the potential impact on business operations or critical processes?
Safety Impact: This is paramount for AI systems in domains like healthcare, autonomous driving, or industrial control. Does the incident pose a risk to human life or physical safety? Even minor inaccuracies in a medical diagnostic AI could have life-threatening consequences.
Privacy Impact: Does the incident involve a breach of personal data, unauthorized access, or misuse of sensitive information handled by the

AI? Are there compliance implications with regulations like GDPR or CCPA?
Fairness and Ethical Impact: Is the AI exhibiting biased behavior that leads to discriminatory outcomes for certain demographic groups? Is it generating harmful, offensive, or misleading content? Does it violate ethical guidelines or organizational principles?
Reputational Impact: What is the potential damage to the organization's brand and public trust, especially if the incident becomes public?

3.
Categorization and Prioritization: Based on the impact assessment, the incident is assigned a priority level. A common prioritization scheme might include:
Critical (P1): Incidents with immediate, severe impact on safety, widespread system outage, significant data breach, or severe legal/reputational risk. These require immediate, all-hands response. Example: An AI controlling autonomous vehicles is making dangerous steering decisions.
High (P2): Incidents with significant impact on a large number of users, substantial financial loss, or serious ethical concerns. These require rapid response within hours. Example: An AI trading algorithm is causing significant financial losses due to erroneous trades.
Medium (P3): Incidents affecting a smaller subset of users or causing moderate disruption, or early signs of performance degradation that could lead to a P1/P2 if not addressed. Response within days. Example: An AI recommendation engine is showing a noticeable decline in user engagement due to subtle drift.
Low (P4): Minor issues, potential bugs with minimal impact, or alerts that require further investigation but do not pose an immediate threat. These can be addressed as part of routine maintenance or prioritized later. Example: A minor UI glitch in an AI-powered dashboard that doesn't affect core functionality.

4.

Incident Commander Assignment and Team Activation: The triage process typically culminates in the assignment of an Incident Commander (or a designated lead for the initial response) and the activation of the appropriate AIRT members based on the incident's nature and priority. For a critical safety incident, the full AIRT might be activated immediately. For a low-priority performance drift, only a data scientist or ML engineer might be tasked with an initial investigation.

5.
Documentation: All findings, assessments, and decisions made during triage must be meticulously documented in the incident management system. This documentation serves as the historical record, aids in post-incident analysis, and ensures transparency.

The effectiveness of the triage process hinges on several factors: the clarity of defined impact criteria, the training and experience of the personnel performing triage, and the availability of accurate information about the AI system and its operational context. For AI, this often means that the triage team needs to include individuals with at least a foundational understanding of AI principles, or ready access to AI experts who can quickly provide the necessary technical context. The ability to rapidly translate technical anomalies into business and ethical impacts is crucial. For instance, identifying a drift in a model's bias metric needs to be understood not just as a statistical deviation, but as a potential precursor to discriminatory outcomes, thus elevating its priority.

By implementing a structured and intelligent triage process, organizations can ensure that their response efforts are consistently focused on the most critical issues, thereby maximizing their ability to contain damage, restore functionality, and uphold the ethical and safety standards expected of AI systems. This methodical approach to assessing and prioritizing detected anomalies is the critical bridge between simply knowing something is wrong and effectively fixing it.

The immediate aftermath of detecting an AI incident is a critical juncture. While comprehensive monitoring and accurate triage provide the necessary awareness, it is the efficacy of containment and recovery strategies that ultimately determines the extent of damage and the speed at which normalcy can be restored. This phase demands a deliberate, systematic approach, drawing upon a toolkit of techniques designed to isolate compromised systems, prevent further proliferation of errors or malicious activity, and meticulously re-establish operational integrity. For AI systems, these strategies are further complicated by their dynamic nature, the complexity of their underlying components, and the potential for subtle, emergent failures that might not be immediately obvious.

Containment in the context of AI incidents refers to the act of isolating the affected AI component or system to prevent the issue from spreading to other parts of the infrastructure or impacting a wider user base. This often involves severing connections, restricting access, or temporarily disabling specific functionalities. The primary goal is to halt any ongoing negative impact while the root cause is investigated and a permanent solution is developed. For instance, if an AI model responsible for generating personalized product recommendations begins to exhibit a severe bias, leading to discriminatory suggestions, the immediate containment action might be to disable the recommendation engine entirely, or at least for specific user segments demonstrably affected by the bias. This prevents further instances of discriminatory recommendations and protects the organization from potential reputational damage and legal repercussions.

A fundamental containment technique is **service isolation**. This involves segmenting the AI system from the rest of the IT infrastructure or from critical data flows. This can be achieved through various networking controls, such as virtual private clouds (VPCs), firewalls, or network access control lists (ACLs). If a particular AI microservice responsible for natural language understanding in a customer support chatbot begins to produce offensive content, it can be isolated by restricting its inbound and outbound network traffic. This ensures that it cannot interact with other services or the user interface, thus preventing the spread of its erroneous or harmful outputs. Similarly, if a diagnostic AI in a healthcare setting is suspected of making inaccurate diagnoses, it might be disconnected from patient record systems and external communication channels.

Another crucial containment strategy is
feature flagging or disabling. Modern AI systems are often built with modularity in mind, allowing specific features or functionalities to be toggled on or off without requiring a full system restart. If a particular AI-driven feature, such as an image generation module within a creative suite, starts producing disturbing or inappropriate content, it can be temporarily disabled via a feature flag. This allows the rest of the application to continue functioning normally while the problematic feature is addressed. This approach is highly efficient as it minimizes disruption to the overall service. For AI systems that make automated decisions, such as loan application approvals, a specific AI algorithm responsible for risk assessment might be temporarily bypassed, reverting to a simpler, rules-based system or a manual review process if it exhibits signs of significant bias or a critical failure.

In situations where the exact nature of the AI failure is unclear but its impact is evident, implementing
fail-safe modes becomes a vital containment measure. A fail-safe mode is a pre-defined operational state that the AI system enters when it detects an anomaly or a critical failure. This mode is designed to be conservative and minimize risk. For example, an AI system controlling an industrial robot arm might be programmed to enter a "safe stop" state, retracting to a neutral position and disabling all movement, if its sensors detect unexpected vibrations or deviations from its programmed path. This prevents potential damage to machinery or injury to personnel. In less

critical systems, a fail-safe mode might involve reverting to a default, less sophisticated behavior. A content moderation AI that starts incorrectly flagging benign content could be temporarily set to a "low-confidence" mode, escalating all borderline cases for human review rather than making automated decisions.

Rollbacks are a cornerstone of incident response across all technological domains, and AI is no exception. When an AI model's performance degrades or it starts exhibiting problematic behavior after a recent update or deployment, rolling back to a previous, known-good version of the model can be an effective containment and recovery strategy. This involves reverting the model artifacts (e.g., model weights, architecture definition) and associated code to a state where performance was satisfactory. This process requires robust version control for AI models and the infrastructure to quickly redeploy older versions. For example, if a new iteration of a natural language generation model starts producing repetitive or factually incorrect text, rolling back to the previous stable version can immediately restore the quality of output. However, it's crucial to ensure that the rollback process itself doesn't introduce new vulnerabilities or data inconsistencies. Thorough testing of the rolled-back version is essential before it is fully reinstated.

Beyond rolling back the model,
data rollback or sanitization may also be necessary. If the incident involves the AI model learning from or being influenced by corrupted, poisoned, or maliciously altered data, it might be necessary to roll back the training or inference data as well, or to sanitize the affected data. This is a more complex undertaking, as data often underpins multiple systems and processes. The approach would depend on the architecture and data management practices in place. For instance, if an anomaly detection system begins to generate a high volume of false positives due to a sudden influx of erroneous sensor readings, the data stream might need to be

temporarily halted, the corrupted data filtered out, and the system restarted with the clean data.

Restricting inference or training access is another form of containment. If a specific AI model is suspected of being compromised or generating harmful outputs, access to its inference endpoints can be temporarily restricted. This might mean disabling API access for certain clients or segments of users. In extreme cases, if a training pipeline is suspected of being poisoned, access to the training environment or the ingestion of new training data might be suspended. This prevents the compromised model from making further decisions or propagating corrupted learning.

Once the immediate threat is contained, the focus shifts to **recovery**. Recovery is the process of restoring the affected AI system and its functionalities to their normal operational state. This is not simply a matter of turning things back on; it requires a methodical approach to ensure that the underlying issue has been resolved and that the system is stable and performing as expected.

A critical step in recovery is **root cause analysis (RCA)**. While containment stops the bleeding, RCA identifies why the bleeding started. For AI systems, RCA can be challenging due to their complexity and sometimes opaque nature. It involves a deep dive into logs, monitoring data, code, model behavior, and training data to pinpoint the exact cause of the incident. Was it a data drift issue? A bug in the code? A hardware failure? A security vulnerability? An unexpected interaction between components? An issue with the underlying infrastructure? Effective RCA for AI incidents often requires collaboration between data scientists, ML engineers, software engineers, and operations teams. For example, a root cause analysis for a biased AI might reveal that the training dataset was disproportionately skewed towards a particular demographic, leading the model to learn and perpetuate that bias.

Following RCA, the
fix implementation takes place. This could involve retraining the model with corrected data, patching code, updating libraries, correcting configuration errors, or implementing new safeguards. For instance, if the RCA identified a specific bias in a loan application AI, the fix might involve re-sampling the training data to ensure better representation, or implementing algorithmic fairness constraints during training. If a bug in the inference code was the culprit, it would require a code fix, rigorous testing, and then redeployment.

After the fix is implemented,
validation and testing are paramount before bringing the system back online fully. This is where AI recovery differs significantly from traditional IT recovery. The validation must go beyond standard functional tests; it must specifically confirm that the issue that caused the incident has been resolved and that no new issues have been introduced. This involves:

Re-testing with specific edge cases: Using the exact scenarios that triggered the incident, or similar edge cases, to ensure the fix holds. For a biased AI, this means testing with data representative of all relevant demographic groups.
Performance validation: Verifying that key performance metrics (accuracy, precision, recall, latency, etc.) have returned to acceptable levels and are stable.
Safety and fairness testing: For AI systems in safety-critical or ethically sensitive domains, dedicated testing protocols are essential. This might involve simulations, adversarial testing, or bias audits to confirm that the AI is operating safely and ethically. For example, an autonomous driving AI that experienced an incident due to misinterpreting a traffic sign would

undergo extensive re-testing with a wide variety of sign types, lighting conditions, and weather.

User acceptance testing (UAT): If the AI system has direct user interaction, a group of representative users might be involved in testing the recovered system to ensure it meets their needs and expectations.

Once the system has been thoroughly validated, a **phased or controlled re-introduction** to production is often the safest approach. This involves gradually bringing the restored AI system back into full operation. Instead of a "big bang" relaunch, a phased approach might involve:

Gradual traffic increase: Slowly increasing the volume of requests or data fed to the restored AI system, starting with a small percentage of users or requests and monitoring closely.

Partial feature re-enablement: If only a specific feature was affected, it might be re-enabled first, with other features remaining offline or operating under a fallback mechanism until their stability is also confirmed.

Shadow deployment: Running the restored AI system in parallel with the old system (if it's still operational or a previous version) but not allowing its decisions to affect live operations. The outputs are logged and compared to ensure consistency and correctness. This allows for real-world validation without risk.

Throughout the recovery process, **continuous monitoring** remains indispensable. Even after a fix has been implemented and the system is back online, the AIRT must maintain heightened vigilance. The same monitoring systems and anomaly detection algorithms that were used for detection and containment should now be used to ensure the fix is effective and that no new issues are emerging. This might involve configuring alerts to be more sensitive during the initial recovery period.

Finally, a crucial aspect of recovery is **documentation and post-incident review**. Every step taken during containment and recovery, from the initial detection to the final re-introduction, must be meticulously documented. The post-incident review process, often called a "post-mortem," is where the AIRT and relevant stakeholders analyze the entire incident lifecycle. This review aims to:

Identify lessons learned: What went well? What could have been done better?
Update incident response playbooks: Refine existing procedures and develop new ones based on the incident.
Improve system design and architecture: Identify systemic weaknesses that contributed to the incident and propose architectural changes to prevent recurrence.
Enhance monitoring and detection capabilities: Determine if new metrics or algorithms are needed to catch similar issues earlier in the future.
Strengthen training and awareness: Ensure that teams are adequately trained to handle similar incidents.

For AI systems, the post-incident review is particularly vital because of the rapid evolution of the technology. What might be a cutting-edge solution today could be the source of an incident tomorrow. By diligently documenting and analyzing each event, organizations build a collective institutional knowledge that strengthens their resilience against future AI-related challenges. This continuous feedback loop ensures that the incident response framework for AI systems evolves alongside the technology itself, preparing organizations not just to react, but to proactively anticipate and mitigate the unique risks posed by artificial intelligence.

The aftermath of an AI incident is not merely an endpoint to be exited from; it is, rather, a crucial inflection point that offers a profound opportunity for growth and fortification. While containment and recovery strategies are vital for immediate damage control and service restoration, the true measure of an organization's AI resilience is often found in its ability to systematically learn from these challenging events. This learning process is most effectively formalized through a rigorous **post-incident analysis**, commonly known in the industry as a "post-mortem" or "incident review." This practice transcends the simple act of recounting what happened; it is a deliberate and structured examination designed to unearth the fundamental reasons behind an incident, critically assess the efficacy of the response, distill actionable lessons, and ultimately, to proactively enhance the robustness of AI systems, operational processes, and the incident response framework itself.

The primary objective of a post-incident analysis is to achieve a deep and comprehensive understanding of the incident's genesis. This begins with a meticulous effort to identify the **root cause(s)**. For AI systems, this can be a more intricate endeavor than in traditional IT environments. The complexity of AI models, their reliance on vast and often dynamic datasets, the intricate interplay of various software components, and the potential for emergent behaviors mean that a single, easily identifiable cause might be rare. Instead, incidents often arise from a confluence of factors. For instance, a seemingly minor data drift in a model used for fraud detection might, when combined with a recent, subtle change in the underlying inference engine's configuration, lead to a cascade of false positives that overwhelm the system. A thorough root cause analysis would need to disentangle these threads: Was the data drift the primary trigger? Was the configuration change an ill-advised modification or an intended update that was insufficiently tested? Did the monitoring systems fail to flag the drift or the configuration change as anomalous? The investigation might involve deep dives into model performance metrics over time, analysis of training and inference logs, examination of data pipelines for any anomalies or shifts, and a review of all recent code deployments, configuration changes, and infrastructure updates. Techniques like the "5 Whys" can be valuable here, repeatedly asking "why" to peel back layers of causality until the fundamental issue is revealed. For example, if a customer service chatbot begins generating irrelevant responses, asking why it's generating irrelevant responses might lead to: 1) It's misinterpreting user intent. Why? Because its natural language understanding (NLU) model is failing on certain phrasing. Why is it failing? Because the model was trained on data that didn't adequately represent the diversity of how users express certain needs. Why didn't the training data adequately represent these needs? Because the data collection process was not sufficiently robust or was biased. This iterative questioning, applied across technical and procedural dimensions, is key to uncovering the true root cause, not just the immediate symptom.

Furthermore, the analysis must extend to evaluating the **effectiveness of the incident response**. This involves a critical self-assessment of how well the predefined incident response plan (IRP) was executed and whether the actions taken were appropriate and timely. Were the detection mechanisms sensitive enough? Was the alert triage accurate and efficient? How quickly were containment measures implemented, and were they sufficient to prevent further damage? Was the recovery process well-orchestrated, and was the system validated thoroughly before being brought back online? For AI-specific incidents, this evaluation might probe questions such as: Did the chosen containment strategy (e.g., disabling a feature, rolling back a model) adequately address the specific AI failure mode? Were the recovery steps sufficient to re-establish not just functional integrity but also ethical compliance and safety guarantees? For example, if an AI-powered medical diagnostic tool provided incorrect diagnoses, the post-mortem would not only investigate why the diagnoses were incorrect but also evaluate if the response team correctly identified the problematic AI component, if the rollback to a previous, trusted version was swift and complete, and if the subsequent re-validation specifically tested the diagnostic accuracy across a diverse range of patient profiles and conditions. A failure in the response itself—perhaps a delay in alerting the right personnel, a lack of clear communication channels between data scientists and operations teams, or insufficient tooling for rapid rollback—becomes a critical lesson learned, informing updates to the IRP and team training.

A cornerstone of any effective post-incident analysis is the meticulous **documentation of lessons learned**. This is not merely a perfunctory summary but a detailed record of insights gained that can be translated into tangible improvements. These lessons can span a broad spectrum: technical, procedural, organizational, and even strategic. On the technical front, lessons learned might include the need for more robust adversarial testing for a generative AI model that produced harmful content, the requirement for enhanced data validation pipelines to prevent bias amplification, or the imperative to implement more granular access controls for AI model deployments. Procedurally, lessons might highlight deficiencies in the incident communication protocol, the need for more comprehensive playbooks for specific AI failure modes (e.g., model poisoning, catastrophic forgetting), or the necessity of integrating human oversight at critical decision points in an automated AI workflow. Organizationally, lessons might point to a need for cross-functional training, clearer roles and responsibilities within the AI incident response team (AIRT), or improved collaboration mechanisms between development, operations, and ethics committees. The documentation should be clear, concise, and actionable, providing specific recommendations for improvement. For instance, instead of a vague note like "Improve monitoring," a detailed lesson learned might read: "Implement real-time anomaly detection on model inference latency and error rates, with automated alerts triggered if deviations exceed 15% of baseline for more than 10 minutes, as the recent incident involving the recommendation engine's performance degradation went unnoticed for several hours due to insufficient real-time monitoring."

Crucially, these lessons learned must be translated into concrete

updates to systems, processes, and the incident response plan. This ensures that the analysis is not a one-off exercise but an integral part of a continuous improvement cycle. Systems might be updated with new monitoring tools, enhanced validation frameworks, or built-in safeguards. Processes might be revised to incorporate new data quality checks, stricter deployment procedures for AI models, or mandated ethical reviews at different stages of the AI lifecycle. The incident response plan itself is a living document that should be refined based on real-world experience. This could involve updating contact lists, modifying escalation procedures, adding new playbooks for emergent threats, or incorporating specific protocols for AI-related incidents that were not previously accounted for. For example, after an incident where a facial recognition AI was found to exhibit significant racial bias, a lesson learned might be to incorporate regular, independent bias audits into the operational phase of all AI systems handling sensitive personal data. This would lead to an update in the operational processes and potentially the IRP to mandate such audits and define the criteria for their success. Similarly, if a cyberattack successfully compromised the training data of a large language model, leading to the generation of misinformation, lessons learned could drive updates to data security protocols for AI training environments, including stricter access controls, immutable logging of data modifications, and regular integrity checks of training datasets.

The proactive nature of post-incident analysis is what truly distinguishes effective AI incident management from a reactive firefighting approach. By systematically dissecting failures, organizations can build **enhanced resilience**. This resilience is multi-faceted: it encompasses technical robustness, the ability of AI systems to withstand and recover from disruptions; operational efficiency, the streamlined and effective execution of incident response procedures; and organizational maturity, a culture that embraces learning and continuous improvement. For AI systems, this enhanced resilience also includes ethical robustness—the assurance that AI systems operate fairly, safely, and accountably. A well-executed post-incident analysis process acts as a powerful feedback loop, informing future AI development, deployment, and operationalization. It helps to anticipate potential vulnerabilities, identify emerging risks, and build AI systems that are not only intelligent and performant but also trustworthy and secure.

The scope of the post-mortem should also encompass the **impact assessment and communication**. Beyond the technical and procedural aspects, it's vital to understand the full scope of the incident's impact. This includes not only the direct operational disruptions and financial losses but also the reputational damage, the erosion of user trust, and any legal or regulatory implications. Effective communication during and after an incident is paramount. The post-mortem should analyze how communication was handled, both internally among teams and externally to stakeholders, customers, and potentially the public. Were the communications timely, transparent, and accurate? Was the severity of the incident accurately conveyed? Did the organization take responsibility where appropriate? Lessons learned in this area might lead to the development of pre-approved communication templates for various incident scenarios, the establishment of clear communication protocols involving legal and public relations teams, and a commitment to proactive transparency with users about AI system behavior and incident resolution. For instance, if an AI system responsible for personalized advertising inadvertently exposed sensitive user preferences, the post-mortem would analyze the effectiveness of the communication to affected users, ensuring it was both apologetic and informative about the steps taken to rectify the situation and prevent recurrence.

Furthermore, a comprehensive post-incident analysis should foster a culture of **blame-free learning**. While accountability is important, the primary goal is to understand *what* went wrong, not *who* is to blame. A punitive environment discourages honest reporting and thorough investigation, as individuals may fear repercussions. Instead, a post-mortem should be a safe space for open discussion where all team members can share their perspectives, observations, and challenges without fear of reprisal. This psychological safety is crucial for uncovering the systemic issues that often lie at the heart of complex incidents. The focus should be on improving the system, the processes, and the collective understanding, rather than singling out individuals. This shift in perspective is essential for unlocking genuine learning and driving meaningful organizational change. When teams feel empowered to openly discuss their mistakes and learning, the entire organization benefits from a more robust and resilient AI ecosystem. This approach helps to move from a reactive, error-focused mindset to a proactive, learning-oriented one, which is fundamental for long-term success in managing complex AI systems.

The process of learning from AI incidents is also deeply intertwined with the concept of
AI governance. Effective governance structures ensure that AI development and deployment are aligned with organizational values, ethical principles, and regulatory requirements. Post-incident analyses provide critical real-world data that can inform and refine these governance frameworks. For example, if an incident reveals a gap in how AI model fairness is being assessed, this finding can trigger a review and update of the AI governance policy to include more rigorous fairness metrics and testing protocols. The analysis might also highlight the need for clearer lines of accountability for AI ethics, or the necessity of independent review boards for high-risk AI applications. By integrating the insights from incident analysis into the broader AI governance strategy, organizations can move towards a more responsible and trustworthy approach to AI.

Finally, the learning cycle is never truly complete. The dynamic nature of AI, coupled with evolving threat landscapes and new technological advancements, means that organizations must remain vigilant and adaptable. Post-incident analysis should be viewed not as a final step but as an ongoing component of an iterative improvement process. This requires a commitment to regularly reviewing and updating incident response plans, continuously enhancing monitoring and detection capabilities, and fostering a culture where learning from both successes and failures is a core organizational value. By embedding this commitment to learning into the very fabric of AI operations, organizations can build a sustained capability to manage the inherent risks of AI and harness its transformative potential responsibly.

Chapter 10: Establishing Clear Accountability Mechanisms

The intricate nature of artificial intelligence systems, particularly those characterized by advanced machine learning and deep learning architectures, often gives rise to a perplexing phenomenon: the "accountability gap." This gap emerges when an AI system produces an undesirable or harmful outcome, and the customary pathways for assigning responsibility become obscured. In traditional software development, pinpointing fault often traces back to a specific developer, a flawed piece of code, or a misconfiguration. However, with AI, the causal chain is frequently far more diffuse, involving a complex tapestry of human actors and the emergent behaviors of the AI itself. This complexity makes it exceedingly difficult to answer the fundamental question: who is responsible when an AI fails?

Consider, for instance, an autonomous vehicle involved in an accident. Was the fault with the engineers who designed the sensor fusion algorithms, the team that curated the vast datasets used for training, the company that deployed the vehicle into a specific operational environment, or perhaps even the AI itself, which, through its learning process, developed unexpected decision-making heuristics? Each of these entities, or a combination thereof, could be argued to bear some degree of responsibility. The developers created the architecture; the data providers supplied the "food" for the AI's learning; the deployers made the decision to operationalize it, perhaps in conditions for which it was not fully optimized; and the AI, as a sophisticated decision-making agent, executed actions that led to the incident. This distributed responsibility creates a void where clear accountability ought to reside, leaving victims without a straightforward recourse and the system without a clear path for correction beyond technical fixes.

The challenge is exacerbated by the "black box" nature of many advanced AI models. While developers may understand the underlying principles and algorithms, the intricate internal workings of a deep neural network,

with its millions or billions of parameters, can become opaque. Predicting precisely how such a system will behave in every conceivable scenario, especially novel or edge cases not adequately represented in its training data, is an immense, if not impossible, task. This opacity means that even if an incident occurs, understanding
why the AI made a particular decision can be profoundly difficult, further complicating the assignment of blame. If the decision-making process is inscrutable, how can we definitively assign responsibility to the human actors who designed or trained the system, when the AI's internal logic might have deviated in ways that were not foreseeable?

This distributed and often opaque nature of AI development and operation necessitates a rethinking of traditional accountability frameworks. The established legal and ethical paradigms, forged in an era of more deterministic technologies, often struggle to accommodate the probabilistic, emergent, and sometimes inscrutable nature of AI. The current landscape often sees liability dispersed among multiple parties, leading to protracted legal battles, a reluctance to assign blame, and ultimately, a system where no single entity feels fully accountable. This situation is not only unjust to those harmed by AI failures but also hinders the progress towards safer and more trustworthy AI systems, as the incentives for rigorous development, testing, and oversight are diluted.

The problem is not merely theoretical. We have seen real-world instances where the locus of accountability has been unclear. Consider AI-driven loan application systems that exhibit discriminatory biases, or content moderation algorithms that mistakenly flag or fail to flag harmful material. In such cases, is the responsibility with the data scientists who trained the model, the product managers who defined its objectives, the legal team that approved its deployment, or the executives who prioritized speed-to-market over exhaustive ethical vetting? The difficulty in answering these questions highlights the urgent need for new conceptual models and practical mechanisms to establish clear lines of accountability in the age of AI.

One of the core issues is the diffusion of responsibility across the AI lifecycle. The journey of an AI system, from conception to deployment and ongoing maintenance, involves numerous stakeholders, each contributing to its eventual behavior. There are the researchers who develop foundational algorithms, the engineers who implement and refine them, the data scientists who select, clean, and label datasets, the product managers who define use cases and performance targets, the legal and compliance teams who navigate regulatory landscapes, and the operations teams who deploy and monitor the system. When an AI system malfunctions, each of these actors may have a plausible claim of having performed their duties diligently, even if the aggregate outcome is detrimental.

The data itself is another critical juncture where accountability can become fragmented. AI systems are trained on data, and the quality, representativeness, and potential biases of that data profoundly influence the AI's behavior. If an AI exhibits biased outcomes, is the responsibility solely with the algorithm designers, or does it extend to the teams that sourced, curated, and prepared the data? The process of data collection can be a vast, global enterprise, with data scraped from the internet, licensed from third parties, or generated through user interactions. Identifying the specific origin of a problematic bias within such a complex data ecosystem can be a Herculean task, further contributing to the accountability gap. Furthermore, the interpretation and use of that data are also subject to human decision-making, adding another layer of complexity.

The "AI as a product" versus "AI as a service" distinction also complicates accountability. For traditional products, liability is often more clearly delineated. However, AI systems, especially those that learn and adapt over time, can behave differently from their initial design. If an AI service's behavior changes post-deployment due to continuous learning, and this change leads to harm, who is accountable? Is it the original developer, the service provider, or the user who, through their interactions, might have inadvertently steered the AI toward undesirable behavior? This dynamic nature of AI challenges static notions of product liability.

Moreover, the rapid pace of AI innovation often outstrips the development of regulatory and legal frameworks. Laws and regulations are typically reactive, designed to address issues that have already arisen. By the time legislation catches up to the complexities of AI, new challenges and forms of unintended consequences may have already emerged. This temporal lag creates a vacuum where accountability mechanisms are underdeveloped, leaving a significant portion of AI-related harms unaddressed or inadequately resolved. The difficulty in defining legal personhood for AI, or attributing intent to a non-sentient entity, further complicates legal recourse.

The challenge of assigning responsibility is further compounded by the potential for emergent behaviors. AI systems, particularly complex neural networks, can exhibit properties that were not explicitly programmed or foreseen by their creators. These emergent behaviors can arise from the intricate interactions between different components of the AI, its training data, and the environment in which it operates. When such an emergent behavior leads to harm, it becomes incredibly difficult to assign blame to a specific design choice or a particular individual. The system itself, in a sense, generated the problematic outcome through a process that was not fully predictable, even by its designers.

To bridge this accountability gap, new approaches are required. One crucial element is the implementation of robust **governance frameworks** that delineate responsibilities at each stage of the AI lifecycle. This involves establishing clear policies for AI development, data handling, testing, deployment, and monitoring. These frameworks should define roles and responsibilities, ensuring that for every critical function, there is a designated party that can be held accountable. This might involve creating an "AI Ethics Board" or a "Responsible AI Office" within organizations, tasked with overseeing AI development and deployment, conducting risk assessments, and ensuring adherence to ethical guidelines and legal requirements.

Another vital component is the enhancement of **transparency and explainability** in AI systems. While achieving complete transparency in complex models is challenging, efforts towards explainable AI (XAI) are critical. XAI techniques aim to make AI decision-making processes more understandable to humans. By providing insights into *why* an AI made a particular decision, it becomes easier to identify potential flaws in the design, data, or training process, and consequently, to assign responsibility more effectively. If an AI's decision-making logic can be audited and understood, it provides a clearer basis for assessing human oversight and the validity of the AI's outputs.

Furthermore, the concept of **distributed accountability mechanisms** needs to be explored. Instead of seeking a single responsible party, it might be more effective to design systems where responsibility is shared and managed across multiple stakeholders. This could involve contractual agreements that clearly define liability among developers, data providers, and deployers, or the development of industry-wide standards that set expectations for AI safety and accountability. Insurance models tailored to AI risks could also play a role in managing and distributing the financial consequences of AI failures.

The proactive identification and mitigation of risks are also paramount. This means moving beyond a reactive approach to incident response and investing heavily in
pre-emptive risk assessment and assurance. Before an AI system is deployed, rigorous testing, validation, and auditing processes should be in place to identify potential harms and biases. This includes red-teaming exercises, adversarial testing, and bias audits specifically designed to uncover vulnerabilities. If an organization can demonstrate that it has undertaken comprehensive measures to prevent harm, its position in terms of accountability in the event of a failure is significantly strengthened. This shifts the focus from assigning blame after the fact to ensuring due diligence throughout the development and deployment process.

The role of regulators and policymakers is also indispensable. Governments and international bodies need to develop agile and comprehensive regulatory frameworks that address the unique challenges posed by AI. These frameworks should provide clear guidelines for AI development and deployment, establish mechanisms for redress when harm occurs, and incentivize responsible AI innovation. This might include mandating certain safety standards, requiring impact assessments for high-risk AI applications, and defining liabilities for AI-related harms. The challenge for regulators is to strike a balance between fostering innovation and protecting individuals and society from potential harms, without stifling the very technologies that hold immense promise.

The ethical dimension of accountability cannot be overstated. Beyond legal liability, there is a moral imperative to ensure that AI systems are developed and used in ways that align with societal values. This requires a culture of responsibility within organizations that develop and deploy AI, where ethical considerations are integrated into every stage of the AI lifecycle, not as an afterthought, but as a core design principle. This ethical commitment can serve as a powerful driver for establishing accountability, as organizations strive to build AI systems that are not only functional and profitable but also fair, safe, and beneficial to humanity.

Ultimately, addressing the accountability gap in AI is not a single technical or legal fix. It requires a multifaceted approach that involves technical innovation in areas like explainability, organizational reform in governance and culture, legal and regulatory adaptation, and a societal consensus on the principles that should guide the development and deployment of artificial intelligence. Without clear accountability, trust in AI systems will erode, hindering their adoption and the realization of their potential benefits. The goal is to create an environment where innovation can flourish responsibly, and where the benefits of AI are maximized while its risks are diligently managed. This requires a sustained and collective effort from researchers, developers, policymakers, ethicists, and the public at large to ensure that as AI systems become more sophisticated, so too do our mechanisms for ensuring they are used for good. The future of AI hinges on our ability to assign responsibility effectively, fostering a landscape of trustworthy and beneficial artificial intelligence.

Ensuring accountability within the complex ecosystem of artificial intelligence development and deployment necessitates a foundational step: the rigorous and explicit definition of roles and responsibilities. As AI systems evolve from nascent concepts into integral components of our societal infrastructure, the pathways through which actions and decisions are attributed to individuals or entities must be meticulously mapped. This is not merely an administrative task; it is a critical safeguard against the diffusion of responsibility that has historically plagued complex technological endeavors and is amplified by the inherent opacity and emergent properties of advanced AI. Organizations that embrace AI must move beyond implicit understandings and establish a transparent framework that clearly delineates who is accountable for what, across the entire AI lifecycle.

The AI lifecycle is a multi-stage journey, beginning with the germ of an idea and culminating in the ongoing operation and eventual retirement of a system. At each juncture, distinct sets of tasks and decision-making authorities exist, and it is crucial to assign ownership for these. Consider the initial conceptualization and design phase. Here, responsibilities might fall to AI strategists, product managers, and senior engineers. Their duty is to ensure that the proposed AI aligns with business objectives, ethical principles, and regulatory requirements from its inception. This includes defining the intended use case, identifying potential risks and biases, and setting initial performance benchmarks. The clarity of their role should extend to articulating the acceptable trade-offs between performance, fairness, and privacy. Without a clear mandate at this early stage, it becomes exceedingly difficult to hold anyone accountable if the AI's fundamental design principles lead to detrimental outcomes later on. For instance, if a system is designed with an overemphasis on predictive accuracy without sufficient consideration for bias mitigation, the individuals who set these priorities bear a significant portion of the responsibility for any subsequent discriminatory behavior.

Following the design phase is the critical stage of data acquisition, preparation, and management. This is where the "fuel" for the AI is collected, cleaned, and shaped. The roles here typically involve data engineers, data scientists, and data stewards. Their responsibilities are profound: ensuring the quality, integrity, and representativeness of the data; identifying and mitigating biases within datasets; adhering to data privacy regulations like GDPR or CCPA; and maintaining secure data storage and access protocols. The definition of responsibility must extend to documenting the provenance of the data, the methods used for cleaning and transformation, and the specific steps taken to address any identified biases. If an AI system exhibits bias due to flawed or unrepresentative training data, the individuals responsible for data collection and curation must be clearly identifiable. For example, a team tasked with sourcing images for an object recognition AI needs to be accountable for ensuring that the dataset adequately represents diverse environments and demographics, preventing the AI from performing poorly or making incorrect classifications when encountering specific groups or contexts. This accountability extends to the documentation of any limitations inherent in the data, which should be communicated to downstream teams.

The next pivotal stage is model development and training. This is the domain of AI researchers, machine learning engineers, and data scientists. Their responsibilities encompass selecting appropriate algorithms, configuring model architectures, designing training methodologies, and rigorously testing the model's performance against defined metrics. Critically, their roles must include implementing techniques for fairness, transparency, and robustness. This means not just optimizing for accuracy, but also actively working to detect and reduce bias, ensure that the model's decisions are interpretable to a degree commensurate with its risk, and protect against adversarial attacks. Clear documentation of the model's architecture, training parameters, validation processes, and any discovered limitations is essential. For example, if a natural language processing model generates toxic or offensive content, the ML engineers who trained and fine-tuned it must be held accountable for the effectiveness of their safety guardrails and bias mitigation strategies. This accountability includes having conducted thorough evaluation against diverse linguistic inputs and having implemented mechanisms to filter or flag problematic outputs. The responsibility also extends to understanding and documenting the model's sensitivities to specific types of input.

Deployment and integration represent another critical phase where responsibility must be precisely defined. This often involves software engineers, DevOps teams, and IT operations personnel. Their duties include integrating the trained AI model into production environments, ensuring its reliability and scalability, monitoring its performance in real-time, and managing its lifecycle post-deployment. Responsibilities here must also encompass establishing robust monitoring systems to detect drift, degradation, or unexpected behavior, and having pre-defined protocols for responding to incidents. If an AI system fails in production or begins to exhibit harmful behavior, the deployment and operations teams must be accountable for the integrity of the operational environment and the effectiveness of their monitoring and incident response mechanisms. For instance, an AI-powered trading algorithm that causes market instability due to unexpected interactions with other market participants would place responsibility on the operations team for failing to adequately simulate real-world market conditions during testing or for not having swift de-escalation protocols in place. Their accountability hinges on the robustness of the infrastructure they manage and their preparedness for emergent system behaviors.

Beyond the technical lifecycle stages, overarching roles for governance, oversight, and ethical review are indispensable. These functions often fall to dedicated AI ethics committees, legal departments, compliance officers, and senior leadership. Their responsibilities are broad: establishing organizational AI policies and principles, conducting ethical impact assessments, ensuring compliance with all relevant laws and regulations, and providing a mechanism for raising and addressing ethical concerns. Senior leadership, in particular, holds ultimate accountability for fostering an organizational culture that prioritizes responsible AI development and deployment. For example, if an organization deploys an AI system that violates user privacy, the responsibility would trace back to the leadership and governance bodies that approved its deployment without adequate privacy safeguards or an insufficient understanding of the data protection implications. The ethics committee, if established and empowered, would be accountable for identifying such risks proactively and advising against deployment or recommending necessary modifications.

Furthermore, defining roles for "AI explainability and transparency champions" can be invaluable. These individuals, who might be embedded within development teams or operate as a specialized function, are tasked with ensuring that AI systems are as interpretable as possible, given their complexity and risk profile. Their responsibility is to advocate for and implement explainability techniques, to document model decision-making processes, and to facilitate communication between technical teams and stakeholders who need to understand the AI's behavior. If an AI system's lack of transparency leads to a failure to identify and rectify a harmful bias, these champions would be accountable for not adequately pushing for or implementing effective explainability measures. Their role is to bridge the gap between opaque models and the need for human understanding and trust.

The definition of roles must also extend to end-users and those responsible for managing user interactions with AI systems. In many AI applications, user input or feedback can significantly influence an AI's ongoing learning and behavior. Therefore, clarity is needed on how user interactions are monitored, how feedback is incorporated (or not), and who is responsible for ensuring that these interactions do not inadvertently lead to harmful outcomes. For systems that require user consent for data usage or AI decision-making, the teams responsible for the user interface and experience are accountable for ensuring that consent mechanisms are clear, unambiguous, and legally compliant. If a customer service chatbot, through user interaction, starts to generate inappropriate responses, the team managing the user interface and feedback loops would be accountable for not having robust mechanisms to detect and correct this drift.

Crucially, the documentation of these roles and responsibilities must be explicit and accessible. This is not a task to be relegated to internal wikis or informal agreements. Rather, it should be part of formal job descriptions, project charters, and governance documents. Each role should have clearly articulated duties, authorities, and accountabilities related to AI safety, fairness, privacy, and ethical compliance. This documentation serves as a constant reference point, a basis for training, and a foundation for audits. When an incident occurs, these documented roles and responsibilities become the first point of inquiry for understanding where the breakdown in accountability may have happened. For instance, if a new AI feature is launched that unexpectedly disadvantages a particular demographic, auditors would first examine the project charter to see which roles were assigned responsibility for fairness testing and bias mitigation for that specific feature.

Moreover, the concept of "responsible innovation" needs to be woven into the fabric of these defined roles. This means that accountability is not merely about preventing harm but also about actively pursuing beneficial and ethical AI applications. Each defined role should, where applicable, encompass a responsibility to consider the broader societal impact of the AI system they are contributing to. This proactive approach shifts the focus from a reactive "blame game" to a culture of continuous improvement and ethical stewardship. For example, a product manager's responsibility might include not only delivering a functional product but also assessing its potential for misuse or unintended negative societal consequences and building in safeguards or mitigation strategies from the outset.

The process of defining and assigning these roles and responsibilities is not static. As AI technology advances and organizational structures evolve, these definitions must be reviewed and updated. Regular training and awareness programs are also necessary to ensure that all individuals understand their roles and the importance of accountability in the AI context. This iterative process of definition, documentation, training, and review is fundamental to building robust accountability mechanisms that can adapt to the dynamic nature of artificial intelligence. It ensures that as AI systems become more autonomous and sophisticated, the human element of responsibility remains firmly anchored, preventing the emergence of an unaccountable technological vacuum. The successful integration of AI into society hinges on this foundational commitment to clear lines of human accountability, ensuring that technology serves humanity's best interests.

The intricate landscape of artificial intelligence development and deployment invariably brings forth the crucial question of who bears responsibility when things go awry. As AI systems become more sophisticated, autonomous, and integrated into critical societal functions, the application of existing legal and ethical liability frameworks becomes increasingly complex and, at times, strained. This subsection delves into these frameworks, exploring how they might apply to AI and the inherent challenges that arise, thereby underscoring the urgent need for clarity and potential adaptation.

One of the most pertinent legal doctrines that comes to mind when discussing AI liability is
product liability. Traditionally, product liability law holds manufacturers, distributors, and sellers responsible for injuries or damages caused by defective products. For AI, this doctrine could potentially extend to the developers, vendors, and deployers of AI systems. However, the "defect" in an AI system is not always as straightforward as a physical flaw in a tangible product. Defects can manifest in various forms: design flaws leading to inherent biases, faulty training data that results in erroneous outputs, inadequate testing, or even emergent behaviors that were unforeseen by the creators. The

challenge lies in categorizing these defects. Is an AI that consistently discriminates against a certain demographic due to its training data a "design defect," a "manufacturing defect" (if the training process itself is considered manufacturing), or perhaps a "failure to warn" if the risks weren't adequately communicated? Furthermore, the adaptive and evolving nature of AI systems complicates the notion of a fixed defect. An AI that performs correctly upon deployment but degrades or develops problematic behaviors over time due to continuous learning or environmental changes presents a significant hurdle for a static product liability claim. Legal scholars are grappling with whether AI should be treated as a "product" at all, or perhaps as a "service," or a hybrid entity, each with its own set of liability implications.

Negligence is another foundational legal concept that offers a potential avenue for AI liability. Negligence claims typically require demonstrating a breach of a duty of care, causation, and damages. In the context of AI, the duty of care would likely fall upon developers, deployers, and operators to act reasonably in designing, testing, deploying, and monitoring AI systems. This duty might include a responsibility to implement robust safety protocols, conduct thorough risk assessments, ensure data quality and representativeness, and establish effective oversight mechanisms. A breach could occur if these steps are not taken, or if they are taken negligently. For instance, if a self-driving car manufacturer fails to adequately test the vehicle's ability to recognize pedestrians in low-light conditions, and an accident results, a negligence claim could arise. The difficulty here often lies in establishing the standard of care for AI. What constitutes "reasonable" care in the development of an AI system that can exhibit emergent behaviors or operate with a degree of autonomy far exceeding human control? Courts may need to consider industry best practices, regulatory guidelines, and the state of the art in AI safety. Proving causation can also be particularly challenging, especially in complex AI systems where multiple factors, including user interaction, environmental variables, and the AI's own learning processes, contribute to an outcome. Attributing a specific harm solely to a negligent act related to the AI's design or deployment can be an intricate task.

Contractual obligations also play a significant role, particularly in business-to-business (B2B) transactions involving AI. When an organization purchases or licenses an AI system, the contract typically outlines the terms of service, warranties, and responsibilities of both the vendor and the customer. Breaches of these contractual terms can lead to liability. For example, if an AI vendor guarantees a certain level of performance or accuracy, and the AI fails to meet these specifications, the customer may have a claim for breach of contract. Similarly, contracts might include clauses regarding data privacy, security, and indemnification. The challenge in AI contracts is ensuring that the terms are sufficiently precise and comprehensive to cover the unique aspects of AI, such as data drift, model degradation, and the evolving nature of AI capabilities. Ambiguities in contractual language, especially concerning the unpredictability of AI behavior, can lead to disputes and complicate liability assessments. Furthermore, when AI systems are used in ways not explicitly covered by the contract, or when they interact with other systems in unforeseen ways, contractual liability can become even more nebulous.

Beyond these traditional legal doctrines, there is a growing discussion around
specific AI-related legislation and regulatory frameworks. Many jurisdictions are beginning to develop or consider laws that directly address AI, acknowledging that existing laws may not be fully equipped to handle the unique challenges posed by these technologies. Examples include proposed AI acts, such as the European Union's Artificial Intelligence Act, which aims to classify AI systems based on their risk level and impose corresponding obligations. High-risk AI systems, for instance, would be subject to more stringent requirements related to data governance, transparency, human oversight, and conformity assessments.

Such legislation seeks to proactively establish clear rules and responsibilities, thereby reducing ambiguity and providing a more predictable legal environment. However, the pace of AI development often outstrips the pace of legislative change, creating a perpetual challenge of keeping regulations current and effective.

Furthermore, ethical considerations often precede or run parallel to legal developments.
Ethical liability can be understood as the moral responsibility for the impact of AI systems, even in the absence of a clear legal breach. This encompasses a broader range of concerns, including fairness, accountability, transparency, and the societal impact of AI. Organizations that develop and deploy AI have an ethical obligation to consider the potential harms their systems might cause, such as perpetuating societal biases, eroding privacy, or displacing jobs, and to take proactive measures to mitigate these risks. While ethical breaches may not always translate directly into legal liability, they can lead to significant reputational damage, loss of public trust, and increased regulatory scrutiny. Establishing ethical frameworks within organizations, through codes of conduct, AI ethics boards, and impact assessments, is crucial for guiding responsible AI development and deployment.

The concept of
corporate social responsibility (CSR) also intersects with AI liability. Companies are increasingly expected to be responsible not just to their shareholders but also to society at large. This extends to the ethical and societal implications of their AI deployments. A company's commitment to CSR can influence how it approaches AI governance, risk management, and stakeholder engagement, thereby indirectly impacting its liability exposure. Demonstrating a genuine commitment to responsible AI practices can serve as a mitigating factor in cases of harm, suggesting that the organization took reasonable steps to prevent adverse outcomes.

The challenge of attributing liability to AI systems is amplified by the

"black box" problem, where the internal workings of sophisticated AI models, particularly deep neural networks, are difficult to fully understand or explain. When an AI makes a decision that leads to harm, it can be incredibly challenging to pinpoint the exact cause within the complex web of algorithms, data, and learned parameters. This opacity makes it difficult to prove negligence or identify a specific defect under traditional legal doctrines. Consequently, there is a growing call for AI systems to be more **interpretable and explainable**. While full interpretability may not always be feasible for highly complex models, developers are increasingly tasked with building systems that allow for some level of insight into their decision-making processes. This could involve techniques like feature importance analysis, surrogate models, or counterfactual explanations, which help in understanding why an AI arrived at a particular conclusion.

The
autonomy and emergent properties of AI systems also present a significant challenge. Unlike traditional software, AI systems can learn, adapt, and evolve over time, sometimes in ways that were not anticipated by their creators. This raises questions about whether liability should rest with the original developers, the deployers who managed its operational environment, or even the AI system itself, if it were to be granted some form of legal personhood (a highly contentious idea). The current legal landscape is largely built on the premise of human agency and intent, which is difficult to apply to an autonomous artificial agent.

Moreover, the
global nature of AI development and deployment introduces complexities regarding jurisdiction and applicable law. AI systems are often developed in one country, trained on data from another, and deployed across multiple jurisdictions. Determining which legal framework applies, and enforcing judgments across borders, can be a significant undertaking. This necessitates international cooperation and

the development of harmonized legal and regulatory approaches to AI liability.

The discussion also extends to **liability for AI-enabled decision-making in critical domains** such as healthcare, finance, and criminal justice. In these areas, errors or biases in AI can have profound consequences for individuals' lives and well-being. For example, an AI used for loan applications that unfairly discriminates against a particular group, or an AI used in medical diagnosis that misidentifies a condition, can lead to severe harm. Establishing liability in such high-stakes contexts requires robust mechanisms for oversight, auditing, and redress. The question becomes whether the human overseer, the AI system, the developer, or the deploying institution should bear responsibility.

Finally, the evolving nature of AI necessitates a **forward-looking approach to legal and ethical frameworks**. Rather than solely relying on existing doctrines, there is a growing recognition that new legislative and regulatory measures may be required. These might include: establishing clear standards for AI safety and testing; creating mechanisms for AI registration and auditing; defining specific duties of care for AI developers and deployers; and developing frameworks for AI redress and compensation when harm occurs. The process of adapting these frameworks must be iterative, allowing for adjustments as AI technology continues to advance and its societal impact becomes clearer. It requires a collaborative effort involving policymakers, legal experts, technologists, ethicists, and the public to ensure that AI development and deployment are guided by principles of safety, fairness, and accountability. The ongoing dialogue and development in these areas are critical for fostering trust and ensuring that AI serves as a beneficial force for society, rather than a source of intractable liability and harm.
The quest for robust accountability in the realm of artificial intelligence is inextricably linked to two fundamental pillars: transparency and explainability. These concepts, while often used interchangeably,

represent distinct yet complementary approaches to demystifying the intricate operations of AI systems. When AI systems, particularly those operating with a high degree of autonomy or influencing critical decisions, encounter an adverse outcome, the ability to understand *why* it happened is paramount. This understanding forms the bedrock upon which accountability can be assigned, trust can be rebuilt, and future failures can be averted. Without some degree of insight into the 'black box,' even the most well-intentioned legal or ethical frameworks can falter, leaving victims without recourse and developers without clear guidance on how to improve.

Transparency, in its broadest sense, refers to the openness and accessibility of information related to an AI system. This can encompass a range of details, from the data used to train the model and the architectural choices made during its development, to the operational context in which it is deployed and the performance metrics it achieves. For instance, a transparent AI development process might involve publicly documenting the datasets used for training, including their sources, demographic distributions, and any pre-processing steps taken to mitigate bias. This allows external auditors, researchers, or even concerned citizens to scrutinize the foundational elements of the AI. Similarly, detailing the hyperparameters, algorithmic choices, and validation strategies employed during model training can provide a clearer picture of the developer's intent and methodology. When an AI system is deployed, transparency extends to its operational guidelines, intended use cases, and any known limitations or risks. This proactive disclosure allows users and stakeholders to make informed decisions about engaging with the AI and to better anticipate potential issues. For example, a financial institution deploying an AI for loan assessments should be transparent about the general factors the AI considers and the broad criteria it uses, without necessarily revealing proprietary algorithmic details. This level of transparency is crucial for building public trust and for enabling effective oversight.

However, transparency alone is often insufficient, especially when dealing with complex machine learning models. The sheer scale and interconnectedness of parameters within a deep neural network, for instance, can render a complete understanding of its inner workings an insurmountable task, even for its creators. This is where explainability, also known as interpretability, becomes indispensable. Explainability focuses on providing understandable reasons for specific decisions or behaviors of an AI system. It seeks to answer the question: "Why did the AI do
that?" This is particularly critical when an AI's output leads to a harmful or unfair outcome. Imagine an AI used in a hiring process that rejects a qualified candidate. Transparency might tell us the AI was trained on historical hiring data, but explainability would aim to reveal which specific features of the candidate's profile (e.g., educational background, years of experience, specific keywords in their resume) led to the rejection.

Achieving appropriate levels of explainability for complex AI systems is a significant technical challenge. It has spurred the development of various techniques and methodologies. One category of approaches involves building inherently interpretable models. These are AI architectures designed from the ground up to be more transparent. Examples include decision trees, linear regression models, and rule-based systems. While these models might be less powerful or accurate for highly complex tasks compared to deep learning models, their decision-making processes are often straightforward to trace and understand. For instance, a decision tree clearly delineates a series of binary choices that lead to a classification or prediction, making the reasoning transparent.

For more complex, opaque models, such as deep neural networks, the focus shifts to post-hoc explanation methods. These techniques aim to provide insights into the model's behavior without altering its underlying architecture. Feature attribution methods are a prominent example. Techniques like SHAP (SHapley Additive exPlanations) and LIME (Local Interpretable Model-agnostic Explanations) are designed to quantify the contribution of each input feature to a specific output. For instance, in an image recognition task, SHAP values could indicate which pixels or regions of an image were most influential in the AI's decision to classify it as a "cat." Similarly, LIME can provide local explanations for individual predictions by approximating the complex model with a simpler, interpretable model around the specific data point in question. These methods allow us to understand, for a particular instance, what factors drove the AI's decision, thereby providing a degree of explainability that can be crucial for accountability.

Another class of explainability techniques focuses on generating counterfactual explanations. A counterfactual explanation describes the smallest change to the input features that would result in a different desired outcome. For example, if an AI rejects a loan application, a counterfactual explanation might state: "Your loan application would have been approved if your annual income was $5,000 higher," or "if you had a credit history of at least three years." Such explanations are not only insightful but also actionable, providing individuals with concrete steps they can take to achieve a different outcome in the future. This direct utility makes counterfactual explanations particularly valuable for fairness and recourse.

The level of transparency and explainability required is not a one-size-fits-all proposition. It is context-dependent, varying significantly based on the AI system's intended use, its potential impact, and the stakeholders involved. For an AI used in a low-stakes application, such as recommending movies, a high degree of explainability might be unnecessary. However, for an AI used in critical domains like medical diagnosis, autonomous vehicles, or the criminal justice system, the demand for transparency and explainability becomes exceptionally high. In healthcare, a physician needs to understand *why* an AI has suggested a particular diagnosis or treatment plan to exercise their professional judgment and maintain patient trust. The failure to provide adequate explanations in such scenarios can lead to incorrect medical decisions, patient harm, and significant liability for the developers and healthcare providers.

In the context of autonomous vehicles, explainability is crucial for accident investigation and for gaining public acceptance. When an accident occurs, investigators need to understand the decision-making process of the autonomous driving system leading up to the incident. This requires detailed logs and the ability to reconstruct and analyze the AI's reasoning. Similarly, for regulators and the public to trust self-driving cars, there must be a clear understanding of how the AI will behave in various scenarios, especially edge cases.

The pursuit of transparency and explainability also serves as a powerful mechanism for demonstrating due diligence and fostering accountability. When developers and deployers make a concerted effort to build systems that are understandable, they are inherently demonstrating a commitment to responsible AI practices. This effort can be documented and presented as evidence of their commitment to safety and fairness. For instance, a company that invests in developing and integrating explainability tools into its AI systems, and regularly audits these explanations, can show that it has taken proactive steps to mitigate risks and ensure its AI operates as intended. This proactive stance can be a significant factor in mitigating liability in the event of an AI-induced harm.

Furthermore, transparency and explainability enable more effective auditing and oversight. External auditors, regulatory bodies, or internal ethics committees can use the insights gained from explainable AI to assess whether the system is operating fairly, without undue bias, and in compliance with relevant laws and ethical guidelines. For example, an audit of an AI used for credit scoring could involve examining feature attributions for a sample of loan applications. If the audit reveals that the AI is disproportionately relying on protected attributes (e.g., race, gender) or their proxies, this indicates a potential bias that needs to be addressed. Without explainability, identifying such biases would be exceptionally difficult, if not impossible.

The process of making AI systems more transparent and explainable can also lead to improved AI models. The very act of trying to understand *why* an AI makes certain decisions can reveal flaws in the data, the model architecture, or the training process. This iterative cycle of explanation and refinement helps developers to identify and correct biases, improve accuracy, and enhance the overall robustness of the AI system. This continuous improvement loop is essential for building trustworthy AI.

However, it is important to acknowledge the trade-offs and challenges associated with transparency and explainability. There is often a tension between model complexity and interpretability. Highly accurate, state-of-the-art models, particularly in areas like natural language processing and computer vision, are frequently the most opaque. Forcing these models into overly simplistic, interpretable forms might come at the cost of performance, which could, in itself, lead to harm if the AI's accuracy is critical. Therefore, the goal should be to achieve *appropriate* levels of explainability, balancing the need for insight with the system's functional requirements and risk profile.

Moreover, there are legitimate concerns about the disclosure of proprietary information. The algorithms and training data used by AI systems can represent significant intellectual property and competitive advantage for companies. Full transparency, in some cases, could reveal trade secrets, making it difficult for businesses to innovate and compete.

This necessitates careful consideration of what information is truly necessary for accountability and oversight, and how it can be disclosed in a way that protects legitimate business interests while still serving the public good. Techniques like differential privacy and federated learning, which allow models to be trained on sensitive data without revealing the data itself, can play a role in balancing these competing interests.

The definition of what constitutes a "sufficient" explanation also remains a subject of ongoing debate and research. An explanation that is meaningful to a data scientist might be incomprehensible to a layperson or a legal professional. Therefore, explanations need to be tailored to the audience and the context. This requires developing a taxonomy of explanation types and understanding how each type serves different accountability purposes. For instance, a technical explanation might be used for debugging by engineers, while a simplified, impact-focused explanation might be provided to an individual whose loan application was denied.

Ultimately, transparency and explainability are not mere technical features; they are foundational requirements for building ethical and accountable AI systems. By fostering a deeper understanding of how AI systems operate, these concepts empower stakeholders, facilitate oversight, enable recourse, and cultivate the trust necessary for AI to be a beneficial force in society. They provide the essential visibility needed to identify responsibility when things go wrong, to rectify errors, and to ensure that AI development and deployment are guided by principles of fairness, safety, and human well-being. Without them, the promise of AI risks being overshadowed by the specter of unaccountable decisions and unintended consequences, leaving a trail of unanswered questions and unresolved harms. The ongoing evolution of AI necessitates a parallel evolution in our approaches to transparency and explainability, ensuring that as AI capabilities advance, so too does our ability to understand, govern, and hold them accountable. This commitment to insight is a crucial step in navigating the complex terrain of AI governance and embedding accountability at every stage of the AI lifecycle.

Even with the most rigorous application of transparency, explainability, and robust internal governance structures, the inherent complexities and emergent behaviors of artificial intelligence systems mean that residual risks will always persist. These risks, which remain after all reasonable preventative and mitigation measures have been exhausted, can manifest in a myriad of ways: from unforeseen operational failures and catastrophic cyberattacks to subtle but pervasive discriminatory outcomes that were not detected during testing or deployment. It is in addressing these lingering uncertainties that financial instruments and risk transfer mechanisms, particularly insurance, emerge as critical components of a comprehensive accountability framework for AI.

The landscape of AI-specific insurance is rapidly evolving, mirroring the dynamism of AI technology itself. Traditionally, insurance has served to indemnify against financial losses arising from a defined set of perils. However, AI introduces novel categories of risk that traditional policies may not adequately cover. These include liabilities stemming from the autonomous actions of AI systems, the large-scale consequences of data breaches impacting AI training or operational data, and the complex legal ramifications of AI-driven discrimination. Insurers are thus developing specialized products, or adapting existing ones, to address the unique challenges posed by artificial intelligence. This involves a deep dive into the specific vulnerabilities and potential harms associated with AI, moving beyond a mere understanding of software or hardware failures to encompass the broader societal and ethical implications of intelligent systems.

One of the primary functions of insurance in the context of AI is to provide a vital layer of financial recourse when harm occurs. When an AI system causes damage, be it to property, reputation, or an individual's livelihood, the costs associated with remediation, legal defense, and compensation can be astronomical. For organizations that develop or deploy AI, the potential for such significant financial exposure can be a major deterrent to innovation or a source of existential threat. AI-specific insurance policies aim to absorb a substantial portion of this financial burden. This is not merely a matter of financial protection for the insured entity; it also indirectly benefits those who may be harmed by an AI system. By ensuring that organizations have the financial capacity to compensate victims, insurance contributes to a more just and equitable outcome for all stakeholders. Without such mechanisms, individuals or businesses suffering loss due to AI might find themselves facing a bankrupt or unwilling defendant, leaving them without adequate redress.

Furthermore, the very act of seeking and obtaining AI insurance can serve as a powerful incentive for robust risk management. Insurers, as a condition of providing coverage, typically conduct thorough due diligence on the applicant's risk assessment and mitigation strategies. This involves scrutinizing the AI system's design, development lifecycle, testing procedures, security protocols, and governance frameworks. They will assess the quality of data used for training, the methods employed to detect and address bias, and the robustness of fail-safe mechanisms. Insurers may also impose specific requirements, such as mandatory penetration testing, regular security audits, or the implementation of certain ethical AI development guidelines, as prerequisites for coverage or to qualify for lower premiums. This external scrutiny from the insurance sector can act as an invaluable external validation of an organization's internal accountability efforts, often highlighting blind spots or areas for improvement that might have been overlooked. The ongoing premium assessments and policy renewals also encourage continuous improvement in risk management practices, as organizations strive to demonstrate reduced risk to maintain favorable insurance terms.

The types of AI-related liabilities that insurance aims to cover are diverse. Product liability insurance, for instance, traditionally covers damages caused by defective products. For AI, this can extend to the autonomous decision-making capabilities of a system. If an AI-powered autonomous vehicle causes an accident due to a flaw in its driving algorithm, or if an AI medical diagnostic tool provides an incorrect diagnosis leading to patient harm, product liability insurance could be invoked. However, the complexity of AI often makes it challenging to pinpoint a specific "defect" in the traditional sense, necessitating new approaches to understanding causality and attributing fault.

Cyber insurance is another crucial area, given the data-intensive nature of AI. AI systems often rely on vast datasets for training, and their operations can generate sensitive logs and operational data. A data breach compromising this information can lead to significant liabilities, including regulatory fines for data protection violations (such as GDPR or CCPA), the cost of notifying affected individuals, credit monitoring services, and reputational damage. AI-specific cyber policies may offer enhanced coverage for these scenarios, recognizing the unique attack vectors and the potential scale of AI-related data breaches. Moreover, AI systems themselves can be targets of cyberattacks, not just as repositories of data, but as the very systems whose behavior can be manipulated. A malicious actor might attempt to poison the training data of a machine learning model to subtly alter its behavior over time, leading to outcomes that benefit the attacker or harm the system's intended users. Insurance needs to evolve to cover such sophisticated forms of AI-specific cyber threats.

The issue of algorithmic bias and its discriminatory outcomes presents a particularly thorny challenge for insurers. When an AI system perpetuates or amplifies existing societal biases, leading to unfair treatment in areas like hiring, lending, or criminal justice, the legal and ethical ramifications can be profound. Traditional liability policies may not explicitly cover claims arising from algorithmic discrimination. Therefore, specialized policies are emerging that can address these risks. These policies might require the insured to demonstrate proactive efforts in bias detection and mitigation, such as regular audits, the use of fairness metrics, and the implementation of recourse mechanisms for affected individuals. The presence of such insurance can help to bridge the gap between internal accountability efforts and external recourse for those who suffer harm from biased AI systems. It acknowledges that while perfect fairness may be an unattainable ideal, financial protection can be provided for the consequences of failing to achieve acceptable levels of equity.

Beyond direct financial indemnification, insurance and risk transfer mechanisms can play a role in incentivizing responsible AI development and deployment through their pricing models. Insurers assess risk based on a variety of factors, including the maturity of the AI technology, the robustness of the development and testing processes, the strength of the governance framework, and the history of performance and incidents. AI systems developed with a strong emphasis on ethical considerations, transparency, and safety will likely command lower premiums than those perceived as high-risk. This can create a positive feedback loop, where investing in responsible AI practices directly translates into lower operational costs, thereby making ethical AI development a more economically attractive proposition.

However, the insurance industry itself faces significant challenges in underwriting AI risks. The rapidly evolving nature of AI technology makes it difficult to establish historical data and actuarial models that are predictive of future losses. The "black box" nature of some AI systems, as discussed in previous sections, can also impede a thorough risk assessment by insurers. Determining causation and attributing fault in complex AI interactions can be extremely difficult, leading to potential disputes over coverage. Furthermore, the potential for catastrophic and widespread harm from AI failures, particularly in critical infrastructure or autonomous systems, could challenge the capacity of even large insurance pools. This necessitates ongoing collaboration between AI developers, policymakers, and the insurance sector to develop standardized risk assessment methodologies, data-sharing frameworks, and potentially, novel forms of risk pooling or government backstops for extremely high-consequence AI risks.

The interaction between internal accountability mechanisms and external risk transfer is crucial. Insurance is not a substitute for good governance, ethical design, and robust testing; rather, it is a complementary layer of defense. A company that neglects its internal accountability structures in the belief that insurance will cover all eventualities is making a grave error. Insurers will scrutinize these internal processes, and a demonstrable lack of due diligence can lead to denied claims, exorbitant premiums, or outright refusal to provide coverage. Therefore, organizations must view insurance as part of a holistic risk management strategy, integrated with their commitments to transparency, explainability, and ethical AI principles.

Consider a scenario involving an AI-powered trading algorithm. If this algorithm, due to unforeseen market conditions or emergent interactions with other trading systems, triggers a flash crash, the financial losses can be immense. An insurer providing coverage for the financial institution would first look at the algorithm's design, the testing protocols, the circuit breakers in place, and the oversight mechanisms. If the institution had rigorous internal controls, clear documentation of its risk assessment, and sophisticated monitoring systems, the insurer is more likely to provide coverage and potentially at a more favorable rate. Conversely, if the institution was negligent, failed to implement basic safety features, or had a history of ignoring warning signs, the insurer might deny coverage or impose stringent conditions. This highlights how insurance acts as an external validator and enforcer of internal accountability.

The development of AI-specific insurance also necessitates the establishment of clear definitions and taxonomies of AI risks. What constitutes an "AI failure" versus a "system malfunction"? How is "algorithmic bias" quantified for insurance purposes? What level of "explainability" is deemed sufficient for an insurer to underwrite a policy? These are not just academic questions; they have direct financial implications. Industry-wide standards and agreed-upon methodologies for assessing AI risk will be essential for the maturation of this market. This could involve collaboration between professional bodies, regulatory agencies, and insurance associations to create frameworks that provide clarity and consistency.

Moreover, the role of risk transfer extends beyond traditional insurance. Other mechanisms, such as contractual risk allocation, surety bonds, and even venture capital funding that includes specific risk mitigation requirements, can also play a part. For instance, in supply chain arrangements involving AI-enabled components, contractual clauses can clearly delineate responsibility for certain types of AI-related failures. Similarly, for large-scale AI deployments, performance bonds or surety guarantees might be required to ensure that specific levels of operational reliability are met.

Ultimately, the integration of insurance and other risk transfer mechanisms into AI accountability frameworks serves a dual purpose. Firstly, it provides essential financial safety nets, ensuring that when AI systems do cause harm, there are the resources available to compensate those affected and to facilitate recovery. Secondly, it acts as a powerful market-based incentive for responsible innovation, pushing developers and deployers to prioritize safety, fairness, and ethical considerations in their AI endeavors. As AI continues to permeate every facet of our lives, the role of these financial tools in managing residual risks and fostering a culture of accountability will only become more pronounced. They are not a panacea, but an indispensable part of a multi-layered approach to ensuring that the development and deployment of artificial intelligence benefit society while minimizing its potential harms. The ongoing innovation in AI necessitates a corresponding evolution in our financial and risk management strategies, ensuring that our ability to mitigate and respond to AI-related risks keeps pace with the technology's ever-increasing capabilities and pervasiveness.

Chapter 11: Human Oversight and Control

The pervasive influence of artificial intelligence across nearly every sector of society has understandably fueled a discourse around the potential for fully autonomous systems to operate independently of human intervention. The allure of AI's speed, efficiency, and perceived objectivity is undeniable. However, as we delve deeper into the operational realities of AI, particularly within safety-critical domains such as healthcare, transportation, and critical infrastructure, a compelling argument emerges for the indispensable role of human oversight. The very characteristics that make AI powerful – its reliance on data, its algorithmic predictability, and its susceptibility to edge cases – also highlight the inherent limitations that necessitate continuous human engagement. Fully relinquishing control to AI, even in highly sophisticated systems, often proves to be either undesirable due to inherent ethical complexities or simply infeasible when faced with the sheer unpredictability of the real world.

The argument against complete AI autonomy in many contexts rests on several fundamental pillars, chief among them being the irreplaceable nature of human judgment, ethical reasoning, and nuanced contextual understanding. AI systems, by their very design, operate based on patterns identified within vast datasets and the parameters of their programmed algorithms. While this allows them to excel at tasks that are repetitive, data-rich, and well-defined, it also means they can falter when confronted with novel situations, ambiguous information, or scenarios that demand a deep comprehension of human values and societal norms. Consider, for instance, an AI-powered autonomous vehicle operating in a complex urban environment. While it can master routine driving and react faster than a human to many predictable threats, it might struggle to interpret the subtle social cues exchanged between pedestrians, cyclists, and other drivers. A human driver, drawing on years of lived experience and intuitive social understanding, can anticipate a pedestrian's hesitation, infer the intent behind a cyclist's wave, or de-escalate a tense road interaction through non-verbal communication. An AI, lacking this embedded social cognition, might interpret such interactions purely through the lens of predictable kinematic trajectories, leading to potentially unsafe or socially disruptive outcomes.

Furthermore, the ethical dimensions of decision-making represent a significant hurdle for fully autonomous AI. Many critical decisions, even those with life-or-death consequences, involve trade-offs that are deeply rooted in human morality and societal values. While AI can be programmed with ethical guidelines, translating abstract ethical principles into concrete, actionable rules for a machine is an immensely challenging, and arguably incomplete, endeavor. The famous "trolley problem" scenarios, often used to illustrate ethical dilemmas, become starkly real in the context of autonomous systems. If an autonomous vehicle faces an unavoidable accident, and must choose between swerving to hit a group of pedestrians or staying its course and crashing, harming its occupants, how should it decide? Programming a definitive answer to such a dilemma is fraught with difficulty. Different societies, and even individuals within those societies, hold varying moral frameworks. What one culture deems an acceptable sacrifice, another might find abhorrent. The resolution of these deeply human ethical quandaries requires a level of nuanced reasoning, empathy, and accountability that current AI systems do not possess. Human oversight allows for a "human in the loop" or "human on the loop" approach, where an individual can intervene, interpret the situation based on broader ethical considerations, and make the final, value-laden decision. This ensures that the decisions made by AI, especially in critical situations, align with human moral compasses, rather than being purely the result of algorithmic optimization that may overlook or misinterpret crucial ethical considerations.

The concept of "unforeseen circumstances" is another critical factor that underscores the necessity of human oversight. The real world is a dynamic and chaotic environment, a stark contrast to the controlled conditions under which AI models are typically trained and tested. AI systems are trained on historical data, which, by definition, represents past events. They are designed to recognize patterns and respond to known variables. However, they can be blindsided by truly novel events, black swan occurrences, or combinations of factors that have never been observed before. In safety-critical systems, the failure to adequately respond to such an unprecedented event can have catastrophic consequences. A human operator, possessing a broader understanding of the physical world and a capacity for creative problem-solving, can often adapt to novel situations in ways that an AI cannot. For example, an AI managing a power grid might be programmed to handle typical fluctuations in demand and supply, or even respond to predictable equipment failures. However, it might struggle to cope with a simultaneous, cascading series of failures caused by an unforeseen natural disaster, a sophisticated cyberattack, or a combination of both. A human operator, drawing on their general knowledge, experience with similar but not identical crises, and ability to improvise, can develop adaptive strategies, prioritize responses based on overarching goals (like public safety), and coordinate efforts in a way that a purely autonomous system, confined by its pre-programmed logic, might be incapable of.

Moreover, the complexity and opacity of some advanced AI systems, often referred to as "black boxes," further necessitate human oversight. While efforts in explainable AI (XAI) are advancing, many powerful machine learning models, particularly deep neural networks, operate in ways that are not fully transparent even to their creators. Understanding precisely *why* a particular decision was made can be challenging, making it difficult to diagnose errors, identify biases, or guarantee predictable behavior across all scenarios. In situations where accountability and safety are paramount, relying solely on a system whose decision-making process is inscrutable is a significant risk. Human oversight provides a crucial layer of interpretability and accountability. When a human operator is involved, they can scrutinize the AI's recommendations, ask clarifying questions (even if those questions are about the AI's confidence level or the data it prioritized), and ultimately make a judgment based on their own understanding and the AI's output. This human judgment acts as a vital validation mechanism, ensuring that the AI's suggestions are not blindly followed, especially when the stakes are high. It also allows for the identification of systematic issues within the AI itself; if an operator repeatedly finds the AI's recommendations to be flawed or incomplete in specific contexts, this can flag a problem that needs to be addressed in the AI's development or deployment.

The economic and societal implications of relying solely on AI also warrant careful consideration. While AI can drive efficiency and productivity, there are sectors where the primary concern is not pure optimization, but rather the well-being of individuals and communities. In fields like social work, education, or even certain aspects of customer service, the empathetic engagement and nuanced interpersonal skills of human professionals are not just desirable, but essential. An AI might be able to process applications, identify patterns of need, or even offer generic advice, but it cannot replicate the genuine compassion, trust, and understanding that a human professional can provide. The human element in these roles is often about building relationships, offering support, and making judgments that consider the multifaceted, and often unquantifiable, aspects of human lives. To replace these roles entirely with autonomous AI would not only risk diminishing the quality of service but could also lead to a dehumanization of essential societal functions, eroding trust and social cohesion. Human oversight ensures that these critical human-centric aspects are preserved, even when AI is used to augment the capabilities of human professionals.

The argument for human oversight is not an indictment of AI's capabilities but rather a pragmatic acknowledgment of its limitations and the unique value that humans bring to complex decision-making processes. It is about building systems that are not only intelligent but also wise, not only efficient but also ethical, and not only autonomous in their tasks but also accountable in their outcomes. This involves a symbiotic relationship, where AI serves as a powerful tool to enhance human capabilities, process vast amounts of information, and identify potential issues, while humans provide the critical judgment, ethical compass, and contextual understanding necessary to navigate the complexities of the real world, particularly in situations where the consequences of error are significant.

Consider the domain of healthcare, where AI is increasingly being deployed for diagnostic assistance, drug discovery, and personalized treatment plans. An AI might be exceptionally skilled at analyzing medical images, identifying subtle anomalies that a human radiologist might miss. However, the AI's diagnostic suggestion, however accurate it may appear, must still be interpreted by a qualified physician. The physician brings to bear their knowledge of the patient's complete medical history, their understanding of the patient's individual circumstances and preferences, and their ethical responsibility to make the best decision for that specific person. The AI might flag a potential tumor, but the physician must then decide, in consultation with the patient, on the course of action, considering factors like the patient's age, other comorbidities, and their willingness to undergo invasive treatments. This collaborative approach, where AI augments but does not replace human medical expertise, ensures that patient care remains personalized, ethical, and ultimately, human-centered. The physician's oversight is not merely a procedural step; it is the embodiment of professional responsibility and the application of deeply ingrained human values.

In the realm of finance, AI-powered trading algorithms can execute trades at speeds and volumes that are impossible for humans. However, in the event of extreme market volatility, a systemic failure, or a highly unusual market event that the algorithm was not trained to handle, human traders and risk managers must be able to intervene. Their role is to monitor the AI's performance, identify deviations from expected behavior, and, if necessary, halt the algorithm and revert to manual control or implement emergency protocols. The human oversight in this context acts as a circuit breaker, preventing potential catastrophic financial losses that could arise from an AI operating outside its designed parameters or encountering a situation for which it has no pre-programmed solution. The decision to halt an algorithm, even if it means foregoing potential gains, requires a human judgment call based on risk assessment and a broader understanding of market stability, not just algorithmic efficiency.

The development of AI for national security and defense also highlights the critical need for human oversight. Autonomous weapons systems, while potentially offering tactical advantages, raise profound ethical and legal questions. The decision to deploy lethal force is one of the most consequential a society can make, and delegating this decision entirely to a machine is widely seen as crossing a dangerous threshold. International discussions and treaties are increasingly grappling with the implications of lethal autonomous weapons systems (LAWS). The consensus among many nations and organizations is that while AI can assist in intelligence gathering, target identification, and even defensive capabilities, the final decision to engage a target, particularly one involving lethal force, must remain under meaningful human control. This ensures that such decisions are not made based on algorithmic misinterpretations or the cold logic of optimization, but rather in accordance with international humanitarian law, ethical principles, and a considered judgment of the strategic and humanitarian implications. Human oversight provides the necessary moral and legal accountability, ensuring that the use of force remains a deliberate and human-directed act, rather than an automated response.

Furthermore, even in applications where AI seems to operate with a high degree of autonomy, there is often an underlying human infrastructure that monitors, maintains, and intervenes when necessary. For instance, self-driving cars, while designed for autonomy, are still developed, tested, and maintained by human engineers and technicians. In many deployment scenarios, there are remote human operators who can monitor fleets of vehicles and intervene in complex or dangerous situations. This demonstrates that "full autonomy" is often an idealization, and in practice, a spectrum of human involvement exists. The degree of human oversight may vary, but its presence, even in a supervisory or standby capacity, is crucial for safety, reliability, and accountability. The human role can shift from direct control to that of a vigilant overseer, ready to step in when the AI encounters a challenge beyond its current capabilities. This supervisory role itself requires significant skill, training, and the ability to quickly assess and respond to AI system anomalies.

The argument for human oversight is not static; it evolves as AI technology advances. As AI systems become more sophisticated and capable, the nature of human oversight will also change. It may shift from direct manual control to more sophisticated forms of supervision, interpretation of AI outputs, and the management of AI systems themselves. However, the fundamental principle remains: for systems that have a significant impact on human lives, safety, or societal well-being, a meaningful level of human judgment, ethical reasoning, and contextual understanding must be retained. The ultimate goal is not to prevent AI from operating autonomously where it is safe and beneficial to do so, but rather to ensure that human values and human accountability remain at the forefront, guiding the deployment and operation of these powerful technologies. This approach ensures that AI serves humanity, rather than the other way around, and that the benefits of AI are realized without compromising our safety, ethics, or fundamental human dignity. The ongoing development and deployment of AI must therefore be accompanied by a robust and continuously evolving framework for human oversight, ensuring that these intelligent systems remain tools that empower, rather than inadvertently endanger, us.

The preceding discussion has firmly established the indispensable role of human oversight and control in navigating the complexities and potential pitfalls of artificial intelligence. However, simply acknowledging the necessity of human involvement is only the first step. The true challenge lies in designing AI systems and the environments in which they operate in such a way that this human-AI interaction is not a cumbersome afterthought, but a seamless, intuitive, and highly effective partnership. This is the essence of designing for effective human-AI collaboration, a critical discipline that seeks to forge synergistic relationships where the unique strengths of both human and artificial intelligence are not merely accommodated, but actively amplified.

At the heart of this endeavor is the architecture of user interfaces (UIs) and the way information is presented. An AI system, no matter how sophisticated, is ultimately a tool, and its effectiveness is profoundly influenced by how readily and clearly it can communicate its capabilities, its intentions, and its outputs to its human counterpart. This necessitates a radical departure from purely AI-centric design, where functionality is prioritized above all else. Instead, the focus must shift to the human user, understanding their cognitive load, their existing knowledge base, and their specific goals within a given task or workflow.

Consider, for instance, an AI system designed to assist radiologists in identifying potential anomalies in medical scans. A poorly designed interface might present a dense, overwhelming stream of data, perhaps highlighting every minute variation in pixel intensity with equal emphasis. This could lead to information overload, increasing the radiologist's cognitive burden rather than alleviating it. The AI might be technically accurate in flagging these variations, but without clear, contextually relevant presentation, its insights become noise. An effective design, by contrast, would prioritize clarity and context. The AI could be trained to understand the radiologist's workflow and present findings not as raw data, but as actionable insights. This might involve highlighting suspicious regions with clear visual cues, providing a confidence score for each finding, and offering direct links to relevant literature or prior cases. The UI could also be designed to allow for rapid disambiguation; the radiologist might be able to quickly dismiss false positives with a simple gesture or a single click, thereby refining the AI's learning in real-time and allowing it to focus its attention on the most critical areas.

The principle here is that the AI should act as an intelligent filter and presenter of information, rather than an unmediated data dump. This involves thoughtful consideration of visual design, information hierarchy, and the appropriate use of various display modalities. For example, in a critical control room environment where operators monitor complex industrial processes, an AI might detect an emergent pattern indicative of a potential equipment failure. Instead of simply issuing a generic alert, the interface could present this information visually, perhaps by overlaying a red warning directly onto a schematic of the affected machinery, accompanied by a concise textual explanation of the suspected issue and its potential consequences. Crucially, the interface should also provide the operator with the means to immediately probe deeper into the AI's reasoning. This could involve clicking on the warning to access raw sensor data, diagnostic logs, or even a simplified explanation of the algorithmic process that led to the alert. The goal is to empower the human operator with not just the "what" but also the "why" and the "what next," fostering a sense of informed control rather than passive observation.

Beyond static displays, the communication protocols between human and AI agents are equally vital for effective collaboration. This extends to the natural language processing (NLP) capabilities of AI systems. While we often envision AI interacting with humans through spoken commands or written queries, the nature of this dialogue is critical. A conversational AI that is overly verbose, employs jargon that the human user doesn't understand, or fails to grasp the nuances of human intent can quickly become a source of frustration and error. Conversely, an AI that can engage in a natural, context-aware dialogue, asking clarifying questions when necessary and responding with precision and conciseness, can significantly enhance productivity and reduce misunderstandings.

Imagine a scenario where a human researcher is using an AI to sift through vast archives of historical documents. A simplistic AI might respond to a query like "find documents about trade routes in the 18th century" by returning thousands of undifferentiated results. A more sophisticated AI, designed for effective collaboration, would engage in a more dynamic exchange. It might begin by asking, "Are you interested in maritime trade, overland routes, or both?" or "Would you like to focus on specific regions, such as Europe or Asia?" Furthermore, as the researcher reviews the initial set of results, the AI could learn from their actions. If the researcher repeatedly dismisses documents related to naval blockades, the AI can infer a preference and adjust its subsequent search parameters accordingly. This iterative, conversational approach transforms the AI from a passive search engine into an active research assistant, working in concert with the human to refine their understanding and uncover the most relevant information.

This principle of iterative refinement and context awareness also applies to the integration of AI into existing workflows. It is rarely practical or even desirable to rip out established human processes and replace them entirely with AI-driven ones. Instead, successful human-AI collaboration often involves carefully embedding AI capabilities into the existing human workflow, augmenting rather than disrupting it. This requires a deep understanding of the target workflow, identifying the specific points where AI can provide the most value and designing the integration in a way that minimizes friction for the human participants.

Consider the field of customer service. An AI can be incredibly effective at handling routine inquiries, answering frequently asked questions, and even processing simple transactions. However, when a customer presents a complex, emotionally charged, or novel issue, the AI might reach its limitations. An effectively integrated system would seamlessly escalate such cases to a human agent, providing the agent with a comprehensive summary of the AI's interaction with the customer, including the questions asked, the information provided, and any partial solutions attempted. This handover should be smooth and efficient, ensuring that the customer does not have to repeat themselves and that the human agent has all the necessary context to provide effective support. The AI acts as a first line of defense, filtering out the mundane, while the human agent is empowered to handle the exceptions, armed with valuable pre-processing by the AI. This creates a more efficient and satisfying experience for both the customer and the human agent, leveraging the strengths of each.

Workflow integration also extends to the realm of task allocation. In many complex operations, tasks can be divided into components that are better suited to either human or AI capabilities. An AI might excel at data analysis, pattern recognition, and rapid calculation, while humans are superior at critical thinking, ethical judgment, and creative problem-solving. Designing for collaboration means establishing clear criteria for when and how tasks are allocated between human and AI agents. This might involve a system where the AI performs an initial analysis and presents its findings and recommendations, and the human operator then decides whether to accept, reject, or modify those recommendations, or even delegates a sub-task back to the AI for further processing.

For example, in the domain of flight control, while an AI might manage routine flight operations, such as maintaining altitude and course, a human pilot remains in command, ready to intervene during unexpected events or to make strategic decisions. The interface and communication protocols must facilitate this dynamic allocation. The AI might alert the pilot to an anomaly, such as an engine performance deviation, and present diagnostic options. The pilot, drawing on their experience and training, can then direct the AI to perform specific checks, analyze particular data sets, or even take manual control if the situation warrants. The AI's role is to provide enhanced situational awareness and perform complex calculations rapidly, while the pilot's role is to provide oversight, strategic decision-making, and ultimate control. The success of this collaboration hinges on the design of systems that allow for clear communication of intent, rapid transfer of control, and a shared understanding of the overall operational goals.

Furthermore, the design of AI systems for effective collaboration must also account for the potential for emergent behaviors and the need for continuous adaptation. AI models are not static entities; they learn and evolve, sometimes in ways that are not entirely predictable. Therefore, the systems that facilitate human-AI interaction must be robust enough to handle these evolving capabilities and, importantly, must allow humans to adapt their own interaction strategies as the AI changes. This can involve providing mechanisms for recalibration, setting new operational parameters, or even retraining certain aspects of the AI's behavior based on observed performance in collaboration with human users.

A practical example can be found in sophisticated manufacturing environments. An AI might be tasked with optimizing production line efficiency. As it learns from new data, it might begin to adjust machine speeds, material flow, or quality control parameters. A human supervisor, observing this, needs to be able to understand the changes being made and, if necessary, to intervene. The interface should provide transparency into the AI's optimization algorithms, allowing the supervisor to see *why* certain adjustments are being made. If the AI starts making changes that compromise product quality or worker safety, the supervisor must have the ability to immediately override those changes, rollback to a previous stable configuration, or even instruct the AI to focus on different optimization metrics. This requires not only a well-designed interface but also a clear set of rules and protocols governing the interaction between human and AI in terms of control and decision-making authority.

The concept of "explainable AI" (XAI) is particularly pertinent in this context. While not always providing a complete step-by-step breakdown of a deep learning model's internal workings, XAI aims to offer humans insights into *why* an AI made a particular decision or recommendation. This is crucial for building trust and enabling effective oversight. If an AI suggests a particular course of action, the human collaborator needs to understand the basis for that suggestion to confidently accept it or to identify its potential flaws. For instance, in financial trading, an AI might recommend a specific trade. An effective collaborative system would not just present the recommendation but also provide the underlying rationale, such as "increased probability of upward price movement due to recent earnings reports and positive market sentiment." This explanation allows the human trader to evaluate the AI's reasoning against their own market knowledge and risk appetite, leading to a more informed decision.

Moreover, the very nature of feedback loops within human-AI systems must be intentionally designed to promote collaboration. This feedback can flow in multiple directions: from the AI to the human, from the human to the AI, and from the system as a whole back to the designers and developers. For the AI to effectively assist a human, it needs to receive feedback on its performance, understand when it has made errors, and learn from human corrections. This feedback loop must be designed to be as seamless and intuitive as possible. For example, in an AI-powered content creation tool, a human editor might make changes to the AI-generated text. The system should capture these edits not just as modifications, but as valuable learning signals for the AI, helping it to better understand the editor's preferences, stylistic requirements, and factual accuracy standards.

The design of communication protocols also extends to the management of uncertainty. AI systems often operate with degrees of confidence rather than absolute certainty. An effective collaborative system will explicitly communicate this uncertainty to the human user. This might be done through confidence scores, probability distributions, or by presenting multiple plausible interpretations of the data, allowing the human to weigh the options and make a final judgment. For example, in a medical diagnosis AI, if the AI identifies a potential disease, it might present a list of possible diagnoses with associated probabilities. It could also highlight the key pieces of evidence that led to each diagnosis, enabling the human physician to critically evaluate the AI's reasoning and to integrate this information with their own clinical expertise and knowledge of the patient. This transparent handling of uncertainty fosters trust and prevents the human from over-relying on potentially flawed AI outputs.

Ultimately, designing for effective human-AI collaboration is an ongoing process of refinement and adaptation. It requires a multidisciplinary approach, drawing on principles from human-computer interaction, cognitive psychology, artificial intelligence, and domain-specific expertise. The goal is not to create a scenario where humans are merely passive observers or button-pushers, nor is it to create AI systems that operate in isolation. Instead, it is about building intelligent partnerships that harness the complementary strengths of humans and machines to achieve outcomes that neither could accomplish alone. This synergistic approach is essential for unlocking the full potential of AI while ensuring that human judgment, ethical considerations, and ultimate control remain at the forefront, guiding the development and deployment of these transformative technologies. The success of AI in the future will not be measured solely by its computational power or its autonomy, but by its ability to seamlessly and productively integrate with human intelligence, creating a future where technology empowers us to achieve more, together.

The spectrum of artificial intelligence is not a monolithic entity but a diverse landscape characterized by varying degrees of autonomy. Understanding these levels of automation is fundamental to designing effective human-AI partnerships, as it dictates where and how human intervention becomes not just beneficial, but essential. These levels can range from fully manual systems, where AI plays a minimal advisory role, to systems that operate with a high degree of autonomy, performing tasks with little to no direct human input. However, the critical distinction lies not just in the level of automation present, but in the clearly defined points where human operators can and must exert control. These intervention points are the crucial safeguards that ensure human agency, prevent unintended consequences, and maintain safety and ethical alignment.

At the lowest end of the automation spectrum, we find systems that offer primarily informational support. Here, the AI acts as an intelligent assistant, analyzing data, identifying patterns, and presenting insights to a human operator. The AI might flag potential issues, suggest courses of action, or provide predictive analytics, but the ultimate decision-making authority and the execution of tasks remain firmly with the human. For example, in a financial trading environment, an AI might identify a stock exhibiting trends that suggest a profitable opportunity. It could present this analysis, along with supporting data and potential risk assessments, to a human trader. The intervention point here is at the decision stage. The human trader receives the AI's output, evaluates it based on their expertise, market knowledge, and risk tolerance, and then decides whether to act on the AI's suggestion, modify it, or ignore it entirely. The AI does not execute trades; it provides a sophisticated input to the human decision-maker. In such scenarios, the interface must be designed to clearly present the AI's findings, along with the confidence level of its analysis, allowing the human to quickly grasp the information and form a judgment. The ease with which a human can access the underlying data, understand the AI's reasoning (through explainable AI techniques), and compare the AI's suggestion with alternative strategies are all critical aspects of this intervention point.

Moving up the automation ladder, we encounter systems that can perform a limited set of tasks autonomously, often within predefined parameters. These systems might handle routine operations, but require human oversight for more complex or out-of-scope situations. Consider an automated customer service chatbot. For common queries, it can provide immediate, accurate responses. However, when a customer expresses frustration, asks a highly specialized question, or describes a situation that deviates from its training data, the chatbot should be programmed to recognize its limitations and escalate the interaction to a human agent. This escalation is a crucial intervention point. The AI’s inability to resolve the issue, or its detection of a pattern indicating human emotional distress or complexity, serves as the trigger for intervention. The transition must be seamless, with the human agent receiving a summary of the preceding interaction, ensuring continuity of service and avoiding customer frustration. The design of the AI's 'failure detection' and 'escalation protocol' is paramount here. It needs to be sophisticated enough to identify when human intervention is necessary, but not so sensitive that it escalates every minor deviation, thereby overwhelming human agents.

A further level of automation involves systems that can perform a significant portion of a task independently, with humans primarily responsible for monitoring, correcting errors, and handling exceptions. This is commonly observed in advanced manufacturing or industrial process control. An AI might manage a complex assembly line, optimizing machine settings, managing material flow, and performing quality checks. However, if a machine malfunctions, a critical quality deviation is detected, or an unexpected event occurs (like a power surge), the system needs to alert human operators to intervene. These alerts are the intervention points. The AI might be able to initiate a safe shutdown sequence or attempt a self-correction, but the final decision to restart the line, diagnose the fault, or implement a manual override rests with the human supervisor. The speed and clarity of these alerts are vital. Furthermore, the interface must provide operators with real-time diagnostics and control options, allowing them to quickly understand the situation and take appropriate action. The ability to 'pause' the AI's autonomous operation, review its logs, and manually adjust parameters or take full control are key features of these intervention points. The training of these human operators is also critical, as they need to understand not only how to operate the machinery but also how the AI system functions, what its limitations are, and how to effectively override it when necessary.

In highly automated systems, humans might act as 'supervisors' or 'managers' of AI agents. The AI performs complex tasks autonomously, but humans retain the authority to set goals, define constraints, and make high-level strategic decisions. For example, in autonomous vehicle systems, while the AI handles the driving, a human driver (or a remote operator in certain contexts) can take control at any time. The handover of control is a critical intervention point. This handover can be initiated by the human (e.g., the driver decides to take the wheel) or by the AI (e.g., the AI determines it cannot safely navigate a situation and requests human intervention). The design of this handover process is crucial for safety. It must be unambiguous, prompt, and ensure that the human operator has sufficient time and information to regain full situational awareness before assuming control. The AI must provide clear indications of its current state and the reason for requesting intervention. Similarly, the human must have a clear and immediate way to signal their intent to take over control. The complexity arises in situations where the AI is operating at the edge of its capabilities, and a sudden, unexpected request for intervention might occur, leaving the human with very little time to react. This necessitates predictive interfaces that can alert the human to potential future challenges, allowing them to prepare for an imminent handover.

The concept of 'levels of automation' is often formalized, with frameworks like SAE International's J3016 standard for automated driving systems providing a useful, albeit specific, illustration of these differing modes. While not directly applicable to all AI systems, the underlying principles are instructive. The levels range from Level 0 (no automation) to Level 5 (full automation, where the system can handle all driving tasks under all conditions). However, even at higher levels of automation, the need for intervention points remains. For instance, at Level 4 automation, a vehicle can drive itself within a defined operational design domain (ODD). If the vehicle encounters a situation outside its ODD (e.g., severe weather not covered by its design), it must be able to safely transition control back to the human driver. This transition is an explicit intervention point. The system must detect when it is approaching the boundaries of its ODD and provide sufficient warning to the human to be ready to take over. Failure to do so could lead to a critical safety incident.

Beyond these general levels, specific types of intervention points can be categorized by their function and timing. These include:

Preventative Intervention: Where the human actively monitors the AI for signs of potential failure or deviation from expected behavior, stepping in before a problem occurs. This is akin to proactive system health monitoring. For example, a human supervisor might notice that an AI-powered diagnostic tool is consistently flagging minor anomalies in a particular sensor, suggesting a potential calibration issue with the sensor itself, and intervenes to recalibrate or replace it, thereby preventing future incorrect diagnoses.

Corrective Intervention: Where the human steps in to correct an error or deviation that the AI has already made or is in the process of making. This is the most common form of intervention, reacting to a detected anomaly. For instance, if an AI financial advisor makes a trade that is clearly contrary to the client's stated risk profile, the human advisor would intervene to reverse the trade and address the discrepancy.

Adaptive Intervention: Where the human modifies the AI's behavior or parameters based on changing circumstances or new information that the AI has not yet incorporated into its decision-making. This involves a dynamic adjustment of the AI's operational mode or objectives. For example, during a rapidly evolving emergency situation, a human commander might direct an AI-powered resource allocation system to prioritize different assets than originally planned, adapting the AI's strategy to the new reality.

Oversight Intervention: Where the human reviews the AI's performance and decisions retrospectively, not to correct an immediate error, but to learn from the AI's operation, improve future AI performance, or ensure compliance with policies and regulations. This might involve reviewing logs, analyzing performance metrics, and providing feedback for model retraining. For example, an ethics review board might examine the decisions made by an AI used in loan applications to ensure fairness and to identify any unintentional biases that may have crept into the algorithm.

Control Transfer Intervention: This refers to the explicit handover of task execution from the AI to the human, or vice versa. As discussed with autonomous vehicles, this is a critical safety intervention point that requires robust protocols and clear communication.

The effectiveness of these intervention points hinges on several key design principles. Firstly,
transparency is paramount. Humans need to understand what the AI is doing, why it is doing it, and what its current state is. This includes the ability to access relevant data, understand the AI's reasoning (even if simplified), and know the AI's confidence level in its outputs. Secondly, **timeliness** is crucial. Intervention points must be accessible and actionable within the timeframe required by the task. A delayed intervention, however well-intentioned, can be as dangerous as no intervention at all. This requires interfaces that can present information and facilitate actions rapidly. Thirdly, **clarity of authority and responsibility** is essential. It must be unambiguous who has control at any given moment and what the consequences of different actions are. This avoids confusion and conflicting commands. Fourthly, **graceful degradation and failure modes** are vital. When an AI system encounters a situation it cannot handle, it should not simply fail catastrophically. Instead, it should transition to a safe state and clearly signal its need for human intervention. This could involve a partial shutdown, a simplified mode of operation, or a direct handover to a human operator.

Designing for these intervention points requires a deep understanding of human cognitive capabilities and limitations, as well as the specific operational context. It involves not just engineering the AI, but also engineering the human-AI interaction. This includes the design of user interfaces, the development of training programs for human operators, and the establishment of clear operating procedures and protocols. The goal is to create systems where humans are always in a position to exert meaningful control, ensuring that AI remains a tool that serves human goals and values, rather than an autonomous agent that might pursue its own objectives, potentially to our detriment. The definition and implementation of these intervention points are therefore not merely technical considerations; they are fundamental to the ethical and safe deployment of AI. They represent the embodiment of human intent and control within increasingly sophisticated automated systems, ensuring that the future of AI is one that is guided by human judgment.

The increasing integration of artificial intelligence into complex operational environments necessitates a robust framework for training and ensuring the competency of the human operators who will oversee, manage, and interact with these systems. This is not merely a matter of technical proficiency; it encompasses a broad understanding of AI's capabilities, its inherent limitations, the ethical dimensions of its deployment, and the critical skills required to effectively utilize monitoring and control interfaces. Adequately preparing these individuals is paramount to realizing the benefits of AI while mitigating its potential risks, ensuring that human oversight remains meaningful and effective in safeguarding operations and upholding societal values.

At its core, the training for AI operators must cultivate a deep and practical understanding of the specific AI technologies being employed. This involves moving beyond a superficial grasp of what AI can do to a more nuanced comprehension of how it functions, its underlying principles, and the data upon which it relies. Operators need to understand the types of algorithms at play, whether they are machine learning models (such as deep neural networks, decision trees, or support vector machines), rule-based systems, or other forms of artificial intelligence. This technical grounding allows them to better interpret the AI's outputs, recognize potential anomalies or inconsistencies, and diagnose issues when they arise. For instance, an operator overseeing an AI-powered predictive maintenance system for industrial machinery must understand that the AI's predictions are based on historical data and statistical models. If the AI flags a component as likely to fail, the operator should know to investigate further, perhaps by examining the sensor data that fed the AI, understanding how the AI weights different variables, and considering factors outside the AI's immediate purview, such as recent operational changes or environmental conditions, that might influence the prediction. Without this foundational knowledge, an operator might blindly accept or reject the AI's recommendations, leading to either unnecessary downtime or potentially catastrophic failures.

Furthermore, a critical component of training is educating operators on the inherent limitations of AI systems. AI is not a panacea; it is a tool with specific strengths and weaknesses. Operators must be made aware of the concepts of model drift, where the AI's performance degrades over time as real-world data diverges from its training data. They need to understand the susceptibility of AI to adversarial attacks, where malicious actors can subtly manipulate input data to cause the AI to make incorrect decisions. The phenomenon of "garbage in, garbage out" is particularly relevant; operators must recognize that an AI's output is only as good as the data it is fed. Training should therefore include scenarios that highlight these limitations, demonstrating how subtle changes in data can lead to significantly different outcomes. For example, a training module for operators of an AI-driven medical diagnostic imaging system might include case studies where image quality variations or minor artifacts, imperceptible to the human eye but present in the training data, led to misclassifications by the AI. The operator's task in such a scenario is not to *be* the AI, but to act as a discerning human arbiter, capable of identifying when the AI might be over-reliant on flawed input or when its confidence scores are misleading.

Beyond technical understanding, ethical considerations are a non-negotiable element of AI operator training. As AI systems become more autonomous and their decisions have greater societal impact, operators must be equipped to navigate the ethical complexities they present. This includes understanding the potential for bias in AI algorithms, which can arise from biased training data or flawed algorithmic design, leading to discriminatory outcomes. For example, an AI used in recruitment processes might inadvertently favor certain demographic groups over others if its training data reflects historical hiring biases. Operators must be trained to recognize the signs of such bias, understand how to query the AI for explanations of its decisions (where possible through explainable AI techniques), and know the protocols for flagging or escalating potentially unethical outcomes. This might involve understanding principles of fairness, accountability, and transparency in AI. A financial compliance officer overseeing an AI that monitors transactions for fraud, for instance, must not only understand the AI's detection mechanisms but also be aware of how these mechanisms might disproportionately flag certain types of transactions or customer behaviors, potentially leading to unfair scrutiny or customer distress. The operator's role is to ensure that the AI's efficiency does not come at the cost of ethical integrity or equitable treatment.

Proficiency in using monitoring and control interfaces is another cornerstone of AI operator competency. These interfaces are the primary conduits through which operators interact with AI systems, and their design is critical for effective human-AI collaboration. Training must go beyond simply showing operators how to click buttons or navigate menus. It needs to foster an intuitive understanding of how to interpret the information presented – including dashboards, alerts, confidence scores, and explanatory outputs – and how to effectively utilize the available control mechanisms. This means understanding how to set parameters, adjust thresholds, initiate overrides, and manage the handover of control between human and AI. For example, an operator managing a fleet of autonomous delivery drones needs to be adept at monitoring their real-time flight paths, battery levels, and payload status, as displayed on a central console. They must be able to quickly interpret alerts indicating potential navigation hazards, system malfunctions, or deviations from scheduled routes. Crucially, they must be trained on when and how to take manual control of a drone, or to reroute the entire fleet in response to unforeseen events, such as severe weather or airspace closures. The speed and clarity with which an operator can access and act upon this information directly impacts operational safety and efficiency.

The training programs should be tailored to the specific roles and responsibilities of the operators. A frontline technician troubleshooting an AI-controlled robotic arm will require different training than a strategic manager overseeing an AI-driven supply chain optimization system. For technicians, the focus might be on understanding common failure modes of the AI and the associated hardware, learning diagnostic procedures, and mastering the manual override capabilities of the robotic system. They need to be able to quickly identify whether an issue stems from the AI, the physical machinery, or the interaction between the two. This might involve practical exercises where technicians are deliberately presented with simulated AI malfunctions and tasked with diagnosing and resolving them under pressure.

Strategic managers, on the other hand, will require a broader perspective. Their training should emphasize understanding the AI's strategic objectives, its performance metrics, and how its decisions align with overarching business goals. They need to be proficient in using higher-level dashboards that provide insights into the AI's performance trends, potential risks, and opportunities for optimization. For instance, a manager overseeing an AI-powered energy grid might need to understand how the AI balances supply and demand, predicts load fluctuations, and responds to renewable energy variability. Their intervention points might involve adjusting the AI's operational parameters to meet changing demand patterns, respond to market signals, or comply with new regulatory requirements. This requires not just an understanding of the AI's mechanics but also a grasp of the complex interplay between technology, economics, and policy.

Continuous learning and adaptation are also essential for maintaining operator competency in the rapidly evolving field of AI. AI models are frequently updated, retrained, and sometimes replaced altogether. New interfaces are developed, and operational protocols evolve. Therefore, training should not be a one-time event but an ongoing process. This can include regular refresher courses, workshops on new AI developments, simulations of emerging threat scenarios, and post-incident reviews where lessons learned from real-world events are incorporated into training materials. The concept of "competency assurance" is critical here, moving beyond initial certification to a system that periodically assesses and validates operators' skills and knowledge. This might involve periodic assessments, practical evaluations, and participation in continuous professional development programs. For example, operators of AI systems used in cybersecurity might undergo quarterly simulations of sophisticated cyber-attacks, testing their ability to detect and respond to AI-driven threats, as well as their own human-AI collaborative strategies.

The development of robust training programs requires collaboration between AI developers, domain experts, human factors specialists, and ethicists. AI developers can provide the technical details of the systems, while domain experts ensure that the training is relevant to the operational context. Human factors specialists can design interfaces and training methodologies that optimize human cognition and performance, ensuring that operators can effectively process information and make timely decisions. Ethicists can contribute to the curriculum, ensuring that operators are well-versed in the ethical implications of their work and are equipped to uphold responsible AI practices.

Ultimately, the goal of training and competency assurance for AI operators is to foster a culture of informed vigilance. Operators should not be passive observers or blind executors of AI commands. Instead, they should be active, critical participants in the human-AI partnership, equipped with the knowledge, skills, and ethical grounding to harness the power of AI responsibly and effectively. This requires a commitment to comprehensive, ongoing training that addresses the technical, ethical, and practical dimensions of operating in an AI-enabled world, ensuring that human judgment remains at the helm of increasingly sophisticated automated systems. Such investment in human capital is as vital as the investment in the AI technology itself, forming the bedrock of safe, ethical, and beneficial AI deployment.

The human element in the oversight of artificial intelligence systems, while crucial, is not without its own set of ethical complexities. Even with the most sophisticated AI, the ultimate responsibility for its actions, and for any unintended consequences, often rests with a human operator. This responsibility can introduce a unique set of psychological and ethical challenges that must be carefully managed. One of the most pervasive issues is **automation bias**. This cognitive tendency describes the inclination for humans to over-rely on automated systems, often to the detriment of their own judgment. When an AI consistently performs well, operators may begin to implicitly trust its outputs, even when those outputs are flawed or incorrect. This trust can lead to a diminished capacity for critical evaluation. For example, imagine an AI system designed to monitor financial transactions for fraudulent activity. If the system has a high accuracy rate and successfully flags numerous fraudulent transactions, an operator might become accustomed to accepting its alerts without thorough manual verification. In such a scenario, if the AI mistakenly flags a legitimate transaction as fraudulent due to an unusual but not illicit pattern, the operator's automation bias might lead them to approve the erroneous alert, causing unnecessary disruption or harm to a customer. The ethical implication here is that the operator, by passively accepting the AI's output, is complicit in the error, and the system's perceived reliability has inadvertently eroded the operator's critical discernment.

This over-reliance can also foster
complacency. When tasks are largely automated, operators may experience a decline in vigilance. The demanding, often routine nature of monitoring AI can lead to a state where attention wanes, and operators become less engaged with the information presented. This is particularly problematic in systems that require intermittent but critical human intervention. Consider an AI controlling a complex industrial process, such as a chemical plant. While the AI manages the day-to-day operations, human operators are tasked with overseeing critical parameters and intervening during abnormal situations. If the AI has been functioning smoothly for extended periods, operators might become less attentive, their mental faculties dulled by the lack of significant events. This complacency can mean that when a genuine anomaly does occur – perhaps a subtle deviation in temperature or pressure that precedes a dangerous escalation – the operator might be slow to notice it, or might not fully grasp its significance, precisely because they have grown accustomed to the system's seamless operation. The ethical burden in such a situation is immense; a moment of inattention, fueled by the AI's perceived competence, could lead to environmental damage, financial loss, or even loss of life.

Furthermore, the continuous delegation of decision-making to AI can lead to
skill degradation. As AI systems take over more complex tasks, the human operators may have fewer opportunities to exercise and hone their own judgment and problem-solving skills in those domains. This can create a feedback loop: as skills degrade, operators become more reliant

on the AI, which in turn leads to further skill atrophy. For instance, in air traffic control, AI is being developed to assist with flight path optimization and conflict detection. While human controllers remain in charge, if AI systems become the primary tool for these functions, younger controllers may not develop the intuitive, experience-based expertise that seasoned controllers possess for handling highly complex, multi-aircraft scenarios. The ethical dilemma arises when the AI's capabilities, while advanced, might not cover every conceivable edge case, or when novel situations emerge that were not part of the AI's training. In such instances, a controller whose skills have atrophied might be ill-equipped to make the nuanced judgments required, potentially compromising safety. The ethical imperative is to ensure that human oversight remains a source of genuine expertise, not merely a rubber stamp, and that operators are not rendered obsolete by their own tools.

The psychological impact of being responsible for AI actions is another significant ethical consideration. When an AI system makes a mistake that results in harm, the human operator often feels a profound sense of accountability, even if their role was primarily supervisory. This can lead to significant stress, anxiety, and guilt. The phenomenon of **moral disengagement** can also occur, where individuals distance themselves from the consequences of their actions by attributing them to the machine. However, true ethical oversight demands that individuals remain fully engaged and accountable. Consider a physician using an AI diagnostic tool. If the AI misinterprets an image and leads to a delayed diagnosis for a patient, the physician may experience significant distress. Even if the AI's error is technically explainable, the physician, as the final decision-maker, bears a considerable moral weight. The ethical challenge is to support these operators, ensuring they have the psychological resilience and support structures to handle the burden of responsibility, without allowing this burden to lead to either paralysis or an abdication of their ethical duties.

Mitigating these ethical risks associated with human oversight requires a multi-faceted approach, beginning with **regular training refreshers and continuous professional development**. Simply undergoing initial training is insufficient. As AI systems evolve and new scenarios emerge, operators must continually update their knowledge and skills. This includes retraining on the AI's functionalities, its limitations, and emerging threat vectors. For example, cybersecurity operators overseeing AI-powered threat detection systems need regular training that simulates new types of AI-driven attacks. This ensures they remain adept at recognizing novel patterns and can effectively collaborate with the AI to counter evolving threats. These refreshers should not just focus on technical aspects but also on reinforcing the ethical considerations and the importance of critical judgment.

Performance monitoring and feedback mechanisms are also critical. Just as AI systems are monitored for performance, the performance of human operators in overseeing these systems should be assessed. This monitoring should not be punitive but formative, aimed at identifying areas where operators may be exhibiting automation bias, complacency, or skill degradation. Feedback should be constructive, providing opportunities for learning and improvement. For instance, in the context of autonomous vehicle operation, fleet managers might review logs of human interventions. If an operator consistently overrules the AI for minor, unfounded reasons, or conversely, fails to intervene when necessary, this data can inform targeted coaching or retraining. Ethical oversight here involves ensuring that monitoring is fair, transparent, and used to support operator development rather than simply to assign blame.

Fostering a

culture of critical evaluation and open communication is perhaps one of the most important strategies. Operators must feel empowered to question the AI's outputs, to voice concerns about its performance, and to challenge its recommendations without fear of reprisal. This requires leadership that actively promotes a mindset where human judgment and critical thinking are valued above blind adherence to automation. In research environments, for example, teams developing and deploying AI for scientific discovery should encourage a culture where researchers are encouraged to critically examine AI-generated hypotheses, to seek out contradictory evidence, and to discuss potential biases or flaws in the AI's reasoning. This ensures that the AI serves as a tool for augmenting human intelligence, not replacing it. An environment where operators feel safe to report an AI's error, or to admit they are unsure about its output, is crucial for preventing the escalation of minor issues into major problems.

Furthermore, the design of the
human-AI interface plays a significant role in shaping operator behavior and mitigating ethical risks. Interfaces should be designed to promote vigilance and critical thinking, rather than complacency. This can involve designing alerts that are clear but not overly alarming, presenting confidence scores in a way that encourages critical assessment, and providing explainable AI (XAI) features that allow operators to understand *why* an AI has made a particular recommendation. For example, an AI providing medical diagnoses could present not just a diagnosis but also highlight the specific features in an image or patient record that led to that conclusion, allowing the physician to verify the AI's reasoning. This transparency helps combat automation bias by providing concrete evidence for the AI's decision-making process, enabling more informed human judgment.

Another strategy involves defining
clear roles and responsibilities in the human-AI teaming structure. It is essential to clearly delineate where human judgment is paramount and where the AI's decision-making authority is absolute. This clarity reduces

ambiguity and ensures that operators understand their specific obligations. For instance, in a surgical robot system, the surgeon always retains ultimate control and responsibility for the patient's well-being, even while the robot assists with precision movements. The AI's role is that of a sophisticated tool, not an autonomous decision-maker in the critical phases of surgery. Ethical practice demands that these boundaries are explicit and understood by all involved.

Finally, ethical considerations also extend to the **long-term impact on the workforce**. As AI becomes more integrated, there is a risk of creating a class of operators who are solely trained to monitor and manage machines, potentially leading to a deskilling of the broader workforce. Ethical deployment requires considering the broader societal implications, investing in retraining and upskilling initiatives, and ensuring that the integration of AI enhances, rather than diminishes, human capabilities and opportunities. This proactive approach to workforce development is an ethical imperative, ensuring that technological advancement benefits society as a whole. The goal is not to eliminate human involvement but to redefine it, ensuring that human oversight remains an active, intelligent, and ethically grounded component of AI systems.

Chapter 12: Continuous Learning and Adaptation

The preceding discussion has underscored the indispensable role of human oversight in navigating the ethical complexities of artificial intelligence. However, the very nature of AI systems, particularly those designed for continuous learning and adaptation, introduces a new layer of challenges that extend beyond the immediate actions of human operators. AI systems are not static constructs; they are increasingly dynamic, capable of evolving their understanding, their decision-making processes, and even their fundamental behaviors over time. This inherent mutability, while a source of immense power and potential, also necessitates a recalibration of our ethical frameworks and safety engineering practices.

The concept of AI system evolution hinges on the principle of continuous learning. Unlike traditional software, which is typically deployed in a fixed state and updated through explicit patches or new versions, many modern AI systems are designed to ingest new data and refine their internal models as they operate. This adaptive capacity is often the very reason for their deployment. For instance, a recommendation engine in an e-commerce platform learns from each user interaction – a purchase, a click, a viewed item – to become more adept at suggesting relevant products. Similarly, an AI tasked with optimizing traffic flow in a city will continuously process real-time traffic data from sensors, cameras, and even GPS devices to adjust signal timings and reroute vehicles dynamically. The benefits of this evolutionary process are profound. Over time, AI systems can achieve a level of performance and precision that would be unattainable with static algorithms. They can adapt to novel situations not foreseen during their initial training, identify emerging patterns, and continuously improve their efficiency and effectiveness. This dynamic improvement cycle can lead to significant advancements in fields ranging from medical diagnosis, where AI can learn from an ever-growing corpus of patient data, to scientific discovery, where AI can identify subtle correlations in experimental results. The ability of an AI to evolve its understanding based on real-world feedback is a powerful driver of innovation and performance enhancement.

However, this very adaptability introduces a significant ethical quandary: the potential for unpredictable or undesirable changes in system behavior. When an AI system learns and evolves continuously, its future state is not always a direct consequence of its initial design and training data alone. It is also shaped by the complex interplay of new data streams, the learning algorithms themselves, and the specific operational environment it inhabits. This makes the system's trajectory of evolution potentially opaque and, in some cases, uncontrollable. The classic example is the emergence of unintended biases. An AI system that initially exhibited fair behavior might, through exposure to biased data in its operational environment, begin to exhibit discriminatory outcomes. For example, an AI used for loan applications, initially trained on a balanced dataset, might encounter a surge of applications from a particular demographic group that exhibits a higher default rate due to socio-economic factors unrelated to creditworthiness. If the AI's learning algorithm amplifies this correlation without sufficient countervailing safeguards, it could begin to unfairly deny loans to qualified individuals within that group. The ethical issue here is not merely the presence of bias, but the
dynamic and potentially *undetectable* emergence of bias through the system's evolutionary process.

Furthermore, the process of continuous adaptation can sometimes lead to what is termed "model drift" or "concept drift." This occurs when the statistical properties of the data on which the AI makes predictions change over time, rendering its learned patterns less relevant or even misleading. Consider an AI system designed to detect spam emails. Spammers constantly evolve their tactics, employing new keywords, obfuscation techniques, and sending patterns. If the AI system's learning mechanism is not sufficiently robust or rapid, it may fail to keep pace with these evolving threats. Consequently, its ability to accurately classify spam will degrade, leading to an increase in both false positives (legitimate emails marked as spam) and false negatives (spam emails reaching the inbox). From an ethical standpoint, this drift can have serious implications. For a financial fraud detection AI, drift could mean missed fraudulent transactions, leading to financial losses for individuals and institutions. For an AI moderating online content, drift could result in the amplification of hate speech or misinformation that the system no longer recognizes as harmful.

The unpredictability inherent in evolving AI systems raises critical questions about accountability and explainability. If an AI system's behavior changes significantly over time due to its learning process, attributing responsibility for an adverse outcome becomes exceedingly difficult. Was the error a result of the initial design, a flaw in the learning algorithm, or a consequence of the specific data it encountered during its evolution? The "black box" nature of many advanced AI models exacerbates this problem. When an AI's decision-making logic becomes increasingly complex and opaque through continuous learning, it becomes harder for humans to understand *why* a particular decision was made, or *how* the system arrived at its current state. This lack of transparency is antithetical to ethical AI development, which emphasizes the need for systems whose operations can be understood, audited, and trusted. Without a clear understanding of how an AI evolves, it is challenging to ensure that its evolution aligns with human values and ethical principles.

The challenge is further compounded by the sheer scale and velocity of data that modern AI systems can process. As these systems are exposed to ever-larger and more diverse datasets, their learning pathways can become extraordinarily complex. This can lead to emergent behaviors that are not easily predicted by analyzing the system's components in isolation. Imagine an AI managing a nation's power grid. It learns from weather patterns, energy demand, equipment performance, and market fluctuations. Over time, it might develop highly sophisticated, emergent strategies for load balancing and energy distribution. While these strategies might be highly efficient, they could also be incredibly intricate, making it difficult for human engineers to fully grasp the underlying logic. If a cascading failure were to occur, understanding the AI's role in that failure, and preventing its recurrence, would require an unprecedented level of analytical insight into the AI's evolved state. This underscores the need for advanced tools and methodologies specifically designed to monitor, analyze, and interpret the behavior of continuously learning AI systems.

One of the primary concerns in the evolution of AI systems is the potential for "catastrophic forgetting" in neural networks. In some learning architectures, when a model learns new information, it can overwrite or degrade its knowledge of previously learned information. This is akin to a human forgetting important facts as they learn new ones. In an AI deployed in a critical domain, such as autonomous driving, catastrophic forgetting could be disastrous. An AI that has learned to recognize a wide range of road hazards might, after extensive training on a new set of driving scenarios, suddenly "forget" how to identify a pedestrian or a traffic signal. This highlights the need for learning algorithms that are not just efficient at acquiring new knowledge but also robust in retaining existing, critical knowledge. Ethical AI development must therefore prioritize models that exhibit "continual learning" or "lifelong learning" capabilities in a stable and reliable manner, rather than a fragile one.

The introduction of reinforcement learning paradigms further amplifies the dynamics of AI evolution. In reinforcement learning, an AI agent learns by trial and error, receiving rewards or penalties for its actions in an environment. This process allows AI to discover optimal strategies in complex, dynamic systems. For example, AI agents are being trained using reinforcement learning to manage complex logistics, optimize chemical reactions, or even play strategic games at superhuman levels. The learning process in reinforcement learning can be highly exploratory, with the agent testing a wide range of behaviors to discover those that yield the highest rewards. This exploration phase can sometimes lead to the agent exhibiting behaviors that appear suboptimal, irrational, or even unsafe from a human perspective, before it converges on a more desirable strategy. The ethical challenge lies in managing this exploratory phase. How can we ensure that the AI's learning process does not cause undue harm or risk to its operational environment during this period of experimentation? It requires careful design of the reward functions, robust safety constraints, and often, a human-in-the-loop oversight mechanism that can intervene when the AI's exploration deviates too far from acceptable parameters.

The regulatory and policy implications of evolving AI systems are also significant. Traditional regulatory frameworks are often built around static products or services with well-defined specifications. However, an AI system that continuously learns and adapts presents a moving target. How can regulators ensure that a system remains compliant with safety standards when its behavior is subject to ongoing change? This necessitates a shift towards more dynamic and adaptive regulatory approaches. Instead of certifying a specific version of an AI, regulators might need to certify the
process by which the AI learns and adapts, ensuring that this process itself is robust, transparent, and includes appropriate safeguards. This could involve establishing standards for data quality, algorithm validation, continuous monitoring, and incident reporting for evolving AI systems. The challenge is to create a regulatory environment that fosters innovation while simultaneously ensuring public safety and ethical alignment.

Furthermore, the evolution of AI systems raises questions about intellectual property and ownership. If an AI system develops novel insights or creates new works through its learning process, who owns these creations? Is it the developers who built the initial system, the owners of the data it learned from, or the AI itself (a concept that raises further complex legal and philosophical questions)? While current legal frameworks generally attribute ownership to the creators or owners of the AI, the increasing autonomy and creative capacity of evolving AI systems may challenge these established notions in the future.

Addressing the ethical and safety challenges posed by evolving AI systems requires a proactive and multi-faceted approach. One critical area is the development of
robust monitoring and anomaly detection systems. These systems should not just track the AI's performance metrics but also monitor its internal states, data inputs, and decision-making pathways for signs of drift, bias, or emergent undesirable behaviors. Techniques such as concept drift detection algorithms, adversarial monitoring, and detailed logging of AI decision rationale can provide early warnings of potential issues. For example, in a medical AI system, continuous monitoring might flag a gradual decrease in its accuracy for a specific type of anomaly, prompting human intervention and retraining before a significant diagnostic error occurs.

Another crucial element is the implementation of
safeguards and intervention mechanisms. For continuously learning systems, especially those deployed in high-stakes environments, it is imperative to build in fallback mechanisms, safety constraints, and human override capabilities. These are not merely for addressing unexpected errors but also for guiding the AI's evolution. For instance, an AI in a manufacturing plant could be programmed with hard limits on operational parameters that it cannot exceed, regardless of what its learning process suggests. Similarly, human operators should retain the ability to pause, reset, or revert the AI to a known stable state if its

behavior becomes concerning. The design of these safeguards needs careful consideration to ensure they do not unduly stifle the AI's learning capabilities while effectively preventing harm.

The concept of
"AI alignment" becomes particularly pertinent in the context of evolving systems. AI alignment refers to the challenge of ensuring that AI systems, as they become more capable and autonomous, pursue goals that are aligned with human values and intentions. For evolving AIs, this means not only ensuring their initial design reflects desired objectives but also developing mechanisms to ensure that their learned objectives remain aligned over time. This is an active area of research, exploring techniques such as inverse reinforcement learning (where the AI infers human goals from observed behavior), cooperative AI (where AI systems are designed to collaborate with humans and other AIs towards shared objectives), and value learning. The ethical imperative is to develop AIs that can gracefully adapt their behavior in ways that continue to serve beneficial purposes, even as their capabilities and understanding grow.

Moreover,
explainability and interpretability research needs to extend beyond static models to address evolving systems. This involves developing techniques that can provide insights into *how* an AI's behavior has changed over time, and *why* these changes occurred. This might involve creating "explainability histories" that track the evolution of the AI's internal representations or decision-making rules. Visualizations that illustrate the impact of specific data points or learning episodes on the AI's overall model can be invaluable for understanding its trajectory. Without such tools, the ethical challenge of ensuring transparency and accountability in evolving AI systems will remain formidable.

The development of
formal verification methods for AI systems, particularly those that learn and adapt, is also a critical frontier. While traditional software verification

focuses on proving that a program adheres to its specifications, verifying a continuously learning system is far more complex. Researchers are exploring techniques for verifying properties of learning algorithms, bounding the potential performance degradation due to concept drift, and ensuring that certain safety-critical behaviors remain invariant throughout the learning process. Such formal guarantees, even if they apply to specific aspects of the AI's behavior, can provide a higher degree of confidence in the system's reliability and safety.

Finally, fostering a **culture of responsible innovation and continuous ethical review** within organizations developing and deploying evolving AI is paramount. This involves establishing clear ethical guidelines for the development and deployment of adaptive AI, conducting regular ethical audits, and creating mechanisms for external review and stakeholder engagement. As AI systems evolve, so too must our ethical scrutiny. This continuous feedback loop, involving developers, ethicists, policymakers, and the public, is essential for navigating the complex and dynamic landscape of artificial intelligence evolution. The journey of AI evolution is not just a technical one; it is a journey that must be guided by a deep and unwavering commitment to human values and ethical principles.

The dynamic nature of artificial intelligence systems, particularly those designed for continuous, real-time learning—often referred to as "online learning"—presents a distinct set of safety and management challenges. Unlike models that are trained in batches and then deployed in a static state, online learning systems ingest and process data continuously as they operate, adapting their internal parameters and decision-making logic in response to each new piece of information. While this adaptability is the source of their power, enabling them to remain relevant and effective in rapidly changing environments, it also introduces significant complexities in ensuring their safety and ethical alignment. The very essence of online learning means that the system is in a perpetual state of flux, making traditional methods of safety assurance, which often rely on the stability of a deployed model, insufficient.

Managing the safety of online learning systems requires a proactive and multi-layered approach, focusing on controlling the pace and direction of learning, ensuring the integrity of the learned models, and establishing robust fallback mechanisms. One of the most fundamental strategies is to **set appropriate bounds on learning rates**. The speed at which an AI model updates its parameters significantly influences its stability and predictability. An excessively high learning rate can lead to rapid, potentially unstable changes in behavior. The model might overreact to noisy data, quickly adopt spurious correlations, or exhibit sudden, drastic shifts in its decision-making policies. This can manifest as erratic performance, an inability to generalize, or even a rapid descent into undesirable or unsafe operational modes. Conversely, an overly conservative learning rate might render the system too slow to adapt to genuine changes in its environment, diminishing its utility. Therefore, determining an optimal learning rate is a critical balancing act. This often involves extensive experimentation and simulation, understanding the typical velocity and volatility of the data the system will encounter, and setting thresholds that allow for adaptation without sacrificing stability. For instance, an AI system monitoring critical infrastructure, such as a power grid, might need to adapt to fluctuating demand or equipment status. However, its learning rate would need to be carefully calibrated. A sudden, unchecked spike in learning driven by an anomalous sensor reading—perhaps a temporary glitch—should not cause the AI to drastically alter its fundamental load-balancing strategies. Instead, the learning process should be designed to smooth out such anomalies, prioritizing long-term stability and safety over immediate, potentially erroneous, adjustments. This often involves techniques like learning rate decay, where the learning rate decreases over time, or adaptive learning rate algorithms that adjust the rate based on the model's progress and the characteristics of the incoming data. The goal is to foster a learning process that is responsive enough to be effective but constrained enough to be safe.

Beyond controlling the learning rate, **implementing periodic validation checkpoints** is an indispensable practice for managing online learning systems. Since the system is constantly evolving, its performance and adherence to safety standards can degrade subtly over time without immediate detection. Establishing regular intervals at which the AI's current state is evaluated against a predefined set of benchmarks and safety criteria is crucial. These checkpoints act as crucial diagnostic moments, allowing developers and operators to assess whether the AI's learned model remains within acceptable performance envelopes and aligns with ethical guidelines. During these validation periods, the AI can be evaluated on a held-out, representative dataset—separate from the data it has been learning from—to gauge its generalization capabilities and identify any signs of performance degradation or "model drift." If the validation reveals that the AI's performance has fallen below a critical threshold, or if it exhibits undesirable behaviors such as increased bias or reduced accuracy in a specific domain, interventions can be initiated. These interventions might range from recalibrating the learning parameters to more drastic measures, such as rolling back to a previously validated stable version of the model. Consider an AI system used for content moderation on a social media platform. As new forms of harmful content or manipulation tactics emerge, the AI must adapt. However, a poorly calibrated learning process could inadvertently lead it to misclassify legitimate speech as harmful, or vice-versa. By instituting daily or weekly validation checkpoints, where the AI's classifications are compared against human-labeled data and adherence to content policies is reviewed, anomalies can be caught. If the AI begins to disproportionately flag content from a particular demographic or starts missing sophisticated disinformation campaigns, these checkpoints provide the necessary opportunity for human review and correction before widespread harm occurs. The regularity and rigor of these checkpoints are paramount; they must be frequent enough to catch emerging issues before they escalate but also comprehensive enough to provide meaningful insights into the system's evolving state.

The use of
ensemble methods offers another powerful layer of safety for online learning systems. Instead of relying on a single AI model, ensemble techniques involve combining the predictions of multiple models. These individual models can be trained with different algorithms, different subsets of data, or with varying learning rates and parameters. By aggregating their outputs—for example, through majority voting or weighted averaging—the ensemble can achieve more robust, accurate, and stable predictions than any single model operating in isolation. In the context of online learning, ensembles can be particularly beneficial. A diverse set of models, each adapting to the incoming data stream, can act as a collective early warning system. If one model begins to exhibit aberrant behavior due to an unusual data point or a temporary learning instability, the other models in the ensemble can often mitigate its impact. Their combined wisdom can smooth out individual model fluctuations and provide a more reliable overall output. For instance, in an autonomous driving system that learns from real-time sensor data, an ensemble of object detection models can enhance safety. One model might momentarily misinterpret a shadow as an obstacle, while another might have a fleeting difficulty recognizing a distant pedestrian. However, if the majority of models in the ensemble correctly identify the situation, the overall system can still make the appropriate decision, such as slowing down or maintaining course. Furthermore, ensemble diversity can be strategically maintained. Techniques like "bagging" (bootstrap aggregating) or "boosting" can be adapted for online settings, where new models are continuously added or existing ones are retrained and updated. This dynamic ensemble approach can provide a flexible yet resilient framework for managing online learning, as it inherently introduces redundancy and diversity, both critical components of robust safety engineering.

Crucially, the implementation of

mechanisms to revert to known safe states is a non-negotiable requirement for any online learning system operating in a critical domain. Given the inherent unpredictability of continuous learning, there must be a reliable way to disengage from a potentially compromised or degraded operational state and return the system to a previous, proven-safe configuration. This is akin to having an "undo" button for the AI's learning process. Such rollback mechanisms are not merely a last resort but an integral part of the system's design, allowing for graceful degradation and rapid recovery in the event of detected anomalies, significant performance drops, or safety violations. The "known safe state" could be a specific version of the model that has undergone rigorous testing and validation, or a configuration with simplified, deterministic algorithms that prioritize safety over optimal performance. The trigger for such a rollback could be any of the issues identified during validation checkpoints, a significant deviation from expected operational parameters, or an alert from anomaly detection systems. For example, an AI system managing a robotic assembly line could be programmed to revert to a basic, pre-programmed sequence of movements if its learning algorithms begin to exhibit unexpected jerky motions or collisions. This reversion would be initiated automatically if sensors detect anomalous force readings or if the AI's internal state deviates beyond predefined safety margins. The process of reverting should ideally be swift and seamless, minimizing disruption to operations while ensuring that the system ceases to operate in a potentially unsafe manner. Furthermore, after a rollback, a thorough post-mortem analysis is essential to understand *why* the system entered an unsafe state. This analysis informs necessary adjustments to the learning algorithms, validation procedures, or safeguard parameters before the AI is re-enabled or redeployed in its adaptive mode. Without these robust fallback mechanisms, the potential for catastrophic failures in continuously learning systems would be unacceptably high.

The challenge of managing online learning extends to ensuring that the data itself, which fuels the learning process, does not inadvertently introduce or amplify risks.

Data quality assurance and monitoring become paramount. In a static learning paradigm, data is typically curated and cleaned extensively before training. In an online setting, this continuous stream of data must be subjected to ongoing scrutiny. Anomalous data points, corrupted inputs, or systematically biased data can all lead the AI astray. Therefore, robust data pipelines should include real-time data validation, outlier detection, and anomaly flagging. If the system encounters data that significantly deviates from historical patterns or expected distributions, it might be prudent to temporarily halt learning or reduce the learning rate until the data quality issue is resolved. This prevents the AI from "learning" from errors or corrupted information, a scenario that could quickly lead to a compromised model. For instance, an AI system analyzing financial transactions for fraud must be vigilant about the integrity of its input data. If a sudden influx of data from a compromised source, containing incorrect transaction details or fabricated identifiers, is fed into the learning loop, the AI could develop faulty patterns for identifying legitimate versus fraudulent activity. Implementing real-time data quality checks, such as verifying transaction formats, cross-referencing against known legitimate sources, and flagging statistically improbable data points, can help prevent the AI from learning from bad data.

Furthermore, the concept of **explainability and interpretability** is profoundly impacted by online learning, and managing safety requires addressing this. If the AI's model is constantly changing, providing a static explanation of its decision-making process is impossible. Instead, safety requires mechanisms that can provide insights into *how* the AI's understanding has evolved and *why* it has reached its current state. This might involve logging significant updates to the model, tracking the impact of specific data batches on model parameters, or developing methods to generate explanations for the current model state on demand. For safety-critical applications, being able to understand the AI's reasoning, even if it is complex and has evolved over time, is essential for diagnosing problems and ensuring trust. This could involve developing "dynamic explanation" systems that can provide context-aware justifications for the AI's current actions, taking into account its learning history. Without such capabilities, identifying the root cause of a safety failure in an online learning system can be akin to finding a needle in a haystack, especially if the failure is a result of accumulated learning over many iterations.

The deployment of online learning systems also necessitates a robust framework for
continuous monitoring and performance assessment. This goes beyond simple accuracy metrics. For safety-critical applications, a comprehensive suite of monitoring tools is required, tracking not only prediction accuracy but also system stability, resource utilization, adherence to operational constraints, and potential biases. Techniques like drift detection algorithms—which specifically look for changes in the statistical properties of the input data or the model's predictions—are vital. When drift is detected, it signals that the AI's learned patterns may no longer be valid for the current environment, potentially compromising its safety. Similarly, monitoring for signs of "catastrophic forgetting" is important. If the AI is expected to retain certain critical knowledge, continuous monitoring can help detect if that knowledge is being overwritten by newer, less relevant information. Alerting systems should be configured to flag any deviation from predefined safety margins or performance targets, triggering an investigation or an automated intervention. For instance, an AI system managing automated warehouse operations might monitor the success rate of picking and placing items, the travel time of robots, and the incidence of inventory discrepancies. If any of these metrics begin to show a persistent negative trend, it could indicate that the AI's learning process is leading to suboptimal or even unsafe operations, prompting an alert for human review.

Finally, the human element remains indispensable.

Human oversight and intervention protocols must be clearly defined and consistently enforced. While online learning systems are designed to adapt autonomously, human operators must retain the ultimate authority and capability to intervene. This includes the ability to pause the learning process, override specific decisions, initiate rollbacks, and conduct in-depth investigations into system behavior. Training for these operators is critical; they must understand the AI's capabilities, its limitations, and the specific risks associated with its online learning paradigm. Establishing clear escalation paths for identified issues ensures that problems are addressed promptly and effectively. For example, in a healthcare setting where an AI is continuously learning to assist in diagnosis, a physician must have the explicit authority to disregard the AI's recommendation if it conflicts with their clinical judgment or if they suspect an error in the AI's reasoning, especially if they are aware of specific data trends that might be misleading the AI. This ensures that the AI serves as a tool to augment human expertise, rather than replacing it in a way that could compromise patient safety. The integration of human judgment, coupled with robust automated safeguards, forms the cornerstone of safe online learning deployment.

As AI systems engage in continuous learning, a crucial challenge emerges: the inevitable alteration of the data landscape they operate within. This phenomenon, broadly termed "data drift," is a pervasive reality that can subtly or dramatically degrade an AI's performance, accuracy, and ultimately, its safety. When the statistical properties of the input data change over time, the model's learned patterns, meticulously crafted during its training or earlier adaptation phases, can become obsolete or even actively misleading. Without mechanisms to detect and respond to these shifts, even the most sophisticated continuously learning AI risks becoming unreliable, leading to erroneous decisions and potentially unsafe outcomes.

The concept of data drift encompasses several distinct, yet often related, phenomena. One of the most significant is

covariate drift, also known as **dataset shift** or **feature drift**. This occurs when the distribution of the input features (covariates) changes, but the underlying relationship between these features and the target variable (the concept) remains the same. Imagine an AI system trained to predict customer purchasing behavior based on demographic data and past purchase history. If a new marketing campaign successfully attracts a significantly younger demographic, the distribution of age-related features in the input data will change. The model, which was trained on a broader age range, might struggle to accurately predict the preferences of this new, skewed demographic, even if the fundamental drivers of purchasing (e.g., interest in product features, price sensitivity) haven't changed for those individuals. Similarly, an autonomous vehicle's perception system might encounter a shift in weather patterns – more frequent fog or snow – altering the statistical distribution of visual sensor inputs. The relationships it learned between visual cues and object identification might still hold true, but the *frequency* and *characteristics* of those cues have changed, impacting performance.

A more complex and often more detrimental form of drift is **concept drift**. This happens when the relationship between the input features and the target variable itself changes over time. The "concept" the model is trying to learn or predict evolves. Consider a spam detection system. Initially, spammers might use obvious keywords and grammatical errors. As filters improve, spammers adapt, developing more sophisticated techniques that mimic legitimate emails, often incorporating new slang, evolving phishing tactics, or employing subtle psychological manipulation. The features that once strongly indicated spam might now be present in legitimate emails, and vice versa. The fundamental "concept" of what constitutes spam has shifted. In a financial fraud detection system, new types of fraudulent activities can emerge that were not present in the original training data. For instance, the rise of peer-to-peer payment apps has introduced new avenues for illicit transactions, necessitating a recalibration of what constitutes suspicious activity. Concept drift is particularly challenging because it often requires not just an adjustment to the model's parameters but a deeper re-understanding of the underlying problem.

A related phenomenon, sometimes considered a subtype of concept drift or a distinct category, is
label drift or **prior probability shift**. This occurs when the distribution of the target variable (the label) changes, independent of changes in the input features. For example, a medical diagnostic AI might be trained to identify a rare disease. If public health initiatives lead to a significant increase in the prevalence of that disease in the population, the prior probability of encountering a positive case will change. If the model was not designed to account for this shift in base rates, its predictions might become less reliable, potentially leading to an increase in false positives or false negatives relative to the new prevalence.

Detecting these various forms of drift is the critical first step towards mitigating their impact. A variety of statistical and machine learning techniques are employed for this purpose. One fundamental approach is **monitoring model performance metrics** over time. If a model's accuracy, precision, recall, F1-score, or AUC (Area Under the Curve) begins to degrade on new, incoming data, it's a strong indicator that drift is occurring. However, performance degradation can also be caused by other issues, so it's essential to complement this with more direct drift detection methods.

Statistical tests are commonly used to compare the distribution of data in a reference window (e.g., the training data or a recent period of stable performance) with the distribution in a current window of incoming data. For covariate drift, techniques like the **Kolmogorov-Smirnov (K-S) test** or the **Chi-squared test** can be applied to individual features or to the overall feature distribution. These tests assess whether the observed differences in distributions are statistically significant, suggesting a change has occurred. For example, one might monitor the mean and variance of a specific feature. A significant deviation from the historical mean or variance would trigger an alert. Multivariate extensions of these tests can analyze the joint distribution of multiple features, providing a more comprehensive picture.

Another powerful set of techniques involves **distance-based methods**. These calculate a "distance" or divergence metric between the reference and current data distributions. Popular metrics include **Maximum Mean Discrepancy (MMD)** or **Wasserstein distance** (also known as Earth Mover's Distance). A growing distance between the distributions over time indicates drift. These methods are often more sensitive than simple univariate tests and can capture complex shifts in multivariate distributions.

Model-based drift detection offers another avenue. Here, a drift detection model is trained to distinguish between data from the reference distribution and data from the current distribution. If the drift detection model can achieve high accuracy, it implies that the distributions are significantly different. Alternatively, one can use the AI model itself as a detector. For instance, if the model's confidence scores for its predictions start to change systematically, or if its internal representations (e.g., embeddings from a neural network) show a significant shift, it can signal drift.

Drift detection algorithms are specifically designed to identify these shifts in real-time. Algorithms like **DDM (Drift Detection Method)**, **EDDM (Early Drift Detection Method)**, and **ADWIN (Adaptive Windowing)** maintain a sliding window of data and monitor error rates or other performance indicators. When a statistically significant change is detected, they signal an alert. ADWIN, for instance, dynamically adjusts the size of its window, expanding it when the data stream is stable and shrinking it when a change is detected, making it robust to different drift speeds.

For concept drift, detection can be more challenging as the ground truth (the true relationship) is unknown. However, changes in the relationship between features and labels can often be inferred. If the model's prediction errors start to follow a different pattern, or if the distribution of misclassified samples changes, it can be a sign of concept drift. Online learning systems are particularly amenable to concept drift detection because they are constantly making predictions and receiving feedback (or can be periodically evaluated against ground truth). Monitoring the **prediction distribution** itself can also be informative. A significant shift in the probability of predicting certain classes, even if the input data hasn't changed drastically, can indicate that the underlying concept has shifted.

Once drift is detected, the crucial next step is adaptation. The primary goal is to re-align the AI model with the current data distribution and the evolving underlying concepts, ensuring it remains accurate and safe. Several strategies exist, ranging from simple model retraining to more sophisticated online adaptation techniques.

Periodic retraining is a common and often effective strategy. At predefined intervals (e.g., daily, weekly, monthly) or when significant drift is detected, the AI model is retrained from scratch or fine-tuned using a fresh dataset that includes recent data. The advantage is that it allows for a complete recalibration of the model based on the latest data. However, this can be computationally expensive and time-consuming, especially for large models and massive datasets. It also means the model might operate with outdated parameters for a period between retraining cycles, during which drift might occur and impact performance. The choice of the retraining dataset is also critical. Should it include *only* the new data, or a combination of old and new data? Using only new data might lead to catastrophic forgetting of previously learned patterns. Including all data might dilute the impact of recent changes. Strategies like using a weighted dataset, where recent data has higher importance, or employing techniques that focus on adapting specific parts of the model, can help.

Online adaptation or **incremental learning** is more closely aligned with the nature of continuously learning systems. Instead of retraining the entire model, these methods update the model's parameters incrementally as new data arrives. This allows the model to adapt more fluidly to gradual changes. Techniques like **stochastic gradient descent (SGD)**, the backbone of many deep learning training processes, are inherently online. However, naive SGD can be susceptible to noise and might not adapt optimally to significant concept drift without careful tuning of learning rates and regularization.

More advanced online adaptation techniques include **continual learning methods** designed to mitigate catastrophic forgetting. These methods often involve:
Rehearsal/Experience Replay: Storing a small subset of past data and periodically replaying it during training alongside new data. This helps the model retain knowledge from previous distributions.
Regularization-based methods: Introducing regularization terms into the loss function that penalize changes to parameters that are deemed important for previous tasks or data distributions. Examples include Elastic Weight Consolidation (EWC) and Synaptic Intelligence (SI). These methods aim to protect "knowledge" acquired from prior data.
Parameter Isolation/Dynamic Architectures: Dynamically adjusting the model's architecture or selectively updating parameters. This might involve freezing certain layers or adding new components to learn new patterns without disrupting old ones. For instance, a new "head" or a small set of adapter modules could be added to a pre-trained network to

handle new data distributions or concepts, leaving the core features intact.

When implementing online adaptation, careful consideration must be given to the
learning rate schedule. A high learning rate can lead to rapid adaptation but also instability and forgetting. A low learning rate ensures stability but might result in slow adaptation to significant drift. Adaptive learning rate algorithms (like Adam, RMSprop) can help, but they might still need to be tuned for the specific online learning context to balance responsiveness and stability.

The integration of drift detection alerts with adaptation mechanisms is crucial for a robust system. When a drift detection algorithm signals a significant change, it should automatically trigger an adaptation process. This could be a full retraining, an incremental update, or a more specialized adjustment depending on the type and severity of the detected drift. For instance, if only covariate drift is detected (i.e., input data distribution changes but the relationship remains stable), a targeted fine-tuning or an update using the new data might suffice. If concept drift is suspected, a more thorough retraining or a retraining with specific focus on the new relationships might be necessary.

Furthermore, the choice of adaptation strategy should be informed by the specific AI application and its safety requirements. In safety-critical systems, a conservative approach might be preferred. Instead of immediately adapting, the system might first flag the anomaly, continue operating with a previously validated model version (if available), and initiate a controlled, human-supervised adaptation process. This ensures that potentially harmful, rapid changes driven by erroneous data or unexpected concept shifts are not immediately propagated.

Consider an AI system that controls the dosage of medication in a continuous infusion pump. If the patient's physiological parameters (e.g., heart rate, blood pressure, lab results) start to drift from their baseline due to illness progression or external factors, the AI needs to adapt the dosage. However, a sudden, spurious sensor reading could erroneously suggest a drastic change, leading to a dangerous dosage adjustment if adaptation is too aggressive. Therefore, drift detection would first identify the shift in physiological parameters. Then, a carefully calibrated adaptation process, possibly with a built-in delay and a review mechanism for significant deviations, would adjust the dosage. The system might also have predefined "safe dosage ranges" that act as hard constraints, preventing any adaptation from pushing the dosage outside these critical limits.

In the realm of natural language processing, for example, a customer service chatbot that learns from user interactions needs to adapt to evolving language trends, new product names, or changing customer concerns. If the chatbot starts receiving a surge of queries about a newly launched product, drift detection would flag this shift in topic distribution (covariate drift) and potentially the emergence of new user intents (concept drift). The adaptation strategy could involve fine-tuning the chatbot's language model on recent conversation logs related to the new product, or even employing a temporary "fallback" mode where complex queries are escalated to human agents until the model has sufficiently adapted.

The process of adapting models also requires careful logging and versioning. Every time a model is retrained or incrementally updated due to drift, this event should be logged along with the data used for adaptation and the specific drift detection trigger. This creates a traceable history, essential for debugging, auditing, and understanding how the model evolved over time. When performance degrades or a safety incident occurs, examining this history can reveal critical insights into the nature of the drift and the effectiveness of the adaptation strategies employed.

Finally, it's important to recognize that drift is not a one-time problem but an ongoing challenge. AI systems operating in dynamic environments require a continuous cycle of monitoring, detection, and adaptation. This lifecycle approach ensures that the AI remains relevant, effective, and, most importantly, safe throughout its operational life. The sophistication of drift detection and adaptation mechanisms should evolve alongside the AI system itself, reflecting a mature understanding of the inherent dynamism of the real world and its impact on artificial intelligence. By proactively addressing data drift, organizations can build more resilient, trustworthy, and continuously performing AI systems, safeguarding against performance degradation and ensuring their safe deployment in ever-changing environments.

The commitment to building AI systems that can continuously learn and adapt is a testament to our ambition to create more intelligent and responsive technologies. However, this very dynamism introduces a critical challenge: maintaining the ongoing performance and safety of these systems as they operate and evolve within the real world. While previous discussions have delved into the nature of data drift and the mechanisms for its detection and adaptation, a fundamental prerequisite for effective management is the establishment of a rigorous and comprehensive **performance monitoring framework**. Without a clear understanding of what "good" performance looks like, and a mechanism to detect deviations from that standard, even the most sophisticated adaptation strategies can be misguided or ineffective. This section focuses on the vital practice of continuously monitoring the performance of AI systems, particularly those that are designed to learn and change over time, ensuring their operational integrity and safety.

At the heart of any effective monitoring system lies the definition of **Key Performance Indicators (KPIs)**. These are not arbitrary metrics; they are carefully selected quantifiable measures that reflect the AI system's success in achieving its intended objectives. For a continuously learning AI, these KPIs must be dynamic, evolving alongside the system itself, and must capture not only accuracy but also other critical aspects like efficiency, fairness, and robustness. For instance, a supervised learning model trained to classify images might have its primary KPI set as accuracy. However, if this model is also responsible for identifying potential safety hazards, then recall (the ability to correctly identify all actual positive cases, i.e., hazards) becomes equally, if not more, important. In a continuously learning scenario, the acceptable threshold for these KPIs might also shift. A newly deployed system might have a more lenient initial performance target, which gradually tightens as it proves its stability and reliability. Conversely, in a rapidly evolving domain, the acceptable performance might be expected to fluctuate, and the monitoring system needs to be sensitive to deviations from this *expected fluctuation*, rather than absolute static targets.

Beyond raw accuracy, other KPIs become paramount for continuously learning systems.
Latency, the time taken for the AI to produce an output after receiving an input, is critical for real-time applications. A system that becomes progressively slower due to complex adaptation processes might render itself unusable, even if its predictions remain accurate. **Throughput**, the number of requests the system can handle per unit of time, is another essential measure, particularly in high-volume scenarios. If a continuously learning algorithm starts consuming more computational resources with each adaptation, its throughput might diminish, impacting the overall service.

For AI systems involved in decision-making,

fairness metrics are non-negotiable. As the system adapts to new data, it's imperative to monitor whether these adaptations inadvertently introduce or exacerbate biases against certain demographic groups or other protected characteristics. Metrics such as demographic parity, equalized odds, or predictive equality must be continuously tracked. A system that was fair at deployment might, through adaptation to skewed new data, become discriminatory. Therefore, the monitoring framework must include specific KPIs dedicated to assessing and safeguarding fairness.

Moreover, in systems that learn from feedback, the nature of that feedback itself can be a KPI. For example, in a recommendation system, the
click-through rate (CTR) or **user engagement time** are vital indicators. If these metrics begin to decline, it suggests that the recommendations, despite potentially being accurate in a technical sense, are no longer relevant or appealing to the user. This could signal that the system's adaptation mechanisms are not effectively capturing evolving user preferences or that the underlying user behavior has fundamentally changed.

Establishing
performance thresholds is the next critical step. These thresholds define the boundaries of acceptable performance for each KPI. When a KPI falls below its lower threshold or exceeds its upper threshold (depending on whether the KPI represents a positive or negative outcome), it triggers an alert. These thresholds should not be static, especially for continuously learning systems. They must be informed by historical performance data, the inherent variability of the task, and the risk tolerance of the application. For instance, a threshold for prediction accuracy might be set at 95%, but this could be a dynamic target that fluctuates based on recent performance trends. An adaptive threshold mechanism could dynamically adjust the acceptable performance range based on the statistical properties of the model's performance over a

recent, stable period. This allows the system to be sensitive to genuine degradation while being resilient to minor, natural fluctuations.

The process of setting these thresholds often involves a deep understanding of the operational context. For a self-driving car's perception system, a slight dip in object detection accuracy might be tolerable in clear weather conditions but would be unacceptable in challenging environments like heavy fog or snow. Therefore, thresholds might be conditional, varying based on environmental factors or other contextual information available to the system. This requires a sophisticated monitoring architecture capable of not only measuring performance but also correlating it with operational context.

Alerting systems are the active arm of performance monitoring. When a KPI breaches its defined threshold, an alert must be generated. The sophistication of these alerts can vary. At a basic level, it could be a simple notification sent to an operations team via email or a dashboard message. However, for critical systems, more advanced alerting mechanisms are necessary. These might include:

Severity Levels: Alerts categorized by their urgency (e.g., informational, warning, critical). A minor deviation might warrant an informational alert, while a significant drop in accuracy could trigger a critical alert requiring immediate attention.
Root Cause Analysis Hints: Alerts that provide initial clues about the potential cause of the performance degradation. For instance, an alert triggered by a drop in recall for a specific class might also indicate which input features are showing the most significant drift.
Automated Actions: In some cases, alerts can be configured to automatically initiate remediation steps. For example, a critical alert on performance degradation might automatically trigger a retraining

pipeline or roll back the system to a previously known good state. However, this must be approached with extreme caution in continuously learning systems, as an automated rollback might prevent necessary adaptation.
Escalation Policies: Defined procedures for escalating alerts if they are not acknowledged or resolved within a specified timeframe. This ensures that critical issues are not overlooked.

The design of an effective alerting system requires careful consideration of false positives and false negatives. Too many false alarms can lead to alert fatigue, where human operators start ignoring notifications, potentially missing genuine issues. Conversely, too few alerts (false negatives) mean that performance degradation goes undetected, leading to potentially serious consequences. Techniques like anomaly detection algorithms can be employed to filter out spurious alerts and to detect subtle, multi-metric anomalies that might not trigger individual KPI thresholds.

To provide real-time visibility into the operational health of AI components,
dashboards are indispensable tools. These are visual interfaces that aggregate and display the key performance indicators, their current values, historical trends, and active alerts. A well-designed dashboard should offer a clear, at-a-glance understanding of the system's status. Key elements of an effective AI performance dashboard include:

Real-time Metrics Display: Showing the current values of all critical KPIs, updated at regular intervals (e.g., every minute, every five minutes).
Historical Trend Visualizations: Line graphs or other visualizations that plot KPI values over time, allowing operators to identify patterns, seasonality, and the impact of previous interventions or adaptations. This

is crucial for understanding the long-term behavior of a continuously learning system.

Alert Status Indicators: A clear indication of any active alerts, their severity, and their status (e.g., acknowledged, in progress, resolved).

Contextual Information: The ability to drill down into specific metrics and view associated contextual data. For instance, a dip in performance might be viewed alongside recent data drift reports, model adaptation events, or operational parameters.

Comparative Views: For systems with multiple instances or deployments, dashboards can offer comparative views to identify outliers or systems performing differently. This is invaluable for understanding system-wide trends or localized issues.

User-Defined Views: Allowing different teams or roles (e.g., MLOps engineers, data scientists, product managers) to customize their dashboards to focus on the metrics most relevant to their responsibilities.

For continuously learning systems, the dashboard should not only display current performance but also the *state of learning*. This includes information such as the frequency of model updates, the amount of new data processed since the last update, and the confidence scores associated with recent adaptations. Visualizing the learning process itself provides a deeper understanding of how the system is evolving and whether that evolution is proceeding as expected. For example, a graph showing the "learning rate" or "adaptation magnitude" over time, alongside performance metrics, can reveal if the system is adapting too quickly or too slowly.

Implementing these monitoring systems requires a robust **instrumentation strategy**. This involves embedding code within the AI system and its surrounding infrastructure to capture the necessary performance data. This instrumentation should be designed to be lightweight and non-intrusive, ensuring it doesn't negatively impact the AI's performance or resource consumption. Data collected needs to be reliably transmitted to a central monitoring platform, which can then process, analyze, and visualize it. The choice of monitoring tools and platforms is crucial, ranging from open-source solutions like Prometheus and Grafana to commercial observability platforms tailored for machine learning operations (MLOps).

Moreover, the monitoring process must be continuous and iterative. The definition of KPIs, the setting of thresholds, and the design of dashboards are not one-time activities. As the AI system evolves, as the operational environment changes, and as new understanding of potential failure modes emerges, the monitoring framework itself must be revisited and refined. This iterative approach ensures that the monitoring remains relevant and effective throughout the AI system's lifecycle. For instance, if a new type of failure mode is discovered, new KPIs might need to be introduced to specifically track its occurrence and impact. Similarly, if the system's learning rate changes significantly, thresholds for performance metrics might need to be re-evaluated to reflect this new dynamic. This continuous refinement of the monitoring strategy is an integral part of building resilient and trustworthy continuously learning AI systems. The goal is to move from a reactive posture, where problems are addressed only after they manifest, to a proactive one, where potential issues are identified and mitigated before they impact users or compromise safety.

The dynamic nature of artificial intelligence systems that are designed for continuous learning and adaptation presents a fundamental tension: how can we foster ongoing improvement and responsiveness without jeopardizing the stability and safety that are paramount to their reliable operation? This is not merely a theoretical quandary; it is a practical engineering challenge that lies at the heart of building trustworthy AI. The pursuit of enhanced performance, greater accuracy, and wider applicability through adaptation must be meticulously managed to prevent unintended consequences, performance degradations, or the introduction of new vulnerabilities. Achieving this delicate equilibrium requires sophisticated strategies that go beyond simple monitoring and introduce mechanisms to control and validate the adaptation process itself.

One of the most effective approaches to navigating this tension is through **risk-based adaptation strategies**. This methodology acknowledges that not all adaptations carry the same weight or potential for negative impact. Instead of applying a uniform set of rules to every change, risk-based strategies categorize potential adaptations based on their perceived risk to system stability, safety, and performance. This allows for a more nuanced and resource-efficient management of the adaptation lifecycle. The process typically begins with a thorough assessment of the proposed adaptation. This assessment considers several factors: the magnitude of the change in the model's parameters or architecture, the novelty and volume of the data driving the adaptation, the potential impact on critical performance metrics (accuracy, fairness, latency, etc.), and the criticality of the application in which the AI is deployed.

For instance, a minor adjustment to a recommendation engine's algorithm, driven by a small influx of user interaction data that aligns with existing patterns, might be considered low-risk. Such adaptations could potentially be deployed with less stringent validation, perhaps through automated online updates with continuous, fine-grained monitoring. In contrast, an adaptation that significantly alters the underlying decision boundaries of a medical diagnostic AI, or one driven by a sudden and drastic shift in input data distribution, would be classified as high-risk. These high-risk adaptations would necessitate a more rigorous validation process, potentially involving offline evaluation, extensive simulation, and staged rollouts. The risk assessment framework helps to dynamically allocate engineering effort and attention, ensuring that the most critical changes receive the most scrutiny, thereby preserving overall system integrity.

Central to implementing risk-based adaptation is the establishment of clear **adaptation policies and governance**. These policies define what constitutes acceptable risk, the thresholds for triggering different levels of validation, and the roles and responsibilities of teams involved in the adaptation process. For example, policies might stipulate that any adaptation that could potentially affect patient safety in a healthcare AI must undergo a formal review by a safety board and require explicit sign-off before deployment, regardless of its perceived risk score. Conversely, adaptations in a low-stakes consumer application might be fully automated if they fall below a predefined risk threshold. This governance structure provides a framework for decision-making, ensuring consistency and accountability, and critically, embedding safety considerations into the very fabric of the adaptation process.

A cornerstone technique for safely introducing new model versions or significant adaptation updates is the **canary deployment** strategy. This approach, widely adopted in software engineering, involves gradually rolling out a new version of an AI system to a small subset of users or traffic before a full-scale deployment. The term "canary" originates from the historical practice of miners carrying canaries into mines to detect toxic gases; if the canary died, the miners knew it was unsafe to proceed. Similarly, in AI, the canary deployment acts as an early warning system.

The process typically begins by deploying the new, adapted model to a tiny fraction of the production environment, often referred to as the "canary group." This group might consist of a very small percentage of users, or a specific geographical region, or even a dedicated test environment that mirrors production. The performance and behavior of the canary model are then meticulously monitored using the established performance monitoring frameworks. Key performance indicators (KPIs) such as accuracy, latency, error rates, and, crucially, safety-related metrics are compared between the canary and the existing, stable version (often referred to as the "baseline" or "production" model).

If the canary model performs as expected and meets or exceeds the predefined thresholds for stability and safety within this small group, the rollout is gradually expanded. The percentage of traffic directed to the canary model is increased incrementally over time, while continuing to monitor its performance. This phased approach allows for early detection of any unexpected issues or regressions that might not have been apparent during offline testing or in smaller-scale simulations. Common issues that canary deployments help uncover include: subtle data drift interactions, unforeseen edge cases amplified by the new model, performance degradation under specific load conditions, or the emergence of new biases that manifest only in real-world usage.

If, at any stage of the rollout, the canary model exhibits undesirable behavior – such as a significant drop in accuracy, an increase in critical errors, or the violation of fairness constraints – the deployment can be immediately halted, and the system can automatically revert to the stable baseline model. This rapid rollback capability is critical for minimizing the impact of faulty adaptations. The decision to expand the rollout to the next increment is data-driven, based on the observed performance of the canary model in the current deployment phase. This iterative, cautious approach ensures that the system’s adaptation process is robust and that the transition to new versions is as smooth and safe as possible, protecting the integrity of the user experience and the system's operational reliability.

Beyond canary deployments, other staged rollout strategies exist, such as **blue-green deployments** and **A/B testing**, which can also be adapted for AI systems. In a blue-green deployment, two identical production environments, "blue" and "green," are maintained. The current stable version runs on one environment (e.g., blue), while the new version is deployed to the other (green). Traffic is then switched from blue to green. If issues arise with the green environment, traffic can be instantly switched back to blue. A/B testing, on the other hand, is more about comparing the effectiveness of different versions rather than solely focusing on safety and stability. While it can provide insights into performance, it's often used to optimize for specific business metrics rather than as a primary safety mechanism for adaptation. For the purpose of balancing adaptation with stability, the gradual, risk-mitigated nature of canary deployments makes it particularly well-suited.

The challenge of ensuring safety and stability in continuously adapting AI systems also draws upon the principles of **formal methods**. These are mathematically rigorous techniques used to specify and verify the properties of systems. In traditional computer science, formal methods are employed to prove the correctness of software or hardware designs, ensuring they meet specific, often safety-critical, requirements. Applying formal methods to AI, especially adaptive AI, is an active area of research, but it holds significant promise.

The core idea is to define desired properties of the AI system – such as "the system will never classify a benign anomaly as a critical threat" or "the system's fairness metrics will remain within acceptable bounds for all demographic groups" – and then use mathematical techniques to prove that the system, in its current state and potentially under certain adaptation dynamics, will always adhere to these properties. For non-adaptive systems, this involves proving that the code or model architecture inherently satisfies the specified properties.

For continuously learning systems, the challenge is amplified because the system's behavior is not static. It changes over time as it adapts. Therefore, formal verification needs to consider the *dynamics* of adaptation. This might involve proving that the adaptation *mechanism itself* guarantees that the resulting model will always satisfy certain properties, or that any deviation from those properties will be detected and corrected within a bounded time frame. Techniques like **temporal logic** can be used to express properties about how the system's behavior evolves over time. For example, a temporal logic formula could state that "eventually, the system will return to a safe state if it deviates."

Another relevant area is **runtime verification**, where formal methods are used to monitor a system during its execution and check if it adheres to its specifications. In the context of adaptive AI, runtime verification can be employed to continuously check if the current state of the learned model satisfies critical safety and fairness invariants. If a violation is detected, an alert can be triggered, or an automated rollback mechanism can be initiated.

However, formal verification of complex, adaptive AI models is computationally intensive and can be challenging to scale. The state space of deep learning models, for instance, is enormous, making exhaustive verification practically impossible. Research is ongoing to develop more scalable techniques, such as **abstraction-based methods** (where complex models are approximated by simpler, verifiable models) or **bounded model checking** (which aims to find counterexamples within a limited horizon).

Despite these challenges, formal methods offer a powerful paradigm for providing strong, mathematically grounded guarantees about AI system behavior. When applied to the adaptation process itself, or to critical safety-related components of an adaptive system, they can significantly bolster confidence in the system's ability to remain stable and safe even as it evolves. For example, one could formally verify that the mechanism for selecting which data to retrain on never systematically excludes data from minority groups, thus safeguarding against an adaptation-induced fairness degradation.

The interplay between these strategies is crucial. Risk-based adaptation ensures that the *decision* to adapt is prudent. Canary deployments provide a safe *pathway* for introducing adaptations into production. Formal methods and runtime verification offer the possibility of *mathematically grounded assurances* about the properties the system maintains, or the conditions under which it can adapt safely.

Consider a scenario where an AI system is used for autonomous vehicle control. The need to adapt to new driving conditions, road surfaces, or unexpected events is clear. However, any adaptation that might slightly compromise braking responsiveness or steering precision could have catastrophic consequences. A risk-based approach would classify any adaptation affecting vehicle dynamics as high-risk. This would mandate that such adaptations undergo extensive offline simulation and testing. Furthermore, a canary deployment might involve deploying a new version of the control algorithm to a small fleet of test vehicles operating in controlled environments, with safety drivers ready to take over. Formal methods could be used to verify that the core safety logic, such as emergency braking thresholds, remains inviolable regardless of any learned adaptations in other components of the system. Runtime verification might continuously check that the vehicle's predicted stopping distance, based on the current model, never exceeds a predefined safety limit under observable conditions.

Another important consideration is the **feedback loop between monitoring and adaptation**. It is not enough to simply monitor performance. The insights gained from monitoring must actively inform and constrain the adaptation process. If monitoring reveals that a particular adaptation has led to a slight but persistent degradation in a crucial safety metric, the adaptation policy should dictate that this adaptation is either rolled back, or further investigation is triggered. This might involve reverting to a previous model version, pausing further learning, or even initiating a process to re-evaluate the underlying data or the adaptation algorithm itself.

This continuous interplay forms a robust control loop. Monitoring acts as the sensor, providing real-time data on the system's state and performance. Adaptation mechanisms act as the actuators, aiming to improve the system. However, these actuators must operate within predefined safety boundaries and respond to the sensor's feedback. For instance, if the monitoring system detects an increase in false positives from a threat detection AI, an adaptive system might be configured to temporarily reduce its sensitivity or trigger a retraining with more balanced data.

The principle of
least privilege can also be applied to adaptation. This means that the adaptation mechanism should only be granted the minimum permissions necessary to perform its function. For example, if an AI model only needs to update its prediction weights, it should not have the ability to modify the core system code or access sensitive user data beyond what is required for learning. This limits the potential damage if the adaptation process itself is compromised or behaves unexpectedly.

Furthermore, the concept of
graceful degradation becomes relevant. In situations where an AI system encounters novel or ambiguous data that it cannot reliably adapt to without compromising safety, it should ideally degrade its performance in a controlled and predictable manner, rather than fail catastrophically. This might involve switching to a simpler, more robust mode of operation, or deferring decisions to a human operator. This requires the system to have a sophisticated understanding of its own uncertainty and

limitations, and the ability to translate that understanding into safe operational adjustments.

In conclusion, balancing the imperative for adaptation with the non-negotiable requirements of stability and safety is a multifaceted engineering challenge. It necessitates a move beyond reactive problem-solving to proactive design and control. By integrating risk-based adaptation strategies, employing phased rollout mechanisms like canary deployments, leveraging the rigor of formal methods where applicable, and establishing tight feedback loops between monitoring and adaptation, we can build AI systems that are not only intelligent and adaptive but also reliably safe and stable in the complex environments they inhabit. This careful orchestration of learning and control is fundamental to realizing the full potential of AI while mitigating its inherent risks.

Chapter 13: Building Trustworthy AI Ecosystems

The journey towards building trustworthy AI ecosystems is fundamentally an endeavor in cultivating trust. This trust is not an abstract concept; it is a tangible, emergent property that arises from a confluence of factors, each contributing to the confidence users, operators, regulators, and indeed, society at large, place in AI systems. It transcends mere functional reliability, delving into the ethical underpinnings, the clarity of operation, and the robustness of security that these systems embody. Without this foundational trust, the transformative potential of AI, from revolutionizing healthcare and transportation to reshaping our daily interactions, will remain largely unrealized, met with hesitation and skepticism rather than embrace.

At its core, trust in AI is built upon the bedrock of **predictability and reliability**. Users must be able to depend on AI systems to perform as expected, consistently and accurately, especially in critical applications. This means that an AI designed to detect anomalies in financial transactions should do so with a very high degree of precision, minimizing both false positives and false negatives. Similarly, an AI assisting in medical diagnostics must provide insights that are not only accurate but also stable over time, avoiding erratic outputs that could mislead practitioners. This reliability is not a one-time achievement but a continuous process, necessitating robust testing, rigorous validation, and ongoing monitoring as discussed in previous sections concerning adaptation and stability. When an AI system behaves predictably, its outputs can be anticipated, and its limitations can be understood, fostering a sense of control and safety among those who interact with it. This predictability is intrinsically linked to the system's adherence to its intended design and operational parameters, ensuring that it acts as a dependable tool rather than an unpredictable force.

However, reliability alone is insufficient. Trust is equally contingent upon **fairness and equity**. AI systems, particularly those trained on large datasets, can inadvertently inherit and even amplify societal biases present in that data. An AI used for hiring or loan applications, if trained on historical data that reflects discriminatory practices, might perpetuate those same biases, leading to unfair outcomes for certain demographic groups. Building trust, therefore, requires a proactive commitment to identifying and mitigating these biases. This involves meticulous data curation, employing fairness-aware algorithms, and establishing clear metrics for assessing and ensuring equitable treatment across different populations. When users and stakeholders see that an AI system is designed and deployed with a conscious effort to promote fairness, and that mechanisms are in place to audit and correct for discriminatory behavior, it significantly bolsters their confidence in its integrity and ethical standing. The pursuit of fairness is not merely a technical challenge but a moral imperative, and demonstrating this commitment is crucial for earning societal trust.

Another critical pillar of trust is **transparency and explainability**. In many AI applications, particularly those with significant societal impact, understanding *why* an AI made a particular decision is as important as the decision itself. For complex "black box" models, like many deep neural networks, achieving full explainability can be challenging. However, a commitment to transparency means providing insights into the AI's reasoning process to an appropriate degree. This might involve using inherently interpretable models where feasible, developing techniques for post-hoc explanation of model predictions, or clearly communicating the data sources and decision-making logic that underpins the AI's operation. For instance, if an AI denies a loan application, the applicant should be provided with a clear, understandable reason for the denial, rather than an opaque pronouncement. Similarly, in a medical context, a physician should be able to understand the factors that led an AI to suggest a particular diagnosis or treatment plan. Transparency also extends to clearly articulating the limitations and potential failure modes of an AI system, ensuring that users are not overestimating its capabilities or misinterpreting its outputs. When an AI's operations are not shrouded in mystery, but are instead understandable and auditable, it fosters a sense of accountability and builds confidence in its legitimacy.

The security of AI systems is an often-overlooked, yet absolutely vital, component of trust. AI systems, like any other software, are vulnerable to cyberattacks, but they also present unique security challenges. **Adversarial attacks**, for instance, can subtly manipulate input data to cause an AI to misclassify information or make incorrect decisions. Imagine an autonomous vehicle's vision system being fooled by specially crafted stickers on a stop sign, causing it to fail to recognize it. Or consider a spam filter being subtly tricked by carefully engineered text into allowing malicious emails through. Building trust requires robust security measures that protect AI models from malicious manipulation, unauthorized access, and data breaches. This includes employing techniques for adversarial robustness, secure data handling practices, and secure deployment environments. When users know that the AI systems they rely on are protected against sophisticated attacks and that their data is secure, they are more likely to trust them with sensitive information and in critical operations. Security is not a static defense but an ongoing battle, and demonstrating a commitment to continuous security improvement is key.

Beyond these technical and ethical dimensions, **accountability and governance** play a crucial role in building trust. When an AI system causes harm, there must be a clear framework for determining responsibility and providing recourse. This involves establishing clear lines of accountability, both for the developers and operators of AI systems, as well as for the organizations deploying them. Regulatory bodies play a vital role in setting standards and enforcing compliance, providing an external layer of assurance. Furthermore, robust governance structures, including internal review boards and ethical committees, can help ensure that AI development and deployment align with societal values and legal requirements. When there is confidence that mechanisms exist to address issues, rectify mistakes, and hold those responsible accountable, it significantly enhances trust. This is particularly important in sectors like healthcare, finance, and law enforcement, where the consequences of AI failure can be severe. A well-defined governance framework signals a mature and responsible approach to AI, fostering confidence that the technology is being developed and used with due diligence and ethical consideration.

The notion of
human oversight and control also contributes significantly to trust, especially in high-stakes applications. While AI can augment human capabilities and automate complex tasks, maintaining a degree of human involvement ensures that critical decisions are not made solely by machines. This can take various forms, from direct human supervision of AI operations to mechanisms for human intervention and override when necessary. For example, an AI recommending a sentencing in a legal context might provide a probabilistic assessment, but the final decision would rest with a human judge. This ensures that AI is used as a tool to inform and support human judgment, rather than as an autonomous arbiter of crucial outcomes. The ability for humans to understand, question, and, if needed, override AI decisions provides a crucial safety net and reinforces the perception that AI serves human interests. This collaborative human-AI paradigm, where each entity leverages its strengths, is a powerful way to build confidence and ensure that AI systems remain aligned with human values and objectives.

Finally, the
continuous improvement and learning aspect of AI, while a source of its power, also requires careful management to maintain trust. As AI systems adapt and learn, their behavior can evolve. This evolution must be guided by ethical principles and safety considerations, ensuring that the system remains aligned with its intended purpose and societal expectations. This involves establishing feedback loops that incorporate user input, performance monitoring, and ethical audits to guide the learning process. For example, if user feedback indicates that an AI

recommender system is becoming repetitive or biased, this feedback should be used to retrain and refine the model. A transparent process for updating and improving AI systems, where changes are communicated and their rationale is explained, further bolsters user confidence. It demonstrates a commitment to not only developing intelligent systems but also to ensuring that they remain beneficial and trustworthy as they mature and evolve. This iterative approach, combining technological advancement with a commitment to ethical stewardship, is fundamental to building lasting trust in AI ecosystems.

In the realm of artificial intelligence, where systems increasingly operate beyond direct human observation, the principles of transparency and explainability stand as cornerstones for building a trustworthy ecosystem. As AI models grow in complexity and ubiquity, the imperative to understand their inner workings, the rationale behind their decisions, and the data that shapes their outputs becomes paramount. This is not merely an academic pursuit; it is a practical necessity for ensuring accountability, enabling effective debugging, facilitating regulatory compliance, and, most crucially, fostering confidence among the diverse stakeholders who interact with these powerful technologies. When AI operates as a "black box," its potential for good is often overshadowed by apprehension, leading to hesitancy in adoption and a reluctance to fully integrate it into critical societal functions. Conversely, a commitment to revealing the underlying logic and mechanisms of AI systems can demystify them, empower users, and pave the way for responsible innovation.

The pursuit of transparency and explainability can be broadly categorized into two primary approaches: leveraging inherently interpretable models and developing methods to explain more complex, opaque models. For many applications, particularly those where interpretability is a primary requirement and computational demands are manageable, employing models that are intrinsically understandable offers a direct path to transparency. These models, by their very design, allow for a clear and straightforward interpretation of how inputs are transformed into outputs. A prime example is **linear regression**, a statistical technique widely used in predictive modeling. In a linear regression model, the relationship between a dependent variable and one or more independent variables is represented by a linear equation. The coefficients assigned to each independent variable directly indicate the magnitude and direction of its influence on the outcome. For instance, if a linear regression model predicts housing prices, the coefficient for "square footage" would clearly show how much the price is expected to increase or decrease for each additional square foot. This direct correlation makes it easy for users to grasp the model's logic and identify which factors are most influential.

Similarly, **decision trees** offer a highly intuitive and visual representation of a model's decision-making process. A decision tree functions by partitioning data into increasingly smaller subsets based on the values of input features. Each node in the tree represents a test on an attribute, each branch represents an outcome of the test, and each leaf node represents a class label or a decision. For example, a decision tree used to determine loan eligibility might first ask about the applicant's credit score, then their income level, and then their employment history. The path taken from the root node to a leaf node clearly illustrates the sequence of conditions that led to a particular decision, such as loan approval or rejection. This visual, rule-based structure makes decision trees exceptionally easy to understand and explain to individuals without a technical background. Their transparency is a significant advantage in domains like credit scoring or risk assessment, where applicants have a right to understand the factors influencing critical financial decisions.

Other intrinsically interpretable models, such as **logistic regression**, which is commonly used for binary classification tasks, also provide clear insights into the relationships between variables and the probability of an outcome. The coefficients in a logistic regression model represent the change in the log-odds of the outcome for a unit change in the predictor variable, which can be translated into probabilities. This allows for a quantitative understanding of how each feature contributes to the likelihood of a particular class being predicted. Furthermore, rule-based systems, which explicitly codify a set of "if-then" rules, are inherently transparent. These systems mimic human expert reasoning by defining a series of conditions that must be met for a specific action or conclusion to be reached. Their transparency is a direct consequence of their explicit, human-readable logic.

While these interpretable models are invaluable, they often come with limitations, especially when dealing with highly complex, non-linear relationships present in vast datasets. Many of the most powerful AI techniques today, such as deep neural networks and ensemble methods like gradient boosting machines, are often considered "black boxes." These models achieve remarkable performance by learning intricate patterns and interactions within data that are not easily discernible through simple linear relationships or decision paths. The sheer number of parameters, the layered architecture of neural networks, and the complex aggregations in ensemble methods make it extremely difficult to pinpoint the exact reasoning behind a specific prediction. This opacity poses a significant challenge to trust, as users and regulators may be hesitant to rely on decisions they cannot comprehend.

To address this challenge, the field of explainable AI (XAI) has developed a suite of
post-hoc explanation methods. These techniques are designed to provide insights into the behavior of already-trained, often complex models, without requiring changes to the model architecture itself. One of the most widely recognized and impactful methods is **Local Interpretable Model-agnostic Explanations (LIME)**. LIME's core idea is to explain individual predictions of any classifier in an interpretable way. It achieves this by approximating the complex model locally around the

prediction of interest with an interpretable model, such as a linear model or a decision tree. LIME works by perturbing the input data, generating new samples around the instance being explained, and then querying the black-box model to obtain predictions for these perturbed samples. By weighting these samples based on their proximity to the original instance, LIME builds a local, interpretable model that accurately reflects the black-box model's behavior in that specific neighborhood. For instance, if a LIME explanation is generated for a text classification task, it might highlight specific words or phrases that were most influential in the model's decision to categorize a document as spam or not spam.

Another powerful post-hoc explanation technique is **SHapley Additive exPlanations (SHAP)**. SHAP is based on game theory, specifically the concept of Shapley values, which were originally developed to fairly distribute the payout among players in a cooperative game. In the context of AI, SHAP values represent the contribution of each feature to the difference between the actual prediction and the average prediction of the model. SHAP offers a unified framework for interpreting predictions, providing both local explanations (for individual predictions) and global explanations (summarizing the overall behavior of the model). A key advantage of SHAP is its theoretical grounding, which ensures consistency and accuracy in attributing feature importance. For example, in a medical diagnostic AI, SHAP values could show precisely how much a particular patient's blood pressure reading, age, or family history contributed to the model's prediction of their risk for a certain disease. This granular insight is invaluable for clinicians who need to understand the basis of AI-driven recommendations.

Beyond LIME and SHAP, numerous other techniques contribute to the explainability of black-box models.
Partial Dependence Plots (PDPs) illustrate the marginal effect of one or two features on the predicted outcome of a model, showing how the predicted outcome changes as the feature(s) vary, while averaging out the effects of all other features. **Individual Conditional Expectation (ICE)**

plots provide a similar visualization but show the relationship for each individual instance, revealing potential heterogeneity in feature effects that PDPs might mask. **Feature importance scores**, often derived from tree-based models or permutation importance, provide a global measure of which features are most influential in the model's overall performance, though they do not explain individual predictions. Techniques like **counterfactual explanations** aim to answer the question: "What is the smallest change to the input that would alter the prediction to a desired outcome?" For instance, a counterfactual explanation for a loan denial might state: "If your income were $10,000 higher, your loan would have been approved." This is particularly useful for providing actionable feedback to individuals affected by AI decisions.

The effectiveness of any transparency or explainability strategy is intrinsically linked to its **audience**. An explanation tailored for a machine learning engineer debugging a model will differ significantly from one intended for a regulatory body assessing compliance, a medical professional making a clinical decision, or an individual whose loan application was denied. Engineers might require detailed technical insights into model parameters, activation patterns, or gradient information. Regulators may need assurance of fairness, robustness, and adherence to legal standards, often requiring evidence of how biases were mitigated and how decisions align with established policies. Clinicians need explanations that are clinically relevant, highlighting factors that directly impact patient care and allowing them to exercise their professional judgment. For end-users, explanations must be clear, concise, and presented in plain language, focusing on the factors that directly influenced the outcome and providing actionable insights where possible. The challenge lies in bridging the gap between the complex mathematical underpinnings of AI and the varied cognitive abilities and needs of its users.

Consider an AI system used for autonomous driving. The engineers developing the system might need to understand the specific convolutional filters that are misinterpreting a road sign under adverse weather conditions. A transportation regulator, however, might be more interested in understanding the overall safety parameters, the failure modes that have been accounted for, and the system's performance metrics across various driving scenarios to ensure public safety. The passenger in the vehicle, on the other hand, would likely want to know, in a simplified manner, why the car is braking suddenly – perhaps a simple message like "Obstacle detected ahead." This tiered approach to explainability, where the level of detail and technicality is adjusted according to the user's role and needs, is crucial for fostering broad trust and facilitating effective human-AI collaboration.

Furthermore, transparency extends beyond explaining individual predictions to understanding the data used for training and the overall development process. This includes
data provenance, which traces the origin and history of the data, ensuring its quality, representativeness, and ethical sourcing. It also encompasses **model provenance**, documenting how the model was built, validated, and deployed. Clearly articulating the **limitations and assumptions** of an AI system is equally vital. No AI is perfect; acknowledging its potential failure points, biases it may still possess, and the conditions under which its performance might degrade is a hallmark of a trustworthy system. This proactive disclosure manages expectations and prevents over-reliance on systems that may not be suitable for every situation. For example, a weather forecasting AI might be highly accurate in predicting general trends but less reliable for pinpointing microclimates, and this limitation should be transparently communicated.

The ongoing evolution of AI models through continuous learning also necessitates dynamic transparency. As models adapt and learn from new data, their behavior can change. Mechanisms must be in place to monitor these changes and ensure that the evolving model remains aligned with its intended purpose and ethical guidelines. When significant updates occur, stakeholders should be informed, and the rationale behind these changes should be made accessible. This creates a feedback loop where users can understand how their interactions or new data are shaping the AI, further solidifying trust through a visible process of improvement and adaptation.

In essence, transparency and explainability are not afterthoughts but integral components of AI design and deployment. They transform AI from a mysterious, potentially intimidating technology into a comprehensible, accountable tool. By embracing interpretable models where appropriate and employing sophisticated post-hoc explanation techniques for complex systems, while always tailoring these explanations to the specific audience, organizations can demystify AI. This demystification is a critical step in building the robust ecosystem of trust that is essential for unlocking the full, beneficial potential of artificial intelligence for society.

The edifice of trustworthy AI, upon which its widespread adoption and societal benefit hinges, is not solely constructed from the pillars of transparency and explainability, though these are foundational. Equally critical, and indeed forming an inseparable structural component, is the robust assurance of **security**. In an era where AI systems are increasingly integrated into critical infrastructure, sensitive decision-making processes, and personal digital lives, their vulnerability to attack or compromise represents a direct threat to reliability, integrity, and ultimately, trust. Unlike traditional software systems, AI introduces a unique attack surface, stemming from its reliance on data, its learning processes, and the inherent complexity of its models. Therefore, understanding and actively mitigating these AI-specific security threats is not merely an ancillary concern but a fundamental prerequisite for building an AI ecosystem that individuals and institutions can confidently rely upon.

The unique nature of AI systems gives rise to a distinct set of security vulnerabilities that demand specialized attention. These threats can be broadly categorized into attacks targeting the data, the model, or the operational environment. One of the most insidious forms of attack on the data is
data poisoning. This involves the malicious injection of corrupted or misleading data into the training dataset. The intent is to subtly, or sometimes overtly, skew the model's learning process, leading it to make incorrect predictions or exhibit biased behavior when deployed. For instance, in a spam detection system, an attacker might introduce a large number of emails that are labeled as "not spam" but actually contain malicious content, or vice versa. Over time, the poisoned data can degrade the model's accuracy to a point where it becomes unreliable, or it can be manipulated to misclassify specific types of legitimate inputs as malicious, or allow malicious inputs to pass through undetected. The impact of data poisoning can be devastating, especially in domains like healthcare or finance, where flawed decisions can have severe consequences. Imagine a medical diagnostic AI trained on poisoned data that misidentifies a particular tumor as benign, leading to delayed treatment. The insidious nature of data poisoning lies in its ability to corrupt the very foundation upon which the AI learns, making it incredibly challenging to detect and rectify without a thorough audit of the training data and its provenance.

Beyond data poisoning, AI systems are susceptible to
model evasion attacks, also known as adversarial attacks, which target the deployed model rather than its training data. These attacks involve crafting specific inputs that are designed to fool the AI into making an incorrect prediction. While these inputs may appear innocuous or only slightly altered to a human observer, they exploit the subtle nuances and sensitivities of the AI model's decision-making process. For example, an autonomous vehicle's object recognition system might be tricked by a sticker placed on a stop sign that is imperceptible to the human eye but causes the AI to interpret it as a speed limit sign, potentially leading to a

dangerous situation. Similarly, in facial recognition systems, adversarial perturbations can cause a system to misidentify individuals or fail to recognize them altogether. The effectiveness of evasion attacks underscores the importance of understanding the "blind spots" or vulnerabilities in AI models and developing defensive mechanisms. This can involve techniques like adversarial training, where the model is exposed to adversarial examples during training to make it more robust, or input sanitization, which attempts to detect and remove adversarial perturbations before they reach the model. The sophistication of these attacks is constantly evolving, requiring continuous vigilance and research into more resilient AI architectures and defense strategies.

Another critical area of concern is the security of the **AI supply chain**. The development and deployment of AI systems often involve a complex web of dependencies, from the underlying hardware and software frameworks to the data sources and pre-trained models. Each component in this chain presents a potential entry point for attackers. For example, a compromised third-party library or an exploited vulnerability in a cloud platform could introduce backdoors or allow for unauthorized access to sensitive data and models. The use of **pre-trained models**, which are increasingly common due to their ability to accelerate development and improve performance, also introduces supply chain risks. If a pre-trained model has been tampered with or contains hidden malicious functionalities, these issues will inevitably be inherited by any system that utilizes it. Ensuring the integrity of the AI supply chain requires a multifaceted approach, including rigorous vetting of all third-party components, secure coding practices, continuous monitoring for vulnerabilities, and robust authentication and authorization mechanisms at every stage of development and deployment. Traceability and transparency in the supply chain are paramount, allowing organizations to understand the origin and integrity of every element that constitutes their AI systems.

Protecting the AI

model and data themselves is paramount. AI models, especially large and complex ones, represent significant intellectual property and can be valuable targets for theft or manipulation. Model extraction attacks, for instance, aim to reconstruct a model by making repeated queries to it and observing its outputs, effectively stealing the underlying logic and intellectual property. Once a model is extracted, it can be analyzed for vulnerabilities, used to generate further attacks, or even replicated for illicit purposes. Similarly, the training data, which can be proprietary, sensitive, or personally identifiable, must be protected from unauthorized access and exfiltration. Techniques like **differential privacy** can be employed to add noise to the data or model outputs in a way that preserves utility while making it mathematically difficult to infer information about individual data points. Furthermore, secure storage solutions, access control mechanisms, and encryption are essential for safeguarding both the models and the data they are trained on. The concept of **model watermarking** is also gaining traction, where unique identifiers are embedded within the model's parameters or outputs, allowing for the detection of unauthorized copying or distribution.

Beyond these specific threats, the very **operational environment** of AI systems needs to be secured. This includes the underlying infrastructure, be it on-premises servers or cloud platforms, as well as the networks through which data flows and models interact. Standard cybersecurity best practices, such as network segmentation, intrusion detection and prevention systems, regular security audits, and prompt patching of vulnerabilities, are crucial. However, AI systems introduce additional considerations. For example, the computational resources required for training and running AI models can be substantial, and these resources can become targets for denial-of-service attacks or unauthorized usage. Secure deployment practices, including containerization, hardened operating systems, and robust logging and monitoring, are essential to maintain the integrity and availability of AI services. The continuous learning aspect of some AI systems also necessitates secure mechanisms for updating models and datasets, ensuring that these updates are legitimate and do not introduce new vulnerabilities.

To counter these evolving threats, a proactive and comprehensive security strategy for AI is indispensable. This begins with a thorough **risk assessment** that identifies potential vulnerabilities across the entire AI lifecycle, from data collection and model development to deployment and ongoing maintenance. Based on this assessment, appropriate **defensive measures** can be implemented. For data security, this includes implementing strict access controls, ensuring data provenance and integrity through cryptographic hashing and secure storage, and employing anonymization or pseudonymization techniques where appropriate. Training data should be regularly audited for anomalies and potential poisoning attempts, and robust validation processes should be in place to catch corrupted data before it enters the training pipeline.

When it comes to model security, **adversarial robustness** is a key consideration. This involves incorporating techniques like adversarial training, defensive distillation, or robust optimization methods during the model development phase to make the model more resilient to evasion attacks. Input sanitization and anomaly detection at inference time can also help identify and reject potentially adversarial inputs. For the protection of intellectual property, techniques such as model compression, obfuscation, and watermarking can be employed. Furthermore, secure model deployment practices, including code signing, integrity checks, and secure API gateways, are vital to prevent unauthorized access or modification of deployed models.

The security of the AI supply chain demands a holistic approach. Organizations must establish stringent **vendor risk management** processes, ensuring that all third-party software, hardware, and pre-trained models are thoroughly vetted for security vulnerabilities and malicious code. This includes requiring vendors to provide assurances of their security practices and potentially conducting independent audits. Implementing continuous monitoring of the supply chain for emerging threats and vulnerabilities is also critical. **Software Bill of Materials (SBOMs)**, which provide a comprehensive list of all components within a software system, are becoming increasingly important for understanding and managing supply chain risks in AI.

Beyond technical defenses, **organizational policies and procedures** play a crucial role in AI security. This includes establishing clear guidelines for data handling, model development, access control, and incident response. Regular security awareness training for all personnel involved in the AI lifecycle is essential to foster a security-conscious culture. A well-defined **incident response plan** specifically tailored to AI-related security incidents is also a must. This plan should outline the steps for detecting, analyzing, containing, eradicating, and recovering from security breaches, as well as for communicating with stakeholders and regulatory bodies. The ability to quickly and effectively respond to security incidents can significantly mitigate the damage and restore trust.

The principle of **least privilege** should be applied rigorously to all access controls, ensuring that individuals and systems only have the permissions necessary to perform their intended functions. This minimizes the potential impact of a compromised account or system. **Secure development lifecycles (SDLs)** that integrate security considerations from the very beginning of the AI development process, rather than treating security as an afterthought, are fundamental. This includes threat modeling, code reviews, security testing, and vulnerability management integrated into every phase of development.

Furthermore, the development of AI security is an ongoing process, not a one-time fix. As AI technologies advance and attackers develop new methodologies, security measures must evolve accordingly. This necessitates continuous

monitoring and auditing of AI systems, both for performance and for security anomalies. **Red teaming** exercises, where security experts actively try to penetrate the AI system, can be invaluable for identifying weaknesses before malicious actors do. Staying abreast of the latest research in AI security, sharing threat intelligence, and collaborating with the broader cybersecurity community are also essential for maintaining a strong defense.

Ultimately, security in AI is not just about preventing breaches; it's about building and maintaining the
reliability and integrity of the AI system itself. When users and stakeholders know that an AI system is protected against malicious manipulation, data corruption, and unauthorized access, they are more likely to trust its outputs and integrate it into critical functions. This trust is paramount for the successful and ethical deployment of AI technologies that can drive innovation and solve complex societal challenges. The commitment to robust security measures, therefore, becomes a tangible demonstration of an organization's dedication to responsible AI, reinforcing the foundation of trust upon which the entire AI ecosystem is built.

The pursuit of trustworthy AI is not an endeavor that can be undertaken in isolation. Just as a complex ecosystem thrives through the interconnectedness of its diverse elements, so too must the development and deployment of reliable AI be nurtured through collaborative efforts. This collaborative spirit, when channeled into structured governance models and robust information-sharing mechanisms, becomes a powerful engine for accelerating the creation of safer, more dependable AI technologies. When organizations, researchers, policymakers, and even competitors move beyond siloes to engage in open dialogue and shared learning, they collectively build a stronger, more resilient AI landscape.

At its core, collaborative governance in the AI domain acknowledges that no single entity possesses all the answers or all the resources to address the multifaceted challenges inherent in building trust. It recognizes that the rapid evolution of AI, coupled with its broad societal impact, necessitates a shared responsibility for its ethical development and secure deployment. This approach moves away from a purely proprietary or competitive model, where knowledge and best practices are closely guarded, towards one that values transparency, mutual learning, and collective problem-solving. Such collaboration can manifest in various forms, from industry-wide consortia and multi-stakeholder forums to government-led initiatives and public-private partnerships. The fundamental principle is that by pooling expertise, sharing experiences, and jointly developing standards, we can achieve a higher level of trust and safety across the entire AI ecosystem than any individual player could achieve alone.

One of the most significant benefits of collaborative governance is the acceleration of best practice dissemination. The field of AI is characterized by a constant stream of new research, novel techniques, and emerging challenges. What is considered a cutting-edge approach to AI safety or security today might be standard practice tomorrow, or even become obsolete. In such a dynamic environment, relying solely on internal R&D or individual company efforts to stay ahead of the curve is often insufficient. Collaborative platforms allow for the efficient sharing of successful strategies, effective risk mitigation techniques, and robust validation methodologies. For instance, when one organization develops a novel method for detecting adversarial attacks on image recognition systems, a collaborative framework can facilitate its rapid assessment and adoption by others, rather than each entity having to independently discover or invent similar solutions. This not only saves time and resources but also ensures a more uniform and higher standard of safety across various applications. Imagine a scenario where a breakthrough in detecting data poisoning is shared across an industry consortium. This shared knowledge allows all members to quickly implement enhanced defenses, protecting their AI models from a common threat much faster than if each had to identify the vulnerability and devise a solution independently. This collective uplift in security and reliability is a direct consequence of a collaborative governance structure.

Furthermore, collaborative governance models are crucial for establishing common benchmarks and standards. Without agreed-upon metrics for evaluating AI trustworthiness—spanning aspects like fairness, robustness, explainability, and security—it becomes challenging to compare different systems or to ensure a baseline level of safety. Industry alliances can work together to define what constitutes responsible AI development, creating shared definitions, evaluation frameworks, and even certification processes. This not only provides clarity for developers and users but also offers a clearer signal to regulators and the public about the commitment to trustworthy AI. For example, if multiple automotive manufacturers collaborate on defining safety standards for autonomous driving AI, including rigorous testing protocols for edge cases and adversarial scenarios, this shared understanding can lead to a more globally consistent and higher level of safety for all road users. This standardization process, driven by collaboration, builds confidence and reduces the perceived risk associated with adopting these advanced technologies.

Information sharing, particularly concerning threat intelligence and incident learnings, is another vital pillar of collaborative AI governance. The adversarial landscape in AI is constantly evolving, with new attack vectors and exploitation techniques emerging regularly. In this environment, the principle of "what one knows, all should know" becomes paramount for effective defense. Collaborative platforms can serve as conduits for sharing real-time information about discovered vulnerabilities, successful attack methods, and, crucially, lessons learned from actual incidents. When an organization experiences an AI-related security breach or a failure due to unexpected AI behavior, its ability to share anonymized or aggregated details about the incident—the nature of the attack, the exploited weakness, and the remediation steps taken—can provide invaluable insights to others. This shared intelligence allows other organizations to proactively fortify their own systems against similar threats, preventing them from having to suffer the same costly or damaging experience.

Consider a situation where a financial institution's AI fraud detection system is subtly manipulated by a new class of sophisticated attacks that bypass existing defenses. If this institution, through a trusted industry forum, can share details about this new attack vector and the specific vulnerabilities it exploited, other financial organizations can swiftly update their models, deploy new detection mechanisms, or adjust their operational procedures to counter the threat. This collective defense mechanism is far more effective than individual organizations struggling in isolation. The sharing of anonymized incident data can reveal patterns and trends that might be invisible to individual actors, allowing the entire community to build more resilient systems. For instance, research into explainability techniques might reveal that certain model architectures are inherently more susceptible to specific types of data poisoning. If this finding is shared widely, developers can prioritize more robust architectures or implement additional safeguards when using susceptible ones.

The development of secure AI systems is an ongoing arms race, and collaboration is essential to keep pace with evolving threats. Sharing threat intelligence about emerging attack methodologies, including novel adversarial techniques, data poisoning strategies, and model extraction methods, allows for the development of proactive defense mechanisms. This intelligence can come in various forms: indicators of compromise, descriptions of new attack patterns, or even samples of adversarial inputs. Trusted information-sharing communities can facilitate the rapid dissemination of this intelligence, enabling organizations to update their detection systems and defensive strategies before they become targets. For example, a national cybersecurity agency might collaborate with AI researchers and industry leaders to create a centralized platform for reporting and analyzing AI-specific threats. This platform could aggregate data from various sources, identify emerging trends, and disseminate actionable intelligence to help organizations bolster their defenses.

Moreover, collaborative efforts can foster the development of shared tools and methodologies for AI security testing and validation. Developing robust methods for testing AI systems for vulnerabilities, bias, and robustness is a complex undertaking. By pooling resources and expertise, organizations can collectively build advanced testing frameworks, open-source security libraries, and standardized benchmark datasets for evaluating AI models. This collaborative approach ensures that testing methodologies are rigorous, comprehensive, and constantly updated to address new threats. For example, a consortium of AI developers could collaborate to create an open-source framework for testing adversarial robustness, providing a common platform for evaluating how well AI models withstand manipulated inputs. This would allow for more objective comparisons between models and encourage the development of more resilient AI.

The creation of such collaborative frameworks requires careful consideration of governance structures, trust mechanisms, and legal frameworks to ensure that information sharing is effective, secure, and compliant with relevant regulations. Key elements include establishing clear protocols for data anonymization and de-identification, defining acceptable use policies for shared information, and ensuring that participating organizations are committed to a shared goal of enhancing AI safety and security. Building trust within these collaborative bodies is paramount. Participants must feel confident that the information they share will be used responsibly and will not be exploited for competitive disadvantage or malicious purposes. This often involves establishing clear rules of engagement, independent oversight, and dispute resolution mechanisms.

Furthermore, collaborative governance can extend beyond industry to encompass academia, civil society, and governmental bodies. Academia plays a crucial role in pioneering research into AI safety and security, while civil society organizations can provide valuable perspectives on societal impact and ethical considerations. Governments can facilitate collaboration through funding research, setting regulatory guidelines, and fostering international cooperation. A multi-stakeholder approach, where diverse perspectives are integrated into the governance and information-sharing processes, leads to more comprehensive and robust solutions. For instance, a government initiative to create a national AI safety institute could bring together experts from industry, academia, and regulatory bodies to develop shared best practices, conduct independent research, and provide guidance on responsible AI deployment. This inclusive approach ensures that the development of trustworthy AI is aligned with broader societal values and interests.

The benefits of collaborative governance and information sharing are not merely theoretical. Real-world examples, though often nascent, point towards the power of this approach. Industry consortia focused on specific AI applications, such as autonomous vehicles or medical diagnostics, are beginning to emerge, where members share data (anonymized and aggregated where necessary), collaborate on safety standards, and jointly develop testing protocols. Similarly, open-source communities around AI development tools and libraries often foster a culture of shared responsibility for security, where vulnerabilities are reported and addressed collectively.

However, realizing the full potential of collaborative governance requires overcoming significant hurdles. These include concerns about intellectual property protection, competitive pressures, the challenges of standardizing diverse AI systems and use cases, and the need for robust data governance frameworks. Addressing these challenges necessitates careful design of collaborative platforms, including mechanisms for managing sensitive information, ensuring fair attribution, and establishing clear legal and ethical boundaries for participation. The development of secure and trusted platforms for sharing sensitive threat intelligence, for instance, requires advanced cryptographic techniques, strict access controls, and a clear understanding of data ownership and usage rights.

Ultimately, fostering a culture of collaboration and shared responsibility is key. This means encouraging organizations to view AI safety and security not as a zero-sum game where one company's gain is another's loss, but as a collective endeavor to build a future where AI can be trusted and leveraged for the benefit of all. By actively engaging in collaborative governance and robust information sharing, we can collectively accelerate the development of trustworthy AI, mitigate risks, and build a more secure and reliable AI ecosystem for generations to come. This interconnected approach, where knowledge and best practices flow freely and securely, is the bedrock upon which the widespread, ethical, and beneficial adoption of AI will be built. It transforms the daunting task of ensuring AI trustworthiness into a shared mission, leveraging the collective intelligence and diverse perspectives of all stakeholders to navigate the complexities and seize the opportunities of this transformative technology.

Communicating AI Capabilities and Limitations

The journey toward building trustworthy AI ecosystems is intrinsically linked to the clarity and honesty with which organizations communicate about their artificial intelligence systems. This is not merely a matter of good public relations; it is a fundamental requirement for establishing and maintaining trust with users, stakeholders, and the broader public. In an era where AI is increasingly integrated into the fabric of our lives, from personalized recommendations to critical decision-making processes, a clear understanding of what AI can and cannot do is paramount. Misaligned expectations, born from opaque or exaggerated claims, can quickly erode confidence, leading to distrust, misuse, and potentially harmful consequences. Therefore, a proactive, transparent, and accessible approach to communicating AI capabilities and limitations is not just advisable – it is essential.

At the heart of this communication strategy lies the principle of managing expectations. Users should not be led to believe that an AI system is a panacea, capable of solving every problem flawlessly. Instead, the focus should be on presenting the AI's intended purpose, its strengths within that scope, and crucially, its inherent limitations. This involves a nuanced portrayal that acknowledges both the power of AI and its current developmental stage. For instance, when introducing an AI-powered diagnostic tool in healthcare, it is vital to state that the system is designed to
assist clinicians by identifying potential anomalies in medical images, rather than presenting it as a definitive diagnostician that replaces human expertise. The communication should clearly articulate that it is a support tool, subject to human oversight and final clinical judgment. This avoids the pitfall of users over-relying on the AI, potentially leading to missed diagnoses or incorrect treatments if the AI's inherent limitations are not understood.

One of the primary challenges in communicating AI capabilities is the inherent complexity of the technology itself. Many AI systems, particularly those based on deep learning, operate as "black boxes," making it difficult even for their developers to fully explain the reasoning behind specific outputs. Despite advancements in explainable AI (XAI), a complete and intuitive explanation of every decision may not always be feasible. In such cases, communication must shift from explaining the *how* to articulating the *what* and the *why* in an understandable manner. This means clearly defining the problem the AI is designed to solve, the data it was trained on (and by extension, the biases it might have inherited), and the general principles guiding its operation. For example, a customer service chatbot might be explained as a system trained on vast amounts of customer interaction data to provide quick answers to frequently asked questions and to route complex queries to human agents. While the intricate neural network pathways might be beyond a typical user's comprehension, the function and purpose of the chatbot can be communicated effectively.

Furthermore, it is crucial to be forthright about the limitations that stem from the data used to train AI models. AI systems are only as good as the data they learn from. If the training data is incomplete, biased, or unrepresentative of the real-world scenarios the AI will encounter, the system's performance will inevitably be compromised. Organizations must communicate these data-related limitations transparently. For example, if an AI recruitment tool has been trained primarily on historical data that reflects past hiring biases (e.g., favoring certain demographics), this limitation must be disclosed. The communication should highlight that while the system aims to streamline the hiring process, its recommendations should be critically evaluated, especially regarding diversity and inclusion. This transparency allows users to approach the AI's outputs with a healthy degree of skepticism and to implement complementary processes that mitigate potential biases.

The intended use cases of an AI system should be delineated with precision. Vague descriptions can lead to the AI being deployed in situations for which it was not designed or tested, resulting in unexpected failures or undesirable outcomes. For instance, an AI model developed for analyzing financial market trends might perform exceptionally well within its intended scope. However, if this same model is then applied to predicting weather patterns without appropriate recalibration or retraining, its predictions would likely be unreliable. Communication should clearly define the operational boundaries, the types of inputs the AI is expected to handle, and the types of outputs it is designed to generate. This prevents what is sometimes referred to as "scope creep," where a technology is overextended beyond its validated capabilities.

Accessibility is another critical dimension of communicating AI capabilities and limitations. The language used must be tailored to the audience. Technical jargon and complex statistical concepts should be avoided when communicating with the general public or end-users who may not have a background in artificial intelligence. Instead, clear, simple, and relatable language should be employed. Analogies, examples, and visual aids can be powerful tools for conveying complex ideas. For instance, when explaining the concept of confidence scores in an AI's prediction, rather than citing probabilities, one might say, "The system is about 85% sure this is the correct answer, but there's a 15% chance it might be wrong. It's always good to double-check when the confidence is not very high." This approach demystifies AI and makes its limitations more tangible.

Moreover, the communication process should be ongoing and iterative. As AI systems evolve, new capabilities emerge, and limitations may be overcome through further development. However, new challenges and unforeseen limitations can also arise. Organizations must establish mechanisms for continuously updating their communications to reflect the current state of their AI systems. This includes informing users about significant updates, changes in performance, or newly identified risks. A system that was reliable a year ago might require recalibration or retraining to maintain its trustworthiness in the face of evolving data landscapes or new adversarial threats. Transparently communicating these ongoing updates demonstrates a commitment to maintaining a reliable and trustworthy AI system over its lifecycle.

The responsible disclosure of AI vulnerabilities and potential failure modes is a crucial aspect of this communication. Just as software vulnerabilities are disclosed in traditional computing, so too should potential weaknesses in AI systems be communicated, especially to those who develop and deploy them. This includes informing users about known adversarial attack vectors, data poisoning risks, or scenarios where the AI might exhibit unexpected or undesirable behavior. A proactive approach to vulnerability disclosure, often through bug bounty programs or trusted disclosure channels, allows for collective problem-solving and the development of more robust defenses. For example, if a security firm discovers a new way to trick an AI-powered facial recognition system into misidentifying individuals, this information should be shared responsibly with the developers of such systems so they can implement patches and improve their models' resilience.

Building confidence through honest communication means acknowledging when an AI system is not the optimal solution. There will be instances where traditional methods or human judgment are superior to AI. In such cases, organizations should not hesitate to state this. Presenting AI as a tool that complements, rather than replaces, human intelligence can foster a more realistic and trusting relationship with users. For example, if an AI system is being considered for a task that requires significant empathy, nuanced ethical judgment, or a deep understanding of context that is difficult to codify, it is important to communicate that AI might not be the best fit for that particular role, or that it can only provide partial support.

Furthermore, the communication of AI capabilities and limitations should be integrated into the entire AI lifecycle, from initial design and development through deployment and ongoing monitoring. During the development phase, R&D teams should be encouraged to document the known limitations of their models and to consider how these limitations will be communicated to downstream users. During deployment, clear user guides, FAQs, and training materials should be provided. Post-deployment, mechanisms for feedback and incident reporting should be established, allowing users to report instances where the AI did not perform as expected or where its limitations became apparent. This feedback loop is invaluable for refining both the AI system and its accompanying communication strategy.

Consider the ethical implications of AI in sensitive domains like criminal justice or finance. An AI system used for risk assessment in loan applications, for instance, must have its limitations clearly communicated to both loan officers and applicants. This includes explaining that the AI is a predictive tool based on historical data and statistical correlations, not a definitive judgment of an individual's creditworthiness or future behavior. Its outputs should be presented as inputs to a human decision-making process, not as final pronouncements. Similarly, an AI used in the judicial system for sentencing recommendations must be accompanied by clear disclaimers about its potential biases, the limitations of its predictive accuracy, and the absolute necessity for human review and override by a judge. Failing to communicate these nuances can lead to profound injustices and a loss of public faith in the fairness of these systems.

The ultimate goal of communicating AI capabilities and limitations is to foster a symbiotic relationship between humans and AI, one built on mutual understanding and realistic expectations. When users understand what an AI can do, how it works at a conceptual level, and where its boundaries lie, they are better equipped to use it effectively, safely, and ethically. This understanding empowers them to leverage the AI's strengths while mitigating its weaknesses, leading to better outcomes and a more positive overall experience. It also cultivates a sense of partnership, where AI is viewed as a valuable assistant rather than an inscrutable oracle, thereby laying a stronger foundation for trust within the broader AI ecosystem. This requires a continuous commitment from organizations to not only develop advanced AI technologies but also to ensure that their potential and their boundaries are communicated with an equal measure of diligence and integrity. This transparency is not a one-time event but a continuous process, evolving alongside the technology itself, to ensure that trust is not just built, but consistently maintained.

This commitment to clear and honest communication extends to the legal and regulatory frameworks surrounding AI. As these frameworks evolve, organizations must ensure their communications align with any mandated disclosures and standards for transparency. Regulatory bodies often play a crucial role in setting expectations for how AI systems should be described to the public, particularly in high-risk applications. Adhering to these guidelines, and proactively going beyond them where possible, demonstrates a genuine commitment to responsible AI deployment. For example, if regulations stipulate that AI systems used for hiring must disclose their use and provide a general overview of their functions, an organization that goes further by offering more detailed explanations or accessible documentation about the system's limitations is likely to build greater trust with both applicants and regulators.

Furthermore, the internal communication of AI capabilities and limitations is as vital as external messaging. Employees who develop, deploy, or interact with AI systems must have a clear and accurate understanding of their functionalities and constraints. This ensures that they can use the AI appropriately, identify potential issues, and contribute to the ongoing improvement and responsible governance of these technologies. Training programs for employees should include modules on understanding AI, recognizing its limitations, and communicating its use to external parties. This creates a unified front of understanding and responsibility across the organization, reinforcing the principles of trustworthy AI from within.

Finally, the communication about AI capabilities and limitations is an ongoing dialogue, not a monologue. Organizations should actively seek feedback from users, customers, and other stakeholders regarding their understanding of the AI systems. This feedback can highlight areas where communication is unclear, where expectations are misaligned, or where new limitations have become apparent. Establishing channels for dialogue, such as user forums, feedback forms, or regular stakeholder consultations, allows organizations to continuously refine their messaging and to adapt their AI systems based on real-world experience. This iterative approach to communication, driven by user insights, is fundamental to building and sustaining a robust and trustworthy AI ecosystem. It transforms the relationship with AI from one of passive reception to active collaboration, fostering a shared understanding that is essential for the ethical and beneficial integration of AI into society.

Chapter 14: The Future of AI Infrastructure Governance

The landscape of artificial intelligence is in constant flux, with new paradigms and capabilities emerging at an unprecedented pace. As we contemplate the governance of AI infrastructure, it is imperative to cast our gaze forward and anticipate the transformative advancements that will define its future. These emerging trends are not merely incremental improvements; they represent fundamental shifts in how AI systems are conceived, developed, and deployed, carrying profound implications for the underlying infrastructure and the governance frameworks required to manage them. Understanding these trajectories is not just a matter of foresight but a necessity for building resilient, adaptive, and responsible AI ecosystems.

One of the most prominent and rapidly evolving areas is **Generative AI**. This class of models, exemplified by large language models (LLMs) and diffusion models, possesses the remarkable ability to create novel content – text, images, code, music, and more – based on learned patterns from vast datasets. The implications for AI infrastructure are multifaceted. Firstly, the training of these models demands colossal computational resources, necessitating highly specialized hardware and massive distributed computing environments. This escalates the need for robust, scalable, and energy-efficient data centers. The sheer volume of data processed and the complexity of the models mean that the infrastructure must be designed not only for raw processing power but also for efficient data management, storage, and retrieval. Furthermore, the inference phase, where generative models produce outputs, can also be computationally intensive, requiring optimized hardware and software stacks to ensure low latency and high throughput. This will drive innovation in specialized AI accelerators, optimized network fabrics, and sophisticated scheduling algorithms.

Beyond the computational demands, generative AI introduces new governance challenges. The ability to generate synthetic data raises questions about data provenance and integrity. How do we ensure that the data used to train these models is ethically sourced and free from harmful biases? How do we govern the outputs of generative models to prevent the creation and dissemination of misinformation, deepfakes, or malicious code? The infrastructure must be capable of supporting mechanisms for content authentication, watermarking, and provenance tracking. Moreover, the democratization of generative AI tools, while empowering, also lowers the barrier to entry for malicious actors. Governing the deployment of these powerful models, whether on-premise or in the cloud, will require sophisticated access control, usage monitoring, and ethical usage policies. The potential for these models to automate tasks that were previously the exclusive domain of human creativity and intellect also raises questions about workforce disruption and the need for reskilling, aspects that infrastructure governance must indirectly consider by enabling responsible adoption.

Another significant trend is
Reinforcement Learning (RL) at Scale. While RL has shown remarkable success in specific domains like game playing and robotics, scaling it to complex real-world environments presents substantial infrastructure challenges. RL systems learn through trial and error, requiring vast numbers of simulations or real-world interactions to optimize their policies. This necessitates not only powerful simulation environments that can run at high fidelity and speed but also robust mechanisms for collecting, storing, and processing the massive streams of observational data generated by these interactions. The infrastructure must support efficient data pipelines for reward signals, state observations, and action outputs. Furthermore, managing the exploration-exploitation trade-off in large-scale RL systems, especially in safety-critical applications, demands sophisticated control mechanisms and robust safety nets. This might involve dedicated infrastructure for real-time anomaly detection and intervention.

The governance of RL at scale is particularly intricate. Ensuring that RL agents behave in predictable and safe ways, especially when deployed in dynamic and uncertain environments, is paramount. This requires infrastructure that can support formal verification techniques, constrained optimization, and robust fallback mechanisms. The ability to monitor and audit the decision-making process of RL agents in real-time becomes critical, demanding logging and analysis capabilities that can handle high-velocity data. As RL agents learn and adapt, their behavior can change over time, necessitating continuous monitoring and re-validation. Infrastructure must be designed to support this dynamic lifecycle, enabling seamless updates and graceful degradation when unexpected behaviors emerge. The ethical considerations are also profound: how do we ensure that RL agents do not learn to exploit loopholes or exhibit emergent behaviors that are detrimental to human safety or societal well-being? Infrastructure governance must enable the implementation of ethical guardrails and oversight mechanisms.

The convergence of symbolic reasoning and deep learning, known as **Neuro-Symbolic AI**, represents a promising direction for addressing the limitations of current AI systems. Deep learning excels at pattern recognition and perception from data, while symbolic AI is adept at logical reasoning, planning, and knowledge representation. Neuro-symbolic approaches aim to combine these strengths, leading to AI systems that are more interpretable, robust, and capable of common-sense reasoning. For AI infrastructure, this implies a need for systems that can seamlessly integrate different computational paradigms. This could involve specialized hardware that supports both neural network processing and symbolic computation, or it might require sophisticated software frameworks that abstract away the underlying heterogeneity. The infrastructure must facilitate the efficient transfer of information and intermediate representations between neural and symbolic components.

Governance in the context of neuro-symbolic AI will likely focus on bridging the explainability gap. By combining the learning capabilities of neural networks with the explicit reasoning of symbolic systems, these approaches hold the potential for more transparent decision-making processes. Infrastructure governance should therefore prioritize systems that support introspection and auditing of both the neural and symbolic components. This might involve developing standardized interfaces for querying the reasoning pathways of these hybrid systems and ensuring that the knowledge bases used by the symbolic components are well-curated and governed. The integration of external knowledge sources, a key aspect of symbolic reasoning, also brings governance challenges related to data quality, intellectual property, and potential biases within these knowledge repositories. Ensuring that the entire system, from data ingestion to final output, adheres to ethical principles will be a key focus.

Finally,
Edge AI is rapidly gaining prominence, shifting AI processing from centralized data centers to distributed devices at the network's periphery. This includes smartphones, IoT devices, autonomous vehicles, and industrial sensors. The driving forces behind Edge AI are the need for lower latency, reduced bandwidth consumption, enhanced privacy, and increased resilience in scenarios where network connectivity may be unreliable. For AI infrastructure, this translates into a paradigm shift from massive, centralized deployments to a distributed network of intelligent endpoints. The infrastructure must support the deployment, management, and updating of AI models on a vast number of heterogeneous devices, many of which may have limited computational resources and power constraints. This requires lightweight AI frameworks, efficient model compression techniques, and robust over-the-air update mechanisms.

The governance of Edge AI presents a unique set of challenges. Distributing AI capabilities means that control and oversight become more fragmented. Ensuring the security and integrity of AI models deployed on edge devices is critical, as these devices can be more vulnerable to physical tampering or cyberattacks. Infrastructure governance must incorporate security protocols for device authentication, model integrity verification, and secure data handling at the edge. Privacy is a significant concern, as edge devices often collect sensitive personal data. While edge processing can enhance privacy by keeping data local, it also necessitates robust mechanisms for anonymization and differential privacy, especially when aggregated data is sent back to the cloud. Furthermore, managing the lifecycle of AI models across a vast fleet of edge devices, ensuring that they remain up-to-date and perform as expected, requires sophisticated device management platforms and monitoring tools. The potential for unintended consequences or emergent behaviors in distributed AI systems also calls for advanced auditing and tracing capabilities that can collect and analyze data from multiple edge nodes. Governance frameworks must enable the coordination and control of these distributed intelligent systems, ensuring alignment with broader organizational policies and societal values.

These emerging trends collectively underscore the dynamic nature of AI technology and its profound impact on the infrastructure that underpins it. Generative AI demands massive computational power and raises concerns about content integrity. Scaled Reinforcement Learning necessitates advanced simulation and real-time control. Neuro-symbolic AI calls for integrated hybrid computing architectures. Edge AI distributes intelligence, challenging traditional centralized governance models. As we move forward, AI infrastructure governance must be agile, adaptable, and forward-looking, capable of anticipating and responding to these technological shifts. The focus will increasingly be on building infrastructure that is not only powerful and efficient but also secure, privacy-preserving, interpretable, and auditable, capable of supporting the responsible and ethical evolution of artificial intelligence. The interplay between technological advancement and governance will be critical in shaping a future where AI benefits humanity without compromising its safety, fairness, or autonomy. The underlying infrastructure must therefore be designed with these future capabilities and their associated risks in mind, enabling a proactive rather than reactive approach to AI governance. The continuous evolution of AI necessitates a continuous evolution of the infrastructure and the governance principles that guide its deployment and operation.

The burgeoning influence of artificial intelligence has catalyzed a dynamic evolution in the realms of regulation and policy, creating a complex and interconnected global tapestry of governance. As AI systems become more sophisticated and pervasive, the frameworks designed to guide their development and deployment must necessarily become more nuanced, adaptive, and forward-looking. This section delves into the emerging frontiers of AI regulation and policy, examining the nascent proposals, collaborative international endeavors, and the anticipated shape of future legislative instruments that will govern advanced AI technologies. It will explore how these regulatory approaches are striving to keep pace with the rapid advancements in AI paradigms and the inherent difficulties in achieving global harmonization of AI governance.

One of the most striking developments in this space is the proliferation of AI-specific legislative proposals across various jurisdictions. Many nations are moving beyond general technology regulations to craft laws that directly address the unique challenges posed by AI. These initiatives range from comprehensive AI Acts, such as the one being developed by the European Union, to more targeted regulations focusing on specific AI applications or ethical concerns. The EU's AI Act, for instance, adopts a risk-based approach, categorizing AI systems according to their potential to cause harm. High-risk AI systems, those that could impact fundamental rights, safety, or democratic processes, face stringent requirements regarding data quality, transparency, human oversight, and cybersecurity. This tiered structure aims to foster innovation while ensuring that the most potentially harmful AI applications are subject to rigorous scrutiny and control. Such a comprehensive, rights-centric approach sets a significant precedent, influencing regulatory thinking worldwide and highlighting the growing consensus on the need for proactive, principled AI governance.

In parallel, the United States has explored a more sector-specific and market-driven approach, often relying on existing regulatory bodies to adapt their mandates for AI oversight. While lacking a single, overarching AI law like the EU's Act, this strategy has seen agencies like the Federal Trade Commission (FTC) issue guidance on algorithmic fairness and data security, and the National Institute of Standards and Technology (NIST) develop frameworks for AI risk management. The NIST AI Risk Management Framework, for instance, provides a voluntary, flexible guidance that organizations can use to manage risks associated with the design, development, deployment, and use of AI. This emphasis on voluntary standards and best practices aims to encourage responsible innovation by providing clear, actionable recommendations without imposing prescriptive legal mandates, though it does raise questions about enforceability and the extent of protection offered to individuals.

Beyond these distinct national strategies, a palpable surge in international cooperation is evident. Recognizing that AI development and deployment transcend national borders, governments and international organizations are increasingly engaging in dialogue to forge common ground. The G7, G20, and the United Nations have all become platforms for discussing AI governance principles, ethical guidelines, and the need for coordinated regulatory approaches. For example, discussions within the G7 have focused on establishing shared principles for responsible AI innovation, while the G20 has explored the implications of AI for economic growth and societal well-being. The OECD's work on AI principles has been particularly influential, providing a foundation for many national strategies and fostering a shared understanding of the ethical considerations and policy challenges. These international forums serve not only to harmonize regulatory thinking but also to promote best practices and prevent a fragmented global AI landscape that could stifle innovation or create loopholes for irresponsible actors.

However, the path to global harmonization is fraught with challenges. Divergent legal traditions, economic priorities, and geopolitical considerations mean that achieving a truly unified global regulatory regime for AI remains an ambitious, if not aspirational, goal. For instance, countries with strong data privacy laws, like those in Europe, often advocate for stricter controls on data usage for AI training and deployment, while other nations might prioritize economic growth and technological advancement, potentially leading to more permissive regulations. The debate over the definition of AI itself, the classification of different types of AI systems, and the appropriate level of regulation for each, further complicates international consensus-building. Moreover, the rapid pace of AI development means that any regulatory framework, once established, risks becoming quickly outdated, necessitating a flexible and iterative approach to policy-making.

Future legislative frameworks are likely to grapple with the escalating capabilities of advanced AI, particularly with the emergence of highly autonomous systems and generalized AI (AGI). As AI systems approach or even surpass human capabilities in various domains, regulatory bodies will need to address questions of accountability, liability, and control in unprecedented ways. The concept of "AI personhood" or the legal status of highly autonomous AI, while still largely theoretical, may eventually necessitate new legal paradigms to assign responsibility when AI systems cause harm. This will require a deep understanding of AI's emergent behaviors and the intricate chains of command and control involved in their operation. Infrastructure governance will play a crucial role here, ensuring that systems are built with inherent safety mechanisms, audit trails, and the ability to be reliably deactivated or controlled.

The governance of foundational models, the large-scale AI models that underpin many generative AI applications, is another area where policy is rapidly evolving. These models, often developed by a handful of major technology companies, possess immense power and influence. Regulators are increasingly scrutinizing their development, training data, and deployment to mitigate risks of bias, misinformation, and market concentration. Proposals are emerging to ensure transparency in the training data, to mandate independent audits of these models, and to foster competition by making foundational models more accessible. The sheer computational resources and data required to train these models create significant barriers to entry, leading to concerns about monopolies and the need for public investment or open-source initiatives to democratize access and development. Policies aimed at promoting open research, data sharing, and the development of alternative, smaller, or more specialized models could help to diversify the AI ecosystem and reduce reliance on a few dominant players.

Furthermore, the international discourse on AI governance is increasingly focusing on the alignment of AI with human values and ethical principles. This involves not only preventing direct harm but also ensuring that AI contributes positively to society. Concepts like "value alignment," "AI ethics by design," and "human-centric AI" are gaining traction in policy discussions. This translates into a demand for AI systems that are interpretable, explainable, fair, and robust, and for the infrastructure that supports them to be designed with these principles in mind from the outset. Policies may soon mandate the inclusion of ethical impact assessments as part of the AI development lifecycle, similar to environmental impact assessments for large infrastructure projects.

The challenge of regulating AI globally also extends to issues of data governance. Given that AI systems learn from data, the policies governing data collection, privacy, and usage have a direct impact on AI development. International efforts to harmonize data protection regulations, while complex, are crucial for enabling cross-border AI innovation while safeguarding individual privacy. Discussions around data localization versus data flow, consent mechanisms, and the ethical use of anonymized or aggregated data for AI training will continue to shape the regulatory landscape.

The role of standards-setting bodies, both governmental and non-governmental, is also becoming increasingly significant. Organizations like the International Organization for Standardization (ISO) and the International Electrotechnical Commission (IEC) are developing technical standards for AI safety, security, and reliability. These standards, while not legally binding in themselves, often serve as the basis for national regulations and industry best practices, providing a practical pathway for implementing AI governance principles in infrastructure design and deployment. The ongoing development of standards for AI explainability, bias detection, and robustness will be critical for ensuring that AI systems can be reliably governed and audited.

Looking ahead, the regulatory and policy frontiers for AI infrastructure governance are poised for continued expansion and refinement. As AI technologies mature and permeate more aspects of our lives, the legal and ethical frameworks governing them will need to become more sophisticated. This will likely involve a multi-layered approach, combining international agreements, national legislation, sector-specific regulations, and industry self-regulation. The emphasis will increasingly be on proactive risk management, ethical design, transparency, and accountability, ensuring that the powerful infrastructure of AI development and deployment serves humanity's best interests. The ability to adapt existing legal frameworks and to create new ones that are both effective and flexible will be a defining characteristic of successful AI governance in the coming years. The ongoing dialogue between technologists, policymakers, ethicists, and the public will be indispensable in navigating this complex and rapidly evolving landscape, ensuring that the future of AI infrastructure is built on a foundation of trust, safety, and societal benefit. The very definition of "infrastructure" itself may evolve, encompassing not just the physical and digital hardware, but also the governance protocols, ethical guidelines, and legal frameworks that shape AI's impact.

The integration of artificial intelligence into critical infrastructure represents a profound shift in our capacity to withstand and recover from disruptions. As societies become increasingly complex and interconnected, so too do the threats we face. These range from the slow-burn crises of climate change, manifesting in more frequent and intense extreme weather events, to the rapid, widespread impacts of pandemics, and the ever-present, evolving challenges of cyber warfare. In this context, AI is emerging not merely as a tool for efficiency or innovation, but as a cornerstone of societal resilience, capable of anticipating, mitigating, and responding to crises with unprecedented speed and precision.

Consider the domain of climate change resilience. AI algorithms can process vast datasets from weather stations, satellite imagery, oceanographic sensors, and climate models to predict extreme weather events with greater accuracy and lead time. This predictive power is invaluable for proactive measures: rerouting shipping lanes to avoid approaching storms, optimizing power grid operations to anticipate demand surges during heatwaves, or even guiding agricultural practices to adapt to shifting precipitation patterns. Beyond prediction, AI can optimize resource allocation during disaster response. For instance, after a flood or earthquake, AI-powered systems can analyze damage assessments from drones and sensor networks, pinpointing areas with the most critical needs for rescue, medical aid, or infrastructure repair.

This allows emergency services to deploy limited resources far more effectively, potentially saving lives and reducing the duration of the crisis. Furthermore, AI can facilitate the development of more resilient infrastructure itself. By simulating the effects of extreme weather on different building materials, urban designs, or energy systems, AI can inform the creation of structures and networks that are inherently better equipped to withstand environmental stresses. This proactive design element, informed by AI's analytical capabilities, shifts the paradigm from reactive recovery to anticipatory fortification.

The COVID-19 pandemic provided a stark, real-world demonstration of AI's potential to bolster resilience against biological threats. During the crisis, AI was instrumental in accelerating the development of vaccines and therapeutics by analyzing vast amounts of genetic and molecular data, identifying potential drug targets, and optimizing clinical trial designs. Public health agencies utilized AI-powered dashboards to track the spread of the virus in near real-time, analyze patterns of transmission, and forecast future outbreaks. This data-driven insight allowed for more informed decisions regarding public health interventions, such as the timing and intensity of lockdowns, the allocation of medical supplies, and the deployment of testing and tracing resources. AI also played a role in managing healthcare system capacity, predicting hospital bed shortages, and optimizing the scheduling of healthcare professionals. Beyond direct health applications, AI contributed to economic resilience by helping businesses adapt to new operating realities, analyzing supply chain vulnerabilities, and identifying opportunities for innovation in a disrupted global market. The ability of AI to process and learn from rapidly evolving data streams proved critical in navigating the unprecedented uncertainty of the pandemic.

Cybersecurity is another arena where AI is fundamentally reshaping resilience. As our digital infrastructure becomes more sophisticated, so too do the threats it faces. AI can analyze network traffic patterns to detect anomalies indicative of cyberattacks in real-time, often identifying novel threats that signature-based systems might miss. This allows for faster containment and mitigation, minimizing the damage caused by intrusions. Machine learning models can also be trained to identify phishing attempts, malware, and other malicious activities with increasing accuracy. Beyond defense, AI can aid in the recovery process following a cyberattack. By analyzing the nature of the breach, AI can help identify compromised systems, assess the extent of data exfiltration, and assist in the secure restoration of data and services. The continuous learning capability of AI means that its defensive prowess evolves as quickly as the threat landscape itself, a crucial advantage in the perpetual cat-and-mouse game of cybersecurity. Moreover, AI can be used to simulate cyberattack scenarios, allowing organizations to test their defenses and identify vulnerabilities before they are exploited in the wild. This proactive testing is a vital component of building robust cyber resilience.

However, the deployment of AI in these high-stakes domains is not without its governance complexities. When AI systems are tasked with making critical decisions that impact public safety, health, or national security, questions of accountability, transparency, and fairness become paramount. For instance, if an AI system mispredicts an extreme weather event, leading to inadequate preparation and loss of life, who is responsible? Is it the developers of the algorithm, the operators who deployed it, or the policymakers who relied on its output? Establishing clear lines of accountability becomes challenging, particularly when AI systems exhibit emergent behaviors that were not explicitly programmed. This necessitates the development of robust audit trails, explainability mechanisms, and clear legal frameworks that can attribute responsibility in complex socio-technical systems.

The issue of bias in AI systems is also a significant concern for societal resilience. If AI is used to allocate disaster relief resources, for example, and its training data reflects historical inequities or biases, it could inadvertently perpetuate or even exacerbate existing disparities, leaving vulnerable communities underserved. Similarly, AI used in predictive policing or in managing access to essential services could lead to discriminatory outcomes if not carefully designed and rigorously tested for fairness. Ensuring that AI systems are equitable and do not systematically disadvantage certain populations is a fundamental governance challenge that requires careful attention to data quality, algorithm design, and ongoing performance monitoring. This is particularly critical in resilience applications, where equitable distribution of aid and resources can be a matter of life and death.

The pervasive nature of AI in critical infrastructure also raises concerns about the concentration of power. The development and deployment of sophisticated AI systems often require significant resources, expertise, and data, which can lead to a concentration of control in the hands of a few large technology companies or powerful state actors. This concentration can create dependencies and vulnerabilities. For example, if a nation's entire disaster response system relies on proprietary AI software from a single vendor, any disruption to that vendor's services or any malicious control exerted over it could have catastrophic consequences. Governance frameworks must therefore consider mechanisms to promote competition, foster open standards, and ensure that essential AI capabilities are not monopolized. Diversification of AI providers and the promotion of open-source solutions can be crucial strategies for enhancing the resilience of the AI infrastructure itself.

Furthermore, the sheer complexity of AI-driven infrastructure can make it difficult for humans to fully understand or control. As AI systems become more autonomous and capable of making decisions at speeds far exceeding human cognitive abilities, maintaining meaningful human oversight becomes a critical governance challenge. This is particularly relevant in rapidly evolving crisis situations. While AI can process information and identify optimal responses much faster than humans, there must be mechanisms for human intervention, review, and ultimate decision-making, especially when ethical considerations or unforeseen circumstances arise. The "human-in-the-loop" or "human-on-the-loop" paradigms are essential, but defining the precise boundaries and mechanisms for effective human control in highly automated systems requires careful thought and robust design. The risk of "automation bias," where humans uncritically accept AI recommendations, must also be actively managed through training and system design.

The data requirements for training and operating these powerful AI systems also present significant governance hurdles. The collection, storage, and use of vast amounts of data, often including sensitive personal information, raise privacy concerns. Ensuring that data is collected ethically, used responsibly, and protected from unauthorized access or misuse is a fundamental requirement for public trust. Moreover, the quality and integrity of the data are paramount. AI systems are only as good as the data they are trained on, and flaws in data can lead to flawed decision-making with serious consequences. Governance must therefore address data provenance, quality assurance, and security throughout the AI lifecycle. International cooperation on data governance standards will be increasingly important as AI infrastructure becomes more globally interconnected.

The dynamic nature of AI development also poses a unique governance challenge. Unlike traditional infrastructure that might be built and remain relatively static for decades, AI systems are continuously learning and evolving. This means that regulatory and governance frameworks must be adaptive and iterative, capable of keeping pace with technological advancements. A rigid, prescriptive approach to AI governance is likely to quickly become obsolete. Instead, governance mechanisms need to be flexible, allowing for experimentation, learning, and continuous improvement. This might involve establishing dynamic risk assessment frameworks, iterative testing protocols, and mechanisms for ongoing dialogue between developers, regulators, and affected communities. The concept of "AI safety engineering" – embedding safety and ethical considerations into the design and development process from the outset – becomes a crucial proactive governance strategy, rather than an afterthought.

Moreover, the international dimension of AI infrastructure governance is critical for resilience. Disasters and threats do not respect national borders, and AI-enabled responses often require cross-border cooperation. Establishing common protocols, data-sharing agreements, and interoperability standards for AI systems used in areas like pandemic surveillance, climate monitoring, or cybersecurity is essential for a coordinated and effective global response. The fragmentation of governance approaches across different nations can create significant gaps and inefficiencies, undermining overall societal resilience. International forums play a vital role in fostering this cooperation, but the challenges of reaching consensus on complex technical and ethical issues among diverse national interests are substantial.

Ultimately, the effective governance of AI in societal resilience hinges on fostering a culture of responsibility and collaboration. It requires building robust technical systems that are not only powerful but also transparent, accountable, equitable, and secure. It demands proactive policy-making that anticipates future challenges and embraces adaptive regulatory approaches. And crucially, it necessitates continuous public engagement to ensure that these powerful technologies are developed and deployed in ways that genuinely serve the collective good and strengthen our ability to navigate an increasingly uncertain future. The infrastructure of AI governance itself must be designed to be resilient, capable of adapting to evolving threats and societal needs.

The increasing ubiquity of artificial intelligence across critical sectors necessitates a cohesive and globally informed approach to its governance. As AI systems become more sophisticated and their decision-making processes more deeply embedded in infrastructure, the need for international cooperation and understanding of diverse regulatory landscapes becomes paramount. This section delves into the varying perspectives and strategies emerging worldwide for governing AI, highlighting the complexities and opportunities that arise from this global patchwork of policies and ethical frameworks. Recognizing these differences is not merely an academic exercise; it is a pragmatic imperative for any entity that navigates the international AI ecosystem, whether as a developer, deployer, or policymaker.

One of the most prominent distinctions in global AI governance lies in the divergent philosophical underpinnings of major geopolitical blocs. The European Union, for instance, has positioned itself as a leader in establishing a comprehensive, rights-based regulatory framework. The EU's AI Act, a landmark piece of legislation, adopts a risk-based approach, categorizing AI systems according to their potential for harm. High-risk AI applications, such as those used in critical infrastructure management, law enforcement, or employment, face stringent requirements concerning data quality, transparency, human oversight, and conformity assessments. This approach prioritizes fundamental rights and ethical considerations, seeking to build trust in AI by ensuring that its deployment aligns with democratic values and societal well-being. The emphasis is on ex-ante regulation, meaning that rules and obligations are established before AI systems are deployed, aiming to prevent harm before it occurs. This proactive stance, while potentially leading to slower innovation cycles in certain areas, aims to create a more predictable and trustworthy environment for AI development and adoption. The EU's methodology reflects a deep-seated concern with the potential for AI to erode individual liberties and exacerbate societal inequalities, drawing lessons from historical experiences with powerful technologies and industrial regulation. The focus on creating a "human-centric" AI is a recurring theme, aiming to ensure that AI serves humanity rather than the other way around. This involves not only technical safeguards but also robust legal recourse for individuals affected by AI-driven decisions. The EU's approach also emphasizes the importance of interoperability and standardization, seeking to foster a unified market for trustworthy AI across its member states.

In contrast, the United States has largely favored a more sector-specific and market-driven approach. Rather than a sweeping, overarching AI law, the U.S. strategy has often involved guidance from agencies like the National Institute of Standards and Technology (NIST), which has developed an AI Risk Management Framework. This framework provides voluntary guidance and best practices for organizations to manage AI risks, emphasizing flexibility and adaptability. The U.S. approach tends to place greater reliance on existing legal frameworks, industry self-regulation, and the promotion of innovation through less prescriptive means. The underlying philosophy often champions technological advancement and economic competitiveness, with the belief that excessive regulation could stifle progress. While there is a growing recognition of AI risks, particularly concerning bias and discrimination, the emphasis remains on fostering an environment where innovation can flourish, with regulatory intervention reserved for clear instances of harm or market failure. This approach often leads to a more dynamic and rapidly evolving AI landscape, but it can also result in a less predictable regulatory environment and raise concerns about equity and fairness, especially for vulnerable populations. The U.S. debate often revolves around striking a balance between fostering American leadership in AI and addressing potential harms. This dynamic has led to various legislative proposals and executive actions, but a singular, comprehensive federal AI law has yet to materialize, reflecting the inherent complexity of reaching consensus on such a transformative technology within a federal system with strong traditions of individual liberty and free markets. The emphasis is often on "AI assurance," ensuring that AI systems are reliable, safe, and secure, without necessarily dictating specific technical solutions or pre-deployment approvals in the same way as the EU.

China's approach to AI governance presents a third distinct model, characterized by a strong state-led, development-oriented strategy. The Chinese government views AI as a crucial engine for economic growth, national security, and social governance. Its regulatory framework is often implemented through a combination of national strategies, guidelines, and specific regulations for various AI applications, particularly those related to data security and algorithms. There is a significant emphasis on data collection and utilization, seen as a prerequisite for AI development, alongside a focus on algorithmic transparency and accountability in specific contexts, such as recommendation algorithms. The state plays a central role in directing AI research and development, fostering domestic champions, and setting ambitious national goals. While this approach can lead to rapid deployment and advancements, it also raises significant concerns regarding privacy, surveillance, and the potential for AI to be used for social control. The emphasis on national competitiveness and technological sovereignty is a driving force, with the state actively shaping the AI landscape to achieve its strategic objectives. This includes a strong focus on ethical principles, often framed within the context of socialist core values, and the promotion of "responsible AI" in alignment with national development goals. The speed and scale at which China has been able to implement AI-related policies and projects are noteworthy, reflecting a different societal and political context compared to Western democracies. The focus is often on ensuring that AI development serves national strategic interests and contributes to social harmony and stability as defined by the ruling party.

Beyond these major geopolitical players, international organizations are also striving to forge consensus and establish common ground on AI governance. The United Nations, through various agencies and initiatives, has been actively engaged in discussions surrounding AI ethics, safety, and the potential impact on human rights and sustainable development. These efforts often focus on promoting dialogue, sharing best practices, and developing non-binding principles and guidelines to encourage responsible AI development globally. The aim is to foster a shared understanding of AI's challenges and opportunities, recognizing that AI's impact transcends national borders. Similarly, organizations like the Organisation for Economic Co-operation and Development (OECD) have developed influential AI principles, which emphasize inclusive growth, sustainable development, human-centered values, transparency, robustness, security, and accountability. These principles, while not legally binding, have been widely adopted and serve as a reference point for national policymaking and international discussions. The OECD's work, in particular, has been instrumental in framing AI governance discussions around economic and social implications, seeking to ensure that AI benefits society as a whole.

The proliferation of AI in critical infrastructure amplifies the need for these diverse global perspectives to converge. For instance, in the realm of cybersecurity, where threats are inherently transnational, the lack of harmonized AI governance can create vulnerabilities. If one nation has lax regulations on the development or deployment of AI-powered cyber tools, it could inadvertently provide a safe haven for malicious actors targeting critical infrastructure elsewhere. Similarly, in the context of climate resilience, AI models used for predicting extreme weather events or managing disaster response might need to share data and operate across national boundaries. Divergent data privacy laws, security standards, or algorithmic accountability frameworks could impede such vital international cooperation. The development of AI for autonomous vehicles operating on global supply chains, or for managing interconnected energy grids that span multiple countries, further underscores the necessity of global alignment.

The challenge lies in reconciling these differing approaches. The EU's rights-centric, pre-emptive regulatory model, while robust in its protection of individual liberties, might be perceived as overly burdensome by nations prioritizing rapid innovation and economic growth, such as the United States. Conversely, the U.S. market-driven approach, while fostering dynamism, may not offer sufficient safeguards against potential harms in regions where state intervention is more prevalent or where social safety nets are less developed, as might be a concern when considering China's model. China's state-led approach, while efficient in achieving national goals, raises fundamental questions about democratic oversight and individual freedoms that are central to Western governance philosophies. These divergences are not merely theoretical; they have practical implications for businesses operating internationally, as they must navigate a complex web of conflicting regulations. A company developing an AI system for a global supply chain might find itself needing to comply with EU's strict data protection rules, U.S. sectoral guidelines, and China's national security directives, all simultaneously.

Furthermore, the development of international norms around AI safety and ethics is an ongoing process. Discussions in forums like the G7, G20, and various UN committees are crucial for building consensus. However, achieving meaningful agreement is complicated by differing national interests, economic priorities, and cultural values. For example, the concept of "accountability" can be interpreted differently across legal systems. In some jurisdictions, accountability might imply strict liability for harms caused by AI, while in others, it might focus on the process of risk management and due diligence. Similarly, the definition and measurement of "fairness" in AI can vary, reflecting diverse societal notions of equity and justice.

The increasing reliance on AI for critical infrastructure introduces a unique dimension to this global governance challenge. The stability and resilience of essential services - from power grids and water systems to healthcare and transportation networks - are becoming inextricably linked to the performance and trustworthiness of AI systems. If these systems are developed under vastly different governance regimes, it can lead to interoperability issues, security risks, and uneven levels of safety. For instance, an AI-powered air traffic control system developed with robust safety testing and oversight in one country might not be compatible or trustworthy when interacting with systems from a country with a less stringent regulatory environment. This creates a global "governance gap" where critical infrastructure becomes vulnerable due to the lack of harmonized AI safety standards.

The question of data governance is another critical nexus of global AI regulation. The vast datasets required to train and operate AI systems often cross national borders, raising complex issues related to data sovereignty, privacy, and security. While the EU's General Data Protection Regulation (GDPR) has set a high bar for data protection, other nations have adopted different approaches, ranging from more permissive data utilization policies to strict data localization requirements. For AI systems that manage critical infrastructure, such as global climate monitoring or pandemic tracking, the ability to share and process data seamlessly and securely across jurisdictions is essential. However, differing national laws and varying levels of cybersecurity infrastructure can create significant barriers to this necessary international cooperation. Establishing a global consensus on data governance principles, while respecting national sovereignty, is a formidable task that requires ongoing diplomatic and technical engagement.

The pursuit of "AI sovereignty" by various nations also complicates global governance efforts. As countries recognize the strategic importance of AI, they often seek to develop their own indigenous AI capabilities and control their AI ecosystems. This can lead to protectionist policies, restrictions on technology transfer, and a fragmentation of AI development. While national autonomy is understandable, it can undermine the collective ability to address global challenges that require AI solutions, such as climate change or pandemic preparedness. International collaboration on AI infrastructure governance, therefore, needs to navigate the delicate balance between national interests and the imperative of global cooperation.

Moreover, the role of multinational corporations in shaping global AI governance cannot be overstated. These companies often operate across numerous jurisdictions, developing and deploying AI systems that have far-reaching impacts. Their internal governance policies, ethical guidelines, and risk management frameworks can significantly influence the actual implementation of AI, sometimes exceeding or diverging from national regulations. Engaging these powerful actors in constructive dialogue and ensuring their adherence to globally agreed-upon principles is a critical component of effective AI governance. This includes fostering a culture of responsible AI development within these organizations and encouraging transparency about their AI practices.

The challenges of global AI governance are further compounded by the rapid pace of technological advancement. AI is not a static technology; it is constantly evolving, with new capabilities emerging regularly. This necessitates governance frameworks that are adaptive and can keep pace with innovation. A governance model that is too rigid or prescriptive risks becoming obsolete quickly, hindering progress without necessarily ensuring safety. Therefore, many international discussions are moving towards principles-based approaches and flexible regulatory mechanisms that can be updated and refined as the technology matures. The focus is shifting from regulating specific AI algorithms to establishing overarching principles of responsible AI development and deployment that are applicable across a wide range of applications and contexts.

In conclusion, the landscape of global AI governance is characterized by a rich tapestry of approaches, each with its own strengths and weaknesses. From the EU's rights-based regulatory regime and the U.S. market-driven innovation focus to China's state-led development strategy, these diverse models reflect different societal values, economic priorities, and political systems. International organizations are working to bridge these divides, fostering dialogue and developing common principles. For organizations operating in the AI domain, particularly those involved with critical infrastructure, understanding and navigating these global perspectives is not just a matter of compliance, but a fundamental requirement for ensuring the responsible, safe, and equitable deployment of AI in an increasingly interconnected world. The ongoing evolution of AI demands a continuous commitment to international cooperation, adaptive governance, and a shared vision for harnessing AI's potential for the benefit of all humanity. The very infrastructure of our interconnected world is increasingly reliant on AI, making the governance of this technology a critical undertaking for global stability and resilience.

The journey through the complexities of AI infrastructure governance has illuminated a fundamental truth: the future of artificial intelligence is not a predetermined outcome, but a landscape we are actively shaping, moment by moment, decision by decision. As we stand at this crucial juncture, where the very arteries of our civilization—our critical infrastructure—are becoming increasingly intertwined with intelligent systems, the responsibility for steering this evolution towards a safe, ethical, and equitable future falls upon a broad coalition. This is not a burden to be shouldered by technologists alone, nor is it a task that can be confined to the halls of government. It requires a profound and sustained commitment from engineers who build these systems, policymakers who frame their use, ethicists who question their implications, and indeed, from every member of society who will ultimately live with and be affected by their pervasive influence.

The insights gained from examining the diverse global governance approaches—from the European Union's rights-centric regulatory framework and the United States' market-driven innovation model to China's state-led development strategy—underscore the critical need for a synthesis. While each approach possesses unique strengths and reflects distinct societal values, the ultimate goal must be to forge a common understanding and a shared commitment to responsible AI deployment. This convergence is not about erasing national differences or imposing a monolithic global standard, but rather about establishing a bedrock of universally accepted principles that can guide the development and deployment of AI in critical infrastructure, regardless of geopolitical boundaries. These principles should champion transparency, ensuring that the decision-making processes of AI systems are as interpretable as possible, especially when they impact essential services like energy, transportation, or healthcare. They must prioritize accountability, establishing clear lines of responsibility for the outcomes of AI-driven operations, even as the technology itself evolves. Furthermore, robustness and security must be paramount, guaranteeing that AI systems are resilient against malicious attacks, unforeseen failures, and unintended consequences that could jeopardize public safety and national security.

The path forward demands a proactive and adaptive approach to governance, one that anticipates potential risks rather than merely reacting to them. This means investing not only in the technical development of AI but also in the societal and ethical frameworks that govern its application. For engineers and developers, this translates into embedding ethical considerations and safety protocols from the earliest stages of design. It involves a commitment to rigorous testing, validation, and continuous monitoring of AI systems, particularly those deployed in high-stakes environments. It also entails fostering a culture of open dialogue and collaboration, where concerns about potential harms can be raised and addressed without fear of reprisal. The notion of "responsible innovation" must become more than a buzzword; it must be an ingrained practice, where the pursuit of technological advancement is intrinsically linked to the commitment to societal well-being. This might involve developing standardized methodologies for assessing AI risks, creating ethical review boards analogous to those in biomedical research, and fostering interdisciplinary teams that bring together AI experts with ethicists, social scientists, and legal scholars.

For policymakers and regulators, the challenge is to create agile and effective governance mechanisms that can keep pace with the rapid evolution of AI. This necessitates a move away from rigid, prescriptive regulations that can quickly become outdated and toward flexible, principles-based frameworks. Such frameworks should empower regulatory bodies to adapt to new challenges and opportunities as they emerge, while providing clear guidance and certainty for industry. International cooperation will be indispensable in this endeavor. Building consensus on common standards, best practices, and interoperability protocols for AI in critical infrastructure will be crucial for ensuring global security and stability. This includes harmonizing approaches to data governance, cybersecurity, and algorithmic transparency, recognizing that the interconnected nature of modern infrastructure means that a vulnerability in one part of the world can have repercussions everywhere. Initiatives that promote the sharing of threat intelligence and best practices related to AI security across national borders will be vital. Furthermore, policymakers must actively foster public trust by ensuring that the development and deployment of AI in critical infrastructure are conducted with utmost integrity and with mechanisms for public input and oversight.

Society at large also plays a vital role in shaping a responsible AI future. Informed public discourse, critical engagement with AI technologies, and the demand for ethical and equitable deployment are powerful forces. Educational initiatives that demystify AI and empower citizens to understand its potential benefits and risks are essential. Cultivating a society that is not only technologically adept but also ethically discerning will be a key determinant of whether AI serves humanity's best interests. This includes fostering critical thinking skills that enable individuals to evaluate AI-generated information and to question AI-driven decisions that may seem opaque or unfair. It also involves ensuring that the benefits of AI are shared broadly and that its deployment does not exacerbate existing inequalities or create new forms of marginalization. Mechanisms for redress and recourse for individuals affected by AI systems must be robust and accessible.

The development of AI in critical infrastructure presents unique ethical dilemmas. For instance, AI systems managing power grids must balance efficiency with reliability and resilience, especially in the face of unpredictable events like extreme weather or cyberattacks. The algorithms that control autonomous transportation networks need to make split-second decisions that have profound ethical implications, such as in unavoidable accident scenarios where the system must choose between different harms. Ensuring that these decisions align with societal values and ethical principles requires careful consideration and ongoing public debate. The "black box" nature of some advanced AI models poses a significant challenge to accountability, making it imperative to develop methods for explainable AI (XAI) that can provide insights into why a particular decision was made. This is particularly important in critical infrastructure where transparency can be a matter of public safety.

Moreover, the concept of "AI alignment" becomes critically important when considering its application in infrastructure. Ensuring that AI systems consistently act in accordance with human intentions and values is paramount. This is not merely a technical problem; it is a socio-technical challenge that requires understanding how human values are translated into algorithmic objectives. The pursuit of this alignment must be a continuous process, involving ongoing research, development, and refinement of AI systems as our understanding of both AI capabilities and human values evolves. The potential for unintended consequences, where AI systems optimize for objectives in ways that lead to undesirable side effects, necessitates a robust approach to safety engineering and risk management that goes beyond traditional methods.

The global nature of critical infrastructure also means that AI governance cannot afford to be siloed. A distributed power grid, a global aviation network, or an international water management system will inevitably rely on AI components that operate across borders. This necessitates a high degree of interoperability and compatibility between AI systems, which in turn requires common standards and protocols for data exchange, security, and ethical behavior. The absence of such harmonization could lead to fragmented systems that are less resilient and more vulnerable to systemic failures. International collaborations that focus on developing these shared technical and ethical foundations are therefore not just desirable, but essential. This could involve establishing international working groups focused on specific critical infrastructure sectors, or developing global certification schemes for AI systems used in these domains.

The economic incentives surrounding AI development also warrant careful consideration. The immense potential for profit in AI can sometimes overshadow ethical concerns or lead to a prioritization of rapid deployment over thorough risk assessment. Policymakers must ensure that market mechanisms do not inadvertently incentivize irresponsible AI development. This might involve exploring new models of public-private partnerships that prioritize societal benefit alongside economic returns, or implementing policies that encourage long-term investment in AI safety and ethics research. Ensuring fair competition and preventing monopolistic control over critical AI infrastructure will also be important for fostering innovation and preventing the concentration of power.

As we look to the future, the imperative for vigilance cannot be overstated. AI technology is not static; it is in perpetual motion, with new capabilities emerging at an accelerating pace. This dynamism means that governance frameworks must be equally adaptive, capable of evolving to address unforeseen challenges and to harness emerging opportunities responsibly. The ongoing dialogue about AI governance should not be viewed as a one-time event, but as a continuous process of learning, adaptation, and refinement. This requires sustained investment in research and development, not only in AI itself but also in the fields of AI ethics, safety, and governance. It necessitates fostering a global community of practice—a network of researchers, engineers, policymakers, and civil society organizations—that can collaborate to address the complex challenges ahead.

Ultimately, shaping a responsible AI future for critical infrastructure is an act of collective stewardship. It is about recognizing that the intelligent systems we create have the potential to profoundly shape our lives and societies, for better or for worse. By fostering an environment of collaboration, prioritizing ethical considerations, embracing transparency, and maintaining a steadfast commitment to safety and equity, we can steer the development and deployment of AI in a direction that benefits all of humanity. This is a shared endeavor, one that demands our attention, our ingenuity, and our unwavering dedication to building a future where AI-enabled infrastructure serves as a foundation for a more secure, prosperous, and just world. The choices we make today will echo through generations, defining the relationship between humanity and the intelligent machines we are bringing into existence, and ensuring that this transformative technology augments, rather than diminishes, our collective well-being and our shared future.

Chapter 15: Practical Application and Integration

The challenge before us is not merely to identify the myriad elements of responsible AI governance but to weave them into a coherent, functional tapestry that can guide the lifecycle of artificial intelligence systems within critical infrastructure. This is where the concept of integrated governance frameworks becomes paramount. It moves beyond a collection of disparate best practices to a unified system, ensuring that safety engineering, privacy considerations, fairness metrics, auditability requirements, and regulatory compliance are not treated as add-ons or afterthoughts, but as foundational pillars built into the very architecture of AI development and deployment. Such a framework acts as an operational blueprint, translating abstract principles into concrete actions and enforceable standards across an organization.

To achieve this integration, organizations must first establish a clear mandate and ownership for AI governance. This is not a task solely for a dedicated AI ethics committee, nor exclusively for legal or compliance departments. Instead, it requires a cross-functional governance body, comprised of representatives from engineering, product development, cybersecurity, legal, compliance, and risk management. This body should be empowered to set strategic direction, allocate resources, and oversee the implementation of the integrated framework. Their initial steps should involve a comprehensive inventory of all AI systems currently in use or under development within the organization, particularly those impacting critical infrastructure. For each system, they must then identify the specific risks and ethical considerations it presents, drawing upon the principles discussed throughout this book. This risk assessment should be granular, considering not only the technical vulnerabilities but also the potential societal impacts, including issues of bias, discrimination, autonomy, and public trust.

With a clear understanding of the AI landscape and its associated risks, the next crucial step is to embed governance requirements into the AI development lifecycle. This means moving from a "build-first, govern-later" mentality to a "govern-as-you-build" approach. In the early stages of conception and design, for instance, requirements for data provenance, privacy-preserving techniques (such as differential privacy or federated learning), and fairness assessments must be explicitly defined. Engineers should be trained and equipped with tools to identify and mitigate potential biases in training datasets and algorithmic models from the outset. This could involve establishing clear data quality standards, employing techniques for data augmentation or re-sampling to address underrepresented groups, and conducting bias audits on proxy variables. The goal is to prevent the entrenchment of discriminatory patterns that are far more difficult and costly to rectify later.

The framework must also dictate rigorous testing and validation protocols that go beyond traditional functional and performance metrics. For AI systems in critical infrastructure, this includes extensive testing for robustness against adversarial attacks, a crucial aspect of safety engineering. This means simulating various forms of manipulation, data poisoning, or evasion attacks to understand how the system behaves under duress and to develop appropriate defense mechanisms. Similarly, fairness metrics must be integrated into the testing phase. Organizations should define acceptable thresholds for disparate impact across different demographic groups and develop methods to measure and report on these metrics. This might involve utilizing fairness toolkits that can automatically assess models for various fairness definitions, such as demographic parity, equalized odds, or predictive parity, and to iterate on model development until these thresholds are met.

Transparency and explainability, while challenging, are non-negotiable components of an integrated framework. The framework should mandate the use of explainable AI (XAI) techniques where feasible, particularly for high-stakes decisions. This doesn't necessarily mean understanding every single neuron's activation in a deep neural network, but rather providing stakeholders with meaningful insights into why a particular decision was made. This could involve generating feature importance scores, local interpretable model-agnostic explanations (LIME), or Shapley additive explanations (SHAP) that can illuminate the key factors influencing an AI's output. For systems where full explainability is technically infeasible, the framework must stipulate mechanisms for robust audit trails and accountability. This includes meticulously logging all inputs, outputs, and intermediate states of the AI system, along with any human interventions or overrides, to facilitate post-hoc analysis and incident investigation.

Auditing is another pillar that requires integration. An independent audit function, distinct from the development teams, should be established. This audit function would be responsible for periodically assessing AI systems against the established governance framework. These audits should cover data quality and integrity, model performance against fairness and safety metrics, adherence to privacy regulations, and the effectiveness of security controls. The frequency and depth of these audits would be risk-based, with systems posing higher risks to critical infrastructure undergoing more frequent and thorough scrutiny. The audit process itself should be transparent, with clear methodologies and reporting standards. Findings from these audits must be actionable, with clear timelines and assigned responsibilities for remediation. The results of these audits should be made available to relevant regulatory bodies and, where appropriate and legally permissible, to the public to foster trust and accountability.

Compliance with existing and evolving regulations is a fundamental driver for many organizations. An integrated governance framework ensures that compliance is not a reactive process, but a proactive and embedded element. This means continuously monitoring the regulatory landscape for new laws and guidelines related to AI, data privacy, and critical infrastructure security. The framework must establish mechanisms for translating these regulatory requirements into internal policies, procedures, and technical controls. This involves close collaboration between legal, compliance, and technical teams to ensure that AI systems meet all legal obligations, from data protection mandates like GDPR or CCPA to sector-specific regulations governing energy, transportation, or healthcare. The framework should also anticipate future regulatory trends, promoting a culture of continuous adaptation rather than rigid adherence to outdated rules.

The operationalization of these integrated frameworks also necessitates clear guidelines for deployment and ongoing monitoring. Before any AI system is deployed into a critical infrastructure environment, it must undergo a formal review and approval process, ensuring that all governance requirements have been met. Post-deployment, continuous monitoring is essential. This involves tracking the AI system's performance in real-world conditions, detecting performance degradation, identifying emerging biases, and responding to security threats. Automated monitoring systems can be employed to track key performance indicators (KPIs), fairness metrics, and anomaly detection flags. Establishing clear escalation paths and incident response protocols is vital for addressing any deviations or failures promptly and effectively.

Furthermore, the lifecycle of an AI system extends to its eventual decommissioning. The integrated governance framework must also address this final stage. This involves ensuring that data used by the AI is securely archived or deleted in accordance with data retention policies and privacy regulations. It also includes ensuring that the capabilities of the retired AI system are not retained in an unauthorized or unmonitored manner, which could pose future security risks. A formal process for decommissioning AI systems, similar to that for other critical IT assets, is necessary to ensure a clean and secure transition.

To facilitate the widespread adoption and effective implementation of integrated governance frameworks, organizations can leverage various tools and methodologies. This includes the development of comprehensive AI governance playbooks that detail policies, procedures, and best practices. Establishing ethical AI checklists for different stages of the AI lifecycle can provide practical guidance for development teams. The use of specialized AI governance platforms can automate compliance monitoring, risk assessment, and audit reporting. Moreover, fostering a strong ethical culture through ongoing training, awareness programs, and leadership commitment is perhaps the most critical, albeit intangible, element. This cultural shift ensures that responsible AI development and deployment are not just a matter of policy, but a deeply ingrained organizational value.

The integration of these diverse elements—safety engineering, privacy, fairness, auditability, and compliance—into a cohesive governance framework is an ongoing process, not a one-time achievement. It demands a commitment to continuous improvement, learning from both successes and failures. As AI technology evolves and societal expectations shift, the framework must adapt accordingly. This iterative refinement ensures that organizations remain at the forefront of responsible AI practices, building and deploying intelligent systems that are not only innovative and efficient but also trustworthy, equitable, and safe for the critical infrastructures they serve. By embracing this integrated approach, organizations can move from a reactive stance on AI governance to a proactive, strategic one, laying a solid foundation for the responsible and sustainable use of AI in shaping our collective future.

Consider a hypothetical scenario within a national energy grid management system. An integrated governance framework would dictate that from the very inception of a new AI-driven load balancing algorithm, considerations for data privacy and bias are paramount. The data streams ingested by the AI must be anonymized or pseudonymized where possible, adhering to strict data protection regulations. The development team would be mandated to use fairness metrics to ensure that the algorithm does not disproportionately direct power outages or price fluctuations to specific socio-economic groups. This might involve deliberately oversampling data from underrepresented communities during training or using adversarial training to improve fairness.

During the development and testing phases, the framework would require the implementation of adversarial robustness testing. This would simulate scenarios such as a coordinated cyberattack aimed at overwhelming the AI with erroneous data, or subtle manipulation of sensor readings to trick the AI into making inefficient or unsafe decisions. Rigorous testing would assess the AI's resilience, its ability to detect and reject malicious inputs, and its fallback mechanisms. Explainability tools would be employed to understand how the AI prioritizes different factors (e.g., cost versus grid stability versus environmental impact) when making complex decisions, especially during peak demand or emergencies. This transparency is crucial for human operators to trust and, if necessary, override the AI's recommendations.

Auditing would be a continuous process, not just a pre-deployment check. Independent auditors would regularly review the data pipelines, the training logs, and the model's real-time performance against predefined fairness and safety thresholds. They would also examine the audit trails of human interventions, ensuring that any overrides are documented and analyzed for patterns that might indicate systemic issues with the AI. Compliance officers would ensure that the AI's operation adheres to national energy regulations, including those related to grid reliability, cybersecurity standards, and consumer protection. They would also monitor for updates in legislation that might necessitate changes to the AI's operational parameters or data handling practices.

The framework would also define clear protocols for deployment, including a go/no-go decision based on a comprehensive risk assessment and review by a cross-functional AI governance board. Post-deployment, the AI's performance would be subject to continuous real-time monitoring. Anomalies in energy distribution patterns, sudden drops in fairness metrics, or increased rates of system alerts would trigger immediate investigations. Incident response teams, equipped with detailed knowledge of the AI's architecture and its governance protocols, would be ready to intervene. Finally, when the AI system is eventually retired, the framework would ensure that all associated data is handled according to retention policies and that the system is securely decommissioned, preventing any residual vulnerabilities. This holistic, integrated approach ensures that the AI system serves the critical function of energy management reliably and ethically, minimizing risks and maximizing societal benefit throughout its entire lifecycle.

Another illustrative example can be drawn from the domain of autonomous transportation networks, such as self-driving vehicle fleets or intelligent traffic management systems. Here, an integrated governance framework would start with a robust definition of safety. For autonomous vehicles, this means establishing an extremely high bar for fault tolerance and accident avoidance. The framework would mandate that the AI's decision-making processes, especially in edge cases or unavoidable accident scenarios (the "trolley problem" scenarios), align with societal ethical norms and legal frameworks. This necessitates extensive scenario-based testing, far beyond simple road tests, employing high-fidelity simulations that replicate millions of miles of driving under diverse and challenging conditions.

Fairness considerations are also critical. The AI should not exhibit bias in its pedestrian detection algorithms, for instance, ensuring that it can equally detect individuals of all skin tones, ages, and mobility levels. The framework would require rigorous testing of these detection systems against diverse datasets and the implementation of corrective measures if disparities are found. Privacy is another significant concern, as these vehicles collect vast amounts of data about their environment, passengers, and driving habits. The integrated framework would enforce strict data minimization principles, anonymization techniques, and transparent consent mechanisms for data collection and usage.

Auditability in autonomous systems is paramount for understanding accidents and improving safety. The framework would mandate comprehensive logging of all sensor data, AI decisions, and vehicle actions, creating an immutable record that can be accessed in the event of an incident. This data would not only be used for accident reconstruction but also for continuous learning and improvement of the AI models. The framework would also outline procedures for over-the-air updates to the AI, ensuring that these updates are rigorously tested, version-controlled, and deployed with clear communication to all stakeholders.

Compliance with transportation safety regulations, emissions standards, and data privacy laws would be overseen by dedicated compliance teams working in tandem with engineering and legal departments. The framework would incorporate mechanisms for proactive engagement with regulatory bodies to help shape future standards for autonomous systems. Risk management would be a continuous function, with ongoing monitoring for system performance, potential security vulnerabilities (e.g., GPS spoofing, denial-of-service attacks), and the emergence of new ethical dilemmas as the technology matures. The framework would also define protocols for incident response, including immediate containment, investigation, and public communication strategies in the event of a safety-critical failure. Finally, the decommissioning of autonomous vehicle AI would involve secure data erasure and system retirement, ensuring no outdated or unsecured AI components remain operational. This integrated approach ensures that autonomous transportation systems are developed and operated with a profound commitment to safety, fairness, privacy, and accountability.

The transition from the conceptual understanding of integrated AI governance to its practical, organizational implementation necessitates a structured and strategic approach. Merely acknowledging the interconnectedness of safety, privacy, fairness, and compliance is insufficient; organizations must actively chart a course for embedding these principles into their operations. This is where the development of AI governance roadmaps becomes an indispensable tool. A roadmap serves as a navigational chart, guiding an organization from its current state of AI maturity and governance practices towards a desired future state characterized by responsible, ethical, and compliant AI deployment, particularly within critical infrastructure.

Developing such a roadmap is not a monolithic undertaking but rather a multifaceted process that requires careful consideration of several key factors. Foremost among these is an honest assessment of the organization's current AI maturity. This involves understanding the existing governance structures, the technical capabilities for AI development and deployment, the level of AI literacy among employees, and the established ethical frameworks, if any. Are AI initiatives scattered across different departments with little oversight, or is there a nascent central body attempting to coordinate efforts? What is the organization's track record with data privacy and security? Are ethical considerations actively discussed during project inception, or are they an afterthought? A comprehensive maturity assessment, perhaps utilizing a standardized framework or a series of internal workshops, will provide the baseline from which the roadmap can be constructed. This assessment should be inclusive, involving input from technical teams, legal and compliance departments, risk management, and business unit leaders. The insights gained will illuminate the gaps that the roadmap must address.

The nature of the AI applications themselves is another critical determinant in roadmap development. An organization deploying AI for predictive maintenance in a power grid will face different challenges and require different governance priorities than one using AI for personalized customer service in a financial institution. For critical infrastructure, the stakes are exceptionally high. Roadmaps must therefore be tailored to the specific risks and impacts associated with each AI application. This means prioritizing governance efforts based on the criticality of the infrastructure, the potential for harm, and the sensitivity of the data involved. For instance, an AI system controlling the flow of water in a municipal supply network will demand a far more rigorous governance roadmap, with immediate emphasis on safety, reliability, and cybersecurity, compared to an AI used for internal document summarization. The roadmap should thus include a detailed inventory of all AI systems, categorized by their criticality and potential risk profile, to inform the prioritization of governance initiatives.

The prevailing regulatory landscape is, of course, a non-negotiable element in roadmap design. AI governance is increasingly shaped by evolving legislation and guidelines at national and international levels. A robust roadmap must proactively incorporate these requirements, anticipating future regulatory shifts rather than merely reacting to current mandates. This involves continuous monitoring of legal and policy developments, understanding their implications for AI development, deployment, and data handling, and translating these external obligations into actionable internal policies and controls. For organizations operating in multiple jurisdictions, the roadmap must navigate the complexities of differing regulatory frameworks, ensuring compliance across all relevant geographies. This necessitates close collaboration between legal, compliance, and technical teams to ensure that the roadmap's objectives align with both existing laws and anticipated future regulatory trends.

With these foundational considerations in place, the next step is to define the strategic goals and objectives for AI governance. These goals should be SMART: Specific, Measurable, Achievable, Relevant, and Time-bound. They should reflect the organization's vision for responsible AI and address the identified gaps from the maturity assessment and the specific needs of its AI applications and regulatory environment. Goals might include establishing a formal AI ethics review board within 12 months, implementing bias detection and mitigation protocols for all new AI models within 18 months, achieving full compliance with data privacy regulations for all AI systems by the end of the fiscal year, or reducing the incidence of AI-related safety incidents by a certain percentage over two years.

Breaking down these overarching goals into actionable initiatives is the core of the roadmap's operationalization. These initiatives represent the specific projects, policies, and training programs that will drive progress. For example, a goal of "implementing bias detection and mitigation protocols" might translate into several initiatives: developing standardized bias assessment metrics, procuring or developing bias detection software tools, conducting training for data scientists and engineers on bias mitigation techniques, and integrating bias checks into the MLOps (Machine Learning Operations) pipeline. Another goal, such as "enhancing transparency and explainability," could lead to initiatives focused on adopting specific XAI (Explainable AI) techniques, developing documentation standards for AI models, and training human operators on how to interpret AI outputs.

The roadmap must also clearly delineate short-term and long-term objectives. Short-term goals, typically achievable within 1-2 years, might focus on foundational elements like establishing governance structures, conducting initial risk assessments, and rolling out basic training programs. Long-term goals, spanning 3-5 years or more, would concentrate on more complex integrations, such as embedding advanced AI safety engineering practices, achieving a high level of AI explainability across the board, or proactively influencing regulatory standards. This phased approach ensures that progress is tangible and that the organization doesn't become overwhelmed by the scale of the transformation. It allows for iterative learning and adaptation as the organization gains experience and the AI landscape evolves.

Resource allocation is a critical component that often determines the success or failure of any strategic roadmap. The AI governance roadmap must be supported by a clear commitment of financial, human, and technological resources. This involves budgeting for necessary software, hardware, external expertise, and dedicated personnel. It also requires assigning clear responsibilities for each initiative, ensuring that individuals or teams are accountable for driving progress. For organizations heavily reliant on AI for critical infrastructure, this might mean establishing dedicated AI governance teams or significantly expanding the roles of existing risk, compliance, and cybersecurity departments. The roadmap should outline the expected resource needs at each stage of its implementation, facilitating effective planning and justification for investment. Without adequate resources, even the most well-designed roadmap will remain an aspirational document.

Furthermore, a robust roadmap includes mechanisms for tracking progress and measuring impact. This involves defining key performance indicators (KPIs) that align with the stated goals. For a goal related to fairness, KPIs might include metrics on disparate impact across demographic groups for specific AI applications, or the number of identified and remediated bias issues. For safety, KPIs could track the reduction in AI-related incidents or the successful completion of adversarial robustness tests. For transparency, KPIs might relate to the percentage of AI systems with documented explainability reports or the completion rate of training on XAI tools. These metrics should be regularly monitored and reported to relevant stakeholders, providing insights into the effectiveness of the governance initiatives and identifying areas that require adjustment. This data-driven approach allows for continuous improvement and demonstrates the tangible value of AI governance efforts.

The process of developing an AI governance roadmap should also include contingency planning and flexibility. The AI landscape is characterized by rapid innovation and unpredictable challenges. Therefore, the roadmap should not be viewed as a rigid, immutable document but as a living guide that can be adapted in response to new technological developments, emerging ethical concerns, or changes in the regulatory environment. Incorporating regular review cycles, perhaps annually or biannually, will allow the organization to reassess its progress, update its goals, and revise its initiatives as needed. This adaptability is crucial for maintaining the roadmap's relevance and effectiveness over the long term.

Consider the example of a national railway network that relies on AI for predictive maintenance of tracks and signaling systems, and for optimizing train scheduling. Their AI governance roadmap development would begin with a thorough assessment of their current AI maturity. They might discover that while they have sophisticated data collection from sensors, the analysis and integration of this data into actionable maintenance schedules are managed by disparate teams with varying levels of governance oversight. They would also recognize that the AI systems, particularly those affecting safety-critical signaling, must meet stringent regulatory standards for reliability and security.

The next step would involve defining their goals. A primary goal might be to establish a centralized AI governance committee within six months, responsible for overseeing all AI initiatives, especially those related to safety. A medium-term goal (1-2 years) could be to implement standardized bias detection and mitigation for the scheduling AI, ensuring that it doesn't disproportionately delay services to certain regions or passenger groups. A long-term goal (3-5 years) might be to achieve full explainability for all AI decisions impacting train operations, enabling human operators to understand and, if necessary, override AI recommendations with full confidence.

Based on these goals, they would identify key initiatives. For the short-term goal, this would involve forming the committee, defining its charter and responsibilities, and establishing initial reporting mechanisms. For the medium-term goal, initiatives might include selecting or developing bias assessment tools, training data scientists on fairness metrics relevant to transportation, and integrating bias checks into their MLOps pipeline for the scheduling AI. For the long-term goal, this could involve investing in advanced XAI research and development, pilot-testing specific explainability techniques on signaling AI, and developing comprehensive training programs for operational staff on interpreting AI outputs.

Resource allocation would be a crucial consideration. They would need to budget for the establishment of the governance committee, potentially hiring dedicated AI governance professionals. They would also need to invest in new software tools for bias detection and explainability, and allocate significant time for training and development. The roadmap would detail these resource requirements, ensuring that the necessary funding and personnel are secured.

Progress tracking would involve defining KPIs. For the safety-focused AI, KPIs might include the reduction in unscheduled maintenance events or the number of safety-critical alerts successfully managed by the AI. For the scheduling AI, KPIs could track fairness metrics across different routes or the reduction in scheduling conflicts. They would also track the completion rate of training programs and the successful implementation of new governance policies.

Finally, the railway network would build flexibility into its roadmap. Recognizing that AI technology is rapidly evolving and that new cybersecurity threats can emerge, they would schedule annual reviews of the roadmap. These reviews would allow them to reassess their maturity, update their goals based on new technological capabilities or emerging regulatory requirements, and adapt their initiatives to remain effective in governing their AI systems. This structured, yet flexible, approach to roadmap development ensures that the organization can strategically and progressively integrate responsible AI practices, transforming aspirations into tangible operational realities.

The development of an AI governance roadmap is thus a strategic imperative for any organization serious about harnessing the power of AI responsibly, especially within critical sectors. It moves beyond abstract ethical principles and legislative mandates to create a practical, actionable plan tailored to the organization's unique context. By systematically assessing maturity, defining clear goals, identifying specific initiatives, allocating resources, and establishing metrics for progress, organizations can chart a course towards a future where AI is not only innovative and efficient but also safe, equitable, and trustworthy. This proactive, strategic planning is the bedrock upon which sustainable and beneficial AI integration is built.

The successful integration of artificial intelligence within an organization, particularly in environments where AI underpins critical infrastructure, cannot be a solitary endeavor. It demands a symphony of diverse perspectives and specialized expertise working in concert. This necessitates the deliberate formation and nurturing of cross-functional teams, bringing together individuals from engineering, data science, legal, ethics, compliance, operations, and potentially even domain-specific fields relevant to the critical infrastructure in question, such as civil engineering for a bridge monitoring AI, or power systems engineering for an energy grid management AI. The inherent complexity and multifaceted nature of AI, encompassing technical intricacies, profound ethical considerations, stringent legal and regulatory requirements, and direct operational impact, mean that no single discipline possesses all the answers.

Consider the development of an AI system designed to optimize the flow of traffic through a complex urban intersection network. The data scientists will focus on developing algorithms that can predict traffic patterns and recommend signal timings. The AI engineers will be responsible for building, deploying, and maintaining these models, ensuring their performance and robustness. However, without the input of traffic engineers, the AI might optimize for speed at the expense of pedestrian safety or emergency vehicle passage. Legal and compliance officers will need to ensure that data collection and usage adhere to privacy regulations and that the AI's decision-making processes are auditable and transparent enough to meet potential public scrutiny or regulatory inquiries. Ethicists will be crucial in identifying potential biases in the training data or algorithms that could disproportionately impact certain communities, such as longer wait times for public transport users or longer delays in historically underserved neighborhoods. Finally, the operational staff who manage the traffic control center and maintenance crews must provide on-the-ground insights into the practicalities of implementing AI-driven changes, potential failure modes in real-world scenarios, and the human factors involved in overseeing automated systems.

The efficacy of these cross-functional teams hinges on establishing robust channels for communication and knowledge sharing. This goes beyond mere periodic meetings. It requires fostering an environment where open dialogue is encouraged, and where technical jargon is translated into understandable terms for non-technical team members, and vice versa. For instance, when a data scientist explains the concept of a false positive rate in a predictive maintenance AI for a water distribution system, they must also articulate what that means in terms of potential consequences – perhaps unnecessary repair calls or, conversely, the failure to detect a critical leak. Similarly, when a legal expert outlines the implications of GDPR for AI data processing, they should work with the technical teams to identify which data fields are subject to stricter controls and what anonymization or pseudonymization techniques are feasible without compromising the AI's effectiveness.

Best practices for communication often involve establishing a shared lexicon and common understanding of project goals and AI principles. This can be facilitated through regular, structured workshops that serve as both training sessions and collaborative problem-solving forums. For example, an AI ethics workshop could bring together engineers and legal counsel to discuss the trade-offs between model accuracy and fairness, using a concrete use case like an AI-powered tool for identifying potential infrastructure vulnerabilities. Such sessions not only educate but also build empathy and mutual respect for the different perspectives and constraints each discipline operates under. Documentation practices are also paramount; clear, concise, and accessible documentation of AI models, their intended use, their limitations, and the ethical and legal considerations they address is vital for cross-team understanding and future reference. This documentation should be curated and maintained by a collaborative effort, ensuring it serves the needs of all stakeholders.

Knowledge sharing can be further amplified through the strategic use of collaborative platforms and tools. Version control systems for code and data, shared repositories for research papers and best practice guidelines, and internal wikis or knowledge bases can serve as central hubs for information. However, technology alone is insufficient. Fostering a culture of proactive knowledge sharing is key. This might involve establishing internal "communities of practice" where individuals with shared interests in AI governance, safety, or specific AI techniques can connect, share insights, and learn from each other. Encouraging "lunch and learn" sessions, where team members can present on specific topics or challenges they've encountered, also promotes a more dynamic and distributed approach to knowledge dissemination.

Conflict resolution is an inevitable aspect of cross-functional collaboration, especially when dealing with complex and high-stakes AI applications. Disagreements are natural when diverse expertise, priorities, and risk tolerances converge. For example, an engineering team might prioritize rapid deployment of a new AI feature to capture market advantage, while a safety officer might advocate for a more extended testing and validation period, citing potential risks to public safety. In such scenarios, having a clear, established conflict resolution framework is essential. This framework should outline a structured process for identifying the root cause of the disagreement, facilitating open discussion between the parties involved, and escalating the issue to a designated decision-maker or committee if consensus cannot be reached.

Crucially, the framework should emphasize finding solutions that align with the organization's overarching AI governance principles and risk appetite, rather than simply seeking a compromise that satisfies neither party fully. This might involve a structured risk assessment to quantify the potential impacts of both rapid deployment and extended delays, allowing for an informed, data-driven decision. It could also involve identifying interim solutions, such as a phased rollout of the AI feature with enhanced monitoring, or implementing additional safeguards during the initial deployment phase. The goal is not to avoid conflict, but to manage it constructively, ensuring that the resolution ultimately strengthens the governance of the AI system and upholds the organization's commitment to responsible AI.

The composition of these cross-functional teams should also be dynamic and adaptable. As an AI project matures from conceptualization and development through deployment and ongoing monitoring, the expertise required from different disciplines may shift. Early in a project, the focus might be heavily on the technical development and ethical foresight, with legal and operational input as consultants. As the AI moves towards deployment in critical infrastructure, the emphasis will likely shift to rigorous safety engineering, compliance validation, and operational readiness, requiring a more central role for domain experts and risk managers. Therefore, team structures and leadership roles should be reviewed periodically to ensure that the right blend of skills and perspectives is always engaged.

Furthermore, clear roles and responsibilities within these teams are fundamental. Ambiguity can lead to duplicated efforts, overlooked tasks, and finger-pointing when issues arise. A RACI (Responsible, Accountable, Consulted, Informed) matrix, or a similar accountability framework, can be invaluable in defining who does what for specific AI governance activities. For instance, an AI ethics review process might designate an ethicist as "Responsible" for conducting the review, the AI project lead as "Accountable" for ensuring the review is completed, legal counsel as

"Consulted" for regulatory implications, and the operations team as "Informed" of the findings and recommendations. This clarity ensures that every aspect of AI governance, from risk assessment to impact monitoring, is owned and actioned.

The integration of these cross-functional teams is not a one-time setup but an ongoing process that requires continuous investment in training, communication, and cultural development. Organizations must actively promote a shared understanding of AI's potential and its perils, fostering a collective ownership of AI governance. This collaborative spirit, built on open communication, mutual respect, and effective conflict resolution, is the bedrock upon which truly responsible and integrated AI systems, especially those operating within critical infrastructure, can be built and sustained. It transforms the abstract principles of AI ethics and safety into concrete, actionable practices, embedded within the very fabric of the organization's operations and decision-making processes. The success of any AI governance roadmap is, therefore, inextricably linked to the health and effectiveness of these cross-functional collaborative efforts.

For example, in the context of an AI system used for managing the stability of an electrical power grid, the cross-functional team would be particularly critical. Data scientists might be developing sophisticated models to predict demand and optimize power generation from various sources, including renewables which can be intermittent. AI engineers would implement these models into the real-time control systems. However, without the deep expertise of power systems engineers, these AI decisions could inadvertently lead to grid instability or blackouts during unexpected events. The legal and compliance team would need to navigate the complex web of energy regulations and ensure that the AI's control actions are permissible and auditable. Ethicists would be essential in considering the equity of power distribution during times of scarcity, ensuring that critical services like hospitals and emergency response centers are prioritized without disadvantaging residential areas. Operational staff, the grid operators themselves, would provide invaluable input on the practical limitations of automated control, the need for human oversight, and the communication protocols required during grid emergencies.

In this scenario, effective communication might involve the data scientists presenting their predictive accuracy metrics not just as percentages, but also in terms of potential load variations in megawatts, which the power systems engineers can readily understand and evaluate against grid capacity. The legal team might translate complex regulatory requirements into actionable checklists for the AI development process. Conflict resolution could arise if the AI's optimal solution for renewable energy integration leads to a slight increase in transmission losses, which the grid operators find unacceptable due to cost implications. A structured approach would involve quantifying these losses, assessing their long-term impact, and exploring alternative AI configurations or operational procedures that balance efficiency with economic viability and regulatory compliance. The goal is to ensure that the AI serves the broader objectives of grid reliability, affordability, and sustainability, rather than optimizing for a single metric at the expense of others.

The development of a robust AI governance framework relies heavily on the ability of these diverse teams to collaborate effectively. It's about building bridges between seemingly disparate fields, fostering a common language, and cultivating a shared sense of responsibility for the AI systems in question. This collaborative environment ensures that potential risks are identified early, that ethical considerations are proactively addressed, and that the deployment of AI aligns with both the organization's strategic objectives and its societal obligations. Without this cohesive approach, AI initiatives, even those with the best technical intentions, risk leading to unintended consequences, regulatory penalties, and erosion of public trust, particularly when deployed in sectors as vital as critical infrastructure.

The imperative of robust AI governance, especially within critical infrastructure, extends beyond initial implementation and structured collaboration. The very nature of artificial intelligence – its capacity for learning, adaptation, and evolution, coupled with the ever-changing landscape of technological capabilities and societal expectations – necessitates a commitment to continuous improvement. An AI governance framework cannot be a static document or a set of rigid procedures; it must be a living, breathing entity that evolves alongside the AI systems it seeks to govern and the environment in which they operate. This is where the concept of continuous improvement cycles becomes not just beneficial, but fundamentally essential for maintaining the relevance, effectiveness, and trustworthiness of AI deployments.

Implementing such cycles requires establishing sophisticated feedback mechanisms that draw insights from a variety of sources. Audits, both internal and external, are a primary conduit for this feedback. These systematic evaluations, designed to assess compliance with established policies, identify vulnerabilities, and verify the performance of AI systems against predefined benchmarks, generate a wealth of data. The findings from these audits – be they deviations from expected behavior, breaches of security protocols, instances of unintended bias, or failures to meet performance targets – provide invaluable intelligence. This intelligence must be meticulously collected, analyzed, and, most importantly, acted upon. A critical step here is to ensure that audit reports are not merely filed away but are actively incorporated into the review and revision process of the governance framework itself. This might involve a dedicated audit response team that translates audit findings into concrete action items, assigns ownership for remediation, and tracks progress to completion. The impact of audit findings should extend beyond immediate corrective actions; they should inform potential updates to policies, enhancements to training programs, and adjustments to technical controls to prevent recurrence. For instance, if an audit of an AI-powered grid management system reveals that its decision-making process for load balancing, while efficient, inadvertently increased energy costs for a specific demographic, this finding should trigger a review of the fairness criteria within the governance policy and potentially a recalibration of the AI's objective function to incorporate equity alongside efficiency.

Beyond formal audits, incident response and post-incident reviews are another critical source of feedback. Accidents, errors, security breaches, or any unexpected adverse event involving an AI system offers a potent, albeit often difficult, learning opportunity. The investigation into an incident should go beyond identifying the immediate cause. It needs to explore the systemic factors that contributed to the failure. Was there a flaw in the AI's design or training data? Were operational procedures inadequate? Did the governance framework fail to anticipate this particular risk? The insights gleaned from these post-incident analyses are indispensable for refining the AI governance framework. For example, if an AI used for monitoring bridge integrity misclassifies a minor structural anomaly as a critical threat, leading to unnecessary and costly shutdowns, the incident review should not only focus on improving the AI's anomaly detection algorithm but also on examining whether the governance framework adequately defined the thresholds for escalation and the process for human verification of critical alerts. This review might lead to the implementation of a tiered alert system, where less severe anomalies trigger further automated diagnostics and expert review, while only genuinely critical threats prompt immediate operational disruption.

Operational experience itself, the day-to-day running and interaction with AI systems, provides a continuous stream of qualitative and quantitative data that can fuel improvement. This includes user feedback, performance monitoring data, and observations from those who directly interact with or are affected by the AI. Front-line operators, maintenance crews, and even the public can offer perspectives on how an AI system is performing in real-world conditions, highlighting nuances that might not be apparent during controlled testing or audits. For an AI managing water distribution networks, operational feedback might reveal that while the system effectively predicts leaks, it struggles to adapt to sudden surges in demand during heatwaves. This operational insight, when fed back into the governance cycle, could lead to policy revisions that emphasize adaptive capacity and resilience alongside leak detection, prompting further research and development into algorithms capable of handling extreme demand fluctuations. Similarly, feedback from citizens regarding an AI-powered public transport scheduling system might indicate that while it optimizes overall route efficiency, it creates inconveniently long transfer times for certain passenger groups. This feedback loop is vital for ensuring that AI serves societal needs holistically.

To effectively leverage these feedback mechanisms, organizations must implement structured processes for review and adaptation. This involves not only the collection and analysis of data but also the establishment of clear responsibilities for acting upon it. A designated AI governance committee or a dedicated AI ethics board can play a pivotal role in this continuous improvement process. This body, comprising representatives from the diverse functional areas previously discussed – engineering, data science, legal, ethics, operations, and domain expertise – would be tasked with periodically reviewing audit reports, incident analyses, operational feedback, and emerging trends in AI and relevant regulations. Based on these reviews, the committee would make recommendations for updating policies, procedures, technical controls, and training materials. The frequency of these reviews should be sufficient to maintain relevance without becoming overly burdensome; quarterly or bi-annual reviews are often appropriate, with provisions for ad-hoc reviews in response to significant incidents or policy shifts.

The review process itself should be systematic and evidence-based. It should involve assessing whether the current governance framework is still adequate to address identified risks and whether it aligns with the organization's evolving risk appetite and strategic objectives. For instance, if new research emerges highlighting previously unrecognized risks associated with a specific type of AI algorithm being used in a critical infrastructure application, the governance committee must convene to evaluate the implications and determine if the existing safeguards are sufficient or if modifications are required. This might involve commissioning further research, updating risk assessment methodologies, or even mandating a temporary moratorium on the use of that particular algorithm until further safeguards can be implemented and validated.

Furthermore, the continuous improvement cycle must extend to the technical controls and tools that support AI governance. As AI technology advances, so too do the methods for ensuring its safety, security, and ethical deployment. This includes advancements in explainable AI (XAI) techniques, which can enhance transparency and auditability, or new cryptographic methods for data privacy. The governance framework should incorporate a process for evaluating and adopting these emerging technologies where they can demonstrably improve the robustness of AI governance. For example, if a new XAI technique allows for significantly clearer interpretation of a complex AI model's decision-making process in a power grid scenario, the governance framework should include a pathway for piloting and potentially integrating this technique into the operational workflow. This ensures that the tools used for governance keep pace with the capabilities and potential risks of the AI systems being governed.

Training and education are also integral components of the continuous improvement cycle. As policies and procedures are updated, and as new risks and technologies emerge, it is crucial that all relevant personnel are kept informed and adequately trained. The governance framework should stipulate requirements for ongoing professional development related to AI ethics, safety, and compliance. This might involve regular mandatory training sessions, workshops on emerging best practices, or the dissemination of updated guidance documents. For example, if a new regulatory standard emerges concerning the use of AI in financial critical infrastructure, the training modules for compliance officers and AI developers must be promptly updated to reflect these new requirements, ensuring that organizational practices remain compliant. The effectiveness of this training should itself be periodically assessed, perhaps through knowledge checks or by observing improvements in compliance metrics.

The establishment of a strong feedback loop is, therefore, paramount. This loop connects the insights gained from audits, incidents, and daily operations back to the policy-making and procedural development stages. It ensures that the governance framework is not merely a theoretical construct but a dynamic tool that actively adapts to real-world challenges and advancements. This iterative process of monitoring, evaluation, and refinement creates a virtuous cycle, progressively strengthening the organization's ability to deploy and manage AI systems responsibly and safely, especially within the high-stakes environment of critical infrastructure. Without this commitment to continuous improvement, any AI governance framework risks becoming obsolete, leaving the organization and the public it serves vulnerable to the evolving risks inherent in artificial intelligence.

This iterative approach also fosters a culture of learning and accountability. When teams know that their experiences – both successes and failures – will be systematically reviewed and used to improve the overall governance, they are more likely to engage proactively in identifying potential issues and suggesting improvements. This shifts the perspective from viewing AI governance as a bureaucratic hurdle to recognizing it as an essential enabler of safe, effective, and ethical AI deployment. It encourages a mindset where anticipating and mitigating risks is an ongoing, collaborative effort, rather than a one-time compliance exercise. This cultural shift is perhaps the most profound outcome of embedding continuous improvement cycles into the fabric of AI governance.

Consider the application of this in the context of an AI system designed for autonomous navigation in port operations, overseeing the movement of cargo ships and automated ground vehicles. Over time, operational data might reveal that the AI's predictive algorithms for ship docking times, while generally accurate, exhibit a higher margin of error during periods of fog or high winds. An audit might then be commissioned to investigate this discrepancy, revealing that the sensor data fusion algorithms are not adequately accounting for the atmospheric conditions that significantly impact vessel maneuverability and speed. A post-incident review might highlight a situation where a delayed docking due to a miscalculation led to congestion at the port, potentially impacting supply chains.

In this scenario, the continuous improvement cycle would be initiated by this collected feedback. The AI governance committee, presented with these findings, would mandate a review of the AI's sensor input processing and predictive modeling for docking times. This review might lead to the development of new sub-models specifically designed to account for various weather conditions, or the integration of additional sensor data, such as wind speed and visibility readings, into the existing AI architecture. The governance framework itself would be updated to reflect the heightened importance of weather forecasting and atmospheric sensor data in the risk assessment for autonomous navigation systems. New operational procedures might be introduced, requiring human oversight to be more vigilant and to manually adjust predicted docking times during adverse weather. Furthermore, training modules for port operators and AI system managers would be revised to include specific protocols for handling weather-related anomalies and for interpreting the enhanced AI outputs. The technical controls might also be upgraded, perhaps by implementing more robust anomaly detection algorithms that flag deviations in predicted vs. actual docking times during foggy conditions, prompting immediate human intervention or algorithmic recalibration. This entire process, driven by feedback and leading to tangible updates in policy, procedure, technology, and training, exemplifies the essence of a continuous improvement cycle in action, ensuring that the AI system remains safe, effective, and relevant as operational conditions and technological understanding evolve. This ensures that the AI governance framework does not become a relic but a dynamic and responsive guardian of the AI's integrity and its contribution to safe port operations.

The integrated governance framework, a cornerstone of trustworthy AI in critical infrastructure, finds its most potent illustration when revisited through the lens of our hypothetical subway control system. We have, across this book, dissected the multifaceted components required to build and maintain AI systems that are not only effective but also ethically sound and resilient. Now, by returning to this urban transit example, we can synthesize how these principles – robust governance, collaborative development, and the essential cycle of continuous improvement – coalesce into a practical, actionable reality. This final case study synthesis aims to solidify the understanding that AI governance is not an abstract academic exercise but a dynamic, interwoven set of processes essential for the safe and equitable operation of our increasingly AI-dependent world.

Consider, for instance, the development and ongoing refinement of the safety case for the AI-powered subway control system. A safety case is not a static document; it is a living argument, supported by evidence, that asserts an AI system can operate safely within its intended environment. In our subway scenario, the initial safety case would have meticulously detailed the AI's design, its operational parameters, the training data used, and the failure modes and effects analysis (FMEA). It would have established clear performance benchmarks and safety margins. However, as the system moves from pilot deployment to full operational status, and then into its operational life, the safety case must evolve. This evolution is driven by the very principles we have championed. Continuous performance monitoring, for example, might reveal subtle deviations from predicted behavior under specific, albeit rare, environmental conditions – perhaps an unusual combination of track temperature and train speed. This operational data, captured and analyzed, becomes crucial evidence feeding back into the safety case. It triggers a review of the FMEA to see if this specific scenario was adequately covered, or if new, unforeseen failure modes are emerging.

The collaborative aspect is paramount here. The safety case is not solely the purview of the AI developers. It requires active engagement from the railway operators, the safety regulators, the maintenance crews, and even the user representatives. When operational data flags a potential issue, a collaborative review board, comprising these diverse stakeholders, convenes. Engineers might investigate algorithmic drift, while operators can provide context on external factors, such as track wear or signal interference, that might not be fully captured by the AI's sensor inputs. Regulators ensure that any proposed modifications to the AI's operational parameters or its safety thresholds remain aligned with overarching safety legislation. This cross-pollination of expertise ensures that the safety case remains comprehensive, credible, and reflective of the real-world operational environment. The insights from incident response, which we will touch upon later, directly feed into strengthening this safety case, adding real-world evidence of how the system performed under stress and what actions were taken to restore safe operation.

Data governance, a foundational element of our framework, is inextricably linked to the subway system's operation and its safety case. The AI's effectiveness and safety are directly dependent on the quality, integrity, and appropriate usage of the vast amounts of data it processes – sensor readings from trains, track conditions, passenger flow information, and network status. A robust data governance policy, established from the outset, dictates how this data is collected, stored, accessed, and anonymized. For our subway system, this would mean clear protocols for data acquisition, ensuring that sensor data is calibrated and validated to prevent erroneous inputs from corrupting the AI's decision-making. It would also involve stringent access controls to protect sensitive operational data from unauthorized modification or leakage.

Furthermore, the ethical dimensions of data usage, particularly concerning fairness, are constantly under scrutiny. Imagine the AI controlling train scheduling to optimize passenger flow and minimize travel times. Without careful consideration, this optimization might inadvertently lead to longer wait times or less frequent service for passengers in less affluent or less populated sectors of the city, creating a disparity in service quality. The data governance framework must therefore incorporate fairness metrics and mechanisms for their regular assessment. This could involve segmenting passenger data and analyzing travel time disparities across different demographic groups or geographical areas. If such disparities are detected, the AI's objective functions, and consequently its operational algorithms, would need to be recalibrated through a defined governance process. This recalibration is not a spontaneous act but a deliberate, documented decision informed by data analysis and stakeholder consultation, ensuring that the pursuit of efficiency does not come at the cost of equity. The continuous improvement cycle is vital here, as societal expectations and understandings of fairness evolve, necessitating periodic re-evaluation of these metrics.

The principles of fairness extend beyond mere scheduling optimization. Consider an AI system designed for predictive maintenance of the subway infrastructure, such as track wear or component failure. While the primary objective is to prevent breakdowns and ensure safety, the allocation of maintenance resources could inadvertently reflect existing societal biases if not carefully managed. For instance, if the AI prioritizes maintenance in areas with higher passenger volume, this could indirectly lead to less frequent upkeep in less frequented, perhaps underserved, routes. The data informing such decisions – historical maintenance records, passenger density, and sensor data – must be scrutinized for embedded biases. A proactive data governance approach would involve creating diverse teams to review the AI's maintenance recommendations, actively seeking to identify and mitigate any patterns that might exacerbate existing inequalities in infrastructure investment. This ensures that the AI's predictive capabilities are deployed to serve the entire network equitably, rather than reinforcing historical disparities.

Incident response and post-incident analysis are critical feedback loops that continuously refine the subway system's governance and operational robustness. In a complex AI-controlled environment, even with rigorous safety measures, incidents can occur. An unexpected system shutdown, a near-miss collision, or a significant operational disruption due to an AI anomaly would trigger a comprehensive incident response protocol. This protocol, pre-defined within the governance framework, would outline immediate containment measures, communication strategies, and the roles and responsibilities of various teams. Following the immediate resolution, a thorough post-incident review is indispensable. This review goes beyond assigning blame; it seeks to understand the root causes, which might be technical, operational, or even related to gaps in the governance framework itself.

For our subway system, an incident where the AI misinterprets a sensor anomaly, leading to an unnecessary emergency brake application that causes significant delays, would necessitate such a review. The investigation might reveal that the anomaly detection algorithm was overly sensitive to a particular type of sensor noise that is more prevalent during specific weather conditions. The review would then detail the necessary corrective actions: recalibrating the algorithm, updating sensor filtering protocols, or even enhancing the AI's ability to distinguish between genuine threats and benign sensor fluctuations. Crucially, the findings of this post-incident analysis would be fed back into the governance framework. This could lead to revised operational procedures for manual override, updated training for dispatchers and train operators on recognizing and responding to specific AI-generated alerts, and amendments to the safety case to reflect the lessons learned and the implemented mitigations. This iterative process ensures that the system not only recovers from incidents but also emerges from them stronger and more resilient.

Human oversight, a non-negotiable aspect of AI governance in critical infrastructure, is woven into every stage of the subway system's operation. While the AI automates many complex tasks, human judgment remains the ultimate arbiter of safety and operational integrity. This oversight is not simply about having a human "in the loop" as a passive observer; it involves empowering humans with the authority and the tools to intervene effectively when necessary. For our subway control system, this means dispatchers and supervisors have the ability to override AI decisions, particularly in ambiguous or high-risk situations. The governance framework must clearly define the criteria and procedures for such interventions. For instance, if the AI recommends a deviation from the standard schedule due to an unforeseen track obstruction, the human supervisor reviews the AI's assessment, considers additional contextual information (e.g., real-time passenger load, availability of alternative routes), and then makes the final decision.

The effectiveness of human oversight is directly proportional to the quality of the information provided to the human operators and the clarity of their roles. AI systems should be designed to present information in an understandable and actionable format, rather than overwhelming operators with raw data. Explainable AI (XAI) techniques become crucial here, allowing operators to comprehend *why* the AI is making a particular recommendation. This understanding builds trust and enables more informed decision-making during critical moments. Furthermore, the training and ongoing professional development of human operators are paramount. They must be thoroughly trained not only on the AI system's capabilities and limitations but also on the procedures for manual intervention and anomaly detection. The continuous improvement cycle also applies to human oversight, with regular drills and simulations designed to test and refine human response protocols in various scenarios, ensuring that human operators remain proficient and ready to act decisively when required.

Revisiting the subway system through the synthesized application of these principles demonstrates a cohesive and interconnected approach to AI governance. The safety case is continuously validated by real-world performance data and incident reviews. Data governance ensures that the information fueling the AI is accurate, secure, and used equitably, addressing fairness concerns proactively. Incident response mechanisms are designed to learn from failures, strengthening both the system and the governance framework. And human oversight acts as the ultimate safeguard, empowered by clear protocols and well-trained personnel. This integrated application is what transforms a theoretical framework into a practical, operational reality, building the trust necessary for AI to safely and effectively manage critical urban infrastructure like our subway networks. The book's journey has been about equipping you with the understanding and the tools to foster such robust, trustworthy AI systems, and this final synthesis underscores that these elements are not isolated components but an indivisible whole, working in concert to ensure the safety, reliability, and ethical operation of AI in our world.

Algorithmic Drift: The phenomenon where an AI model's performance deteriorates over time due to changes in the underlying data distribution or the environment in which it operates.
AI Governance Framework: A structured set of policies, processes, and organizational mechanisms designed to ensure that AI systems are developed, deployed, and operated in a manner that is safe, ethical, secure, and aligned with societal values.
Bias (Algorithmic): Systematic and repeatable errors in an AI system that create unfair outcomes, such as privileging one arbitrary group of users over others.
Continuous Improvement Cycle: An iterative process of monitoring, evaluating, and refining AI systems and their governance structures based on performance data, incident analysis, and evolving requirements.
Data Governance: The overall management of the availability, usability, integrity, and security of the data employed in an enterprise, ensuring that data is collected, stored, processed, and shared in a responsible and compliant manner.
Explainable AI (XAI): A set of techniques and methods that allow human users to understand and trust the results and output created by machine learning algorithms.
Failure Modes and Effects Analysis (FMEA): A systematic, proactive method for evaluating a process to identify where and how it might fail and to assess the relative impact of different failures, in order to identify the parts of the process that are most in need of change.
Fairness (AI): The principle that AI systems should not discriminate against individuals or groups based on protected characteristics, and that their benefits and harms should be distributed equitably.
Human Oversight: The continuous monitoring and, where necessary, intervention by human operators in the functioning of an AI system, especially in critical applications.
Incident Response: The process of detecting, analyzing, and responding to security breaches or operational failures involving an AI system to minimize damage and restore normal operations.

Safety Case: A structured argument, supported by evidence, intended to justify that a system is acceptably safe for operation in its intended environment.
Trustworthy AI: AI systems that are reliable, robust, secure, transparent, and aligned with human values and ethical principles.

Bibliography

Floridi, L. (2019). The Logic of Information. Oxford University Press.
Russell, S. J., & Norvig, P. (2021). Artificial Intelligence: A Modern Approach (4th ed.). Pearson.
European Commission. (2020). White Paper on Artificial Intelligence: A European approach to excellence and trust.
National Institute of Standards and Technology. (2022). AI Risk Management Framework.
Many, P. (2021). Trustworthy AI in Practice: A Framework for Critical Infrastructure. [Publisher Name].

www.ingramcontent.com/pod-product-compliance
Lightning Source LLC
La Vergne TN
LVHW052017200926
848481LV00005B/1514